THE
HUMAN BRAIN
COLORING BOOK

Also Available in the Coloring Concepts Series

Zoology Coloring Book by L. M. Elson

Marine Biology Coloring Book by T. M. Niesen

Human Evolution Coloring Book by A. L. Zihlman

Botany Coloring Book by P. Young

Computer Concepts Coloring Book by B. M. Glotzer

Biology Coloring Book by R. D. Griffin

THE HUMAN BRAIN COLORING BOOK

by
Marian C. Diamond
Arnold B. Scheibel
Lawrence M. Elson

HarperPerennial
A Division of HarperCollins*Publishers*

This book was produced by Coloring Concepts, Inc.
P.O. Box 324, Oakville, CA 94562

The book editors were Joan Elson and Jeanne Flagg
Layout and design of illustrations were by the authors
The copy editor was B. F. Emmer
Type was set by ComCom, A Division of Haddon Craftsmen
Page makeup and production was by C. Linda Dingler
The proofreader was Rainé Young

THE HUMAN BRAIN COLORING BOOK

ISBN: 0-06-460306-7

94 95 96   19 18 17

Marian C. Diamond, Ph.D., is Professor of Anatomy at the University of California at Berkeley. She teaches general human anatomy and neuroanatomy and has conducted numerous lines of research into the effect of the environment and hormones on the forebrain. Dr. Diamond is perhaps best known for her investigations into structural changes in the cerebral cortex induced by an enriched environment and structural lateralization of the cortex as influenced by sex steroid hormones.

Arnold B. Scheibel, M.D., is Professor of Anatomy and Psychiatry at the University of California Medical School at Los Angeles and a member of the Brain Research Institute. Dr. Scheibel teaches courses in neurosciences and psychiatry. He has published numerous articles on his investigations into the parts of the brain involved in consciousness and higher mental function.

Lawrence M. Elson, Ph.D., is a consultant and lecturer on the anatomical basis of injury, author of several books, and producer of the Coloring Concepts series of scientific, educational coloring book texts. Dr. Elson has taught anatomy at Baylor College of Medicine, University of California Medical School at San Francisco, and the City College of San Francisco.

Cinthea Vadala, who finished the illustrations in Units Five through Nine, is a scientific illustrator in the San Francisco area.

Janice Aspelin Schwegler, who finished the illustrations in the first four units, is a certified medical illustrator in Long Beach, California.

With love to Catherine,
Rick, Jeff, and Ann
and
To the young of every age who seek
the foundations of human behavior

—M.C.D./A.B.S.

To Kathy Dahl, for her unmatched con-
tribution to the completion of this book

—L.M.E.

CONTENTS

Unit Three: EARLY DEVELOPMENT OF THE CENTRAL NERVOUS SYSTEM

Unit Four: SPINAL CORD

Unit Five: BRAIN

Unit Six: CRANIAL NERVES

Unit Seven: SURVEY OF SPINAL NERVES

Unit Eight: SURVEY OF THE VISCERAL NERVOUS SYSTEM

Unit Nine: SUPPORT SYSTEMS OF THE CENTRAL NERVOUS SYSTEM

Index

PREFACE

May knowledge of the brain provide people of all nations with greater tolerance, empathy, and appreciation of human behavior

This coloring book has been written for everyone who wishes to learn about the brain—from the beginner to the professional. It represents a distillate of several decades of experience that the three authors have had in teaching medical students, graduate students, and undergraduates, as well as the lay public.

Developed in graded degrees of complexity, this book offers the beginner an introduction to the nervous system, while more advanced individuals can benefit from the greater details. Middle school students can learn from the first few plates of each unit. Pupils at secondary levels will benefit by continuing further, whereas undergraduates, and specifically graduate students, will wish to complete the sequence of plates in their entirety.

We believe that this selection of material and type of organization will satisfy the needs not only of basic science, psychology, and health science students but also of public health workers, sociologists, lawyers, nurses, optometrists, physical therapists, pharmacists, dentists, and physicians and surgeons of all kinds. Specialists from other professions, such as physicists, molecular geneticists, and those involved with artificial intelligence, who are finding the nervous system the ultimate challenge, may discover these plates a very useful way to begin.

The organization of this book follows the authors' course outlines. It can be used in conjunction with most neurobiology courses. However, by coloring one plate each day or night, any informal learner can develop a personal and useful knowledge of the nervous system in a reasonable period of time.

In limited space, we have tried to interweave classical neural structure with recent research findings. The subject matter ranges from the basic anatomical characteristics of the nerve cell through developmental patterns to connections within the highest levels of the brain. Today, psychological and behavioral concepts are beginning to find grounding in the structure of the nervous system. For example, wakefulness and sleep, pleasure and pain, psychotic illness, epilepsy, stroke, paralysis, and speech are being linked to their organic foundations. A person who is interested in any of these areas of behavioral function or dysfunction can *begin* to appreciate their structural basis as these plates are colored. The development, maturation, and aging of regions of the brain; the flow and focusing of consciousness; the response of the cerebral cortex to challenge; and the brain's own way of suppressing pain are representative of subjects that are addressed in these pages.

The Coloring Concepts format of coloring by direction seems particularly applicable to a subject as complex as the brain. The enormous number of components and their interconnections constitute an entirely new vocabulary. By replacing rote memory with the act of coloring, a visual-motor component is introduced into the process of learning, enhancing long-term retention. By selecting and physically applying the color of choice to the name (title) of a structure and then to its pictorial representation, one actively participates in the process, sustaining the desire and motivation to learn. The final product serves as a perpetual review as well as a satisfying and aesthetic creation.

As we administer the finishing touches to our work in this book, we look back with appreciation to those who helped so much to make this book a reality. We are grateful to our students, families, and friends whose invariable question "Is the book finished yet?" over the last three years provided constant evidence of interest and support for the need of such a project. Warm thanks are owed to Professor Richard Eakin of the University of California at Berkeley, Drs. Ian Monie and Henry ("Pete") Ralston III at the University of

California Medical School in San Francisco, and Dr. Jackson Wagner of the College of Medicine at Texas A & M University for their patience and their criticisms while reviewing the manuscript. Special thanks go to Joan Elson, our editor, who scrupulously attended to technical accuracy with respect to use of subscripts and exponents. She scrutinized every manuscript page and colored every plate of this book three and four times, unceasingly demanding didactic clarity. We have had the pleasure of working with two talented artists, Cinthea Vadala and Janice Aspelin Schwegler, who rendered with polish and refinement our working illustrations. We are grateful to Robert Griffin, M.S., for the use of his concept illustrated in the lower part of Plate 1–6.

And to you, dear colorer, we wish fulfillment of all your aspirations. It will be by the use of your brain that you will achieve such fulfillment. May the knowledge and insights gained from the coloring of this book bring your potential closer to reality.

M.C.D., A.B.S., and L.M.E.
November 1984

HOW TO USE THIS BOOK:
COLORING INSTRUCTIONS

1. INTRODUCTION

a. This is a book of illustrations (plates) and related text pages in which you (the colorer) color the name (title) of a structure and use the identical color for its structural representation. The titles are listed on the plate, and following each title is a letter printed in small type (subscript). In some cases, a number (exponent) is added to the subscript. In most cases, titles are arranged in alphabetical order of the subscripts, starting with A. The structure that corresponds to a title receives the same subscript and exponent as the title. Upon coloring a title and its corresponding structure identically, the relationship between the two is apparent at a glance. As more and more structures and their titles are colored, relationships become apparent and visual orientation is developed, setting the stage for understanding the related text. It is the experience of one of the authors (Elson) that retention of material learned by directed coloring is generally gained more quickly and more securely than by passive reading.

b. You will need coloring instruments. Colored pencils or colored felt-tip pens are recommended. Laundry markers (with waterproof colors) and crayons are not recommended, the former because they stain through the paper, the latter because they are coarse and messy and produce unnatural colors.

c. Note that each plate has a colorable rectangular thumb index on the right margin and that all the indexes of any one unit are arranged at the same horizontal level. Once colored (see ahead), the thumb indexes, as well as the titles in the upper right corner of the plate, make it possible to find a specific plate simply by flipping pages.

d. Scan the table of contents to get an idea of the organization of presentation of topics. Note that the plates are numbered by unit and plate number: 1-1, 1-2, and so on. To reinforce the arrangement of subjects in this book, the name of each unit can be colored in the table of contents. Choose contrasting colors for these names, and apply these same colors to the rectangular thumb indexes on the right margin of each page.

e. To achieve maximum benefit, you should color the plates in each unit in the order presented. The simpler and broader concepts are presented in the first few plates of each unit. As the plates progress within a unit, more detailed concepts and structures are considered, and the plates may appear more complex. These may seem intimidating at first glance; however, once you begin coloring the plate in accordance with the instructions (in bold-faced type) and read the corresponding text, the illustrations will take on meaning and the relationships of different parts will become clear.

2. SUGGESTED WAYS OF USING THIS BOOK

a. If you are an informal learner and are not following any specific course-related organization, it is recommended that you begin with Plate 1-1 and color the subsequent plates *in order of presentation*. Each plate can be thoughtfully colored and read in 30 to 45 minutes. Unless you have had a formal course in neuroanatomy, neurobiology, neuropsychology, or neuroscience, coloring isolated plates at random without first coloring developmental or introductory plates may prove self-defeating. The organization of this book is based on the authors' overall perspective of the subject and represents, in their opinion, the most effective way to engage the subject. Frequent reference to the index will make possible an integration of structure, function, and disorder which have been presented in a number of different and seemingly unrelated plates.

b. The plates most applicable for use by middle and high school students are listed here. Each of these plates can be colored and the text read and understood in about 30 minutes. The 46 plates listed represent about 30 hours of work; the 28 plates listed in italics represent the most basic plates in the book: about 15 hours of work.

Unit 1: *1-1 through 1-4* (4)
Unit 2: *2-1, 2-3,* 2-4, 2-6, 2-9 (5)
Unit 3: *3-1, 3-2, 3-6, 3-7,* 3-8, 3-9, *3-12* (7)
Unit 4: *4-1, 4-2,* 4-5, 4-9 (4)

Unit 5: *5-1*, *5-2*, 5-3, *5-13*, 5-20, 5-24, *5-29*, 5-30, 5-33, 5-38, *5-44* (11)
Unit 6: *6-1*, 6-6, 6-7, 6-11, 6-25 (5)
Unit 7: *7-1*, 7-3, *7-4* (3)
Unit 8: *8-1* (1)
Unit 9: *9-1*, *9-2*, *9-3*, *9-10*, *9-11*, *9-12* (6)

c. The plates recommended for consideration in lower-division undergraduate courses of instruction, as well as related courses in schools of nursing, physical therapy, and so on, are listed below. The 81 plates listed represent approximately 55 hours of work, equivalent to 5 hours per week in an 11-week quarter or 3 to 4 hours per week in a 15- to 17-week semester. For reduced loads, consider the recommendations in paragraph b.

Unit 1: all (6)
Unit 2: 2-1 through 2-9, 2-12 (10)
Unit 3: 3-1, 3-2, 3-6 through 3-12 (9)
Unit 4: 4-1 through 4-5, 4-9 (6)
Unit 5: 5-1, 5-2, 5-3, 5-12, 5-13, 5-16, 5-20, 5-24, 5-26, 5-29 through 5-34, 5-35, 5-37, 5-40, 5-41, 5-44, 5-46 (21)
Unit 6: 6-1, 6-2, 6-4, 6-6, 6-7, 6-8, 6-11, 6-15, 6-17, 6-18, 6-19 (11)
Unit 7: 7-1, 7-3 through 7-6 (5)
Unit 8: all (4)
Unit 9: 9-1 through 9-4, 9-9 through 9-13 (9)

d. For upper-division students and students of graduate or professional schools such as medicine, chiropractic, psychology, and dentistry, who are all presumed to have had a solid background in biological science, the more detailed plates may be particularly applicable. Plates of particular significance to these students include 2-5 through 2-8, 2-10 through 2-12, 3-11, 4-4 through 4-13 (CNS pathways), and all of Units Five through Nine (115 plates, representing approximately 60 to 70 hours of work).

e. Professionals in the neurosciences or related fields, with neuroanatomy experience, may find useful Plates 2-5, 2-11, 3-11, 5-12, 5-19, 5-27, 5-28, 5-32, 5-34, and 9-4 through 9-8. An excellent review of the brain stem and cerebral hemispheres can be had by coloring Plates 5-4 through 5-11 and 5-35 through 5-48. For a review of circuits among brain stem and cerebral structures, see the table of contents and the index.

f. Frequent use of the index is strongly recommended for all users.

3. TIPS FOR COLORING THE PLATES

a. As you come to each plate, look over the entire illustration to get your bearings. Note the arrangement and order of titles. Contemplate a number of color arrangements before starting. Count the number of subscripts to find the number of colors you will need. Subscripts with exponents may receive the same color as the parent subscript, a shade of the same color, or a different pattern of the same color. Scan the coloring instructions on the text page for further guidance on choosing colors. In some cases, you may want to color related forms with different shades of the same color; in other cases, contrast is desirable. The more thought you put into the use of colors, the more information you will derive from the plate.

b. Read the coloring instructions. Follow the directions. These instructions have been developed after many coloring trials, and they work. The most important consideration is to link a structure and its title (printed in large outline or blank letters) with the same color. It is recommended that you color the title first and then its corresponding structure.

c. It is wise to scan the text before coloring. After coloring according to the directions, read the related text for color-reinforced learning. Then go to the next set of coloring instructions and continue as before. In the text, certain words are set in *italics*. The title of any structure to be colored will be set this way when it is first discussed in the text. This is to enable you to spot quickly the title of a structure to be colored. New terms may also be italicized when they are introduced.

d. In some cases, a plate of illustrations will require more colors than you have in your possession. Forced to use a color twice or three times on the same plate, you must take care to prevent confusion in identification and review by employing such a color on areas well separated from one another. Consider the use of different patterns of the same color (dots, dashes, etc.) to eliminate confusion.

e. On some plates, structures will require colors that were used for the same structures on a previous plate (this is especially true in Unit Three). In such cases, color the titles of the repeated structures first, regardless of where they appear on the plate. Then go back to the top of the title list and begin coloring in the usual sequence. In this way, you will be prevented from using a color already specified for another structure.

f. Now turn to any plate in the book and note the following aspects:

(1) Areas to be colored are bounded by heavy lines, and each such area usually has a pointer (leader) with a letter (subscript). Some boundaries between coloring zones may be represented by a dot or two or dotted lines. These represent a division of names (titles) and indicate that an actual structural boundary may not exist or, at best, is not

clearly visible. Lighter lines represent background, suggest texture, or define form and should be colored over if they exist within the confines of a heavier line. A light-line structure outside a heavy-line boundary, often marked with a no-color sign ($-\frac{1}{1}-$), should not be colored.

(2) Any outline-lettered word followed by a subscript should be colored. The main title of the plate receives a black color, indicated by the symbol (●). Subheadings, which are used for organizational reasons, are indicated by a (★) and should be colored gray. An outline-lettered word followed by a subscript and parentheses, as A( ), is not represented by a single structure to be colored but by a composition of parts whose titles are listed below it with the same letter but different exponents. This word can be colored with a mixture of the colors used for its parts.

(3) If structures are duplicated on a plate, as in left and right parts, branches, or serial (segmented) parts, only one may be labeled with a subscript. If you come upon a structure bounded by a heavy line without a subscript, look for its complementary structure above it, below it, or on the other side of the midline: you will find the subscript there.

g. Throughout this book, and others of the Coloring Concepts Series, the following symbols are employed:

●	=	color black; generally reserved for headings and subheadings
★	=	color gray; generally reserved for subheadings
$-\frac{1}{1}-$	=	do not color
A( )	=	as a subscript, signals that this structure is composed of the parts whose titles are listed below it with the same subscript but different exponents; receives same color or mosaic of colors used for parts; only its parts are labeled in the illustration
A^1, A^2, etc.	=	identical letter with different exponents implies parts so labeled are sufficiently related to receive same color or shade of the same color
N.S.	=	not shown

h. As a general rule, large areas should be colored with light colors, and dark colors should be used for small areas. Test your colors before you use them on this book. Take care with very dark colors; they obscure detail, texture lines, stippling, and subscripts (in the event they are located within the area to be colored).

i. In some cases, a structure will be identified by two subscripts (e.g., A + D). This indicates you are looking at one structure overlying another. In such a case, consider using two light colors or a pattern of lines or dots of one color superimposed over another.

THE
HUMAN BRAIN
COLORING BOOK

The human brain is the most complex mass of protoplasm on earth—perhaps even in our galaxy. A product of heredity and environment, operative for many tens of millions of years, this three-pound collection of cells is still of virtually unknown potential; yet what a history of achievement and what incredible promise for the future! Certainly no other group of cells sends travelers to the moon and soon beyond, creates the Declaration of Human Rights, reengineers genes, produces a Mozart sonata or a Turner landscape. In our search to understand the brain, we cannot expect simple answers to our questions.

What is the most significant achievement of this organ small enough to be held in one's hands? Perhaps it includes the ability to conceive of a universe a billion light-years or more across or a microcosmic world out of reach of our senses—in other words, to model worlds completely separate from the reality we can see, hear, feel, and smell.

Certainly one significant achievement is the ability of the brain to change in response to cultural diversity—with measurable chemical and structural changes! Indeed, our brains literally add nerve cell branches in response to training and learning, no matter what our age. Conversely, the brain is learning to reshape the environment in which we live and will both benefit from and suffer the consequences as it does.

The brain and its expressions are unique for every individual who has ever lived. Almost every organ of the body has the potential for being transplanted into another person. With the acceptance of each organ, the "persona" of the individual remains the same—except in the case of the brain. Transplant the brain, transplant the person, for the brain is the person. However, the brain does not carry out its functions alone; it is part of a total unit, the human body. The body is the support system for the brain and the brain for the body. The brain is dependent on the heart, liver, kidneys, lungs, and the immune system all working together.

Color the earth (A), in the upper left corner of the plate, and its title, Outer World. Then color the title Inner World (★) gray.

The *outer world* (A), represented by the globe, is the world of our external reality experienced by our sense organs and reported to our brain. The activity of our brain, in turn, constructs the inner world. It is the constant interaction between events in the two worlds that determines our survival. The concepts and ideas created in the inner world of the brain are translated into the realities of the outer world, and it is within the cerebral hemispheres that such activities take place.

Color the lobes of the cerebral hemisphere (B through E) and the related titles and activity representations.

The external surface of one cerebral hemisphere is seen here from the side. The hemispheres are subdivided into lobes, each of which is characterized by unique functional capacities. The planning of the future, represented here by the exploration of space, utilizes the *frontal lobes* (B). Musical masters have created concerti that are heard and appreciated through the action of the *temporal lobes* (C). The *occipital lobes* (D) of the hemispheres are responsible for the visual capacities necessary to construct the architectural monuments of the world. The logic of mathematics, representing perhaps the most abstract of neural functions, is derived in part from the *parietal lobes* (E).

In the next plate, the external, undissected structure of the brain as seen from the side is introduced as a means of further orientation.

INTRODUCTION TO THE HUMAN BRAIN.

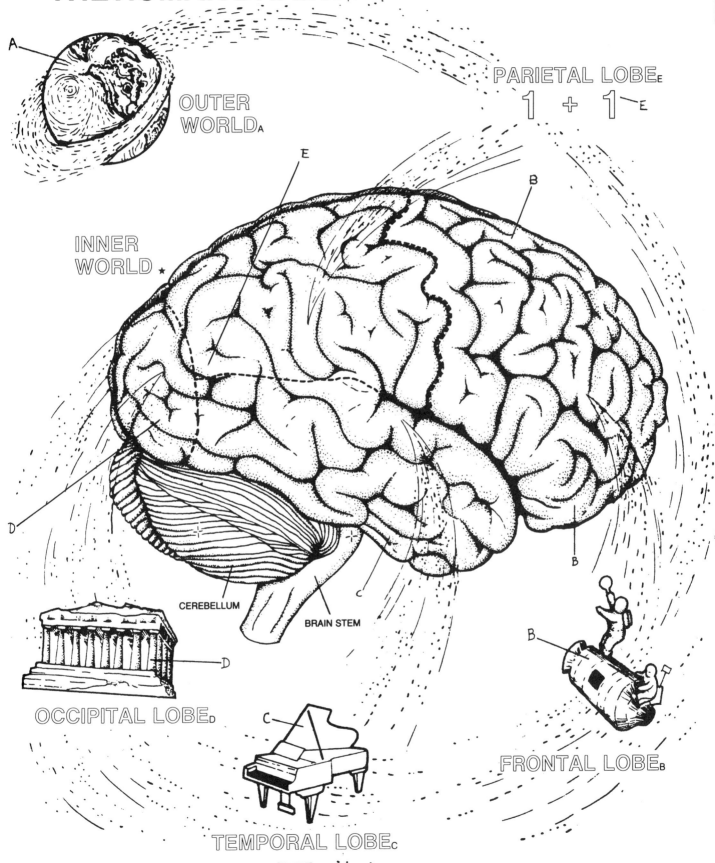

OUTER WORLD_A

PARIETAL LOBE_E

1 + 1_E

INNER WORLD ★

CEREBELLUM

BRAIN STEM

OCCIPITAL LOBE_D

TEMPORAL LOBE_C

FRONTAL LOBE_B

This plate elaborates on some structural landmarks and functional areas of the hemispheres, which are part of the forebrain, and describes some major parts of the hindbrain, as a further introduction to the brain. A more complete treatment is provided in Unit Five. Structures in this illustration that were shown in the previous plate have been given the same subscripts and should be colored identically to those in Plate 1-1.

Reserve the colors used for B, C, D, and E in the previous plate and use them here for the same structures. Color the heading Forebrain, titles A through D, and related structures. Different shades of the same color are recommended for structures that have the same subscript but different exponents. The fissures A and G and sulcus (F) are exaggerated in size for coloring.

The cerebral hemispheres are separated into right and left halves by a deep groove called the *longitudinal fissure* (A). Other prominent grooves (fissures or sulci) separate the hemispheres into lobes. Two such grooves are the *central sulcus* (F; also called *fissure of Rolando*) and the *lateral fissure* (G; also called *fissure of Sylvius*). The central sulcus runs from the top (vertex) of the hemisphere downward and forward about midway between the front and rear poles of the hemisphere. The lateral fissure runs backward and slightly upward, appearing as a deep groove between the temporal and parietal lobes.

The part of the hemisphere in front of the central sulcus is the *frontal lobe* (B). It constitutes about one third of the hemispheric surface. A major part of the frontal lobe is concerned with planning ahead, prediction, and programming for an individual's needs. The lower portion of the frontal lobe, primarily on the left side, is specialized for articulation of speech (*speech area,* B^1). A thin strip of frontal lobe just in front of the central sulcus (*motor area,* B^2) specifically controls discrete movements of the body. Injury to this area can cause paralysis of the opposite side of the body.

The part of the hemisphere below the lateral fissure is the *temporal lobe* (C), the uppermost part of which is concerned with the sense of hearing. Damage to this part of the brain results in impaired hearing or deafness. The inner surface of the temporal lobe plays a role in memory processing. Much of the remaining temporal lobe may be involved with the integration of multiple sensory functions such as auditory, visual, and touch.

The part of the hemisphere behind the central sulcus is the *parietal lobe* (E), the precise boundaries of which are difficult to delineate. Nerve impulses related to the sensations of pain, temperature, touch, and pressure enter the portion of the parietal lobe just behind the central sulcus (*primary sensory area,* E^1). Investigators have demonstrated that structural abnormalities localized in the lower regions of the parietal lobe are associated with reading disabilities. Stimulation of parts of this lobe in conscious patients produces gustatory (taste) sensations.

The *occipital lobe* (D) is behind the parietal and temporal lobes and is separated from them on the illustration by a vertical dotted line drawn between a fissure above and a notch below. A dotted line drawn from the end of the lateral fissure back to this vertical line completes the separation of parietal and temporal lobes. Visual information is processed in the occipital lobes; damage to this area results in partial or complete blindness. Visual mechanisms in the brain constitute one of the most intensely studied subjects in neuroscience.

Color the heading Hindbrain, titles H, I, and J, and related structures.

The lowest part of the hindbrain, the *medulla oblongata* (J), is continuous with the spinal cord. This 2.5-centimeter-long region controls such vital functions as respiration and heart rate. Just above the medulla is the *pons* (H; pons, bridge), which serves as part of a relay between the cerebral hemispheres and the *cerebellum* (I). The cerebellum can be identified clearly from the overlying cerebral hemispheres by its more finely folded surface. The cerebellum deals with muscle coordination and balance involved in such action as writing and walking.

INTRODUCTION TO BRAIN STRUCTURE I.

FOREBRAIN ★
 LONGITUDINAL FISSURE$_A$
 CENTRAL SULCUS$_F$
 LATERAL FISSURE$_G$
 FRONTAL LOBE$_B$
  SPEECH AREA$_{B^1}$
  MOTOR AREA$_{B^2}$
 TEMPORAL LOBE$_C$

PARIETAL LOBE$_E$
 PRIMARY SENSORY AREA$_{E^1}$
OCCIPITAL LOBE$_D$

HINDBRAIN ★
PONS$_H$
CEREBELLUM$_I$
MEDULLA OBLONGATA$_J$

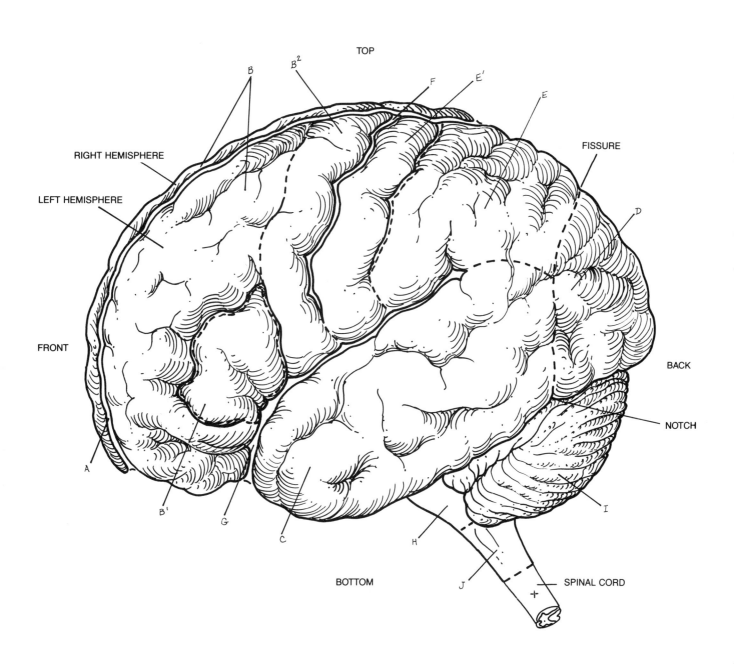

The introduction to the brain continues with this "exploded" view of the brain and upper spinal cord. You have become acquainted with the cerebral hemispheres on the two previous plates, and here you can visualize them in relation to the rest of the brain. Again, structures in this illustration that were shown earlier have been given the same subscripts and should be colored as before.

Reserve the colors used for B, C, D, E, H, I, and J in the previous plate and use them here for the same structures. Color the heading Cerebral Hemisphere, titles B through F, and related structures in the two upper illustrations.

The cerebral hemispheres consist of five lobes, four of which you have colored in a side view of the brain. Here you see those lobes as you look into the inside (medial) surface of the right hemisphere. In this case, the left hemisphere has been completely removed to permit such a view. Moving backward from the front one can see the medial surfaces of the *frontal* (B), *parietal* (E), and *occipital* (D) lobes, overlapping from the outer or lateral surface. The view also shows the underside of the *temporal lobe* (C) and the collarlike *limbic lobe* (A; *limbic*, "of a margin or border") arranged around the junction of the cerebral hemisphere with the brain stem. Some functions of the frontal, temporal, parietal, and occipital lobes have been presented on Plates 1-1 and 1-2. The limbic lobe is involved with sexual and emotional aspects of behavior and with the processing of memory.

Beneath the surface of the hemispheres are great masses of fibers (not shown) conducting impulses in all directions and large groups of cells forming discrete bodies at the base of each hemisphere: these are the *basal ganglia* (F; sing. *ganglion,* "knot"). Their major role seems to be the programming and execution of movement (motor activity). Diseases of the basal ganglia are manifested by tremors and uncontrolled movements.

Color the heading Upper Brain Stem, titles G through L, and related structures.

The uppermost part of the brain stem (tucked away into the concave bases of the hemispheres) consists largely of the *thalamus* (G), *hypothalamus* (K; *hypo-,* "below"), and *pineal gland* (L). The thalamus serves as the sensory gateway to the cerebral hemispheres. The pathways for all senses except smell stop in the thalamus before proceeding into the hemispheres. The hypothalamus packs a remarkable roster of functions into its small size (barely larger than four peas). It controls the visceral nervous system, which stimulates contraction of muscle fibers and glandular secretions in the internal organs; it regulates appetite, thirst, and temperature; and it controls the hormonal secretions from the pituitary gland and, thereby, many of the endocrine glands of the body.

The small pineal gland, located behind the thalamus, functionally resembles a biological clock, regulating body rhythms and sexual activity.

Color the rest of the headings, titles M through N, and related structures.

The middle portion of the brain stem is the *midbrain* (M), which, in part, controls automatic (reflex) patterns associated with the visual and auditory systems. Its deeper parts are concerned with other important movement patterns. The lower brain stem is a part of the hindbrain and consists of the *medulla* (J) and *pons* (H), which have been presented in Plate 1-2. The *cerebellum* (I) is the other part of the hindbrain, and its function has been described in Plate 1-2 as well.

The *spinal cord* (N) is continuous with the medulla at the base of the skull and is enclosed in the neural canal of the spine or vertebral column. It includes both ascending (generally sensation-related) and descending (generally movement-related) pathways for the conduction of impulses to and from the brain. As the most primitive portion of the human nervous system, the spinal cord receives sensory information from all parts of the body (except the face) and sends commands for motor activity.

INTRODUCTION TO BRAIN STRUCTURE II.

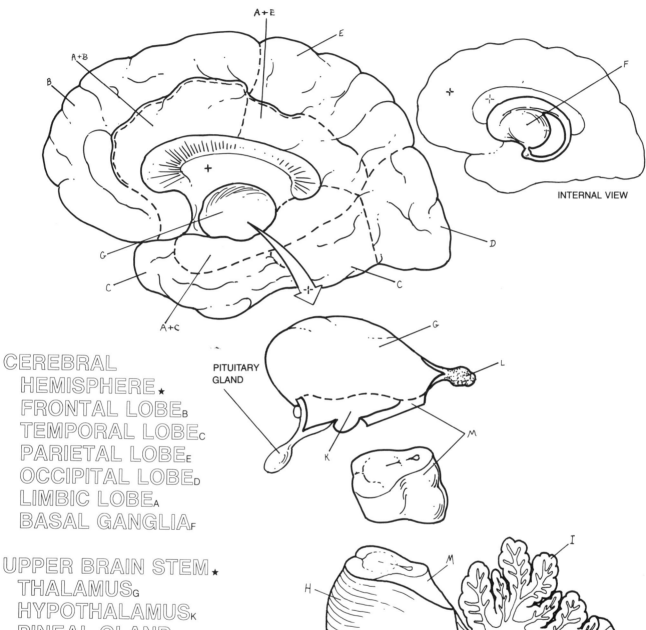

A+E

A+B

B

E

G

C

A+C

C

D

INTERNAL VIEW

F

PITUITARY GLAND

G

L

K

M

CEREBRAL
    HEMISPHERE ★
    FRONTAL LOBE B
    TEMPORAL LOBE C
    PARIETAL LOBE E
    OCCIPITAL LOBE D
    LIMBIC LOBE A
    BASAL GANGLIA F

UPPER BRAIN STEM ★
    THALAMUS G
    HYPOTHALAMUS K
    PINEAL GLAND L

MIDDLE BRAIN STEM ★
    MIDBRAIN M

LOWER BRAIN STEM ★
    PONS H
    MEDULLA J
CEREBELLUM I
SPINAL CORD N

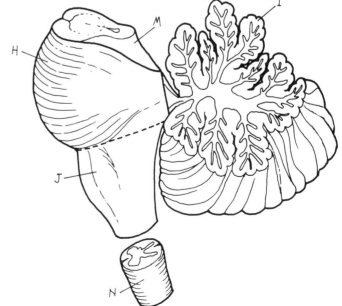

I

M

H

J

N

It is important to recognize that the cerebral hemispheres, though exciting structures in their own right, are not the entire human nervous system. In this plate, as an aid to orientation, we introduce the scheme of the entire nervous system: central, peripheral, and visceral.

Color the titles and structures A through C, contrasting the colors among the three systems.

The human nervous system consists of both central and peripheral parts. The *brain* (A^1), reposing in the cranial vault, and the *spinal cord* (A^2), encased within the neural arches of the vertebral column, constitute the *central nervous system,* or *CNS.* Not only are they centrally located, but they are also the centers of neural functions. The brain is the focus of Unit Five. The major components or areas of the brain have been introduced in the previous plate. The cerebral hemispheres are certainly the largest structures of the brain, but they are still only a part. The hemispheres are dependent on other components of the nervous system to receive information and to transmit and modify its commands.

The junction of the brain with the spinal cord occurs at the foramen magnum (not shown but see Plate 6-2), the large hole (foramen) at the base of the skull. The spinal cord is the subject of Unit Four. Pathways that transit both spinal cord and brain are also included in that unit.

The *peripheral nervous system,* or *PNS,* consists of *cranial* (B^1) and *spinal nerves* (B^2), and their components are located outside the CNS. Of the 12 paired cranial nerves, all but the first arises from the brain stem. Four cranial nerves on one side of the brain stem are diagrammatically represented here. Cranial nerves are largely concerned with the head and are the subject of Unit Six.

The 31 paired spinal nerves (several of which on one side are diagrammatically represented here) arise from the spinal cord and, like cranial nerves, consist of nerve cell processes conducting sensory-related impulses and/or processes conducting movement-related (motor) impulses. Spinal nerves are concerned with the entire body except the areas of the head that are supplied by the cranial nerves; they are the topic of Unit Seven.

The *visceral nervous system,* or *VNS* (C; also called *autonomic nervous system,* or *ANS*), is concerned with the motor innervation (nerve supply) of cardiac muscle and of glands and smooth muscles of cavity-containing body organs (viscera), as well as with the sensory innervation of viscera. Viscera include the organs of the thoracic, abdominal, and pelvic cavities, certain structures of the head and neck, as well as blood vessels, sweat glands, and hair-raising muscles throughout the skin. Components of the VNS include parts of the brain and spinal cord, cranial and spinal nerves, as well as their own specialized parts. Shown here is a part of a chain of VNS nerve cells located in the thoracic, abdominal, and pelvic cavities and connected to the spinal cord by parts of spinal nerves. Processes of these VNS motor nerve cells are directed to visceral structures. The motor component of the VNS is the subject of Unit Eight. The sensory component of the VNS is more diffusely arranged than the motor component and cannot be structurally distinguished from sensory axons to somatic (musculoskeletal and skin) structures. See the index, under VNS, for a complete list of plates considering both sensory and motor components.

In essence, all three divisions of the nervous system are constantly interacting with each other. They are presented separately only because each has some specific characteristics.

ORGANIZATION OF THE NERVOUS SYSTEM.

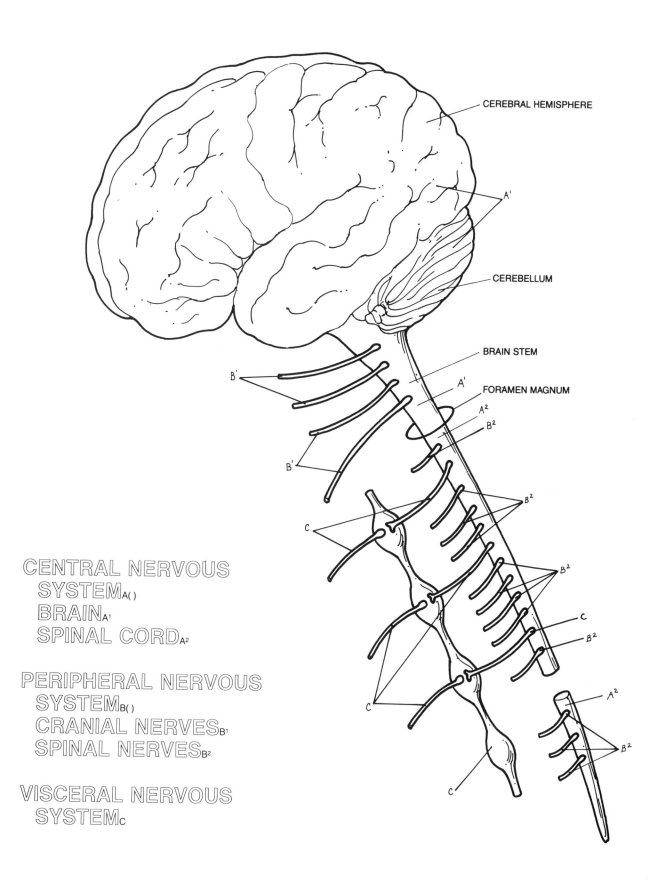

CEREBRAL HEMISPHERE

A^1

CEREBELLUM

BRAIN STEM

A^1

FORAMEN MAGNUM

A^2

B^2

B'

B'

B^2

C

B^2

C

B^2

C

A^2

C

B^2

CENTRAL NERVOUS
SYSTEM$_{A(\ )}$
BRAIN$_{A^1}$
SPINAL CORD$_{A^2}$

PERIPHERAL NERVOUS
SYSTEM$_{B(\ )}$
CRANIAL NERVES$_{B^1}$
SPINAL NERVES$_{B^2}$

VISCERAL NERVOUS
SYSTEM$_C$

The brain is an organ of complex shape and orientation, and a number of special terms of position and direction are helpful in describing its structure. Such terms are employed universally in anatomy, medicine, and biology and are well worth learning at the outset of one's study of the nervous system. Once learned, they will facilitate a degree of precision in description that will always be useful to you. In this plate, we begin with terms that apply to quadrupeds (four-footed animals) and then relate them to terms applied to the brain and spinal cord. Other terms used in reference to the nervous system are also introduced.

Color the heading Quadruped, subheadings Head End, Tail End, Back and Belly, titles A through D, and the arrows relating to the horse.

In the four-legged animal, such as the horse, the anatomic terms of direction are based on the four basic reference points: head in front, tail behind, back up, and belly down. Such terminology presupposes that the animal is in a standing position. The classic terminology for these four basic reference points comes from the Latin or Greek.

The head or front end of the animal is said to be *anterior* ("front") or *rostral* (*rostrum*, "beak, mouth") or *cranial* (A; *cranium*, "head").

The tail or hind end is said to be *posterior* ("behind") or *caudal* (B; *cauda*, "tail").

The back of the animal is said to be *dorsal* (C; *dorsum*, "back").

The belly of the animal is said to be *ventral* (D; *venter*, "belly").

Color the heading Bipedal, titles A^1 through D^1, and the arrows relating to the brain and spinal cord. Then color the titles E through J and their related arrows.

With the development of the upright or bipedal posture of human beings, the four basic reference points of the body in three-dimensional space change through a full 90 degrees. In the standing person, therefore, the front is also the belly side and the hind end is also the back.

The head end becomes the upper end: *cranial* (A^1) or *superior* (A^2; "upper"). In some areas of the brain (but not the brain stem nor spinal cord), the term *dorsal* (C^1) is sometimes carried over from the quadruped to mean "upper."

The tail end becomes the lower end: *inferior* (B^2; "lower") or *caudal* (B^1). The term *caudal* is used with reference to the brain stem or spinal cord but not the cerebrum. In some areas of the brain (but not the brain stem nor spinal cord), the term *ventral* (D^1) is sometimes carried over from the quadruped to mean "lower."

The back of the brain and spinal cord is *posterior* (B^3). In the case of the brain stem and spinal cord (as well as the body in general), the term *dorsal* (C^1) is used synonymously with *posterior*. Although both terms are seen in descriptive anatomy, *posterior* is generally preferred.

The front of the brain and spinal cord is *anterior* (A^4) or *rostral* (A^3). In the case of the brain stem and spinal cord (as well as the body in general), the term *ventral* (D^1) is used synonymously with *anterior*. Both terms are seen in descriptive anatomy, but *anterior* is generally preferred.

Referring to the human figure, a few additional terms of direction are shown. If a structure is on the same side as a reference point, it is said to be *ipsilateral* (E; *ipsi*, "self"). If it is on the opposite side of the reference point, it is said to be *contralateral* (F; *contra*, "against"). For example, movement of your left hand is initiated by the contralateral hemisphere.

When comparing two structures, the structure closer to the midline is said to be *medial* (G) to the other, which is *lateral* (H). Thus the important medial lemniscus of the spinal cord and brain stem is closer to the midline than the lateral lemniscus.

The terms *proximal* (I) and *distal* (J) refer to relative distances from a reference point, proximal being closer and distal being farther. In the illustration, *proximal* is closer to the root of the limb, and *distal* is farther away. For example, damage to the radial nerve of the upper limb is more likely proximal to the elbow than distal.

TERMS OF DIRECTION.
QUADRUPED.
HEAD END★
  ANTERIOR/ROSTRAL/
    CRANIAL$_A$
TAIL END★
  POSTERIOR/CAUDAL$_B$
BACK★   BELLY★
  DORSAL$_C$ VENTRAL$_D$

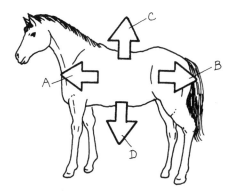

QUADRUPED.

BIPEDAL.
CRANIAL$_{A^1}$/
SUPERIOR$_{A^2}$/
DORSAL$_{C^1}$

ROSTRAL$_{A^3}$/
ANTERIOR$_{A^4}$

INFERIOR$_{B^2}$/
VENTRAL$_{D^1}$

POSTERIOR$_{B^3}$

CAUDAL$_{B^1}$

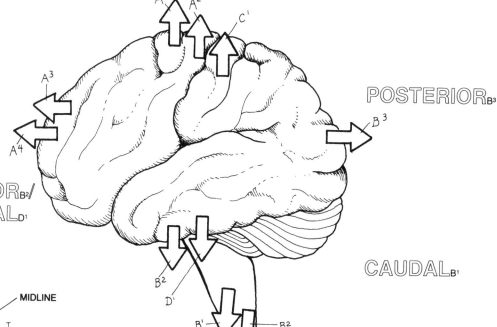

IPSILATERAL$_E$
CONTRALATERAL$_F$
MEDIAL$_G$
LATERAL$_H$
PROXIMAL$_I$
DISTAL$_J$

REFERENCE POINT

MIDLINE

BIPEDAL.

Exploration of the structure of the central nervous system has for more than a century been based on the detailed study of slices or sections cut through brain substance in one or another group of specified orientations. Thus our understanding of internal structure or the relationship of structures is dependent on a knowledge of the planes of sections illustrated here.

Color the heading Planes, titles A through E, and the related structures in the three uppermost illustrations.

The *median plane* (A) divides a structure (in this case, the brain) along its longitudinal axis into left and right halves. Median or *midline* sections of the hemispheres are used frequently to study structure immediately adjacent to the midline (see Plate 1-3).

The *sagittal plane* (B; *sagitta,* "arrow") runs along the longitudinal axis parallel to the median plane. Sagittal sections of the hemispheres, brain stem, or cerebellum are often employed to study internal structure (see Plates 5-41 through 5-44).

The *coronal* or *transverse plane* (C; *corona,* "crown") divides a structure perpendicular to the long axis. Coronal sections (slices) of the hemispheres are frequently used to study internal structure (see Plates 5-35 through 5-40). The term *cross section* (D) is also applied to transverse sections of the spinal cord and brain stem.

The *horizontal plane* (E) is perpendicular to both the coronal and sagittal planes and is parallel with the earth's horizon. Horizontal sections of the hemispheres are often employed to study internal structure (see Plates 5-45 through 5-48).

Color the heading Relative Dimensions, titles F through J, and the related vertical bars and abbreviations. Bright, contrasting colors are recommended here. Note the relative diameters of the structures indicated along the upper border of the diagram.

All descriptions of the nervous system that include quantitative statements about size (linear dimensions, volume, weight) are expressed in the metric system. The length and thickness of structures and their apparent distance from each other are important aspects of all descriptive science. The basic unit of linear measurement in the metric system is the *meter* (F), about 10 percent longer than the yard. The various units of this system differ from each other by multiples of ten. Thus, a *decimeter* (seldom used) is $\frac{1}{10}$ meter, a *centimeter* (abbreviated cm, written 10^{-2} m) is $\frac{1}{100}$ meter, and a *millimeter* (G; abbreviated mm, written 10^{-3} m) is $\frac{1}{1000}$ meter.

In the field of cellular biology, we deal with structures of the order of a thousandth of a millimeter (*micrometer,* H; abbreviated μm, written 10^{-6} m; formerly called a *micron,* abbreviated μ) and a millionth of a millimeter (*nanometer,* I; abbreviated nm, written 10^{-9} m). The next smallest order of magnitude, a ten-millionth of a millimeter, is the *angstrom* (J), abbreviated Å and written 10^{-10} m. The angstrom is named after Swedish physicist Anders J. Angström. It is infrequently used today. The term *picometer,* abbreviated pm, is more commonly used.

As you color the plates on the nervous system, you will find it interesting to turn back to this plate when dimensions are given and relate the size of the structure to the examples given at the upper border of the lowest diagram on this plate.

PLANES OF SECTION AND RELATIVE DIMENSIONS.

PLANES.
MEDIAN/MIDLINE_A
SAGITTAL_B
CORONAL/TRANSVERSE_C
CROSS SECTION_D
HORIZONTAL_E

RELATIVE DIMENSIONS.
METER_F
MILLIMETER_G
MICROMETER_H
NANOMETER_I
ANGSTROM_J

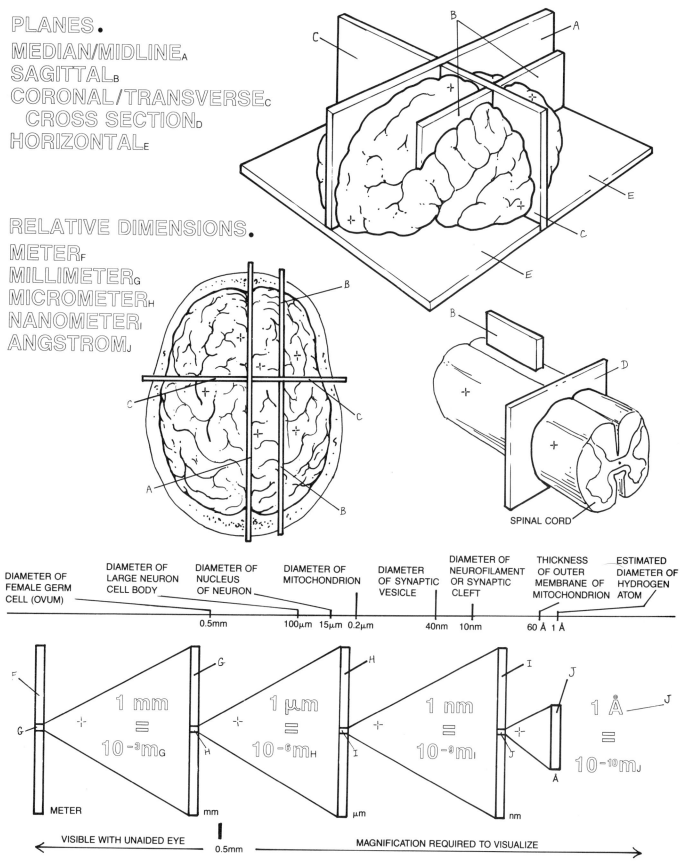

SPINAL CORD

DIAMETER OF FEMALE GERM CELL (OVUM)	DIAMETER OF LARGE NEURON CELL BODY	DIAMETER OF NUCLEUS OF NEURON	DIAMETER OF MITOCHONDRION	DIAMETER OF SYNAPTIC VESICLE	DIAMETER OF NEUROFILAMENT OR SYNAPTIC CLEFT	THICKNESS OF OUTER MEMBRANE OF MITOCHONDRION	ESTIMATED DIAMETER OF HYDROGEN ATOM
	0.5mm	100μm 15μm	0.2μm	40nm	10nm	60 Å	1 Å

$1\ mm = 10^{-3}m_G$

$1\ \mu m = 10^{-6}m_H$

$1\ nm = 10^{-9}m_I$

$1\ Å = 10^{-10}m_J$

METER

mm

μm

nm

VISIBLE WITH UNAIDED EYE

0.5mm

MAGNIFICATION REQUIRED TO VISUALIZE

The neuron (nerve cell) is the basic information-processing unit of the nervous system. Several hundred billion of these cells, integrated into a functional mosaic by untold billions of interconnections, make possible the recognition and interpretation of a myriad of sensory stimuli (understanding), retention of experience (memory), and the elaboration of an enormous range of responses (behavior).

Color the headings Neuron and Processes, titles A through E⁴, and related structures in the upper neuron. Then color the parts of the magnified neuron below. The nucleus (B) is being viewed through the wall of the cell body (A) and therefore receives A and B colors (consider crosshatching or dotting with both colors). Use different shades of the same color for E through E⁴.

The neuron consists of a *cell body* (A; also called *soma*) with its *nucleus* (B) and a number of processes (polar extensions or branches). The neurons shown here have a number of such processes projecting from their cell bodies and are therefore called multipolar neurons. Seven processes are shown: six are *dendrites* (C) and one is an *axon* (E).

   The dendrites spread out from the cell body like the branches of a tree and greatly increase the surface area of the neuron, thereby making more space available to receive contacts from other neurons. Here the dendrites have been trimmed back. These dendrites, which depend on the cell body for their survival (nutrition, DNA-directed growth and repair activities, and so on), range from a few tens of micrometers to as much as several millimeters in length. Like radio antennas, dendrites collect incoming (afferent) information from other neurons or sensory receptors. The dendrites receive these incoming impulses directly on their surface membrane or on tiny projections of membrane called *dendritic spines* (D), which project outward for a few micrometers like forests of tiny lollipops. The afferent information reaches the neuronal cell body in the form of membrane electrical disturbances (to be discussed in Plate 2-7).

   The neuron and its various parts constitute a highly plastic entity, capable of a good deal of growth and reshaping, especially at the ends of the dendritic tree. But the dendritic spines are thought to be the most plastic elements of the entire neuron—arising out of the membrane, growing, changing shape and size, and probably disap-

pearing, all in response to shifting patterns of information coming onto the neuron.

   Impulses are conducted away from the neuronal cell body by a single process called the axon, with the exception of a few neuron types known to function without axons. The axon emerges from the cell body as a conical protrusion called the *axon hillock* (E¹). The course the axon then follows depends on the nature of the parent neuron and the target element to be reached. Axons are very short (100 micrometers or less), while others have very long courses (up to more than 1 meter). Axons are covered by a cellular *sheath* (F; Schwann cells in the PNS, oligodendrocytes in the CNS) with or without a lipoprotein insulating material called *myelin*.

   Most axons develop side branches along the route. These are called *axon collaterals* (E²) and help to bring information to several parts of the nervous system simultaneously. When the target neural elements are reached, the axon (and collaterals) end in a small number of *terminal branches* (E³). Important specialized structures called *synaptic terminals* (E⁴) are usually found at the tips or terminal ends of the axons. The synaptic terminals transmit nerve impulses from one neuron to the next, thereby providing one of the primary means of intercommunication in the nervous system. That specialized site of the target neuron or other cell type (such as muscle) upon which the terminal impinges constitutes one of the most important anatomical and functional entities in the entire nervous system: the synapse (Plates 2-4 and 2-5).

Color the heading Dendritic Tree Organization, titles G through K, and the related structures in the upper neuron.

The parts of a dendrite can be identified by the sequence of their branching pattern (branch order). In the present case, using what is technically called a centrifugal notation, we can call the first part or shaft of the dendrite (as it leaves the cell body) the *first-order segment* (G). The first branching (*first bifurcation,* H) produces *second-order segments* (I). The *second bifurcation* (J) produces *third-order segments* (K), and so on. Note that there are very few spines on first-order dendrites, so any terminals here would be likely to make contact directly with the dendrite shaft. Spines become more numerous on second- and third-order segments, and so on, but decrease again in number as the most peripheral (farthest out) branches are reached.

THE NEURON.

NEURON ★
  CELL BODY_A
  NUCLEUS_B
PROCESSES ★
  DENDRITE_C
  DENDRITIC SPINE_D

AXON_E
  AXON HILLOCK_{E1}
  SHEATH_F
  AXON COLLATERAL_{E2}
  TERMINAL BRANCH_{E3}
  SYNAPTIC TERMINAL_{E4}

DENDRITIC TREE
ORGANIZATION ★
FIRST-ORDER SEGMENT
(SHAFT)_G
FIRST BIFURCATION_H
SECOND-ORDER SEG._{□I}
SECOND BIFURCATION_J
THIRD-ORDER SEG._{□K}

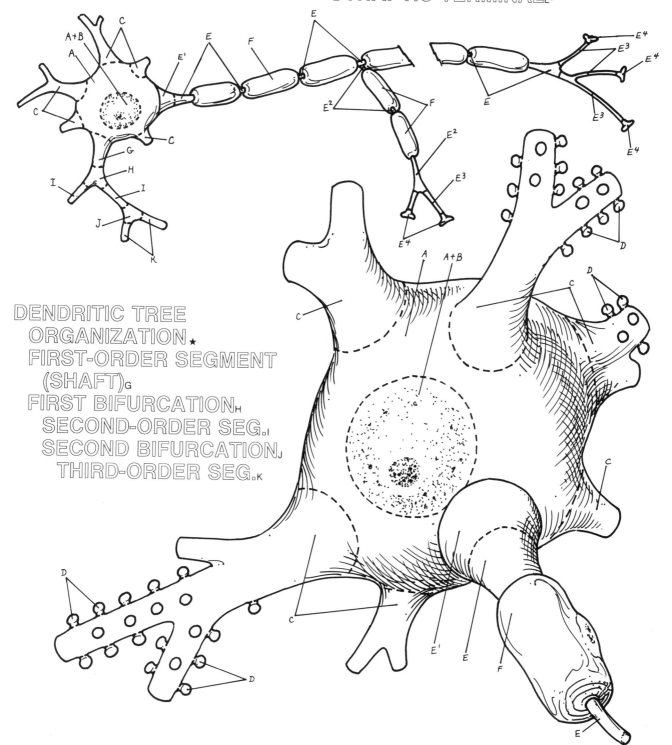

The whole neuron and its processes were considered in the preceding plate. Here we concentrate on the fine or smaller structures of the neuron that are usually studied with electron microscopes. The integrative functioning of these units makes possible the generation and conduction of nerve impulses so basic to nervous activity.

Reserve the colors used for A and B in Plate 2-1 and use them for these structures here. Color the heading Neuron, titles A through B³, and related structures in the larger illustration.

The neuron is bound by a triple-layered, highly pliable, lipoprotein-rich *cell membrane* (A). This membrane is capable of incredibly rapid inpocketings and outpocketings to ingest and expel neurotransmitters and other substances in the moment-to-moment activity of the cell. The interior of the neuronal cell body consists of a dense, chemical gel called cytoplasm. Within the cytoplasm, there is a nucleus (karyon) and numerous organelles ("little organs").

The *nucleus* (B) is the administrative center of the cell, bound by a porous *nuclear membrane* (B¹). The pores covered by a granular ultrastructure act as passageways between the interior of the nucleus and the cytoplasm. The interior of the nucleus is called the *nucleoplasm* (B²), consisting largely of chromatin, the hereditary material that directs the operations of the cell. Via the pores of the nuclear membrane, the chromatin (not shown) communicates with cytoplasmic organelles, largely with regard to the production of structural protein. The nuclei of neurons are generally quite large; this is probably related to the metabolic load involved in supporting the immense amount of protein in the surface membrane of the multiple, treelike processes of the neuron. The *nucleolus* (B³), a mass of protein and ribonucleic acid, stands out boldly in the pale-staining nucleus and is intimately involved in ribosomal synthesis. In active neurons, there may be many nucleoli.

Ordinarily, the nucleus is located centrally in the cell body. In a few cell types, however, the nucleus is eccentrically situated. In an injured neuron, the nucleus is invariably found at the periphery of the cell—one of the indications sought by pathologists and other investigators in examining injured or destroyed nerve tissue.

Color the heading Cytoplasm, titles C through E, and related structures in the main illustration.

The cytoplasm of a neuron contains many of the same organelles found in other cells. *Mitochondria* (C), concerned with cell respiration and energy dynamics, are prominent in all parts of the neuron, especially in the cell body and in the synaptic terminals (Plate 2-4). Numerous rows of platelike membranous sacs, called the *endoplasmic reticulum* (D; also known as *ER* or *Nissl substance*), are found in the cell body and shafts of the dendrites. Often covered with small granular bodies (ribosomes), these structures are important in the synthesis of proteins. *Golgi bodies* (E) are stacks of membrane-lined canals involved in the packaging of proteins in vesicles for transport or discharge, as in the case of neurotransmitters.

Color the title and structure of the microtubule (F) in the larger illustration. Then color the heading Intracellular Transport, titles G and H, and the related structures in the lower illustration. The title Neurofilament and related structure receive no color.

The products of protein synthesis migrate into the farthest reaches of the axon and dendrites via axoplasmic and dendroplasmic flow or transport. A spectrum of transport rates, from slow (1–10 mm/day) to fast (100–400 mm/day) has been described for the innumerable liquid and solid constituents of the neuron. More rapid rates of transport may be associated with long, tubelike filaments called *microtubules* (F) and neurofilaments (F¹). These are synthesized in the cell body and extend, skeletonlike, throughout the neural processes. Intracellular transport occurs in both directions: *Somatofugal* (G) transport moves away from the cell, and *somatopetal* (H) transport moves toward the cell. The mechanical basis for this plasmic flow is not well understood.

Pigment of various types (not shown) is found in many neurons, including a fat-protein complex called lipofuscin, which accumulates with age, and melanin, a black pigment that occurs normally in the neurons of specific regions of the brain.

FINE STRUCTURE OF THE NEURON.

NEURON.★
  CELL MEMBRANE$_A$
  NUCLEUS$_{B( )}$
    NUCLEAR MEMBRANE$_{B^1}$
    NUCLEOPLASM$_{B^2}$
    NUCLEOLUS$_{B^3}$

CYTOPLASM.★
  MITOCHONDRIA$_C$
  ENDOPLASMIC RETICULUM$_D$
  GOLGI BODY$_E$
  MICROTUBULE$_F$
  NEUROFILAMENT$_{F^1}$✛

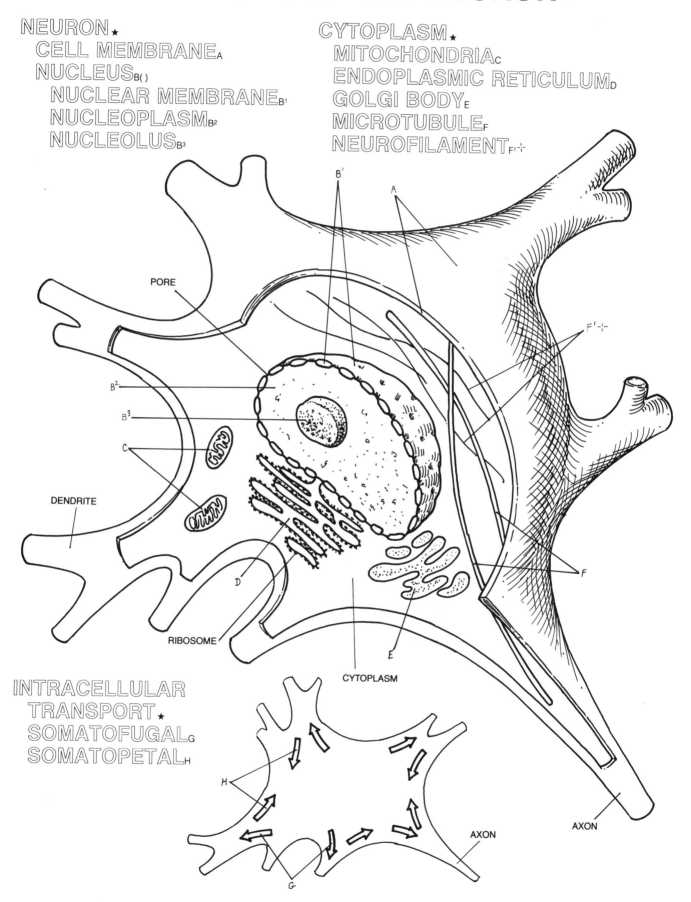

PORE

DENDRITE

RIBOSOME

CYTOPLASM

AXON

AXON

INTRACELLULAR
TRANSPORT.★
  SOMATOFUGAL$_G$
  SOMATOPETAL$_H$

Each part of the nervous system is microscopically characterized by the size, shape, and arrangement of the neurons composing it. Even though some neurons have many internal characteristics in common, their forms vary tremendously. Within that variety, neurons are generally classified according to structure, function, and type of neurotransmitter. This plate is concerned with structural and functional classifications.

It is not unusual for the cell bodies of neurons to be collected into masses or groups. Groups of unencapsulated neuronal cell bodies in the CNS are called *nuclei* (sing. *nucleus*); in the PNS, such groups, generally encapsulated, are called *ganglia* (sing. *ganglion*). In the CNS, masses of neuronal cell bodies and neuroglia largely contribute to the gray matter of the brain and spinal cord.

The long fibers or axons of neurons are also often grouped. In the CNS, bundles of axons carrying information or motor commands of one kind are called *tracts*. Tracts make up the white matter of the CNS. In the PNS, discrete bundles of axons bringing information to the CNS from peripheral structures and conducting motor commands to muscles and glands are called *nerves*.

Color the heading Structural, titles A through C², and related structures and arrows.

Neurons may be classified structurally according to the numbers of their processes. Those without processes or with only one are seen in embryonic neural tissue (Plate 3-3). Such neurons are termed *apolar* and *unipolar* (not shown here). Neurons with two fused processes that appear as one are called *pseudounipolar* (A; *pseudo*, "false") and are generally restricted to groups of sensory neuron cell bodies located outside the CNS (ganglia). In these neurons, the short, single process (stem) branching off from the cell body splits into a central process conducting impulses toward the spinal cord and a peripheral process conducting impulses toward the cell body. Impulses moving along the peripheral process probably pass into the cell body before entering the central process. Peripheral and central processes, as well as the stem of the pseudounipolar neuron, are axonal in structure and function.

Bipolar neurons (B), are limited to two processes, usually one dendrite and one axon, occasionally two dendrites. Bipolar neurons are found in selected areas such as the ganglia of the VIII cranial nerve, the retina, and the olfactory epithelium (receptor cells in the roof of the nasal cavity).

Multipolar neurons (C) are characterized by one axon and two or more dendrites. They are the most common neurons in the nervous system. *Golgi I neurons* (C¹) are multipolar cells whose axons extend considerable distances to their target cells. They are found throughout the nervous system, examples here being the pyramidal cell of the cerebral cortex, the Purkinje cell of the cerebellum, and the anterior horn cell of the spinal cord. Multipolar neurons with short axons terminating quite close to the cell body of origin are called *Golgi II neurons* (C²). They are typified by the stellate (shown here) or granule cells of the cerebral cortex. Of all the neurons, the multipolar seem to exhibit the greatest variety of shapes and sizes.

Color the heading Functional, titles D, E, and F, and related arrows.

Neurons are functionally classified as sensory, motor, or interneuron.

Sensory neurons (D) conduct impulses from receptors to the brain and spinal cord, such impulses being informational (vision, sound, touch, pain, and so forth). Sensory neurons are the sensory (afferent) components of spinal and cranial nerves; their cell bodies largely make up the spinal (posterior root) and cranial ganglia. Sensory neurons are typically pseudounipolar or bipolar.

Motor neurons (E) conduct impulses from the brain and spinal cord to effectors (muscles and glands), resulting in the contraction of muscle fibers or the secretion of gland cells. Motor neurons are the motor (efferent) component of spinal and cranial nerves. In practice, they are often called lower motor neurons. They are generally multipolar.

Interneurons (F) are neurons whose cell bodies and processes remain within the CNS; in other words, they have no direct contact with peripheral structures (receptors and effectors). One important group of interneurons, whose axons descend and terminate on motor neurons in the brain stem and spinal cord, are called upper motor neurons. Interneurons are responsible for the modification, coordination, integration, facilitation, and inhibition that must occur between sensory input and motor output. They are the source of the seemingly unlimited array of responses to our environment. Interneurons are generally multipolar in structure.

CLASSIFICATION OF NEURONS.

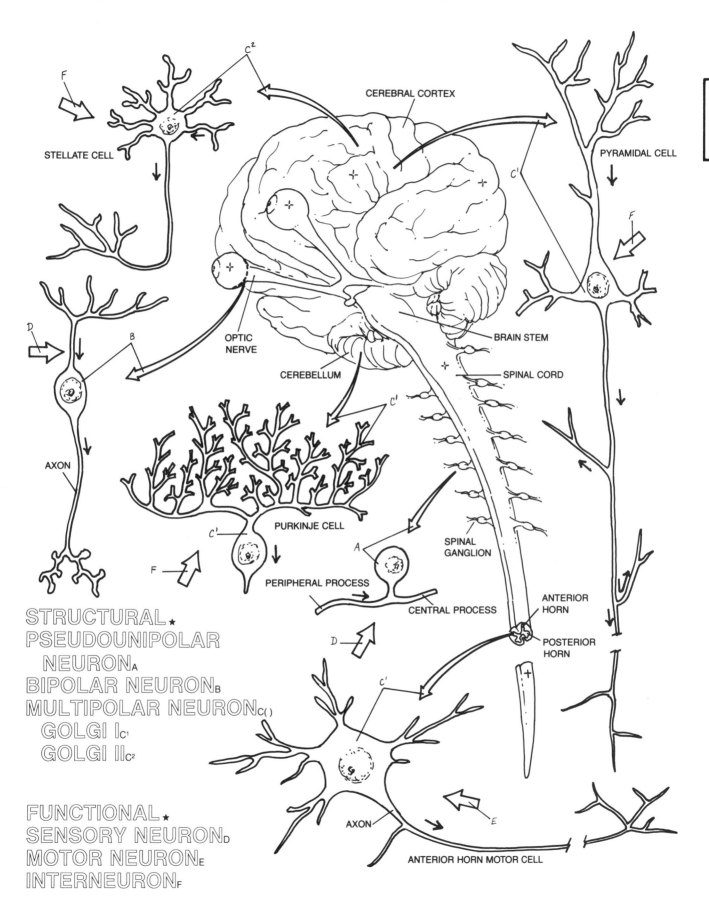

STELLATE CELL

CEREBRAL CORTEX

PYRAMIDAL CELL

OPTIC NERVE

BRAIN STEM

CEREBELLUM

SPINAL CORD

AXON

PURKINJE CELL

SPINAL GANGLION

PERIPHERAL PROCESS

CENTRAL PROCESS

ANTERIOR HORN

POSTERIOR HORN

STRUCTURAL ★
PSEUDOUNIPOLAR
   NEURON_A
BIPOLAR NEURON_B
MULTIPOLAR NEURON_C( )
   GOLGI I_C1
   GOLGI II_C2

AXON

ANTERIOR HORN MOTOR CELL

FUNCTIONAL ★
SENSORY NEURON_D
MOTOR NEURON_E
INTERNEURON_F

The role of the neuron is to communicate, and the role of the nervous system is to generate behavior, both by virtue of interneuronal connections. Neurons communicate with neurons at sites called *synapses* (A; "clasps") or synaptic junctions. The structural details of these communication links are of central importance in understanding how the brain works. In this and the next plate we will examine the basic structure of a synapse, the types of synapses, and the fine detail of the synaptic elements and their functions.

Color the titles A through C[1] and related structures in the upper part of the plate. The Synaptic Cleft title and area (E) should be left uncolored).

Every synaptic junction is made up of a part of a neuron (*presynaptic terminal*, B; *pre-*, "before") that conducts an impulse to the synapse and a part of another neuron (*postsynaptic structure*, F; *post-*, "after") that receives the stimulus at the synapse. The stimulus must cross a narrow (approximately 20 nm) gap, the *synaptic cleft* (E), which separates pre- and postsynaptic structures. Since the synapse does not involve a physical contact between the neurons, a chemical carrier (called a *neurotransmitter*, D[1]) is generally required to bridge the gap. Such synapses, characterized by the release of neurotransmitters from presynaptic terminals, are the most common type in mammalian nervous systems.

Chemical synapses are recognized with the electron microscope by the presence of many small, bubblelike *synaptic vesicles* (D) in the presynaptic terminals. Frequently shown to contain neurotransmitters, synaptic vesicles come in many sizes (20–120 nm in diameter) and shapes (spherical or elliptical with dense or clear cores or centers). Vesicles of a certain size or shape are sometimes associated with specific transmitters. Energy for the release of the transmitter is generated in the *mitochondria* (C) of the presynaptic terminal. Binding of the neurotransmitter to receptors of the postsynaptic membrane produces changes in permeability of that membrane. Depending on the nature of the neurotransmitter and of the postsynaptic receptor, the effect may be either excitatory or inhibitory. *Mitochondria* (C[1]) are also found in the postsynaptic structure.

Color the heading Neuronal Elements in Synaptic Transmission, titles G through I, and related structures, including F[1], associated with the large central neuron. Then color the heading Chemical Synapse and titles J through R. Starting at the upper left part of the large neuron, color the Type I synapse (J) arrow and parts. Work to the right and clockwise around the neuron, coloring each kind of synapse (arrow and parts). Stop at the electrotonic synapse (S); do not color it at this time. If it is necessary to use the same color twice, space its use to prevent confusion when reviewing the plate.

Chemical synapses are generally named for the neuronal elements (*axon*, G; *dendrite*, H; *dendritic spine*, H[1]; *cell body* or *soma*, I) of which they are composed. Chemical synapses are generally considered to be asymmetrical (*Type I*, J) or symmetrical (*Type II*, K). Asymmetrical synapses are characterized by a difference in the density of the presynaptic and postsynaptic membranes, the *postsynaptic density* (F[1]) being the thicker. This density consists of a protein material that is applied to the postsynaptic membrane and may be associated with postsynaptic receptors. In symmetrical synapses, the opposed presynaptic and postsynaptic membranes are of the same thickness.

As you can see in the main illustration (from upper center, moving clockwise around the neuron), synapses can be formed between axon and soma (*axosomatic*, L); axon and dendrite (*axodendritic*, M); axon and dendritic spine (*axospinodendritic*, N); axon and axon (*axoaxonal*, O); dendrite and dendrite (*dendrodendritic*, P); and soma and soma (*somatosomatic*, Q). More complex combinations of several of these elements, often surrounded by a neuroglial sheath, are called *glomeruli* (R; sing. *glomerulus*, "skein, ball").

Color the title Electrotonic Synapse (S) and its parts in the bottom illustration.

Another major type of synapse, first described in invertebrates but now recognized with increasing frequency in mammalian vertebrates, is the *electrotonic synapse* (S). In this synapse, pre- and postsynaptic processes are contiguous, and the stimulus is thus able to pass directly from one cell to the next without chemical mediation.

THE SYNAPSE: STRUCTURE AND TYPES.

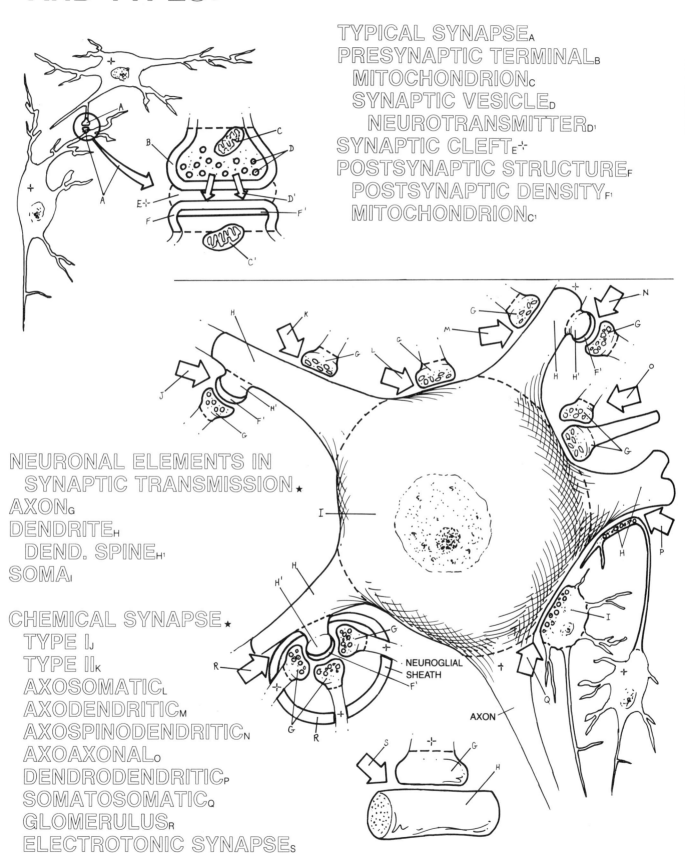

TYPICAL SYNAPSE_A
PRESYNAPTIC TERMINAL_B
MITOCHONDRION_C
SYNAPTIC VESICLE_D
NEUROTRANSMITTER_{D¹}
SYNAPTIC CLEFT_E
POSTSYNAPTIC STRUCTURE_F
POSTSYNAPTIC DENSITY_{F¹}
MITOCHONDRION_{C¹}

NEURONAL ELEMENTS IN
SYNAPTIC TRANSMISSION ★
AXON_G
DENDRITE_H
DEND. SPINE_{H¹}
SOMA_I

CHEMICAL SYNAPSE ★
TYPE I_J
TYPE II_K
AXOSOMATIC_L
AXODENDRITIC_M
AXOSPINODENDRITIC_N
AXOAXONAL_O
DENDRODENDRITIC_P
SOMATOSOMATIC_Q
GLOMERULUS_R
ELECTROTONIC SYNAPSE_S

NEUROGLIAL
SHEATH

AXON

A great deal has been learned about the fine structure and the modes of action of chemical synapses over the last 30 years. Not only are they transmitters of neural information, but they also produce and discharge chemical substances called neurotransmitters. Further, they may gather up the remnants of this material and reprocess and repackage it for future use. In this plate, we consider the dynamics of the movement, discharge, uptake, and reformation (resynthesis) of a neurotransmitter, such as acetylcholine, as a part of the process that conveys a stimulus from one neuron to another.

Color the heading Presynaptic Terminal, titles A through I and C¹, and the related structures in the large illustration.

Some *neurotransmitters* (C), such as peptides, are produced in the cell body, packaged within *vesicles* (B) that migrate down the axon by axoplasmic flow (perhaps along the *neurotubules,* A) to the presynaptic terminal, where they are called *synaptic vesicles* (B¹). In an alternative process, the transmitter substance, such as acetylcholine, may be produced from precursor substances ("building blocks") in the immediate vicinity of the presynaptic terminal. In either event, it is critical for the synaptic vesicles to be adjacent to the *presynaptic membrane* (F).

When an impulse reaches the presynaptic terminal, it is accompanied by the entry of *calcium ions* (Ca++; D) into the neuronal cytoplasm from the tissue fluids outside the neuron (extracellular space). Calcium ions, which have passed through the cell membrane, bind to a carrier molecule called *calmodulin* (E). The Ca++ enhances the migration of some of the synaptic vesicles toward the presynaptic membrane. The membrane of each vesicle undergoes *fusion* (G) with the presynaptic membrane, followed by rapid expulsion (*exocytosis,* H; *exo-,* "outside"; *cyt-,* "cell") of *free neurotransmitter* (C¹) into the *synaptic cleft* (I). Recent data indicate that acetylcholine may also exist unencapsulated in the cytoplasm of the presynaptic terminal.

Color title J, the heading Postsynaptic Structure, titles K through N, and the related structures, including the lower right inset of the magnified view of the postsynaptic membrane and its constituent receptor molecules (L) and the ion-specific channel (L¹).

The free neurotransmitter released into the synaptic cleft interacts directly with the *receptor molecules* (L) in the *postsynaptic membrane* (K). By such an interaction, a number of *ion-specific channels* (L¹) are believed to be opened. This permits an electric current, carried by charged ions, to flow through the postsynaptic membrane, affecting the electrochemical status of the membrane in the immediate area of the channel. In this way, the electrical excitability of that tiny patch of membrane can be increased or decreased (through electrical depolarization or hyperpolarization of the membrane, a topic covered in Plate 2-8). Individual electrical disturbances in the postsynaptic membrane exert an effect on the membrane potential of the neuron, which can lead to the generation of a nerve impulse.

Once released into the synaptic cleft, the neurotransmitter is, in some cases, quickly inactivated (broken down) by specific enzymes. The resulting *neurotransmitter fragments* (J) are either washed away or recycled through a process called *endocytosis* (M; *endo-,* "within") in which case the fragments are incorporated into a new vesicle formed from the presynaptic membrane. Such a structure is called a *coated vesicle* (N) and is somewhat different in appearance from the synaptic vesicle. It is interesting to note that the venom of the black widow spider, *Lactrodectus mactans,* causes rapid fusion of synaptic vesicles to the synaptic membranes and prevents the re-formation of coated vesicles.

Neurotransmitter fragments taken up by endocytosis are ultimately resynthesized as the complete neurotransmitter. In other cases, as with amine-containing transmitters such as norepinephrine, the neurotransmitter in the synaptic cleft is not fragmented but is reclaimed, in its entirety, through the presynaptic membrane into the presynaptic terminal.

Color title O and the related structures in the illustration at lower left.

The ultrastructure of the pre- and postsynaptic membranes is still incompletely understood. Many investigators believe that the presynaptic membrane is associated with a *presynaptic grid* (O) made up of alternating thick and thin filamentous elements arranged with almost crystalline regularity. This grid has much to do with guiding synaptic vesicles from the pool of vesicles to their point of fusion with the presynaptic membrane.

THE SYNAPSE: STRUCTURAL AND FUNCTIONAL DYNAMICS.

PRESYNAPTIC TERMINAL ★
   NEUROTUBULE$_A$
   VESICLE$_B$
   SYNAPTIC VESICLE$_{B^1}$
     NEUROTRANSMITTER$_C$
   CALCIUM IONS (Ca^{++})$_D$
   CALMODULIN$_E$
   PRESYNAPTIC MEMBRANE$_F$
   FUSION$_G$
   EXOCYTOSIS$_H$

SYNAPTIC CLEFT$_I$
   FREE NEUROTRANSMITTER$_{C^1}$
   NEUROTRANS. FRAGMENT$_J$

POSTSYNAPTIC
   STRUCTURE ★
   POSTSYNAPTIC
     MEMBRANE$_K$
   RECEPTOR MOLECULE$_L$
   ION-SPECIFIC CHANNEL
     (OPEN)$_{L^1}$

ENDOCYTOSIS$_M$
COATED VESICLE$_N$

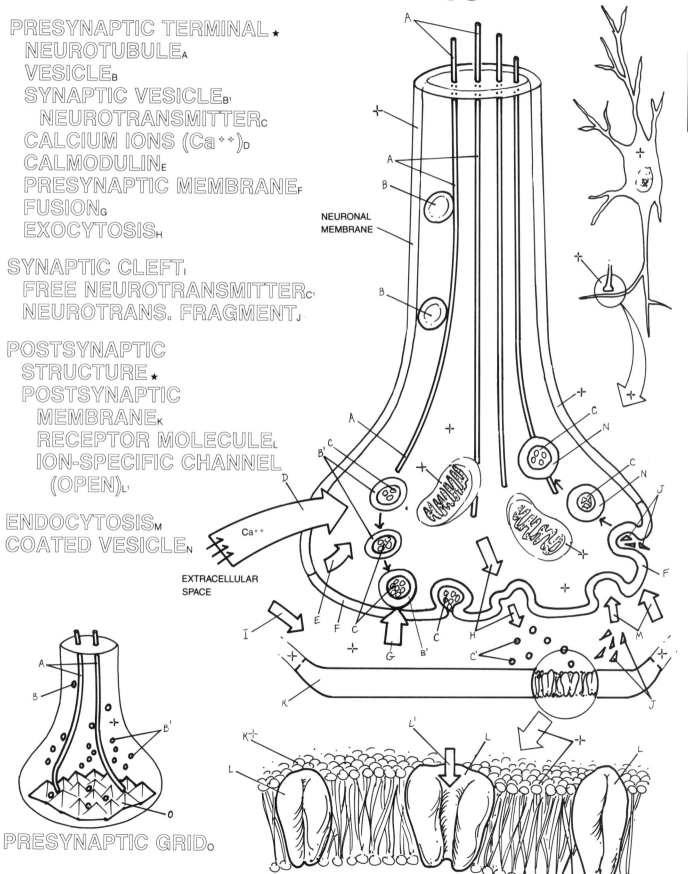

NEURONAL
MEMBRANE

Ca^{++}

EXTRACELLULAR
SPACE

PRESYNAPTIC GRID.

In carrying out their role, the neurons depend on a population of cells called *neuroglia (neuro-,* "nerve"; *glia,* "glue"; also called *glia* or *glial cells*). In the CNS, these include macroglia, microglia, and ependymal glia. In the PNS, they include satellite and Schwann cells. Developing glia (glioblasts, radial glioblasts) are considered in Plates 3-4 and 3-11.

Neuroglia support the function of neurons. In part, they regulate the concentration of ions (atoms with an electrical charge, such as potassium) in the extracellular spaces of the brain and spinal cord, and they may play a role in the blood-brain barrier. In addition, they are involved in several other functions discussed in this plate.

Unlike most neurons, neuroglia are capable of cell division after birth. In fact, they are often the structural element in slow-growing tumors of the brain. Further, neuroglia do not form synapses. Although they do participate in slow, electrical phenomena, they are not capable of transmitting impulses.

Color the heading Central Nervous System (A★) and the brain and spinal cord at left gray. Color the title Blood Vessel (B) and the corresponding structure red. Color the neurons and axons in the center gray; they have no title. Then color the heading Macroglia, titles C through E³, and related structures. Shades of the same color are recommended for structures with the same subscript but different exponents.

The macroglia include the *astrocytes* (C through C²) and the *oligodendrocytes* (E through E³).

Astrocytes (*astro,* "star") are the most common type of glia found in the *CNS* (A★). They are of two kinds, *protoplasmic* (C¹) and *fibrous* (C²). Protoplasmic astrocytes are found primarily in gray matter (unmyelinated areas, consisting largely of the cell bodies and dendrites of neurons) and are characterized by numerous branching processes. Fibrous astrocytes are found primarily in white matter (bundles of myelinated axons) and exhibit long, thin, relatively unbranched processes. Both types are larger than oligodendrocytes.

Some processes of astrocytes terminate in expansions called "end feet" or attachments. They are applied to the surfaces of *blood vessels* (B) (*capillary end feet,* D), to dendrites (*dendritic attachments,* D¹), and to the pia mater (*pial attachments,* D²), the innermost covering of the brain and spinal cord. Capillary end feet may be involved in transporting substances between blood vessels

(capillaries) and neurons. Dendritic attachments are applied to the parts of dendrites not covered by synapses and may be involved in metabolic support of the neuronal membrane. The pial attachments of the astrocytes form a functionally protective membrane with the pia mater called the pia-glial membrane.

Oligodendrocytes (oligo, "few"; *dendro,* "tree," meaning "few treelike processes") are smaller than astrocytes and have fewer processes. *Satellite "oligos"* (E¹) are found close to the neuronal cell membranes. *Interfascicular (inter-,* "between"; *fasciculus,* "small bundle") *"oligos"* (E²) are known to form myelin around the axons of neurons of the CNS. The counterpart of the oligodendrocyte in the peripheral nervous system (PNS) is the *Schwann cell* (J); the two differ in that the Schwann cell myelinates one fiber at a time, whereas the "oligo" can myelinate several fibers simultaneously. Occasional oligodendrocytes with perivascular attachments (*vascular oligodendrocytes,* E³) are seen adjacent to capillaries.

Color titles F and G and the related structures.

Microglia (F) are the smallest of the neuroglia. They actively proliferate in response to injury within the CNS. During the resting stage, they have small, dark, elongated nuclei and scanty cytoplasm. When activated (as in scavenging for foreign bodies or injured tissue), microglia swell up with ingested material. In this condition they are known as "gitter cells" (*gitter,* "lattice", referring perhaps to the spongelike or porous appearance of distended microglia).

Ependymal glia (G) are the cells that line the cavity of the brain and spinal cord (the ventricles and central canal). They are discussed in Plate 3-4.

Color the heading Peripheral Nervous System (H★) and its representative structure, the spinal nerve and its roots, gray. Then color titles I and J and related structures in the magnified view of the spinal ganglion.

The neuroglia of the *PNS* (H★) are the *satellite cells* (I; surrounding the neuronal cell bodies of the spinal ganglia) and the Schwann cells (J; enveloping the axons of the PNS). Satellite cells appear to serve the same nutritive and supportive functions as the macroglia of the CNS. Schwann cells play an important role in nerve regeneration (Plate 7-6).

NEUROGLIA.

CENTRAL NERVOUS
   SYSTEM$_A$ ★
BLOOD VESSEL$_B$

MACROGLIA ★
   ASTROCYTE$_{C()}$
      PROTOPLASMIC$_{C^1}$
      FIBROUS$_{C^2}$
      CAPILLARY END FEET$_D$
      DENDRITIC ATTACH.$_{D^1}$
      PIAL ATTACH.$_{D^2}$

OLIGODENDROCYTE$_{E()}$
   SATELLITE OLIGO.$_{E^1}$
   INTERFASCIC. OLIGO.$_{E^2}$
   VASCULAR OLIGO.$_{E^3}$
MICROGLIA$_F$
EPENDYMAL GLIA$_G$

PERIPHERAL NERVOUS
   SYSTEM$_H$ ★
SATELLITE CELL$_I$
SCHWANN CELL$_J$

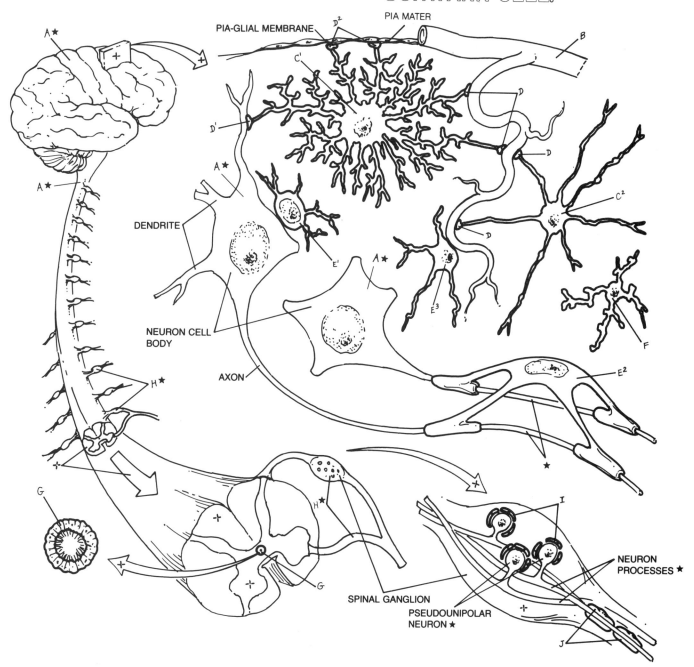

MEMBRANE POTENTIAL

The human body is approximately 60 percent water (by weight) in which a number of salts are dissolved. Salts in solution are dissociated into atoms with electrical charges (ions or electrolytes). The molecular arrangement and properties of cell membranes throughout the body create a barrier to the flow of certain ions through those membranes, resulting in a difference in proportion of ionic charges between the two sides of the membrane. A potential difference (or voltage; "potential" for short) is thus created across the membrane.

All cell membranes demonstrate a reasonably stable *resting potential* (A) between the outside of the cell and the inside. Certain cells, specifically nerve and muscle cells, have excitable membranes. In response to a stimulus, the membrane potential of these cells undergoes a series of rapid changes, called an action potential, resulting in the formation of a nerve impulse. Nerve impulses are the currency of the nervous system and will be considered in the next plate. This plate visually explores the basis for the resting membrane and action potentials.

Two longitudinal sections of one axon are illustrated on this plate. In each drawing, an oscilloscope is shown with wires leading to two recording electrodes that measure the voltage inside and outside the cell. The voltage values, in thousandths of a volt, or millivolts (mV), are indicated by small horizontal bars at the left side of the oscilloscope screen and are represented on the oscilloscope screen by a line.

Color the titles in the upper part of the plate and related structures in the upper two drawings. Use a light color for C and F. Color over the positive and negative charges with the colors of your choice. Scan the following paragraph before coloring.

The membrane resting potential is created by the selective permeability of the *cell membrane* (B) to certain ions in the *extracellular fluid* (C) and *intracellular fluid* (F) compartments. In the resting state, the cell membrane is virtually *impermeable* (D^1, G^1) to *sodium ions (Na +)* (D) and *protein ions (Pr −)* (G) largely concentrated outside and inside the cell, respectively. It is much more *permeable* (E^1, H^1) to *chloride ions (Cl −)* (E) and *potassium ions (K +)* (H), which are largely concentrated in the extracellular and intracellular fluids, respectively.

As a result of the selective permeability of the membrane and the imbalance in concentration of the K +, the potassium ions flow outward from the cell interior. The net movement of K + out of the cell creates a resting potential across the nerve cell membrane of about −70 mV with an excess of *negative charge* (−) inside and an excess of *positive charge* (+) outside the cell. It is the energy of this resting potential that the neuron taps each time an impulse is generated.

Color the heading Action Potential, the titles at the bottom of the plate, and related structures in the lower two drawings. Start with the Depolarization Phase (D through H^1) illustrated on the left half of the lower axon segment, coloring the outer perimeter (I) first. Then continue with the Repolarization Phase (J through H^2) and Hyperpolarization Phase (K), beginning with the outer perimeter (J) of the right half of the segment. Color over the positive and negative charges with the colors of your choice. Color the cell membrane and fluid compartments as you did before. Then color the illustration at the right.

Following a stimulus, there is a sudden change in *permeability* (D^2) of the membrane to Na + (opening of channels to sodium), which rushes into the cell interior, causing a rapid alteration in the voltage at the membrane from −70 mV to +35 mV. This reversal in the polarity of the charge at the membrane is called *depolarization* (I). Note the arrangement of charges at the membrane during this time; they are reversed. After 0.8 millisecond, the Na + channels close; at the same time, an increased number of potassium channels open (potassium *permeability,* H^1), and intracellular K + escapes to the outside. This event drives the membrane potential back toward its initial value, −70 mV, a phenomenon called *repolarization* (J). During this stage, there is a brief *hyperpolarization* (K) or "overshooting" of the membrane potential.

The restorative process is made complete by the *sodium and potassium pumps* (D^3, H^2), which move Na + and K +, respectively, out of and into the cell. These ions are moved against their gradients by these metabolic, energy-utilizing, enzyme-operated pumps until a stable, resting membrane potential of about −70 mV is once again achieved.

MEMBRANE POTENTIAL.

RESTING POTENTIAL$_A$
CELL MEMBRANE$_B$
EXTRACELLULAR FLUID$_C$
SODIUM ION (Na$^+$)$_D$/
IMPERMEABILITY$_{D^1}$
CHLORIDE ION (Cl$^-$)$_E$/
PERMEABILITY$_{E^1}$
POSITIVE CHARGE (+)

INTRACELLULAR FLUID$_F$
PROTEIN ION (Pr$^-$)$_G$/
IMPERMEABILITY$_{G^1}$
POTASSIUM ION (K$^+$)$_H$/
PERMEABILITY$_{H^1}$
NEGATIVE CHARGE (−)

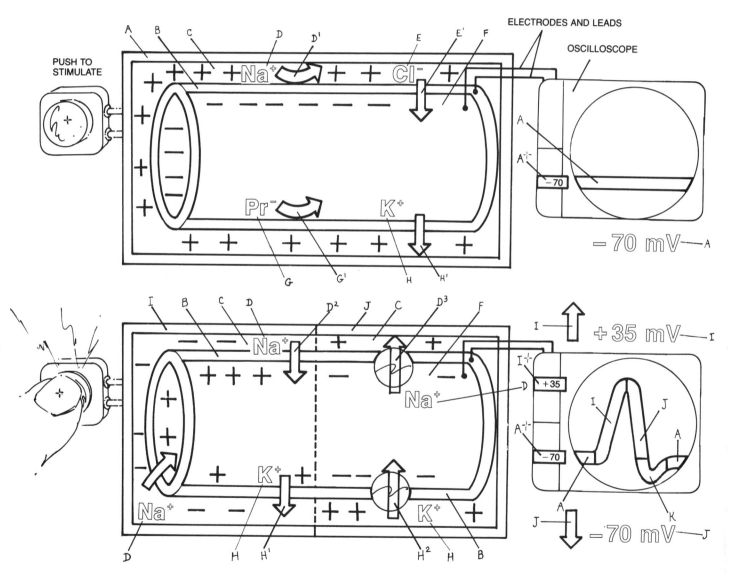

ACTION POTENTIAL.★
DEPOLARIZATION PHASE$_I$
Na$^+$$_D$/PERMEAB.$_{D^2}$
K$^+$$_H$/PERMEAB.$_{H^1}$

REPOLARIZATION PHASE$_J$
Na$^+$ PUMP$_{D^3}$
K$^+$ PUMP$_{H^2}$
HYPERPOLARIZATION PHASE$_K$

It is not sufficient that a nerve cell membrane be capable of simply firing an action potential; that potential must be conducted along the length of the membrane as well. In many cases that membrane is part of an axon, and that axon may be as long as 1 meter! Further, the conduction of the action potential must take place quite rapidly. How long does it take you to be aware of pain after you have stepped on a sharp object? Consideration of the mechanism for conduction of the action potential (nerve impulse) and structural factors that enhance the velocity of impulse conduction are the subjects of this plate.

Color the titles in the upper half of the plate and the related structures in the upper illustration of the axon. Consider using the same colors for the structures repeated on this plate from the Plate 2-7 (A, B, I, J, and charges). Begin coloring area A opposite the Start arrow and work to the left. Color all the structures in each area of electrical activity (A, I, J, and A) before going to the next. Charges with a broken line are transient, consistent with the refractory state (E). After coloring section I, color the nerve impulse (D). Read the text before going on to the lower illustration.

Conduction of the nerve impulse along the *cell membrane* (B) depends on a series of local electrical events, each of which is triggered by the one immediately preceding it.

Depolarization (I) of a patch of membrane causes a local interchange of ions with an adjacent patch (A, to the right of I), which, if sufficient to depolarize that patch to a threshold level, results in a full-fledged action potential there. This transfer of depolarization is generated by a *current flow* (C) created by the movement of *positive charge* (+) (ions) into an area of *negative charge* (−) (see the intracellular arrows) and the extracellular surge of positive ions into the region of depolarization (extracellular arrows). The current spreads along the axon, seeking a pathway of least resistance; the higher the membrane resistance, the farther the current flows along the axon. The result is a self-propagating *nerve impulse* (D) moving along the membrane without loss of speed or energy.

In theory, the nerve impulse moves in both directions; in practice, it probably does not, as the patch (J) behind the most recently depolarized area (I) is recovering from the depolarized state (*repolarization,* J) and therefore still likely to be in a nonresponsive or *refractory state* (E). The existence of such refractory periods immediately following

the passage of impulses also explains why every axon has a maximum rate of impulse conduction beyond which it cannot conduct. Following the refractory state, the membrane returns to a *resting potential* (A, the section of the axon farthest to the left).

Color the heading and titles F and G at the bottom of the plate. In the lower illustration, color the myelin sheath (F) around the axon and the arrows pointing to the interspace between sheaths (nodes of Ranvier, G). Then color the positive charges in the extracellular space at right, followed by the current flow (C) arrows to the extracellular negative charges. Proceed to the intracellular positive charges, then to the current flow arrows (C) and the intracellular negative charges. Finally, color the movement arrow (D) representing impulse conduction.

Axons of the PNS greater than 1 micrometer in diameter have a lipoprotein-rich membrane coat called the *myelin sheath* (F). Produced and maintained by Schwann cells (not shown), myelin sheaths are interrupted at the interface between these cells. Such interruptions are called *nodes of Ranvier* (G), and here the axon is naked, making the nodes preferential sites for impulse generation and propagation. Myelin, being a fatty substance, resists the flow of current through it, and the number of Na^+ channels in the underlying axonal cell membrane is limited. Where the myelin sheath is absent, at the node of Ranvier, the Na^+ channels are packed into the membrane more densely than in any other region of the neuronal membrane. Nodes of Ranvier are also found in the CNS.

When excitation of a myelinated axon occurs, the action potential literally jumps from node to node (saltatory conduction; *saltare,* "to jump"). Note how the intracellular current flow moves from one node to the next. The myelin sheath prevents the current from leaking back across the membrane as it is "booted" to the next node. The greater the distance between nodes, the faster the speed of conduction. In general, the larger the axon, the greater the impulse velocity.

Impulses in certain large, myelinated sensory and motor fibers may travel as fast as 100 meters per second (m/s); the smallest myelinated axons conduct impulses at 3 m/s or more. The more numerous nonmyelinated axons —without nodes and therefore without saltatory conduction—conduct impulses more slowly.

NERVE IMPULSE AND SALTATORY CONDUCTION.

CELL MEMBRANE_B
RESTING POTENTIAL_A
  POS./NEG. CHARGES_{+,−}
DEPOLARIZATION_I
  CURRENT FLOW_C
  POS./NEG. CHARGES_{+,−}
  NERVE IMPULSE_D

REPOLARIZATION_J
REFRACTORY STATE_E
  POS./NEG. CHARGES_{+,−}
RESTING POTENTIAL_A
  POS./NEG. CHARGES_{+,−}

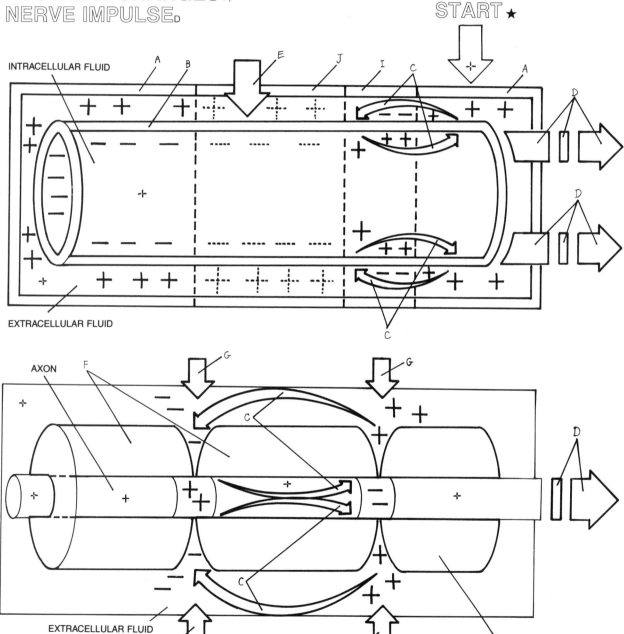

INTRACELLULAR FLUID

START ★

EXTRACELLULAR FLUID

AXON

EXTRACELLULAR FLUID

SALTATORY CONDUCTION ★ NODE OF RANVIER_G
MYELIN SHEATH_F

GENERAL SENSORY RECEPTORS OF THE BODY SURFACE

Stimuli from the external environment are constantly impinging on our body surface. These stimuli are sensed by specialized endings of sensory neurons called *receptors* and are then transmitted by these neurons to the spinal cord or, in the case of cranial nerves, to the brain for interpretation and response. Various kinds of stimuli are sensed by receptors of the skin, ranging from touch (tactile sensation) and temperature to pressure and pain. Some of these receptor types have been shown to be specialized for one or more specific kinds of stimuli.

Receptors are essentially transducers; that is, they receive the energy of the stimulus in one form and transform that energy into another form. In the case of the majority of receptors in the skin, mechanical energy presses on, displaces, or deforms the receptor (mechanoreceptor), which converts the energy into an electrochemical event, resulting in a nerve impulse. There are many kinds of receptors. The most common classification of receptors (proposed by Sherrington in 1906) organizes receptors according to their position in the body. "Exteroceptors" receive stimuli on the surface of the body; "proprioceptors" receive stimuli from muscles, tendons, and joints (Plate 2-10); and "interoceptors" receive stimuli from internal surfaces, such as walls of viscera and blood vessels. Here we consider representative exteroceptors of the cutaneous (skin) and subcutaneous areas. Exteroceptors are further classified by the kinds of stimuli to which they respond (touch, pressure, etc.) and the structure of the receptor (encapsulated, unencapsulated, etc.).

Color the headings Skin (A★) and Unencapsulated Exteroceptors, titles B through E¹, and the related structures. Color titles H and I and related structures associated with receptors B, C, and D. Then color the heading Sources of Stimulation, titles J, K, and L, and the related arrows.

Unencapsulated nerve endings terminate as *free* (B), branched fibers in the epithelial layer of the *skin* (A★), wrap around the lower shafts of hair (*perifollicular,* C), or form flattened discs (*Merkle's disc,* D) abutted against *modified epithelial cells* (E). Free nerve endings are the simplest type of receptor. As the parent *axon* (H) reaches the epithelial layers, it loses its *Schwann cell sheath* (I) and forms numerous branches, which ramify throughout the

deep layer. Free nerve endings are receptive to stimuli that may be interpreted as *touch* (J), *temperature* (K), and *pain* (L).

Touch a hair on your arm or head and note the tactile sensation. The nerve endings responsible are of the perifollicular (*peri-,* "around"; *folliculus,* "cavity, sac") type and are generally filamentous, like the free nerve endings. One parent axon approaches a nest of hairs, loses its sheath, and breaks up into as many as 100 branches, innervating as many hairs.

Certain receptors consist of nerve endings shaped like flattened discs, each of which encloses the base of an epithelial cell. Each of these Merkle's discs lies adjacent to *vesicles* (E¹) within the epithelial cell. There is some evidence that light pressure (touch) on the epithelial cell releases from the vesicles a transmitter that stimulates the Merkle's disc.

Color the heading Encapsulated Exteroceptors, titles F and G, and the related structures, as well as the axons and sheaths associated with them. Color titles M and N and the related arrows.

There is a large family of encapsulated endings, of which *Meissner's corpuscles* (F) and the *Pacinian corpuscles* (G) are typical examples.

Meissner's corpuscles are distributed in the hairless parts of the skin, most commonly in the epithelial layer in the fingertips, the palms of the hands and the soles of the feet, the nipples, and the external genitals. Meissner's corpuscle consists of a laminated capsule of connective tissue cells surrounding a spiral-coursed naked nerve ending in the center of the capsule. The sheaths of the nerve blend with the connective tissue capsule, at which point the myelin covering is lost. Meissner's corpuscles are particularly receptive to mechanical shear forces applied to the skin and probably participate in two-point discrimination.

The Pacinian corpuscle is the most widely distributed of the encapsulated receptors. It is also the largest; in fact, it is visible with the naked eye (1 by 2 mm in size). The laminations of the connective tissue capsule resemble a slice of onion with the laminae separated from one another by clear fluid and tiny blood vessels. Known to respond to *pressure* (M) stimuli, Pacinian corpuscles may also be sensitive to *vibratory* (N) stimuli in the upper and lower limbs.

GENERAL SENSORY RECEPTORS OF THE BODY SURFACE.

SKIN꜀ ★
UNENCAPSULATED
   EXTEROCEPTORS ★
   FREE_B
   PERIFOLLICULAR_C
   MERKLE'S DISC_D
   MODIF. EPITHELIAL CELL_E
      VESICLE_E'

ENCAPSULATED
   EXTEROCEPTORS ★
   MEISSNER'S CORPUSCLE_F
   PACINIAN CORPUSCLE_G
AXON_H
   SCHWANN C. SHEATH_I

SOURCES OF STIMULATION. ★
   TACTILE_J
   TEMPERATURE_K
   PAIN_L
   PRESSURE_M
   VIBRATION_N

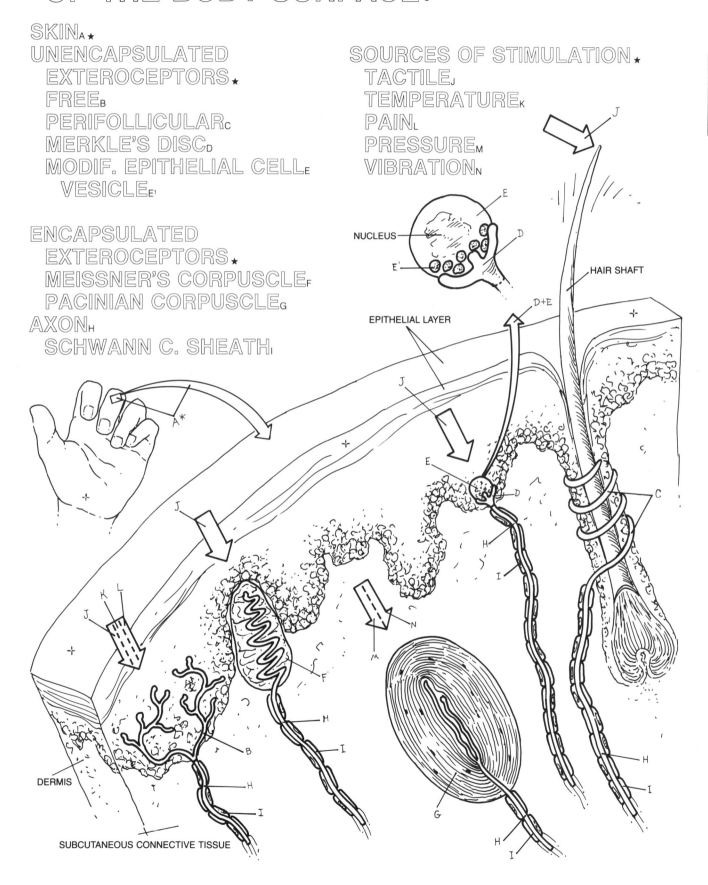

NUCLEUS
EPITHELIAL LAYER
HAIR SHAFT
DERMIS
SUBCUTANEOUS CONNECTIVE TISSUE

Special receptors are needed in muscles, tendons, ligaments, and joints to provide information about muscle and joint movements and position. In this plate, two encapsulated proprioceptors, called *neuromuscular* or *muscle spindles* (A) and *neurotendinous* or *Golgi organs* (J), are considered. They are activated by the stretching of the muscles and tendons, respectively, within which they are located. Impulses from these receptors reach several regions of the CNS (via the spinal nerves or cranial nerves), such as the cerebellum, to result in the coordination of muscle activity during movement.

Color titles A through D, the heading Intrafusal Fiber, and the related structures in the upper right and center illustrations. Carefully plan your coloring scheme before starting.

Neuromuscular spindles are numerous in the muscles of the limbs and especially the small muscles of the hands and feet. Scattered throughout the contractile parts (belly) of each muscle, muscle spindles are long, slender, *connective tissue–encapsulated* (B) receptors averaging 2 to 4 millimeters in length. They lie parallel to the surrounding skeletal muscle fibers and are attached at each of their ends to the connective tissue envelope (not shown) of the adjacent skeletal muscle. The central part of each spindle contains a considerable amount of fluid, giving it a swollen appearance. Within each spindle there are 2 to 12 long, slender, specialized skeletal muscle fibers called *intrafusal fibers* (intra-, "within"; *fusal,* "fusiform, slender"). Intrafusal fibers are different from the more numerous extrafusal muscle fibers: they are smaller, and their contractions put tension on the spindle only. Unlike extrafusal fibers, they do not contribute to the movement of bones around joints. Intrafusal fibers are of two types, *nuclear bag fibers* (C) and *nuclear chain fibers* (D). Nuclear bag fibers are relatively large; exhibit saclike, nuclei-filled central portions; extend beyond the capsule ends (shown beyond the lower end of the spindle capsule and labeled C); and contract relatively slowly. Nuclear chain fibers each contain a single row or chain of nuclei and are each attached at their ends to the bag fibers.

Color the heading Innervation Pattern, titles E through H[1], and the related axons and endings. Note that the alpha motor axon (I-¦-) is not to be colored.

Muscle spindles are supplied by axons of both sensory and motor neurons. The sensory axons are of two kinds: large myelinated fibers (E; classified group Ia or class A *primary* muscle spindle *afferents*) that come into the spindle and terminate around the nuclear bag and chain fibers with wraparound or *annulospiral endings* (E[1]) and smaller myelinated axons (F; group II or class A *secondary* muscle spindle *afferents*) that terminate primarily around nuclear chain fibers with *flowerspray endings* (F[1]). The sensory endings of these axons are sensitive only to the stretch or elongation of the intrafusal fibers that occurs when the extrafusal muscle mass is stretched (as occurs during stretching movements or exercises). They are not sensitive to extrafusal muscle contraction. The motor axons to muscle spindles are specialized, relatively small myelinated efferents (G; classified A *gamma* [γ] *efferents*), unlike the axons of the larger A or alpha (α) motor neurons (I) to the extrafusal muscle fibers. Gamma efferents have two kinds of endings: a leash of fine filaments called *trail fibers* (G[1]), which innervate both nuclear bag and nuclear chain fibers, and discrete *end plates* (G[2]) located at the ends of the nuclear bag fibers. In addition, certain motor axons to extrafusal fibers, designated *beta* (β) *efferents* (H), innervate the nuclear bag fibers just outside their connective tissue capsule via *beta end plates* (H[1]). Gamma efferents cause the contraction of intrafusal fibers in response to involuntary commands from the central nervous system, resulting in a resetting of afferent nerve-ending sensitivity to extrafusal muscle and muscle spindle stretch (see Plates 4–11 and 4–12).

Color the titles and headings relating to the Neurotendinous Organ (J through O) and associated structures in the drawings at the left.

Neurotendinous (Golgi) organs (J) are encapsulated receptors found in most (if not all) *tendons* (N). Tendons are the noncontractile ends of *muscles* (O) and consist of cords or sheets of connective tissue (collagen) fibers attached to bones (and their sheaths) or other tendons. The capsules of these receptors are tightly layered *cellular sheets* (K). The receptors consist of twisted braids of small *collagen* fibers, called *fibrils* (L), intertwined with *group Ib afferents* (M). It is believed that tension on the tendon during muscle lengthening or shortening stretches the twisted fibrils, tightening them and deforming the entrapped axons sufficiently to generate an action potential.

STRETCH RECEPTORS.

MUSCLE SPINDLE A
  C. T. CAPSULE B
    INTRAFUSAL FIBER ★
      NUCLEAR BAG F. C
      NUCLEAR CHAIN F. D
    INNERVATION PATTERN ★
      PRI. AFFERENT AXON E
        ANNULOSPIRAL ENDING E¹
      SEC. AFFERENT AXON F
        FLOWERSPRAY ENDING F¹
      GAMMA EFFERENT AXON G
        TRAIL FIBER G¹
        END PLATE G²
      BETA EFFERENT AXON H
        BETA END PLATE H¹
    ALPHA MOTOR (EFF.) AXON I

NEUROTENDINOUS
  (GOLGI) ORGAN J
    CAPSULE ★
      CELLULAR SHEET K
    RECEPTOR ★
      COLLAGEN FIBRIL L
      GRP. Ib AFFER. AXON M
TENDON N
MUSCLE FIBER O

TENDON

MUSCLE BELLY

BONE

JOINT

BONE

EXTRAFUSAL
FIBERS (SKELETAL
MUSCLE CELLS)

NERVE

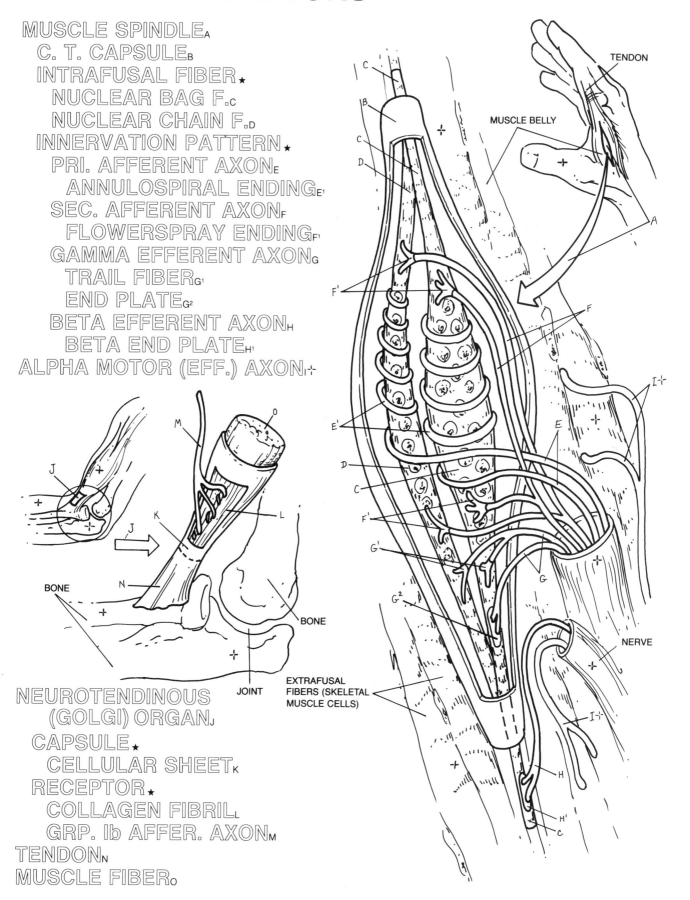

MUSCLE SPINDLE/ TENDON ORGAN DYNAMICS

This plate is concerned with the function of the *muscle spindles* (C) and the *neurotendinous organs* (D), the structure and pattern of innervation of which were introduced on the previous plate. To gain maximum advantage of the contents of this plate, it is important that Plate 2-10 be colored first.

Six figures of muscle spindle/neurotendinous organ activity states are shown. Each activity takes place at the lower end of a muscle at the musculotendinous junction (see inset at upper right). In each figure the full complement of nerve fibers to the receptors is shown; however, only the fibers that are active in a given muscle state are to be colored.

Color titles A through D and related structures (except C^1 and C^2) in the upper right corner. Then color the same structures (including C^1 and C^2) in Figures 1 through 6, noting the shapes of the extrafusal muscles (thin, thick) in stretch and contraction, respectively. Also note the two conditions of the muscle spindles, tense and relaxed. Shades of the same color are recommended for structures that have the same subscript but different exponents. Color titles E through I and related axons in Figures 1 through 6. Watch carefully for the no-color symbols ($-\vert-$). After coloring each figure, read the appropriate text.

In the state of contraction (Figure 1), a variable number of *extrafusal muscle* (A) fibers are stimulated to shorten by the alpha motor neurons (*alpha efferent axon*, H). *Muscle contraction* (A^1) puts the *tendon* (B) under tension and moves the bone. In this situation the contraction of the extrafusal fibers takes the tension off the resident muscle spindle. This action removes the stimulus for activation of the afferent endings around the intrafusal fibers, and the *afferent axons* (E and F) of the spindle do not fire. The neurotendinous organ within the tendon is stretched, however, and it fires impulses along the *tendon afferent axon* (G) to the spinal cord.

If a muscle is stretched and then contracted (Figure 2), the conditions are no different from the preceding situation. During the stretch phase, the spindle is tensed, and the afferent endings begin to fire (not shown). Once the alpha efferent axon fires, however, the extrafusal fibers contract, taking the tension off the muscle spindle, and the afferent endings do not fire. The neurotendinous organ is stimulated in both cases, as the tendon is tensed in stretch and in contraction.

In a state of steady, unwavering (static) *stretch* of the *extrafusal muscle* (A^2; Figure 3), the muscle spindle is put under stretch, and both primary and secondary endings fire. Studies have shown that the secondary afferent axons have an increased rate of firing over the primary (annulospiral) afferents during sustained stretch, suggesting that the *nuclear chain fibers* (C^2) are more sensitive to changes in length than in the rate of change in lengthening (stretching). In static stretch, the neurotendinous organ fires as before, but there is no activity in the efferent axons.

In a state of varying degrees of lengthening or dynamic stretch (Figure 4), the primary afferents fire at a faster rate than the secondary axons; in fact, the rate of firing of the secondary axons does not change significantly during variations in muscle stretch. This suggests that the *nuclear bag fibers* (C^1) are more sensitive to changes in rate of stretch (velocity, acceleration) than the nuclear chain fibers, which seem sensitive only to the lengthening itself. To make this point, the secondary afferent axon (F) in Figure 4 is not to be colored; however, it could be colored very lightly to suggest that, although active, it is not transmitting information of a dynamic nature.

It is important that the CNS have the capacity to alter the sensitivity of the spindles in the face of changing lengths of extrafusal muscle fibers, so as to have a continual, updated input on the position and activity of the body musculature. It does so through the gamma efferent system of neurons. As the spindle is stretched (Figure 5), the afferent endings fire, and the CNS is informed of the stretch via the primary and secondary afferent axons, as well as by the tendon afferent axon (see Plates 4–7 and 4–8). In succeeding stretches and contractions, the *gamma efferents* (I) fire and stimulate contraction of the intrafusal fibers, tensing up the spindle and enhancing its sensitivity to changing conditions (see Plate 4–12). Although gamma efferents fire during muscle stretching, it is probable that they also fire during contractions (Figure 6), making possible a continuum of muscle-state information to the CNS throughout a spectrum of muscle activity.

MUSCLE SPINDLE/ TENDON ORGAN DYNAMICS.

EXTRAFUSAL MUSCLE$_{A()}$
  CONTRACTED STATE
    (ACTIVE)$_{A^1}$
  STRETCHED STATE
    (PASSIVE)$_{A^2}$
TENDON$_B$
MUSCLE SPINDLE$_C$
  BAG FIBER$_{C^1}$
  CHAIN FIBER$_{C^2}$
NEUROTENDINOUS ORGAN$_D$
  PRI. AFFERENT AXON$_E$

SEC. AFFERENT AXON$_F$
TENDON AFFERENT AXON$_G$
ALPHA EFFERENT AXON$_H$
GAMMA EFFERENT AXON$_I$

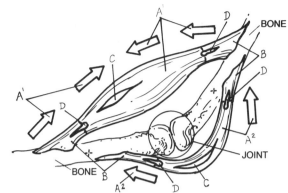

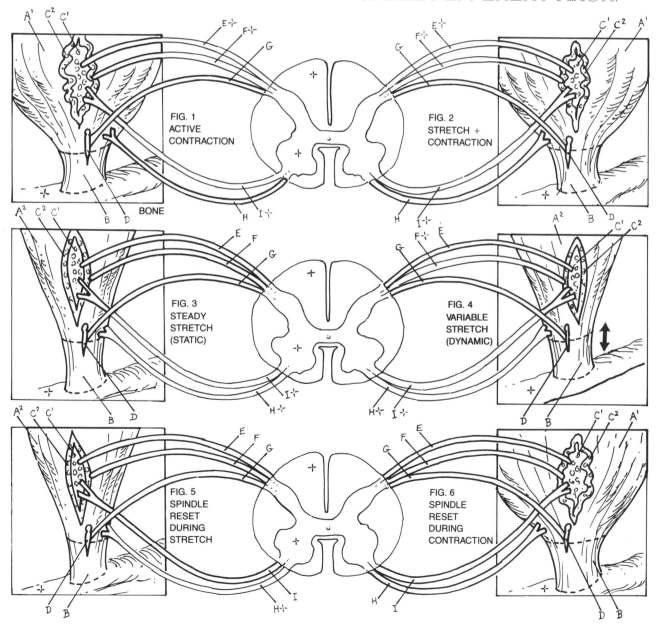

FIG. 1
ACTIVE
CONTRACTION

FIG. 2
STRETCH +
CONTRACTION

FIG. 3
STEADY
STRETCH
(STATIC)

FIG. 4
VARIABLE
STRETCH
(DYNAMIC)

FIG. 5
SPINDLE
RESET
DURING
STRETCH

FIG. 6
SPINDLE
RESET
DURING
CONTRACTION

Muscles must be stimulated to contract. In the case of skeletal muscle (the muscle making up the form of the body), the stimulation is in the form of a neurotransmitter released by nerve endings. The microscopic site of "contact" between muscle and nerve is called a *neuromuscular* or *myoneural junction,* the topic of this plate. Although the discussion here is limited to skeletal muscle, it should be understood that smooth muscle (of the walls of internal organs) also has neuromuscular junctions of lesser complexity than described here. The neuromuscular junctions of cardiac muscle are less well known, but in certain cases they are similar to those of smooth muscle.

Color titles A through E and related structures in the two uppermost illustrations. Shades of the same color are recommended for structures that have the same subscript but different exponents.

The upper illustration depicts a *skeletal muscle* (A) of the arm and its source of stimulation, a *motor nerve* (B). The middle illustration depicts a branch of that nerve giving off an *axon* (B^1) ensheathed in *myelin* (C) and a *Schwann cell* (D). The axon divides into *branches* (B^2), each of which terminates in a number of *neuromuscular junctions* (E) with *muscle cells* (A^1; also called fibers). The number of muscle fibers supplied by one axon and its branches varies from four (in the muscles of the orbit, which track the eyeball) to several hundred (as in the gluteus maximus muscle of the buttock). A motor neuron and the muscle fibers it supplies constitute a *motor unit.*

Color titles B^3 through G and the related structures in the lower illustration (circled inset).

Each axon branch terminates on a muscle fiber by forming an expanded ending called an *axon terminal* (B^3). The circled illustration depicts the appearance, as seen in an electron micrograph, of an axon terminal adjacent to the specialized region of a muscle cell membrane called the motor end plate. Before the axon branch reaches the motor end plate, it loses its myelin sheath but retains its Schwann cell covering, which flows over and covers the myoneural junction. At this level of magnification, it can be seen that the axon terminal does not enter the muscle fiber but appears to lie in a trough of the fiber, flush against its cell membrane or *sarcolemma* (A^2; *sarco,* "flesh"; *lemma,* "lining").

Color the heading Motor End Plate, titles A^2 through A^5, including I and F^1, and the related structures in the inset illustration. The title Synaptic Cleft (H-¦-) and related area should be left uncolored.

The *presynaptic membrane* (B^5) of the axon terminal, an extension of the *cell membrane* (B^4), is separated from the sarcolemma by a space 20 to 60 nanometers wide. This space is the synaptic cleft (H; also called *synaptic gutter* or *trough*). The sarcolemma adjacent to the cleft exhibits convolutions, called *junctional folds* (A^3), which project into the *sarcoplasm* (A^4; muscle cell cytoplasm). Neurotransmitter *receptor sites* (I) are found on the sarcolemma between junctional folds.

Neurotransmitter, released from *synaptic vesicles* (G) in the axon terminal, is cast by the presynaptic membrane into the synaptic cleft, from which it can stimulate the receptor sites. At these sites it induces an increased permeability to sodium ions, resulting in depolarization of the muscle fiber and subsequent contraction. The acetylcholine remaining in the synaptic cleft is rapidly inactivated by an enzyme (acetylcholinesterase). The choline is taken back up by the axon terminal for resynthesis of the transmitter. The energy for this transfer of stimulus and related events is developed within the *mitochondria* (F, F^1).

Diseases involving profound muscle weakness are often related to disturbances in neurotransmitter release, uptake, or clearance. In the case of myasthenia gravis (*myo,* "muscle"; *asthenia,* "weakness"), fewer receptor sites between the junctional folds are found. As a result, only feeble muscle contractions can take place.

EFFECTORS:
THE NEUROMUSCULAR JUNCTION.

SKELETAL MUSCLE_A
MUSCLE CELL_{A¹}

BONE

MOTOR NERVE_B
AXON_{B¹}
MYELIN SHEATH_C
SCHWANN CELL_D
AXON BRANCH_{B²}
NEUROMUSCULAR
JUNCTION_E

AXON TERMINAL_{B³}
CELL MEMBRANE_{B⁴}/
PRESYNAPTIC
MEMBRANE_{B⁵}
MITOCHONDRION_F
SYNAPTIC VESICLE_G

SYNAPTIC CLEFT_H⁺

MOTOR END PLATE ★
SARCOLEMMA_{A²}
JUNCTIONAL FOLD_{A³}
RECEPTOR SITE_I
SARCOPLASM_{A⁴}
MITOCHONDRION_{F¹}
NUCLEUS OF MUSCLE CELL_{A⁵}

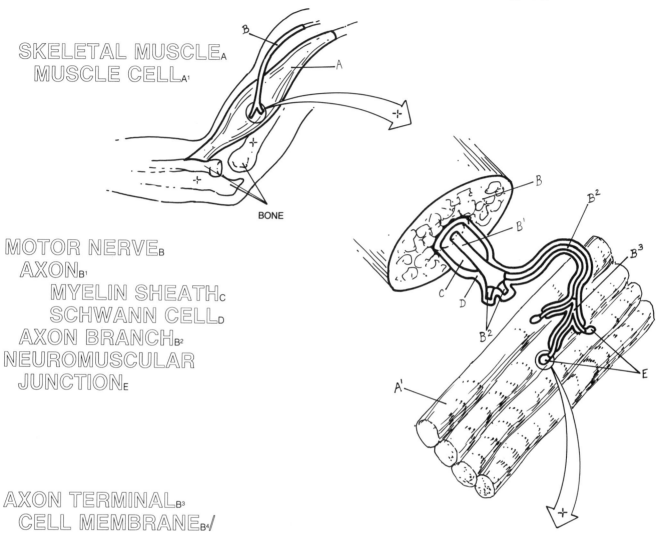

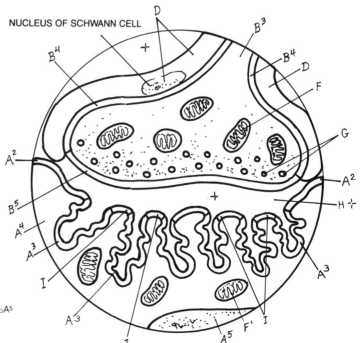

NUCLEUS OF SCHWANN CELL

We begin this unit with the first stages of human development, as understanding them will enhance your appreciation of the growth and maturation of the nervous system.

Color titles A through F¹ and related structures. In coloring A, avoid coloring over the developing germ cells (B), their follicles (C, C¹), and the corpus luteum (C³). Light pastel colors for A and E are recommended.

As in all mammals, formation of a human being takes place in the reproductive system of the female. The *ovary* (A), about the size and shape of an almond, lying deep in the pelvis and supported by ligaments, is the site of the *developing germ cell* (B), which will mature to become an ovum at fertilization. Of the several hundred thousand germ cells formed before birth, only a few hundred are destined to reach maturity during the 35 to 40 reproductive years of the female. Through a series of preparatory steps within the ovary, the cells surrounding the germ cell take the form of (differentiate into) a solid *developing follicle* (C) or ball of cells. This follicle soon develops a cavity in which the germ cell is partly surrounded by a fluid pool, the liquor folliculi. The follicle is now called a *Graafian* or *mature follicle* (C¹). The mature follicle increases in size as it moves toward the ovarian surface and discharges the immature germ cell encased in a zona pellucida (not shown) and a layer of *follicle cells* (C²). This process is called *ovulation* (D). The remaining ovarian follicle then differentiates into a fatty, secretory body called the *corpus luteum* (C³), which supplies essential hormones for the maintenance of the reproductive tract for a period of time.

The mobile *fimbria* (E¹; "fingers") clasp the surface of the ovary and guide the discharged germ cell into the *Fallopian* or *uterine tube* (E). Here, currents, produced by the beating of hairlike cilia along the tubal surface and the contractions of smooth muscle in the tubal walls (not shown), draw the germ cell and its coverings toward the *uterus* (I). Penetration of the still immature germ cell by a single *sperm* cell (F¹), in a process called *fertilization*

(F), occurs in the first third of the uterine tube. By this act, one set of paternal genes is added to the maternal set, a key event in the continuing developmental process of the individual.

Color titles G through N and the related structures. Consider coloring the embryos (G through G²) different shades of the same color. A light color for I is recommended.

The fertilized ovum divides into two daughter cells (blastomeres), which form a *2-cell embryo* (G). This embryo develops within the first 24 to 30 hours following conception, dividing again into a *4-cell embryo* (G¹) in approximately 40 to 50 hours and again into a *8-cell embryo* (G²) in about 60 hours. This process continues, resulting (in about 72 hours) in a small multicellular sphere called a *morula* (H; "mulberry"). During this phase there is an increase in numbers of cells without appreciable increase in size.

By the time the 32-cell stage is reached, the ball of cells begins to develop a central cavity and is called a *blastocyst* (J; *blast,* "developing"; *cyst,* "sac"). The outer cells or wall of the blastocyst constitute the *trophoblast* (N). The trophoblast will serve strictly as part of the embryonic support system by becoming intimately associated with the uterine lining and its blood vessels to form the placenta (not shown). Within the blastocyst itself, attached at one pole, is a group of cells called the *inner cell mass* (K). This mass of cells soon flattens to become, in large part, the embryonic disc, which consists, at the outset, of two basic layers, the *future ectoderm* (L; also called *epiblast*) and *future entoderm* (M; *hypoblast*). Of these, the future ectoderm will form the epidermis and its derivatives (outer part of skin) and, most important for our purposes, the nervous system.

The development of the third germ layer (mesoderm) from the future ectoderm in the embryonic disc and its influence on the formation of the neural tube will be seen in the next plate.

THE BEGINNING.

OVARY_A
  DEVELOPING GERM CELL_B
  DEVELOPING FOLLICLE_C
  MATURE FOLLICLE_{C^1}/
    FOLL.CELL_{C^2}
  CORPUS LUTEUM_{C^3}
  OVULATION_D

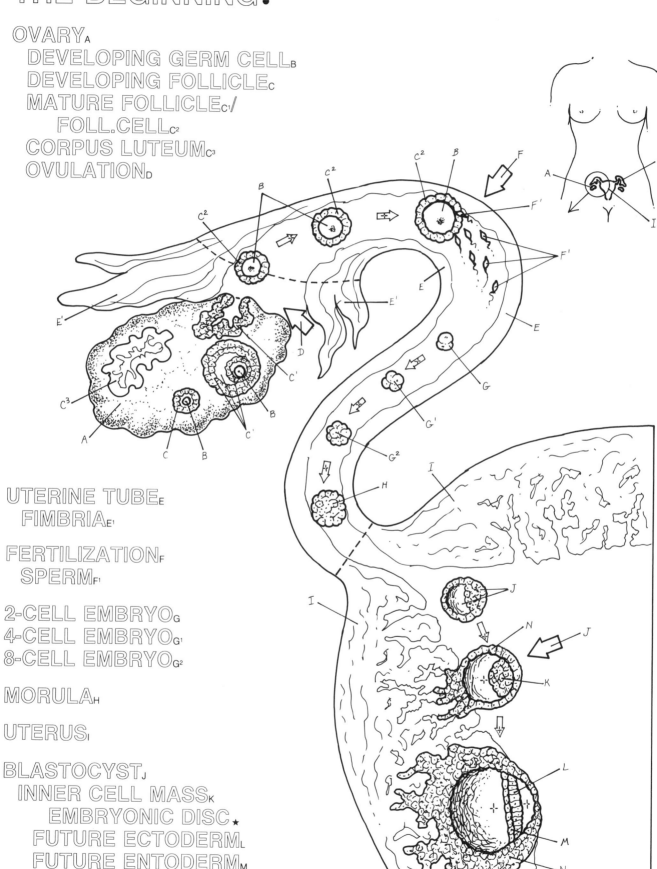

UTERINE TUBE_E
  FIMBRIA_{E^1}

FERTILIZATION_F
  SPERM_{F^1}

2-CELL EMBRYO_G
4-CELL EMBRYO_{G^1}
8-CELL EMBRYO_{G^2}

MORULA_H

UTERUS_I

BLASTOCYST_J
  INNER CELL MASS_K
    EMBRYONIC DISC_★
    FUTURE ECTODERM_L
    FUTURE ENTODERM_M
  TROPHOBLAST_N

The differentiation of the embryonic disc into two and subsequently three layers—ectoderm, mesoderm, and entoderm—is an initial step leading to development of the entire body. In this plate we concentrate on the formation of the neural tube, which will become the brain and spinal cord when fully developed.

Set aside the colors used in Plate 3-1 for structures L and M and use them for the same structures here. The subscript N is not used on this plate. Color the heading Embryonic Disc, titles L through O, and related structures in Figures 1 through 6, as applicable. Color the heading Mesodermal Differentiation, titles O^1 and O^2, and related structures in the applicable figures. Different shades of the same color are recommended for structures with the same subscript but different exponents.

You will recall from Plate 3-1 that two layers formed from the inner cell mass of the early embryonic disc, *future ectoderm* (L) and *future entoderm* (M). Newly differentiated cells split off from the underside of the future ectodermal layer to form the third germ layer, the *mesoderm* (O). Cells from this layer now form a midline ropelike *notochord* (O^1), while other mesodermal components spread out laterally to form the *somites* (O^2), precursors of muscles and bones. In later development, the notochord will form the central portion of the intervertebral disc (nucleus pulposus; not shown).

At about 16 days of age, the notochord appears to induce the single-layered, overlying ectoderm to change structurally, forming a plate of multilayered, newly differentiated cells, the *neural plate* (A; Figure 2). This plate of neural ectoderm will become the source of the entire nervous system.

Color the heading Neural Ectoderm Differentiation, titles A through F, and related structures in Figures 1 through 6. Select carefully the colors for structures E and F, as they will be used again for the same structures in the plates ahead. It is essential that you use a light pastel color for F.

Development of the early neural tube is initiated by an indentation along the midline of the neural plate (A; Figure 2), forming the *neural groove* (B^1; Figures 3 and 4). Deepening of the groove creates the flanking *neural folds* (B^2); continued deepening (Figure 4) ultimately leads to the roofing over and formation of the *neural tube* (E; Figure 5), which is pinched off from the overlying ectoderm. In this manner, the cavity or *lumen* (F) of the tube (Figure 5) is formed.

A special group of cells breaks off from the neural folds during the formation of the neural tube and can be seen as a thin, irregular layer at the angle between the newly formed tube and the overlying ectoderm bilaterally (on both sides) (Figure 5). These are the *neural crest cells* (C); they will migrate laterally to form a series of cell clusters alongside the lengthening tube, a subject developed in Plate 3-5.

The *anterior* and *posterior neuropores* (D, D^1; Figure 6) are temporary openings at the ends of the undeveloped neural tube. This condition exists because the roofing process is initiated in the center of the embryonic disc. Then, like two zippers moving away from each other, the roofing-over process continues in anterior and posterior directions, eventually closing the neuropores. If normal closure is not achieved, malformation of the nervous system results. Failure of anterior closure causes anencephaly (lack of brain formation, not shown) which is fatal. Improper closure of the posterior neuropore can result in a variety of structural abnormalities (not shown) ranging from a lower spinal cord that is absent (amyelia) or exposed (spina bifida) to the more benign but often painful pilonidal sinus (cyst) over the coccyx or tailbone.

FORMATION OF THE NEURAL TUBE.

EMBRYONIC DISC★
 FUTURE ECTODERM$_L$
 ECTODERM$_{L^1}$
 FUTURE ENTODERM$_M$
 ENTODERM$_{M^1}$
 MESODERM$_O$

MESODERMAL
 DIFFERENTIATION★
NOTOCHORD$_{O^1}$
SOMITE$_{O^2}$

NEURAL ECTODERM
 DIFFERENTIATION★
NEURAL PLATE$_A$
DEV. NEURAL TUBE$_B$
 NEURAL GROOVE$_{B^1}$
 NEURAL FOLD$_{B^2}$
NEURAL CREST$_C$
ANT.$_D$/POST. NEUROPORE$_{D^1}$
NEURAL TUBE$_E$
 LUMEN$_F$

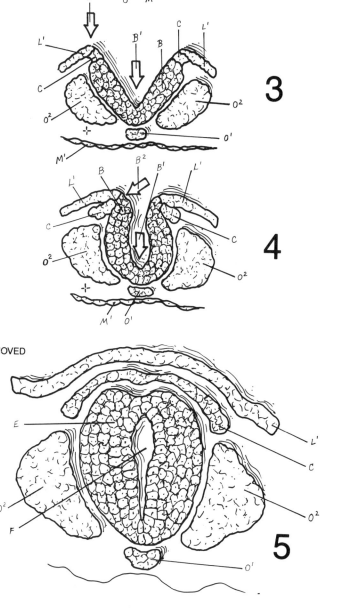

PLACENTAL MEMBRANES

16-DAY EMBRYONIC DISC WITH CAUDAL PORTION SECTIONED

1

2

3

4

5

OVERLYING ECTODERM AND NEURAL CREST REMOVED

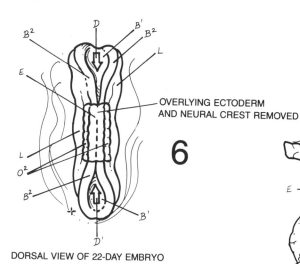

6

DORSAL VIEW OF 22-DAY EMBRYO

All the cells of the brain and spinal cord (central nervous system, or CNS) develop from the walls of the *neural tube* (E). The neural ectoderm cells making up this tube are called *neuroepithelia* (A; sing. *neuroepithelium*), and their mitotic divisions produce the more than 100 billion neurons and neuroglia of the CNS. With a few exceptions, neurons are not produced after birth. Here we explore how neurons are formed before birth from the neuroepithelia of the neural tube.

In this and the following plates of this unit, assignment of subscripts has been designed to maximize the concept of structural continuity throughout development of the nervous system. Thus, structures seen in two or more plates of this unit will carry the same subscript throughout and, where feasible, should be colored identically.

Set aside the colors used for E and F on the previous plate and use them for the same structures here. Color the list of titles E through E^1 and the related structures, where applicable, in the inset at upper right, the left (smaller) hemisection of the neural tube, and the cutout section at left. Then color the title Neuroblast (G) and its structure in the cutout section at left. Read the following paragraph before and after coloring.

The *neuroepithelia* (A) of the neural tube at 23 days of age are found between the *lumen* (F) and *outer limiting membrane* (E^1). At this age, the neuroepithelial cells alternate in activity between cell division or mitosis (*mitotic cell,* A^1) and synthesis of the genetic material DNA (*DNA synthesizing cell,* A^2). In any given cycle, a neuroepithelial cell divides; the nucleus of each newly formed daughter cell moves away from the lumen of the neural tube toward the outer limiting membrane (*nuclear movement,* B). The nucleus undergoes DNA synthesis or generation of genetic material. The nucleus of this DNA synthesizing cell then moves back toward the lumen, and the cell becomes mitotic once again. These to-and-fro cycles occur over a time span of 5 to 24 hours. Once the cycles cease, differentiation of the neuroepithelia into *neuroblasts* (G) begins. These neuroblasts break their attachments and migrate away from the lumen starting at about day 35.

Now color the structures on the right side of the hemisection and the cutout section at right, as well as the neuron and its title (H).

The neuroepithelial layer reduces in size as the neuroblasts migrate away from the lumen to form a new, outer *mantle layer* (C), which becomes the gray matter (primarily nerve cell bodies and dendrites) of the spinal cord and brain. Here the neuroblasts mature into *neurons* (H). The outward extension and migration of axons from the developing neurons form the outermost or *marginal layer* (D) of the neural tube. This layer becomes the white matter of the spinal cord and much of the brain. The term "white matter" reflects the appearance of this layer, the axons of which are largely ensheathed by a white fatty material (myelin; not shown).

Another source of neurons is the neural crest cells, a topic explored in Plate 3-5.

ORIGIN OF NEURONS.

NEURAL TUBE$_E$
  LUMEN$_F$
  NEUROEPITHELIAL LAYER$_A$
    MITOTIC CELL$_{A^1}$
    DNA SYNTHESIZING CELL$_{A^2}$
      NUCLEAR MOVEMENT$_B$
  MANTLE LAYER$_C$
  MARGINAL LAYER$_D$
  OUTER LIMITING
    MEMBRANE$_{E^1}$

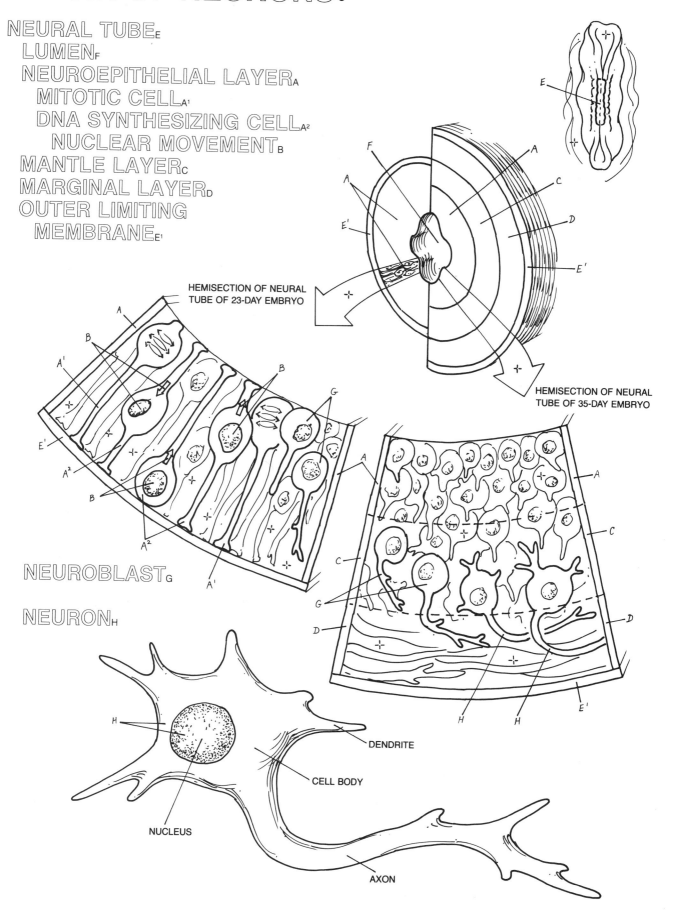

HEMISECTION OF NEURAL TUBE OF 23-DAY EMBRYO

HEMISECTION OF NEURAL TUBE OF 35-DAY EMBRYO

NEUROBLAST$_G$

NEURON$_H$

DENDRITE

CELL BODY

NUCLEUS

AXON

Neuroglia (recall Plate 2-6) make up a very appreciable part of the central nervous system and probably exceed in number the more familiar neurons. In this plate, we consider the differentiation of those glial cells arising from the neuroepithelia of the developing neural tube. Not considered here are the satellite and Schwann cells of the PNS, which are derived from neural crest cells (Plate 3-5). The microglia (not shown) are derived from mesoderm and probably migrate into the developing neural tube to take up a phagocytic (scavenger) function.

Use the same coloring scheme from Plate 3-3 for the list of titles E through E^1 and related structures. As before, start with the inset at upper right, followed by the smaller hemisection on the left side, and the two cutout sections (on the left and in the middle). Color the heading Neuroglia, titles H and H^1, and the related structures in the middle cutout section.

It is not possible at 23 days of age to distinguish neuroglia from neurons. Both originate in the *neuroepithelial layer* (A) of the *neural tube* (E). In their development, glia follow the same *mitotic cell* (A^1)—*DNA synthesizing cell* (A^2)—*nuclear movement* (B) cycle as the developing neurons but may continue in this stage for a longer period. About the time the newly formed neuroblasts begin to migrate out to form the *mantle layer* (C), primitive glial cells (*glioblasts,* H) lengthen by maintaining their attachments to the *lumen* (F) surface and the *outer limiting membrane* (E^1) as the neural tube thickens. Most of these

cells will become *radial glioblasts* (H^1), arranged around the neural tube like spokes on a wheel. In this way, they probably serve as guides along which neuroblasts will migrate outward to the mantle and *marginal layers* (D) of the developing tube (recall Plate 3-3).

Now color the hemisection of the neural tube on the right side. Note that in this case the innermost layer is ependymal (G) instead of neuroepithelial (A), as it was in Plate 3-3. Here we follow the development of glial cells in the ependymal layer or innermost part of the neuroepithelia of the primitive neural tube, whereas in Plate 3-3 we were concerned with neuronal development from the entire neuroepithelial layer. Color titles G^1, I, J, and K. Then color the cutout section at right, followed by the individual neuroglia at the bottom of the plate.

As the radial glioblasts continue to mature, they begin to lose contact with their attachments to the lumen surface and the outer limiting membrane. A small number remain attached to the surface of the lumen to become *ependymal cells* (G^1). These cells form an *ependymal layer* (G) of single-cell thickness, lining the lumen of the central canal of the spinal cord and the ventricles of the brain. The vast majority of elongated glioblasts round up within the expanding mantle layer to become monopolar or bipolar cells; these soon differentiate into mature neuroglia: *protoplasmic* (I) and *fibrous astrocytes* (J) and *oligodendrocytes* (K).

ORIGIN OF NEUROGLIA.

NEURAL TUBE_E
  LUMEN_F
    NEUROEPITHELIAL LAYER_A
      MITOTIC CELL_{A1}
        DNA SYNTHESIZING CELL_{A2}
          NUCLEAR MOVEMENT_B
    EPENDYMAL LAYER_G
    MANTLE LAYER_C
    MARGINAL LAYER_D
    OUTER LIMITING
      MEMBRANE_{E1}

NEUROGLIA★
  EPENDYMAL CELL_{G1}
  GLIOBLAST_H
    RADIAL GLIOBLAST_{H1}
  PROTOPLASMIC
    ASTROCYTE_I
  FIBROUS ASTROCYTE_J
  OLIGODENDROCYTE_K

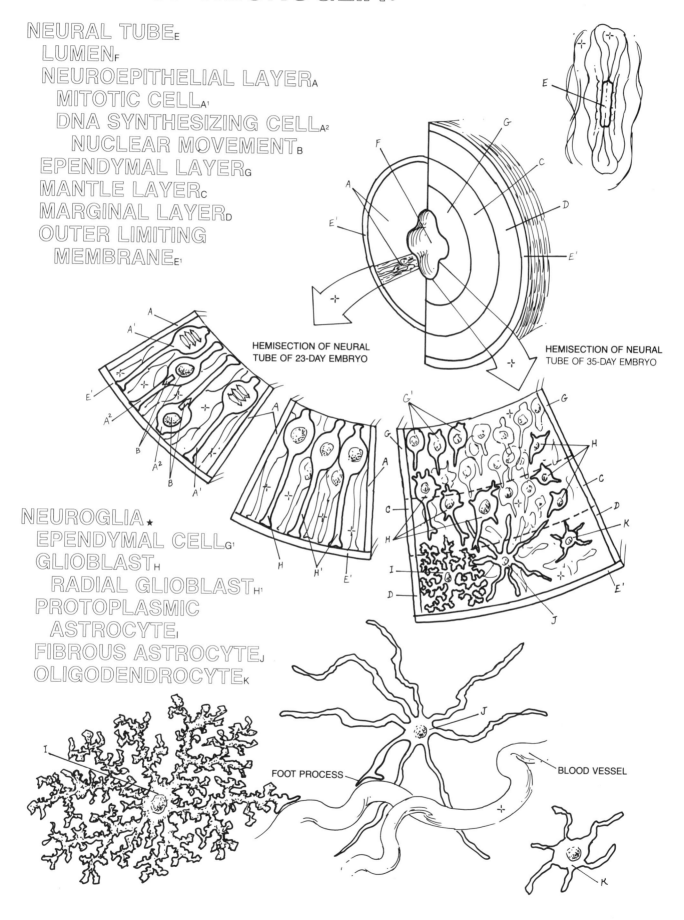

HEMISECTION OF NEURAL
TUBE OF 23-DAY EMBRYO

HEMISECTION OF NEURAL
TUBE OF 35-DAY EMBRYO

FOOT PROCESS

BLOOD VESSEL

Neural crest cells (A; recall Plate 3-2) migrate to various areas of the body, changing form as they do so, and mature to play out their specific roles. The migratory pattern of these cells is presented here.

Color titles A and A¹ and the related structures and arrows in the uppermost illustration. Then color the heading Derivatives of Neural Crest, titles B through C only, and the related structures in the two large middle illustrations.

Many neural crest cells begin an early migration from the sheet of cells adjacent to the neural tube; others remain as a linear series of cell groups along each side of the neural tube from the future midbrain to the end of the future spinal cord. These cell groups are called cranial and *spinal ganglia* (B; sing. *ganglion*, "swelling"; also called *posterior root ganglia;* see middle illustration) and develop largely into *cell bodies* (B²; lower illustration) of developing *sensory neurons* (B¹) of cranial and spinal nerves. These are pseudounipolar neurons (recall Plate 2-3) from the cell bodies of which central processes extend into the neural tube and peripheral processes project out to sensory receptors. The lower illustration shows only one sensory neuron in the nerve and its posterior sensory root; in fact, each root contains thousands of sensory neurons. Neural crest derivatives also surround the sensory neuron cell bodies and become *satellite cells* (C; lower illustration). These cells are a kind of neuroglia and offer physical and chemical support to the neurons.

Color titles D through D³. Starting with the cells labeled D¹ in the upper middle illustration, color those cells and the related arrows A¹, cells D² and related arrows, and the arrows and cells (D³) around the primitive gut. Then go to the lower middle illustration and color the D¹ and D² cells in the sympathetic chain and nerve and around the artery.

Cells of the neural crest and the anterior gray matter of the neural tube form a chain of motor neurons whose multipolar cell bodies are collected together in series along each side of the developing spinal cord and anterior to the spinal ganglia. These are *paravertebral (sympathetic) ganglia* (D¹; middle and lower illustrations; *para-,*

"alongside"). The vertebral column (not shown) will subsequently take form around and enclose the spinal cord and its spinal nerve roots, separating them from the sympathetic chain of ganglia on each side. Some neural crest cells will continue to migrate anteriorly from the paravertebral chains toward the abdominal aorta (major artery of the abdominal cavity) immediately anterior to the vertebral column. These cells form masses of multipolar cell bodies, called *prevertebral (sympathetic) ganglia* (D²; lower illustration) around branches of the aorta.

Some neural crest cells migrate into the walls of abdominal and pelvic organs to form small masses of multipolar motor neurons called *intramural (parasympathetic) ganglia* (D³; middle illustration; *intra-,* "within"; *mural,* "wall"). Other neural crest cells form parasympathetic ganglia in the head region (not shown). The neurons of the ganglia are connected by synapses to motor neurons in certain parts of the spinal cord and brain and innervate smooth muscles and certain glands throughout the body.

Color titles E and F. Color the cells (E) lateral to the neural tube in the upper middle illustration, then their mature derivatives (E) in the spinal nerve of the lower middle illustration. Color the cells (F) and related arrows (A¹) in the upper middle illustration, then their mature derivatives (F) in the boxed illustration at lower left.

Schwann cells (E) are a peripheral kind of glial cell that migrate along the axons growing into all parts of the body (lower illustration) and form individual sheaths about each of them. Most Schwann cells differentiate from neural crest cells; some may emerge from the neural tube by way of the motor roots of spinal nerves. Schwann cells produce myelin coverings around certain axons in the peripheral nervous system.

Some neural crest cells migrate laterally from the prevertebral (sympathetic) ganglia (D²) to invade the outer cells (cortex) of the developing adrenal gland. These cells come to occupy a central position within the gland and constitute the *adrenal medulla* (F). These cells liberate chemical substances (such as epinephrine, also called adrenaline) that mimic the action of substances from the sympathetic nerves (increase heart rate, etc.).

FATE OF THE NEURAL CREST.

NEURAL CREST CELL_A
MIGRATION PATH_{A¹}

DERIVATIVES OF NEURAL
CREST.★
SPINAL GANGLION_B
SENSORY NEURON_{B¹}
CELL BODY_{B²}
SATELLITE CELL_C
VNS GANGLIA_{D( )}
PARAVERT. (SYMP.) G._{D¹}
PREVERT. (SYMP.) G._{D²}
INTRAMURAL
(PARASYMP.) G._{D³}
SCHWANN CELL_E
ADRENAL MEDULLA_F

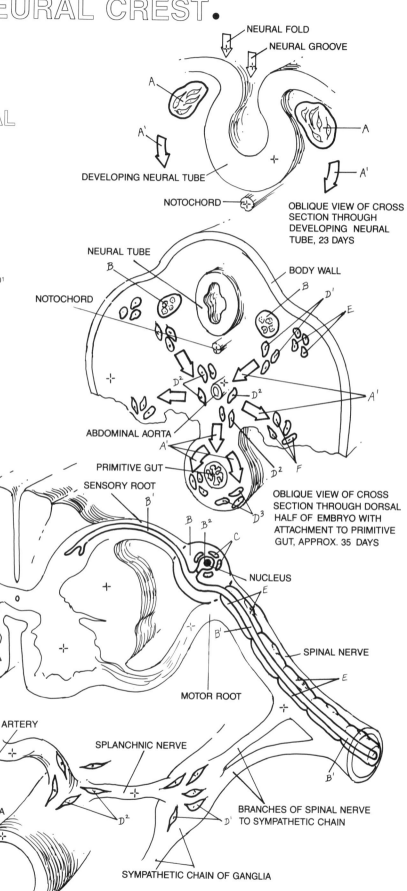

NEURAL FOLD
NEURAL GROOVE
DEVELOPING NEURAL TUBE
NOTOCHORD
OBLIQUE VIEW OF CROSS SECTION THROUGH DEVELOPING NEURAL TUBE, 23 DAYS

NEURAL TUBE
BODY WALL
NOTOCHORD
ABDOMINAL AORTA
PRIMITIVE GUT
OBLIQUE VIEW OF CROSS SECTION THROUGH DORSAL HALF OF EMBRYO WITH ATTACHMENT TO PRIMITIVE GUT, APPROX. 35 DAYS

SENSORY ROOT
NUCLEUS
SPINAL NERVE
MOTOR ROOT
OBLIQUE VIEW OF CROSS SECTION OF MATURE SPINAL CORD, NERVE, AND ROOTS

ADRENAL CORTEX
KIDNEY

ARTERY
SPLANCHNIC NERVE
ABDOMINAL AORTA
BRANCHES OF SPINAL NERVE TO SYMPATHETIC CHAIN
SYMPATHETIC CHAIN OF GANGLIA

The modifications that take place in the cranial third of the neural tube (the *future brain,* E) are presented in this plate. Unlike the relatively equal distribution of alar and basal plates in the spinal cord, the alar plate derivatives of the brain increase considerably, whereas the motor related basal plate derivatives do not. The cerebral hemispheres, representing 80 to 90 percent of the total mass of the brain, are entirely sensory in origin.

Set aside the colors used for D, D¹, E, and F in Plate 3-2 and use them for the same structures in this plate. Color titles E, D and D¹ and the related structures in Figure 1. Color the title F and the related cavity in Figures 1 through 5; use one color throughout the lumen of the entire brain for now.

The cranial end of the neural tube begins to exhibit a series of swellings along its longitudinal axis at about three weeks of age. The *lumen* (F) of the tube is not yet closed, and the *anterior* and *posterior neuropores* (D and D¹) can be seen at both ends (Figure 1). By the end of four weeks, the tube is essentially closed. The growth of the future brain is reflected to some degree in the changes observed in the brain cavity (lumen or ventricles) throughout the developmental period (Figures 1 through 5).

Color the heading Brain, the titles of each of the three major brain regions listed (A, J, and L), and the related regions in Figure 2. Then color the titles listed under Forebrain (B through I) and the related regions and cavities in Figures 2 through 5. Complete the coloring of each structure through all applicable figures before going to the next structure. Color, dot, or crosshatch over the already colored ventricles (F) of each region (C and G) with the color used for that region.

The future brain develops into three distinct, spherical vesicles (see Figure 2): the *forebrain* (A), the *midbrain* (J), and the *hindbrain* (L). With few exceptions, such as the pineal gland of the forebrain (not shown), each of these three vesicles will form bilateral structures. Early anatomists named the forebrain *prosencephalon* (A; *pro-,* "in front"; *encephalon,* "brain"). The prosencephalon soon divides into three parts, the two-part *telencephalon* (C; *tel,* "head end"; Figure 3) and the *diencephalon* (G; *di-,* "be-

tween"). The paired telencephalic vesicles bulge out laterally from the midline diencephalon. The midline, rostral-most wall of the early telencephalon is the *lamina terminalis* (B; "terminal layer"; Figures 2, 3, and 4). The lamina terminalis is the most rostral part of the original neural tube and represents the tissue that covered the anterior neuropore (D¹). Seen in a median section of the developed brain (Plate 5-26), it serves as a kind of "surveyor's benchmark" or point of reference from which one can visualize the dramatic expansion of the telencephalic vesicles into the massive *cerebral hemispheres* (C¹). The lumen of this region becomes the *lateral* (first and second) *ventricles* (F+C, Figures 3 and 4).

The diencephalon becomes somewhat compressed between the proliferating hemispheres, reflected by the relatively flattened shape of its cavity, the *third ventricle* (F+G, Figure 3). The *optic stalks* (H; Figure 3), outgrowths from the ventral diencephalon, expand into the *optic cups* (I), which give rise to the retina and optic tracts.

Color all remaining titles and the related structures, cavities, and arrows in Figures 2 through 5.

The midbrain is named *mesencephalon* (J; *mes,* "middle") and does not undergo further visible division. The lumen of this region retains its tubular character and is called the *cerebral aqueduct* (F+J; Figures 3 and 4). During a period of rapid and unequal growth, taking place largely in the cerebral hemispheres, the developing brain bends at the midbrain, creating the *cephalic flexure* (K; Figures 2, 4, and 5).

The hindbrain is named the *rhombencephalon* (L; *rhombus,* "diamond shape") and divides into a more rostral *metencephalon* (M; *meta-,* "change") and a more caudal *myelencephalon* (O; *myel-,* "spinal"). The lumen of the hindbrain becomes the *fourth ventricle* (F+M and F+O, Figures 3, 4, and 5). The increasing cephalic flexure induces a temporary flexure in the opposite direction on the anterior surface of the metencephalon. This is the *pontine flexure* (N; Figure 5). The bulge formed becomes the pons of the metencephalon. Another bend occurs between the myelencephalon and the more caudal spinal cord, called the *cervical flexure* (P; Figures 4 and 5). All of these flexings of the developing brain serve to fit the rapidly growing brain within the more slowly growing cranial cavity of the skull.

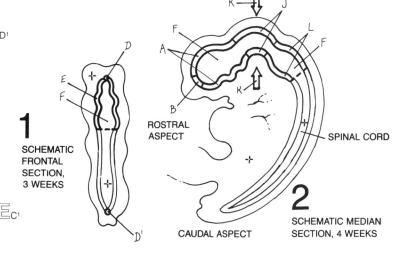

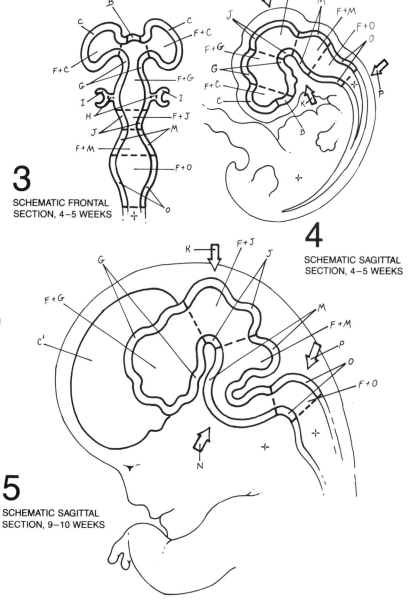

FORMATION OF THE BRAIN.

FUTURE BRAIN$_E$
ANT.$_D$/POST. NEUROPORE$_{D^1}$
LUMEN$_F$

BRAIN.★
FOREBRAIN/
PROSENCEPHALON$_A$
LAMINA TERMINALIS$_B$
TELENCEPHALON$_C$/
CEREBRAL HEMISPHERE$_{C^1}$
LATERAL VENTRICLE$_{F+C}$

DIENCEPHALON$_G$
THIRD VENTRICLE$_{F+G}$
OPTIC STALK$_H$
OPTIC CUP$_I$

MIDBRAIN/
MESENCEPHALON$_J$
CEREBRAL AQUEDUCT$_{F+J}$
CEPHALIC FLEXURE$_K$

HINDBRAIN/
RHOMBENCEPHALON$_L$

METENCEPHALON$_M$
FOURTH VENTRICLE$_{F+M}$
PONTINE FLEXURE$_N$

MYELENCEPHALON$_O$
FOURTH VENTRICLE$_{F+O}$
CERVICAL FLEXURE$_P$

1 SCHEMATIC FRONTAL SECTION, 3 WEEKS
ROSTRAL ASPECT
CAUDAL ASPECT
SPINAL CORD
2 SCHEMATIC MEDIAN SECTION, 4 WEEKS
3 SCHEMATIC FRONTAL SECTION, 4–5 WEEKS
4 SCHEMATIC SAGITTAL SECTION, 4–5 WEEKS
5 SCHEMATIC SAGITTAL SECTION, 9–10 WEEKS

Here we examine the development of major derivatives of the wall and lumen of the brain vesicles (except the telencephalon). Stemlike relative to the expanded telencephalon, the lower four vesicles, excluding the cerebellum, are known as the *brain stem*. In this plate, cross sections taken through each of the four regions are shown. In each cross section, the alar and basal plate distribution is to be colored on the right, and the major derivatives of these plates are to be colored on the left.

Set aside the colors used for F, A, B, C, and I in Plate 3-6 and O, M, J, and G in Plate 3-7 and use them for the same structures on this plate. Use the same color for the ependymal layer (D) here as you did for this layer in Plate 3-6. Start by coloring the heading Brain Stem Derivatives/Cerebellum and the lead titles for each region of the brain stem (O, M, J, and G). Color the related bars and letters on the uppermost illustration (indicating the planes of section shown below) and the letters above each of the cross sections. Now color the headings Lumen (F) through Roof Plate (I) and the related structures and arrows in the cross sections, beginning with O. Color each structure or arrow in all the applicable figures before moving on to the next structure. Note that roof plates that are substantially ependymal receive two colors.

The *lumen* (F) of the brain stem regions, lined by the *ependymal layer* (D), changes size and shape regionally during the subsequent developmental period. The *roof plates* (I) of the brain stem vesicles are substantially ependymal (I + D), except in the *mesencephalon* (J). In the *myelencephalon* (O), *metencephalon* (M), and *diencephalon* (G), the ependymal layer becomes intimately associated with small blood vessels in the overlying pia mater, a thin covering around the neural tube (not shown). The combination of these form the *choroid plexus* (E), the site of cerebrospinal fluid formation.

The *sulcus limitans* (A), a longitudinal groove on each side of the lumen of the neural tube, extends into the brain stem and continues to divide the mantle layer of the tube into the posterior *alar* (B) and anterior *basal plates* (C). The alar plates develop into sensory areas, except in the

telencephalon, where some motor areas develop as well. The basal plates develop into areas of motor neurons. The roof and floor plates are devoid of neurons, with certain exceptions. Although the alar and basal plates are shown on only one side of the cross sections here, they are, of course, bilateral.

Color the titles listed under each heading of a brain stem section (O, M, J, and G). Color the related structures and arrows in each brain stem section, then the upper sagittal section.

The myelencephalon expands laterally during growth, stretching the roof plate to a thin membrane. For the most part, the alar plate region forms columns of sensory nuclei associated with cranial nerves in the area. The basal plate forms columns of motor nuclei. Cranial nerves VIII through XII (not shown) are found in the myencephalon, which develops into the *medulla oblongata* (O^1).

The metencephalon forms the *cerebellum* (M^1) from the rostral half of the roof plate and part of the alar plates. Cell masses from the basal plates form the pontine nuclei. Axons from these nuclei bend laterally around the brain stem and project to the cerebellum. In so doing, they form the *pons* (M^2). Cranial nerve nuclei V, VI, VII, and part of VIII (not shown) develop in the metencephalon.

The alar plates of the *mesencephalon* (J) form the *corpora quadrigemina* (J^1). Within the basal plates, large masses of axons pass down from the forebrain to form the *crura cerebri* (J^3; sing. *crus cerebri*). The more central portions of the alar and basal plates, called the *tegmentum* (J^2), form discrete masses of relay, sensory, and motor nuclei. The axons of the motor nuclei form the III and IV cranial nerves (not shown).

The diencephalon (G) is the rostralmost region of the brain stem. The *thalamus* (G^1) is derived from the alar plate on each side. These masses of largely sensory nuclei are separated from the basal plate–derived *hypothalamus* (G^2) by the hypothalamic sulcus (see sagittal section), a groove similar to but probably not the same as the sulcus limitans. The roof and alar plates give rise to the epithalamus (of which the pineal gland is a part; not shown). Cranial nerve II (optic, not shown) arises from the optic cup (not shown), a derivative of the diencephalon.

BRAIN WALL DEVELOPMENT: BRAIN STEM.

LUMEN_F
EPENDYMAL LAYER_D
CHOROID PLEXUS_E
SULCUS LIMITANS_A
MANTLE LAYER_★
  ALAR PLATE_B
  BASAL PLATE_C
  ROOF PLATE_I

BRAIN STEM DERIVATIVES/
  CEREBELLUM_★
MYELENCEPHALON_O( )
  MEDULLA OBLONGATA_O¹

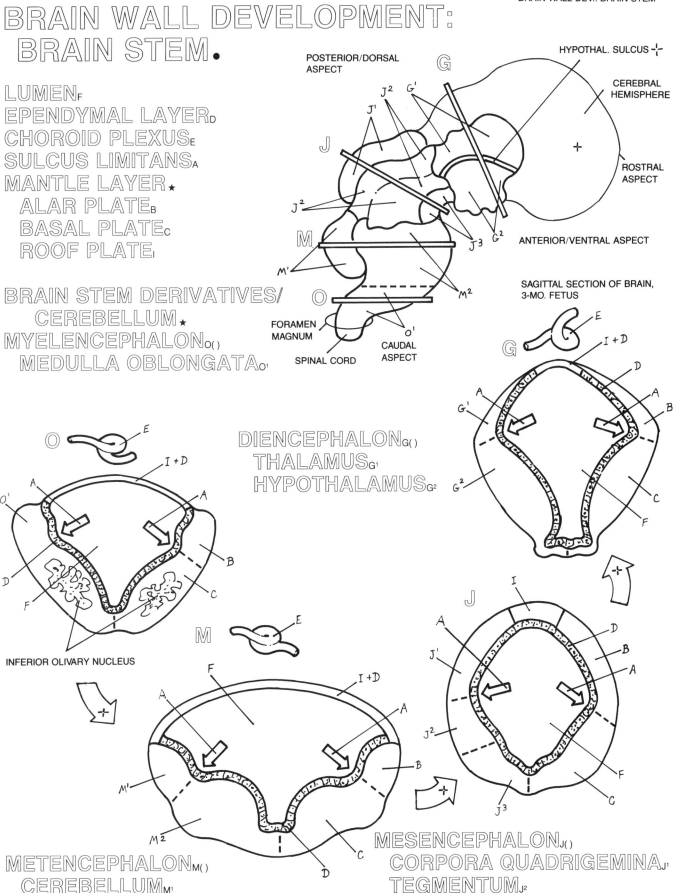

POSTERIOR/DORSAL ASPECT

G

J²
J¹
G'

J

J²

M

M'

O

O'

FORAMEN MAGNUM

SPINAL CORD

CAUDAL ASPECT

J³

G²

ANTERIOR/VENTRAL ASPECT

M²

HYPOTHAL. SULCUS

CEREBRAL HEMISPHERE

ROSTRAL ASPECT

SAGITTAL SECTION OF BRAIN, 3-MO. FETUS

G
E
I + D
D
A
G'
B
G²
C
F

DIENCEPHALON_G( )
THALAMUS_G¹
HYPOTHALAMUS_G²

O
E
I + D
A
O'
A
D
B
F
C

INFERIOR OLIVARY NUCLEUS

M
E
F
I + D
A
A
M'
B
M²
C
D

J
I
A
D
J'
B
A
J²
F
C
J³

METENCEPHALON_M( )
  CEREBELLUM_M¹
PONS_M²

MESENCEPHALON_J( )
CORPORA QUADRIGEMINA_J¹
TEGMENTUM_J²
CRUS CEREBRI_J³

BRAIN WALL DEVELOPMENT: CEREBRUM (PART 1)

The formation of the cerebrum (cerebral hemispheres) from the early telencephalic vesicle is developed in this and the following plate. Both plates can be worked together. For ease of reference, the illustrations are numbered Figures 1 through 9.

Set aside the colors used for A in Plate 3-3, G in Plate 3-6, and B and F in Plate 3-7, and use them for the same structures in this plate. Color the figure numbers, 1 through 9 (on this and the next plate), black or dark gray. Color the headings and titles from the top of the list through Ependymal Layer (G) and the related structures as follows: A, B, C, D, and F in Figure 1 only and G in Figures 6 and 8.

The telencephalic vesicles develop as lateral outpocketings from the forebrain during the fifth week of embryonic life (Figure 1). The landmark structure for these outgrowths is the *lamina terminalis* (B) at the rostral end of the neural tube (recall Plate 3-7). The wall of each vesicle, from the *lumen* (F) outward, consists of the *neuroepithelial layer* (A) and the developing gray *(mantle layer)* and white *(marginal layer)* matter (C; Figure 1). The basal part of the brain wall is the *future corpus striatum* (D; considered in the next plate). As the neuroblasts and glioblasts migrate outward, a *layer of ependymal cells* (G) is left lining the ventricles (Figures 6 and 8). The pattern of gray and white matter development familiar to you from Plate 3-6, however, occurs only initially in the growing cerebrum. Owing to the demands of the more complex cerebral cortex, the developmental process in the brain wall here changes significantly.

The massive growth of the cerebral hemispheres is a result of rapid proliferation of neurons and glia in the brain wall and at the base or floor of each of the hemispheres. In this plate, we focus on the development of the brain wall, especially the outer layer of gray matter. In the subsequent plate, the subcortical areas are considered.

Color the heading Pallium/Cerebral Cortex, titles E through I, the related directional-growth arrows in Figures 2 and 3, and the structures and arrows in Figure 4. Structure E can be colored in Figures 5 and 6; so can structures E^1, E^4, and E^5 in Figure 8 in the next plate. Different shades of the same color are

recommended for structures with the same subscripts but different exponents.

The outer few millimeters of gray matter covering the cerebral hemispheres are called the cerebral cortex ("bark") or pallium ("cloak"). On the basis of evolutionary age (phylogenetically and ontogenetically), the pallium is subdivided into three areas: the archipallium, (*archi-*, "ancient"), the *paleopallium* (J; *paleo-*, "old"), and the *neopallium* (E; *neo-*, "newest").

The neopallium is the largest and fastest-growing cortical area, expanding anteriorly to form the *frontal lobes* (E^1), pushing upward and bilaterally to form the *parietal lobes* (E^2), expanding posteriorly and downward to form the *occipital lobes* (E^3), and curving around in a reverse C shape on each side to form the more lateral *temporal lobes* (E^4) (Figures 2, 3, and 4). One area of neocortex grows relatively slowly while the overlying frontal, parietal, and temporal lobes develop more rapidly and ultimately cover it. In the process, it is left as a cortical island, called the *insular cortex* (E^5; Figure 4).

The cortex initially develops as a smooth-surfaced layer of cells (Figure 3). By the sixth month of fetal life, however, the rapidly dividing cells of the cortex must fit into the confining cranium. Thus the smooth surface begins to form folds or convolutions (*gyri;* sing. *gyrus*) separated by indentations or depressions (*sulci;* sing. *sulcus*) in accommodation to its tight quarters (Figure 4). The formation of convolutions results in a considerable increase in cortical surface area. The process is so extensive that two-thirds of the mature cortex is buried in the floors and walls of the sulci. The *central sulcus* (H) and the *lateral sulcus* (I) are the first sulci to appear (Figure 4). Growth of the neocortex is the subject of Plate 3-11.

Now color titles J and J^1 and related structure in Figures 2, 3, and 4 here and Figures 6 and 7 in the next plate.

While the neopallium continues to thicken and spread out as just described, the paleopallium makes its appearance on the underside of the frontal lobes, having originated from the floor of the ventricles (not shown). The paleopallium refers to the olfactory brain or rhinencephalon and will be discussed in more detail as a mature structure in Plate 6-5. In this and the next plate, only the *olfactory bulb* and *tract* (J^1) and adjacent paleopallium are illustrated.

BRAIN WALL DEVELOPMENT: CEREBRUM (PART 1).

TELENCEPHALON.
BRAIN WALL.★
   NEUROEPITHELIAL LAYER$_A$
   LAMINA TERMINALIS$_B$
   MANTLE/MARGINAL LAYER$_C$
   FUTURE CORPUS
     STRIATUM$_D$
LUMEN/VENTRICLE$_F$
EPENDYMAL LAYER$_G$

PALLIUM/CEREBRAL
   CORTEX.★
   NEOPALLIUM/NEOCORTEX$_E$
   FRONTAL LOBE$_{E^1}$
   PARIETAL LOBE$_{E^2}$
   OCCIPITAL LOBE$_{E^3}$
   TEMPORAL LOBE$_{E^4}$
   INSULAR CORTEX$_{E^5}$
   CENTRAL SULCUS$_H$
   LATERAL SULCUS$_I$

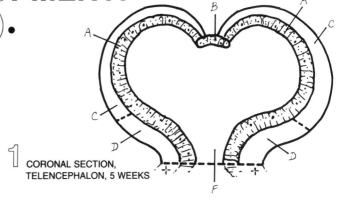

1 CORONAL SECTION, TELENCEPHALON, 5 WEEKS

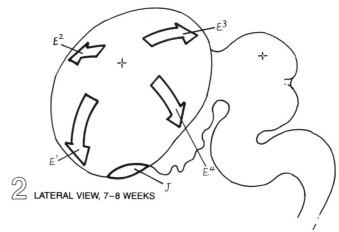

2 LATERAL VIEW, 7–8 WEEKS

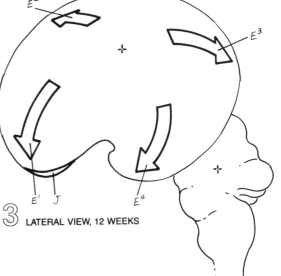

3 LATERAL VIEW, 12 WEEKS

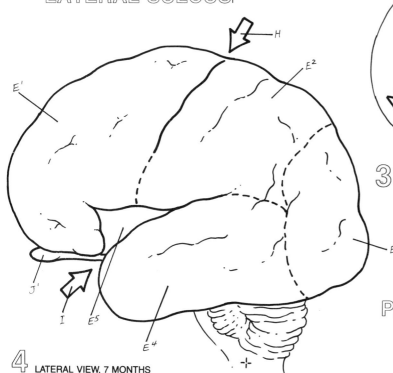

4 LATERAL VIEW, 7 MONTHS

PALEOPALLIUM/
RHINENCEPHALON$_J$
OLFACTORY BULB/TRACT$_{J^1}$

The development of the archipallium, the corpus striatum, the lateral ventricles and choroid plexus, and the subcortical white matter are presented in this plate, which is the second part of a two-plate discussion. You will find here certain structures with subscripts (G, E, J, and J^1) assigned in the previous plate.

Color the heading Pallium, titles K through K^3, and the related structures in Figures 5 through 9. With each structure to be colored, start with the first applicable figure and work to the last before coloring another structure. As before, different shades of the same color are recommended for structures with the same subscripts but different exponents.

The *archipallium* (K) arises on the medial wall of each hemisphere and at the early stage is called the *hippocampal ridge* or formation (K^1; Figures 5 and 6; *hippocampus,* "seahorse"). Bulging into the lateral ventricles, the neuronal cell bodies of the ridge migrate posteriorly and then arc around into the temporal lobes (Figure 9) to form the *dentate gyrus* and *hippocampus* (K^2; *dentate,* "toothed"). Somewhat like comets with arched fiery tails, the clusters of hippocampal cells leave a trail of axons in their path from the medial wall of the hemisphere to the temporal lobe. This "trail" of white matter is called the *fornix* (K^3; "arch"; Figures 8 and 9).

Color titles D through D^4 and the related structures in Figures 5 through 9 in the same manner as before. Use the same basic color for D through D^4 as you did for D in the previous plate.

The *corpus striatum* (D; "striated body") begins as a thickening in the base of each hemisphere just below the lateral ventricles and to either side of the third ventricle (Figure 1). As the corpus striatum enlarges, one part, called the *caudate nucleus* (D^1; *caudate,* "tail-like"), bulges into the lateral ventricle lateral to the *interventricular foramen* (L; Figures 5 and 6). As each hemisphere is stretched back over the diencephalon (recall Figures 2 and 3 of the previous plate), the corpus striatum is drawn back as well. The curved extremity of the caudate (*tail of the caudate,* D^2) is swept around to the temporal lobes as the

latter are formed, to lie over the hippocampus (Figure 9).

At the same time, bundles of axons migrating through the base of the hemispheres divide the corpus striatum into the caudate nucleus and *lentiform nucleus* (D^3; *lentiform,* "lens-shaped"; Figure 8). It is the weaving of the white matter through the gray, forming visible striations, that gives the corpus striatum its name; it is that same process that yields the shape of the caudate and lentiform nuclei for which they are named. The lentiform nucleus is subdivided further into smaller nuclei (not shown), which will be considered later (Plate 5-24).

The *amygdaloid nucleus* (D^4; *amygdala,* "almond"; *-oid,* "shaped"; Figures 8 and 9) is the first part of the corpus striatum to appear; it is also the most complex of that body. The amygdala begins as a thickening (not shown) on the floor of each interventricular foramen. As the temporal lobe forms, the amygdala fuses to the tail of the caudate and finally settles at the rostral (forward) end of the temporal lobe above the tip of the inferior horn of the lateral ventricle (Figures 8 and 9).

Color titles F^1 through N and the related structures in Figures 5, 6, and 8 in the same manner as before.

The *lateral ventricles* (F^1) undergo considerable alteration with the expansion of the hemispheres. Initially, they balloon out lateral to the third ventricle (Figure 6). The connecting passages between the lateral and the third ventricles are retained during growth and are called the interventricular foramina (L; *foramina,* "holes"). The lateral ventricles then follow the direction of growth of the hemispheres, projecting into the frontal and occipital lobes and even bending around into the temporal lobes (inferior horn, seen between K^2 and D^4 at the bottom of Figure 8; see also Plate 9-11). The roof of the lateral ventricles is invaded by small blood vessels to form (along with the overlying pia mater) the *choroid plexus* (M; Figures 6 and 8; recall Plate 3-8).

The *subcortical white matter* of the cerebrum (N; Figures 6 and 8) consists of myelinated fibers coming from and going to the cell bodies of the cerebral cortex. As you can see in Figure 8, the white matter takes up a considerable amount of the volume of the hemispheres. It is the subject of Plate 5-33.

BRAIN WALL DEVELOPMENT: CEREBRUM (PART 2).

PALLIUM★ (CONTINUED)
ARCHIPALLIUM_K( )
   HIPPOCAMPAL RIDGE_K1
   HIPPOCAMPUS/DENTATE
     GYRUS_K2
   FORNIX_K3

CORPUS STRIATUM_D( )
   CAUDATE NUCLEUS_D1
    TAIL OF THE CAUDATE_D2
   LENTIFORM NUCLEUS_D3
   AMYGDALOID NUCLEUS_D4

LATERAL VENTRICLE_F1
INTERVENTRICULAR
   FORAMEN_L
CHOROID PLEXUS_M
SUBCORTICAL WHITE
   MATTER_N

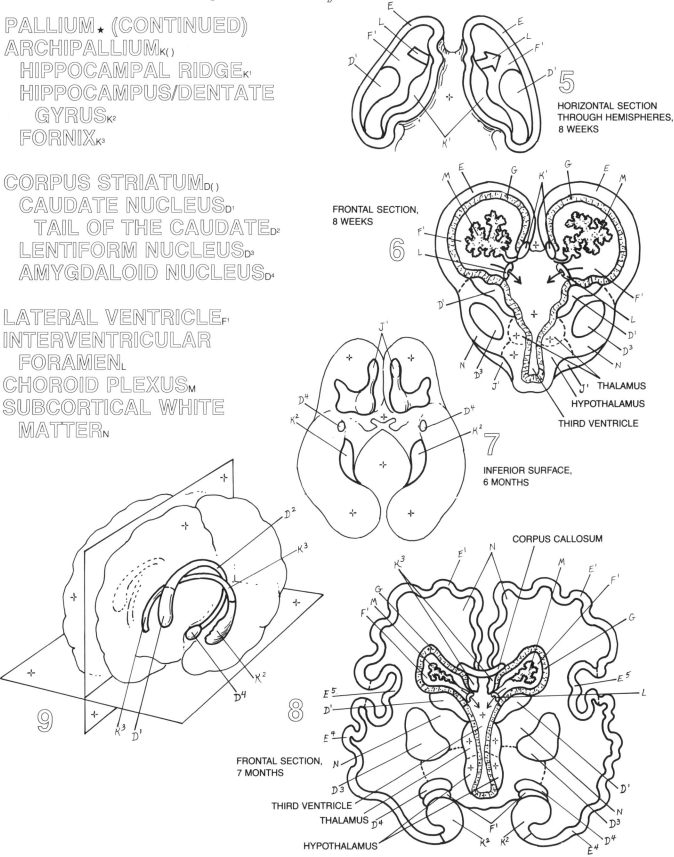

5 HORIZONTAL SECTION THROUGH HEMISPHERES, 8 WEEKS

6 FRONTAL SECTION, 8 WEEKS

THALAMUS
HYPOTHALAMUS
THIRD VENTRICLE

7 INFERIOR SURFACE, 6 MONTHS

9

CORPUS CALLOSUM

8 FRONTAL SECTION, 7 MONTHS

THIRD VENTRICLE
THALAMUS
HYPOTHALAMUS

In this plate we pursue the maturation of the cerebral neocortex, the most sophisticated of neural structures, in which lies hidden most of the intellectual power of humankind.

Reserve the colors used for C, D, F, G, and H^1 from Plate 3-4, A and E from Plate 3-9, and N from Plate 3-10 for use here. Color the heading Telencephalic Vesicles, titles B through F^1 at upper left, and the related structures in the section of the telencephalic vesicles at upper left and on the left side of the large cortical maturation diagram. Also color the headings Radial Glioblast (H^1) and Neuroblast (I) and related structures in the five-week and three-month sections of the maturation diagram. The subscripts H and M are not used in this plate.

The early telencephalic *vesicle wall* (B), from *lumen* (F) outward, consists of the *neuroepithelial layer* (A), the *mantle layer* (C), and the *marginal layer* (D). This vesicle wall develops by virtue of a rapidly proliferating layer of *neuroblasts* (I) in the neuroepithelial layer (see the five-week and three-month sections of maturation diagram). These cells then move up into and form the mantle and marginal layers. However, a second phase of migration of the recently developed neuroblasts occurs, characterized by the generation of successive waves of primitive neurons threading their way through groups already in place and proceeding with their own differentiation. This inside-out process of migration resembles the settling of the American West whereby each successive wave of immigrant settlers had to pass through already established communities to find the open frontier lands beyond. The result of such a growth pattern is quite different from that seen in the spinal cord (recall Plate 3-6) and even the brain stem (Plate 3-8).

One interesting mechanism for the inside-out process seems to depend on the presence of *radial glioblasts* (H^1) the processes of which extend outward to and help form the outer limiting membrane of the cortex. Neuroblasts apparently use these stalks as guides, literally flowing amoebalike along them to their eventual positions (see the five-week and three-month sections). The cell bodies of these glia remain as the developing *ependymal layer* (G; bottom of five- and eight-month sections).

Color the heading Microstructure of Brain Wall, titles G through E^6, and the related structures,

Roman numerals, and vertical bars in the five-week and eight-month sections of the main diagram. Different shades of the color used for E are recommended for E^1 through E^6. Color the heading Neuron Types, titles J, K, and L, and the related cell types, including the neuroblasts, in the five-week and eight-month sections. Finally, color the coronal section of the eight-month cerebrum at the upper right.

The positions that these neurons ultimately take, along with their shape, size, and arrangement of axonal and dendritic patterns, are such that six layers of the cerebral neocortex can be distinguished. Consistent with the inside-out migration pattern just described, the cells of the deepest layers (V and VI, E^5 and E^6) are the first to reach their position. The neurons of layer VI are typically *fusiform* (J; "spindle-shaped") or *pyramidal* (K) and contribute axons to the projection system of fibers in the *subcortical white matter* (N). The layer itself, however, seems the least organized of all the layers of the neocortex. The cells of layer V eventually develop into large pyramidal neurons whose axons contribute to the major efferent component of the projection system just mentioned as well as association fiber systems (see Plate 5-33). Pyramidal cells are characterized by (1) a single apical dendritic shaft and (2) a group of shorter basilar dendrites emerging from around the axon at the lower angles of the cell body.

The cells contributing to layer I (E^1) also arrive in position early and usually mature well before those of layers II, III, and IV (E^2, E^3, and E^4). In fact, layer I appears to begin functional operation before birth and then degenerates one or two years after birth. As the layer I cells die, they are replaced by horizontally arranged glial cells and dendrites of cortical cells in deeper layers.

The cells of layers II and III develop into small and medium-sized pyramidal cells, and their axons will remain in the hemisphere of origin, pass into the other hemisphere via a commissural fiber system (corpus callosum), or leave the cerebrum via the projection system (Plate 5-33).

The majority of neuroblasts reaching layer IV become *stellate* (L; "star-shaped") or granule cells characterized by fairly short axons with strictly local connections (Golgi II cells). These cells receive ascending (sensory-related) fiber systems.

The details of neuronal organization vary from area to area in the neocortex, but the picture presented here is reasonably representative.

BRAIN WALL DEVELOPMENT: CEREBRAL NEOCORTEX.

TELENCEPHALIC VESICLES.★
VESICLE WALL$_B$
  NEUROEPITHELIAL LAYER$_A$
  MANTLE LAYER$_C$
  MARGINAL LAYER$_D$
  LUMEN$_F$/VENTRICLE$_{F^1}$

MICROSTRUCTURE OF BRAIN
  WALL★
  EPENDYMAL LAYER/CELL$_G$
  SUBCORTICAL WHITE M.$_N$
  NEOCORTICAL LAYERS:$_E$
  I$_{E^1}$ II$_{E^2}$ III$_{E^3}$ IV$_{E^4}$ V$_{E^5}$ VI$_{E^6}$

NEURON TYPES:★
  FUSIFORM N.$_J$
  PYRAMIDAL N.$_K$
  STELLATE N.$_L$

RADIAL GLIOBLAST$_{H^1}$
NEUROBLAST$_I$

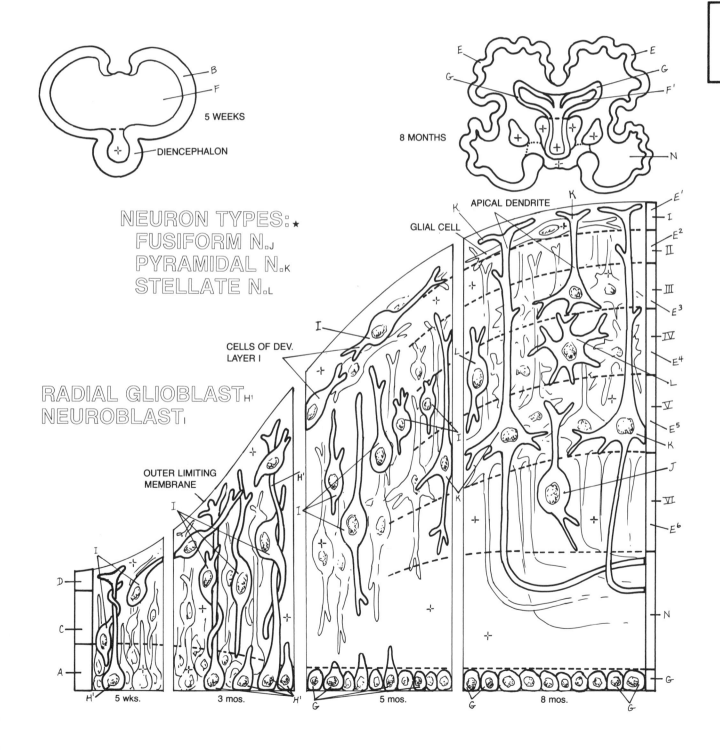

5 WEEKS

DIENCEPHALON

8 MONTHS

APICAL DENDRITE

GLIAL CELL

CELLS OF DEV.
LAYER I

OUTER LIMITING
MEMBRANE

5 wks.   3 mos.   5 mos.   8 mos.

The data illustrated in this plate suggests a capacity of the nervous system for responsiveness to the environment throughout the lifetime of the individual. Considering the changes we go through in our life, learning and remembering, collecting experiences with each additional day of life, the neurons of our brain must undergo some very significant adaptations.

Start with the upper section. Color the heading Neuron Loss in Development and titles A and B. The numbers of neurons and neuroglia (B) in the lumbar region of the developing spinal cord (A) are compared between chick embryos 12 days and 5 days before hatching. Color structures A and B in the chick embryo first, then the chick. Color the graph last.

Proliferation of neurons and neuroglia is incredibly rapid during the early stages of nervous system development (recall Plates 3-3 and 3-4). However, the death rate of these cells during the latter stages of development is equally incredible, as the graphs portray. The experimental animal here is the chick, a representative of advanced organisms. Note the tremendous loss of *neurons and glia* (B) in the *spinal cord* (A) of the embryonic chick over a period of just 7 days during the total 21-day developmental (gestational) span. The cause or significance of this loss is not known. The survival or death of cells in the brain and spinal cord is influenced by many variables such as availability of oxygen and nutrients, growth factors, hormones, and cell density.

Color the heading of the middle section: Neuron Loss with Aging, and titles C, C[1], and B[1]. The numbers of neurons and neuroglia (B[1]) in the occipital cortex (C[1]) of the brain (C) are compared between 26-day-old and about 2-year-old rats. Color structures C, C[1], and B[1] in the younger rat and then the older. Color the graph (B[1]) last.

Studies with rats, a common experimental animal, have shown that the most significant loss of neurons and glia occurs early in life and not after the attainment of adulthood. In this set of experiments, neuron counts were obtained in the *occipital cortices* (C[1]) of 11 to 15 young (26-day-old), young adult (108-day-old), elderly (650-day-old), and very old (900-day-old) rats. As the graph shows, the most significant loss of *neurons and glia* (B[1]) occurs before 100 days of age. The loss between 108 days and 900 days is considered insignificant by standard statistical methods. How do these data relate to the generality that millions of our neurons die each day of our lives? That aging is associated with slowed reflexes and loss of memory? Are these changes chemical ones and not related to neuronal death? The answers to these questions have yet to come in. We do know that neurons require healthy support systems to survive—good nutrition, a continuous supply of oxygen, and freedom from stresses that can translate into chemical harm. In this environment, neurons will function well for a lifetime.

Color the heading of the lowest section: Cortex Thickens with Training, and titles D and E. The effect of environmental enrichment on the thickness of the cerebral cortex (E) is compared with the thickness of the cerebral cortex of nonenriched animals (D). Color structures D at left, then the arrow (D and E) and the title Enrichment. Then color structures E at right. Color the graph (D and E) last.

It has been shown in studies (not shown here) that neuronal size and complexity and numbers of glia increase in the cerebral cortices of animals exposed to enriched environments (characterized by large cages and exposure to objects that arouse curiosity and stimulate exploratory activity). Presumably, such increases in neuronal complexity and neuroglial numbers imply a greater adaptability of the organism to its environment, possibly a greater capacity for storage of memory, and enhancement and modification of reflexes (in substance, "smarter animals").

The data illustrated here corroborate such theories. "Enriched" rats housed in large cages and exposed to toys and stimulus objects were compared with nonenriched (control) rats of the same age. After varying periods of enrichment (6–26, 60–90, 600–630, and 766–900 days), the cerebral *cortices of enriched animals* (E) were seen to be significantly thicker than the *cortices of control animals* (D), presumably reflecting increases in neuronal complexity and numbers of neuroglia of the trained rats.

From such data we may infer that experience, whether formal education or adventure, is to some degree reflected in the structure of our brains. The evolutionary implications of such a phenomenon are staggering, both in history and in the future.

PLASTICITY OF THE DEVELOPING AND AGING NERVOUS SYSTEM.

NEURON LOSS IN DEVELOPMENT.
SPINAL CORD_A
NO. OF NEURONS AND GLIA_B

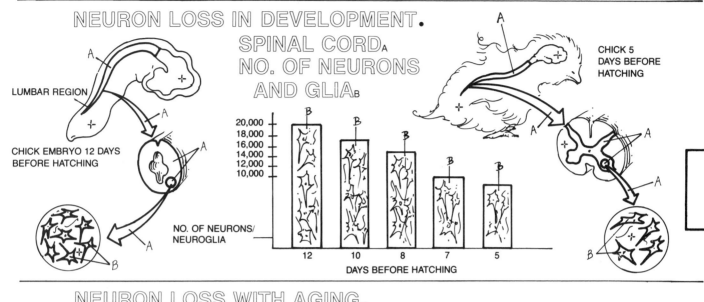

LUMBAR REGION

CHICK EMBRYO 12 DAYS BEFORE HATCHING

NO. OF NEURONS/ NEUROGLIA

DAYS BEFORE HATCHING

CHICK 5 DAYS BEFORE HATCHING

NEURON LOSS WITH AGING.
BRAIN_C/OCCIPITAL REGION_C'
NO. OF NEURONS AND GLIA_B'

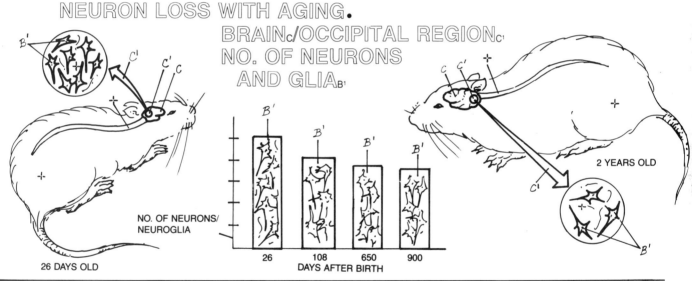

NO. OF NEURONS/ NEUROGLIA

DAYS AFTER BIRTH

26 DAYS OLD

2 YEARS OLD

CORTEX THICKENS WITH TRAINING.
CONTROL CORTEX_D
ENRICHED CORTEX_E

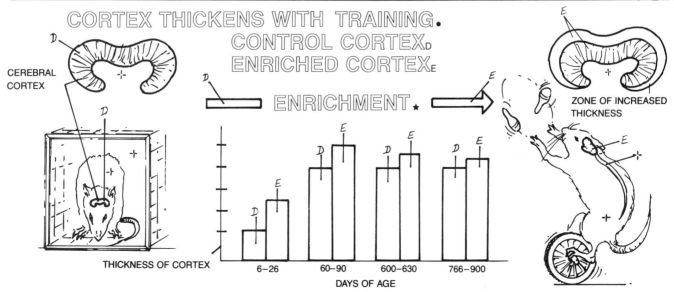

CEREBRAL CORTEX

ENRICHMENT ★

THICKNESS OF CORTEX

DAYS OF AGE

6-26   60-90   600-630   766-900

ZONE OF INCREASED THICKNESS

The spinal cord is the caudal two-thirds of the central nervous system, approximately 45 cm in length in males (about 2 cm less in females), and housed within the vertebral canal of the vertebral column. It begins rostrally at the *foramen magnum* (A) of the skull and ends at the level of the first or second lumbar vertebra as the *conus medullaris* (B). The spinal cord is subdivided into levels corresponding to the vertebral regions surrounding it. Within each level, the cord is further subdivided into segments, corresponding to the segmental appearance of the spinal nerves. This plate introduces you to the regional and segmental organization of the cord.

Color titles A and B at the top right of the page, and the related structure and arrow at either end of the spinal cord. Then color the Cervical titles C through D, the titles Gray Matter (F) and White Matter (G), the cervical segments in the spinal cord (C¹ through C⁸), the arrow D pointing to the cervical enlargement, and the C5 segment (cross section) of the cord at the top left of the page.

The *cervical level* (C), consisting of eight *segments* (C1 through C8), is characterized by an *enlargement* (D) or swelling from C4 to T1 that reflects the large amount of neurons and fibers associated with the innervation of the upper limb. The cross-sectional appearance of the cervical cord (C5) shows the *gray matter* (F; nerve cell bodies, dendrites, glia, and blood vessels) appearing as a butterfly circumscribed by a field of *white matter* (G; largely myelinated axons, glia, and blood vessels). In comparing the section of the cervical cord with the other sections shown, note the differences in the configuration of the gray and white matter. Also observe the oval, relatively large size of the cervical section with its bulging anterior horns, indicative of the large number of anterior horn motor neurons dedicated to the upper limb. The white matter in the cord here is extensive; it includes all the fibers ascending to the brain, collected from all the nerve cells below, as well as all the axons descending from the brain, which terminate on neurons at the various levels of the spinal cord.

Color the titles and segments of the thoracic level as well as the cross section of T7.

The *thoracic level* (T) of the cord is considerably thinner than the cervical cord and contains a smaller amount of gray matter due to the lesser innervation density (number of receptors and effectors per unit area) of the thoracic and abdominal walls, and mid back. The thoracic *segments* (T1 through T12) are easy to distinguish (see the cross section, T7) because of the thin posterior and anterior horns, as well as the presence of the lateral horns, which are seen from the first thoracic segment (T1) to about the third lumbar segment (L3). The white matter, of course, is still quite extensive, for the reason given previously.

Color the lumbar, sacral, and coccygeal titles (L through Co1), segments (L1 through L5, S1 through S5, and Co1), and cross sections (L3, S3, and Co1), and the arrow (E) pointing to the lumbar enlargement.

The massive numbers of neurons in the *lumbar level* (L) of the cord involved in the lower limb is reflected in the *lumbar enlargement* (E) and in the enlarged anterior and posterior horns, as seen in the cross section (L3). The amount of white matter left in this region, committed only to the lower limbs and pelvis, is considerably reduced. The lumbar level of the cord consists of five *segments* (L1 through L5).

The *sacral* (S) and *coccygeal* (Co) *levels* of the cord are smaller than the levels rostral to them. The posterior horns of the sacral segment (see the cross section, S3) are particularly large, due probably to the great influx of sensory fibers from the genitals and pelvis and the relatively small amount of white matter. The sacral level consists of five *segments* (S1 through S5), the coccygeal level one *segment* (Co1 is concerned only with the area around the bony coccyx). The caudal part of the coccygeal level tapers to a point (conus medullaris) as the last of the gray and white matter disappears.

The meningeal coverings and blood supply of the spinal cord are presented in Plate 9-13.

SPINAL CORD: LEVELS AND SEGMENTS.

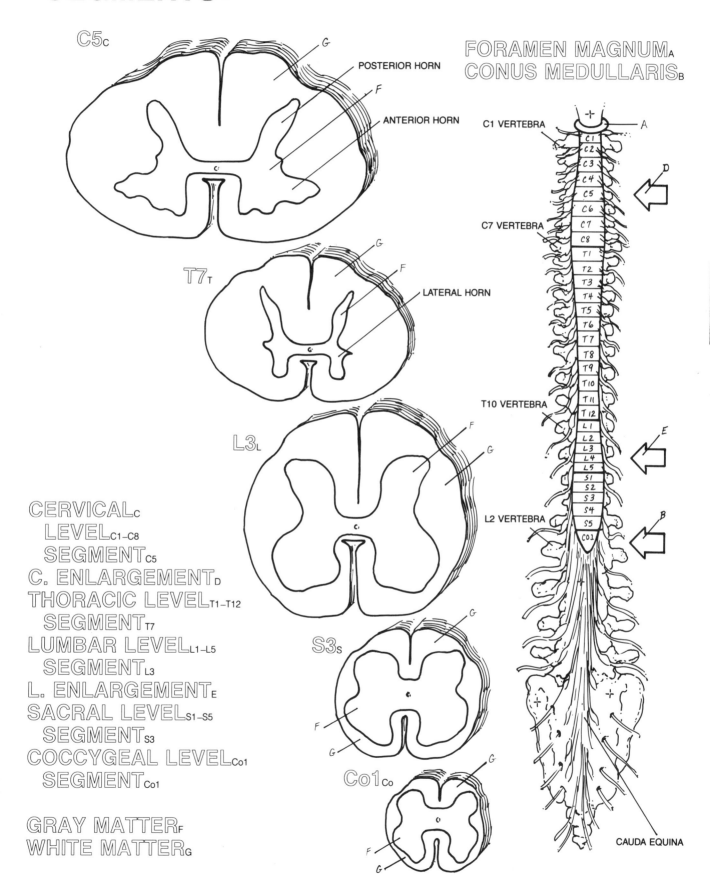

C5c

FORAMEN MAGNUMA
CONUS MEDULLARISB

POSTERIOR HORN

ANTERIOR HORN

T7T

LATERAL HORN

L3L

C1 VERTEBRA

C7 VERTEBRA

T10 VERTEBRA

L2 VERTEBRA

S3s

Co1Co

CAUDA EQUINA

CERVICALc
   LEVELC1–C8
      SEGMENTC5
C. ENLARGEMENTD
THORACIC LEVELT1–T12
      SEGMENTT7
LUMBAR LEVELL1–L5
      SEGMENTL3
L. ENLARGEMENTE
SACRAL LEVELS1–S5
      SEGMENTS3
COCCYGEAL LEVELCo1
      SEGMENTCo1

GRAY MATTERF
WHITE MATTERG

This plate is concerned with identification of external landmarks that assist in organizing the internal structure of the spinal cord and with the internal structure itself. Armed with an understanding of the cord framework, you can more easily localize the various tracts and nuclei that will be the subjects of the following plates of this unit.

Color the heading Landmarks, titles A through F, and the related arrows pointing to external markings of the cord. Color the heading White Matter, its titles G through J, and the related areas on the segment of the cord. Color the heading Gray Matter, its titles K through U, and the related areas on the cord segment. Note that the major divisions of the gray matter are shown on the left side and the subdivisions are shown on the other.

The various grooves *(sulci, fissures)* and lines *(septa;* sing. *septum)* can generally be seen throughout the cord. The *posterior median sulcus* (A) marks the position of the *posterior median septum* (B), a line of neuroglia, which extends down to the level of the gray commissure. The white matter, in the cervical and upper thoracic cord on either side of the septum, is divided into two masses of fibers by the *posterior intermediate septum* (C). The *posterior* (D) and *anterior lateral sulci* (E) mark the entrance and exit sites of the posterior and anterior roots, respectively, of the spinal nerves. The *anterior median fissure* (F), with an infolding of pia, reaches to the depths of the white commissure to separate the anterior white matter into left and right halves.

The white matter of the cord is divided into three large divisions or *funiculi* (sing. *funiculus,* "cordlike"): *posterior* (G), *lateral* (I), and *anterior* (J). These funiculi are further divided into smaller, separate functional divisions called fasciculi (sing. *fasciculus,* "bundle"). One example of such a bundle is *Lissauer's* (dorsolateral) *fasciculus* (H), which actually fits between the posterior and lateral funiculi. In the following plates of this unit, the arrangement of a number of fasciculi or specific bundles of axons will be illustrated.

The gray matter of the cord is arranged into *posterior and anterior horns* (K and R) or columns. These columns are further subdivided into layers or laminae. In the thoracic region, small lateral horns (not shown) project from lamina VII (see Plate 4-1).

Lamina I (L), also called the *posterior marginal nu-*

cleus, is at the outermost tip of the posterior horn. Cells in this layer respond to primary afferent axons carrying certain aspects of pain and temperature sensations. Many neurons here give rise to axons of the spinothalamic tract, the subject of Plates 4-5 and 4-6.

Lamina II (M), also called the *substantia gelatinosa,* is an area that appears gelatinous when examined in the fresh state. Lamina II receives afferent fibers from Lissauer's fasciculus, carrying impulses important in transmission of pain, touch, and temperature.

Laminae III and IV (N), sometimes called the *nucleus proprius,* contain interneurons that receive touch and pressure stimuli. The dendrites of some of these neurons extend into the adjacent lamina II, while axons of certain neurons here cross to the opposite side and contribute to the spinothalamic tract.

Lamina V (O) is located at the neck of the posterior horn. Neurons here receive input from afferent axons conveying both painful and nonpainful stimuli. As in laminae III and IV, axons of interneurons located here cross to the contralateral side and contribute to the spinothalamic tract.

Lamina VI (P) is located at the base of the posterior horn in the cervical and lumbar enlargements only and receives afferent input from central processes of primary sensory neurons.

Lamina VII (Q), also called the *intermediate zone,* consists of interneurons of which one prominent group (in the thoracic and upper lumbar segments) is the dorsal nucleus of Clarke (Clarke's column; not shown) associated with the posterior spinocerebellar tract (Plate 4-7). Lateral projections of lamina VII in the thoracic part of the cord constitute the lateral horn.

Lamina VIII (S) is generally found at the base of the anterior horn, but its position varies from one region of the cord to another. Axons of descending tracts are known to synapse among the interneurons here.

Lamina IX (T) of the anterior horn is made up of columns of large motor neurons (anterior horn cells) the axons of which form the anterior roots of spinal nerves.

Lamina X (U), also called the *gray commissure,* is the gray matter surrounding the central canal. It consists of small interneurons.

Much of present-day research on the spinal cord is concentrated on the interaction among neurons of various spinal laminae, rostral interneurons, and motor and primary sensory neurons.

SPINAL CORD ORGANIZATION.

LANDMARKS ★
POST. MEDIAN SULCUS$_A$
POST. MEDIAN SEPTUM$_B$
POST. INTERMED. SEPTUM$_C$
POST. LATERAL SULCUS$_D$
ANT. LATERAL SULCUS$_E$
ANT. MEDIAN FISSURE$_F$

WHITE MATTER ★
POST. FUNICULUS$_G$
LISSAUER'S FASCIC.$_H$
LAT. FUNICULUS$_I$
ANT. FUNICULUS$_J$

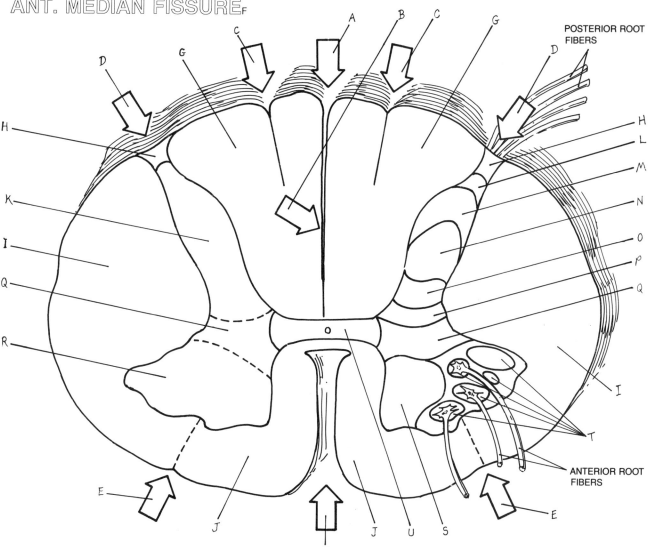

POSTERIOR ROOT FIBERS

ANTERIOR ROOT FIBERS

GRAY MATTER ★
POST. COLUMN/HORN$_K$
LAMINA I/POST. MARG. NUCLEUS$_L$
LAMINA II/SUBST. GELAT.$_M$
LAMINAE III, IV/NUC. PROP.$_N$
LAMINA V$_O$
LAMINA VI$_P$

LAMINA VII/INTER. ZONE$_Q$

ANT. COLUMN/HORN$_R$
LAMINA VIII$_S$
LAMINA IX$_T$

GRAY COMMISSURE$_{U( )}$
LAMINA X$_U$

4-3
SPINAL REFLEXES

A reflex (*re,* "back"; *flex,* "bend") arc is a programmed unit of behavior in which a certain type of stimulus from a receptor (the input side of the arc) automatically leads to the response of an effector (the output side of the arc). Although the human nervous system is capable of developing vastly more complex and innovative (voluntary) actions, reflex activities still remain at the root of much human behavior and are perhaps most obvious at times of stress and danger. Many spinal cord and brain stem mechanisms involved in control of somatic and visceral activities are essentially reflexive. The circuitry that generates these patterns varies greatly in complexity, depending on the nature of the reflex. We shall examine two of the simpler spinal reflexes as models.

Color the heading Myotatic (Stretch) Reflex, titles A through G, and the related structures and arrow in the upper illustration. Begin at the knee. Different shades of the same color are recommended for structures with the same subscript but different exponents.

The myotatic (stretch) reflex is one of the simplest known, depending on just two neurons and one synapse (a monosynaptic reflex). The sharp tap of the physician's reflex hammer (*stimulus,* A) on the *tendon* (B^1) of the quadriceps femoris muscle as it crosses the knee joint causes a brief stretch of the tendon and muscle belly where the neurotendinous organ and muscle spindle (*stretch receptors,* B) are stimulated. The subsequent volley of impulses reaches the spinal cord primarily over the large (Ia) *peripheral* (C^1) and *central processes* (C^2) of the *afferent neurons* (C). Although some impulses may head up the cord via *ascending branches* (C^3), the majority reach the *synapses* (D) with ipsilateral *efferent* (motor) *neurons* (E) of the anterior horn controlling the muscle that has been lengthened. Impulses are conducted along the *axons* (E^1) of these efferent neurons to the *neuromuscular junctions* (F), exciting the *effectors* (G, quadriceps femoris muscle) and causing a brief, weak contraction resulting in a momentary straightening of the leg ("knee jerk").

This example is one of a large number of reflex shortening responses built into the connections between extensor muscles and the central nervous system. Extensors are principally antigravity muscles, straightening our back and lower limb joints, among others, to keep us upright in the gravitational field in which we live. A sudden unexpected lengthening of an extensor muscle is interpreted as a possible loss of antigravity tone and sets off an immediate shortening reaction (stretch reflex) to "take up the slack."

Color the headings Flexor Withdrawal/Crossed Extensor Thrust Reflex and Ipsilateral Pathway and titles H through I, leaving G^1 uncolored. Then color the related structures (C^1 through G, beginning with OUCH!) in the lower illustration on the left side only. Color the facilitatory pathway (H, E, E^1, F, and G) first, then the inhibitory interneuron (I). The motor neuron and effector (E, E^1, F, and G) following the inhibitory neuron are not colored. Color the heading Contralateral Pathway, titles H^1 through I^1, and related structures on the right side of the lower illustration, as you did on the left. Start with H^1 in the gray commissure. Do not color G^3.

A flexor withdrawal/crossed extensor thrust reflex is a good example of one involving more than one synapse (polysynaptic reflex). It is demonstrated when a stimulus is applied to one leg, causing its (flexor) withdrawal "out of harm's way" while the contralateral limb extends (extensor thrust) to stabilize the body and prevent falling.

Afferent neurons convey impulses from the site of stimulus to an array of interneurons in the gray central laminae of the spinal cord. On the ipsilateral side, a *facilitatory interneuron* (H) synapses with both the efferent neuron and an *inhibitory interneuron* (I). The efferent neuron stimulates *contraction* (G) of the "hamstring" *muscles, flexing* the leg at the knee joint. The inhibitory interneuron generates an inhibitory neurotransmitter (e.g., gamma aminohydroxybutyric acid, or GABA) at the synapse with the efferent neuron to the extensor muscle, resulting in its inactivation (G^1-).

On the contralateral side, a *facilitatory interneuron* (H^1) receives a stimulus from a branch of the afferent neuron, synapses with another *facilitatory interneuron* (H^2), which synapses with an *inhibitory interneuron* (I^1) and an efferent neuron. In this case, the efferent neuron stimulates *contraction of the extensor muscle* (G^2), and the (E, E^1) inhibitory interneuron *inactivates* the efferent neuron to the antagonistic flexor muscles (G^3-), resulting in rapid (reflexive) extension of the knee joint.

This model of synaptic inhibition, in which an interposed interneuron reverses the mode of synaptic action from facilitation to inhibition, is no longer considered the only acceptable model. It has become increasingly clear that inhibition and facilitation may be at least as dependent on the nature of the postsynaptic membrane receptor as on the presynaptic transmitter molecule.

SPINAL REFLEXES.

MYOTATIC (STRETCH) REFLEX ★
STIMULUS_A
STRETCH RECEPTOR_B / TENDON_B¹
AFFERENT NEURON_C
  PERIPH. PROCESS_C¹
  CENTRAL PROCESS_C²
  ASCENDING BR._C³
SYNAPSE_D
EFFERENT NEURON_E
  AXON_E¹
NEUROMUSC. JUNCTION_F
EFFECTOR (MUSCLE)_G

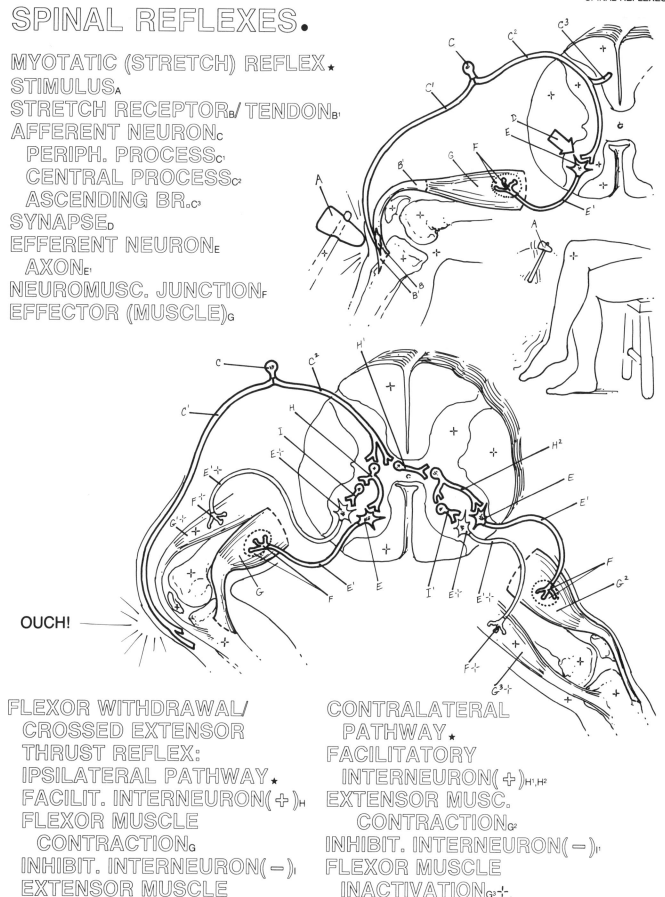

OUCH!

FLEXOR WITHDRAWAL /
  CROSSED EXTENSOR
  THRUST REFLEX:
  IPSILATERAL PATHWAY ★
FACILIT. INTERNEURON(+)_H
FLEXOR MUSCLE
  CONTRACTION_G
INHIBIT. INTERNEURON(−)_I
EXTENSOR MUSCLE
  INACTIVATION_G¹

CONTRALATERAL
  PATHWAY ★
FACILITATORY
  INTERNEURON(+)_H¹,H²
EXTENSOR MUSC.
  CONTRACTION_G²
INHIBIT. INTERNEURON(−)_I¹
FLEXOR MUSCLE
  INACTIVATION_G³

ASCENDING PATHWAYS: POSTERIOR COLUMNS

In this and the following several plates, the major ascending and descending pathways of the spinal cord, brain stem, and cerebrum are presented. In each ascending pathway, you can color a sequence of neurons from receptor to cerebrum or cerebellum (primary, secondary, and sometimes tertiary neurons). In descending pathways, you can color one or more neurons in sequence from the cerebral cortex or brain stem to effectors. On each plate of pathways, a small diagram of the neuron or neurons involved is included.

This plate is concerned with the posterior columns (fasciculi gracilis and cuneatus of the posterior funiculus) and the medial lemnisci, which convey impulses concerned with well-localized (epicritic) touch and with the sense of movement and position (kinesthesis). Important in moment-to-moment (temporal) and point-to-point (spatial) discrimination, the posterior columns make it possible for you to put a key in a door lock without light or visualize the position of any part of your body without looking. Lesions (pathologic wounds from destructive tumors, hemorrhage, scar tissue, swelling, infections, direct trauma, etc.) of this system abolish or diminish tactile sensations and movement or position sense.

Color titles A through B². Color the primary neuron (B) in the diagram at the upper left. In the figure at the lower left, color the arrow (A), which points to an area of stimulated receptors during the movement shown. Then color receptor A in the lower right corner, followed by the primary neuron (B) and related structures B¹, B², C, and D in the two lowest sections.

The cell bodies of the *primary neurons* (B) in the posterior column pathway are in the spinal ganglion. The peripheral processes of these neurons begin at receptors in joint capsules (*joint capsule receptor,* A) and muscles as well as skin (tactile and pressure receptors, not shown).

The central processes of these neurons enter the cord and pass directly into the posterior funiculus without synapsing. Fibers coming in from the lumbosacral region enter the lowest (most caudal) part of the posterior columns and therefore occupy their most medial portions, close to the posterior median septum. Fibers entering progressively higher up the cord occupy more lateral po-

sitions within the columns. These lateral fibers (from the thoracic and cervical regions of the cord) are separated from the more medial lumbosacral axons by the posterior intermediate septum; the more medial group becomes known as the *fasciculus gracilis* (B¹; *gracilis,* "slender") and the more lateral group as the *fasciculus cuneatus* (B²; *cuneatus,* "wedge"). The fibers of the two fasciculi ascend to the medulla oblongata of the brain stem, where they synapse with the cell bodies of the *secondary neurons* (E) in their respective *nuclei, gracilis* and *cuneatus* (C and D).

The total length of the processes of the primary neurons can be very long: the longest can be over 2 meters from receptors in the big toe to the medulla oblongata!

Color the rest of the titles. Color the secondary and tertiary neurons in the diagram at the upper left; then color the related structures in the main illustration, starting in the second lowest section with the internal arcuate fibers (E¹) and finishing in the cerebral cortex (J). Different shades of the same color are recommended for E¹ and E².

From the nuclei cuneatus and gracilis in the mid medulla, the axons of the secondary neurons sweep down and across to the contralateral side as the *internal arcuate fibers* (E¹) and ascend in the brain stem as the *medial lemniscus* (E²; *lemniscus,* "ribbon"). The relationships of the medial lemniscus will be illustrated in Unit Five. The axons of the secondary neurons terminate in the *ventral posterior lateral nucleus of the thalamus* (G), where they synapse with the *tertiary* (third-order) *neurons* (F). The axons of these neurons pass rostrally through a great boomerang-shaped band of fibers, the *internal capsule* (H), and on through certain radiations of the subcortical white matter, the *corona radiata* (I; *corona,* "crown"). In this manner they reach the neurons of the *postcentral gyrus* (J), where many body sensations are processed.

Fibers bringing sensations from the lower part of the body project to the superior aspect of the cortex; fibers from the thoracic and cervical regions end in the more inferior aspect of the cortex. This arrangement contributes to an inverted representation of the contralateral body half on the cortex known as the homunculus ("little man"; not shown).

ASCENDING PATHWAYS: POSTERIOR COLUMNS.

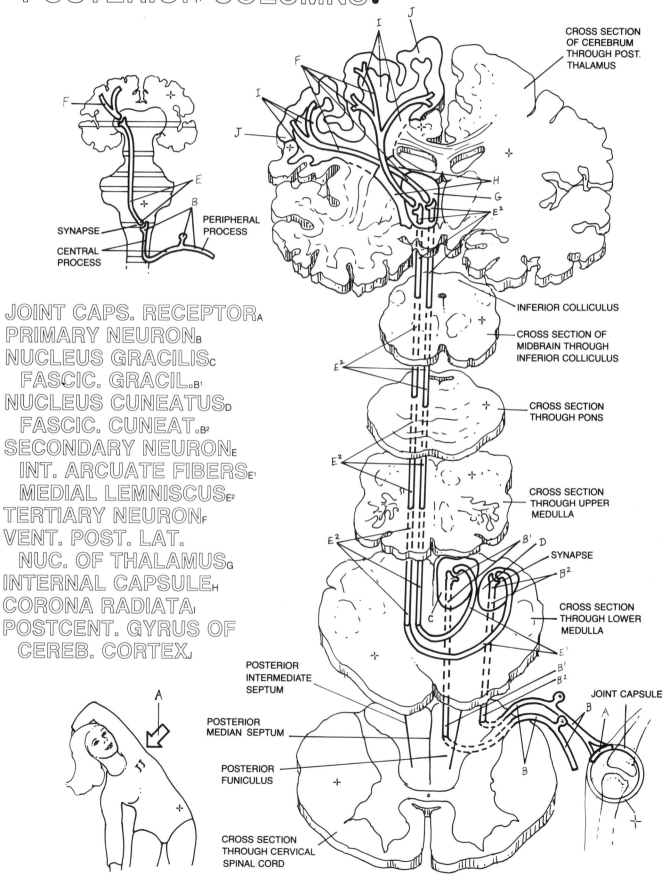

CROSS SECTION OF CEREBRUM THROUGH POST. THALAMUS

SYNAPSE

CENTRAL PROCESS

PERIPHERAL PROCESS

JOINT CAPS. RECEPTOR_A
PRIMARY NEURON_B
NUCLEUS GRACILIS_C
FASCIC. GRACIL._{B¹}
NUCLEUS CUNEATUS_D
FASCIC. CUNEAT._{B²}
SECONDARY NEURON_E
INT. ARCUATE FIBERS_{E¹}
MEDIAL LEMNISCUS_{E²}
TERTIARY NEURON_F
VENT. POST. LAT. NUC. OF THALAMUS_G
INTERNAL CAPSULE_H
CORONA RADIATA_I
POSTCENT. GYRUS OF CEREB. CORTEX_J

INFERIOR COLLICULUS

CROSS SECTION OF MIDBRAIN THROUGH INFERIOR COLLICULUS

CROSS SECTION THROUGH PONS

CROSS SECTION THROUGH UPPER MEDULLA

SYNAPSE

CROSS SECTION THROUGH LOWER MEDULLA

POSTERIOR INTERMEDIATE SEPTUM

POSTERIOR MEDIAN SEPTUM

POSTERIOR FUNICULUS

JOINT CAPSULE

CROSS SECTION THROUGH CERVICAL SPINAL CORD

The lateral spinothalamic tract carries sensations of pain and temperature from receptors throughout the body (except the face) to the brain. Both of these sensations are modified (as are others) by our emotional state and altered by our cultural surroundings, a fact exemplified by the soldier who, though suffering a traumatic wound, feels no pain, and the yogi who, reposing in quiet meditation, lies on the points of a thousand nails (pathways for inhibition of pain are presented in Plate 5-34). Different organs exhibit varying degrees of pain: A passing stone in the bile duct or ureter can bring excruciating pain, whereas an intravenous injection with a needle brings little discomfort.

It should be noted that the distinction between the lateral and anterior spinothalamic tracts is now thought to have little anatomical significance. Although the pathways are separated here (anterior spinothalamic tract is presented in the next plate), we alert you to the fact that this separation is no longer so clearly defined.

Use the same color scheme here as you did on Plate 4-4, where applicable. Color titles A through C. Color the primary neuron (B) in the upper right diagram. Color the arrow (A) at the lower left. Color the receptor A in the lower right corner, followed by the primary neuron (B) and fasciculus (C) in the two lowest sections. Then color the titles relating to the secondary and tertiary neurons (E through K) and their related structures in the two diagrams above and the main illustration, as applicable.

Free nerve endings (Plate 2-9) are now thought to be the principal *receptors* (A) for both pain and temperature. The related impulses are conducted to the cell bodies of the *primary neurons* (B) in the spinal ganglion along thin, myelinated and unmyelinated peripheral processes. The short central processes of the primary neurons enter *Lissauer's fasciculus* (C) and ascend at least one segment before entering the posterior horn to synapse with the *secondary neurons* (E). Some fibers ascend ipsilaterally (not shown) within Lissauer's fasciculus and reach the thalamus.

There are numerous pools of secondary neurons (interneurons) in the posterior horn, just as there are numerous areas of terminations in the thalamus. For example, secondary neurons associated with the lateral spinothalamic tract are found primarily in laminae I, IV, V, and VII of the spinal cord and project to the ventral posterior lateral nucleus of the thalamus; neurons in the intermediate zone project to the intralaminar nuclei of the thalamus.

The axons of the secondary neurons cross the midline in the anterior white commissure and ascend as the *lateral spinothalamic tract* (E^1) in the anterior part of the lateral funiculus. Fibers relating to the lower body are located in the lateral part of the tract (*peripheral fibers,* E^2), while those relating to the upper body are added successively to the medial part of the tract (*medial fibers,* E^3). This laminated axon pattern is important to the surgeon in the event that spinothalamic fibers in the cord need to be selectively severed to control severe pain in one part of the body. As these medial and lateral fiber bundles ascend, many give off *branches* (E^4), particularly to the *reticular formation* (L) of the brain stem and the *periaqueductal gray* (L^1) of the midbrain. It is possible that sharp, well-localized pain is expressed through direct spinothalamic fibers while deeper, dull, aching, poorly localized pain is conducted via the slower ascending fibers in the reticular formation. The collaterals from the spinothalamic tract to the reticular formation and periaqueductal gray are in a position to activate the pain-inhibitory system and thus start an intrinsic pain-suppression mechanism (see Plate 5-34).

As the spinothalamic tract ascends, it migrates from a lateral position (lower medulla, Plate 5-4) to a posterolateral position (upper medulla, Plate 5-6). In the midbrain, the tract lies adjacent to the medial lemniscus. The axons of the secondary neurons terminate in one of a number of centers in the thalamus, including the *ventral posterior lateral nucleus* (G), the posterior (PO) region adjacent to the medial geniculate body (not shown) and the *intralaminar nuclei* (G^1; see Plate 5-19). Pain impulses ascending through the reticular formation reach the PO and intralaminar nuclei of the thalamus.

Axons of *tertiary neurons* (F) project through the *internal capsule* (H) and *corona radiata* (I) to the *postcentral gyrus of the cerebral cortex* (J), with the exception of axons from the thalamic PO region, which project to the *secondary sensory cortex* (K) within the lateral fissure.

ASCENDING PATHWAYS:
LATERAL SPINOTHALAMIC TRACT.

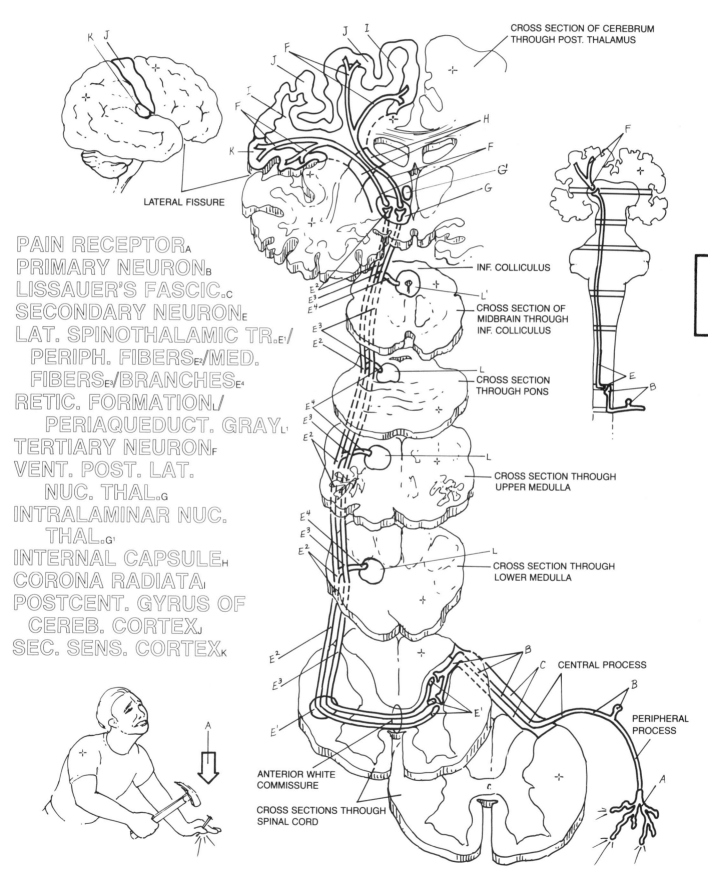

CROSS SECTION OF CEREBRUM
THROUGH POST. THALAMUS

LATERAL FISSURE

INF. COLLICULUS

CROSS SECTION OF
MIDBRAIN THROUGH
INF. COLLICULUS

CROSS SECTION
THROUGH PONS

CROSS SECTION THROUGH
UPPER MEDULLA

CROSS SECTION THROUGH
LOWER MEDULLA

CENTRAL PROCESS

PERIPHERAL
PROCESS

ANTERIOR WHITE
COMMISSURE

CROSS SECTIONS THROUGH
SPINAL CORD

PAIN RECEPTOR_A

PAIN RECEPTOR$_A$
PRIMARY NEURON$_B$
LISSAUER'S FASCIC.$_C$
SECONDARY NEURON$_E$
LAT. SPINOTHALAMIC TR.$_{E^1}$/
PERIPH. FIBERS$_{E^2}$/MED.
FIBERS$_{E^3}$/BRANCHES$_{E^4}$
RETIC. FORMATION$_L$/
PERIAQUEDUCT. GRAY$_{L^1}$
TERTIARY NEURON$_F$
VENT. POST. LAT.
NUC. THAL.$_G$
INTRALAMINAR NUC.
THAL.$_{G^1}$
INTERNAL CAPSULE$_H$
CORONA RADIATA$_I$
POSTCENT. GYRUS OF
CEREB. CORTEX$_J$
SEC. SENS. CORTEX$_K$

The anterior spinothalamic tract conducts impulses related to sensations of light, poorly localized (protopathic) touch. Light touch sensations originate in hairless areas of the skin; drawing a wisp of cotton lightly across the palm of the hand or caressing the soft fur of a stuffed animal demonstrates this sensation. Although bilateral destruction of this tract results in little or no general tactile impairment, there is often a reduction in itching, tickling, and sexual sensations.

Color this plate as you did the two preceding plates, using the same color scheme.

Axons (peripheral processes) of the *primary neurons* (B) conduct impulses of light touch from *receptors* (A) in the hairless areas of the skin to the cell bodies located in the spinal ganglia of spinal nerves. The central processes of these primary neurons reach into the posterior horn and intermediate gray, ranging throughout laminae IV through VII. Here they synapse with *secondary neurons* (E), the axons of which cross in the anterior white commissure and turn rostrally to form the *anterior spinothalamic tract* (E¹) in the anterolateral part of the spinal white matter. In the medulla, this tract appears to merge with the lateral spinothalamic tract, posterolateral to the inferior olivary nucleus. At this level, *branches* (E² and E³) from the tract project to the *reticular formation* (C) and to the *lateral reticular nucleus* (D), a processing station en route to the cerebellum. The branching is so extensive, in fact, that only a third of the fibers in the tract actually reach the thalamus.

The axons of the secondary neurons terminate in the *ventral posterior lateral nucleus* (G) and the posterior (PO) region of the thalamus (not shown), where they synapse with the *tertiary neurons* (F). The axons of the tertiary neurons project to the *postcentral gyrus of the cerebral cortex* (J), as before, through the *internal capsule* (H) and *corona radiata* (I).

It is well to point out that the lateral spinothalamic tract is phylogenetically a newer tract in mammals, providing somewhat more precise sensations of pain and temperature; the anterior spinothalamic tract is historically older and is characterized by larger, more diffuse receptive fields with less precise qualities of tactile sensations. In the mid medulla and above, the anterior and lateral spinothalamic tracts on each side appear as one and are generally designated the spinothalamic tract.

ASCENDING PATHWAYS: ANTERIOR SPINOTHALAMIC TRACT.

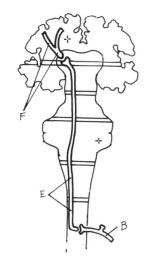

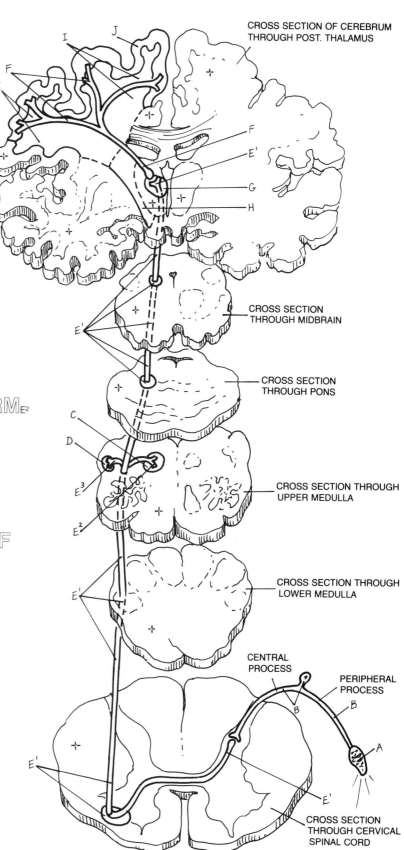

CROSS SECTION OF CEREBRUM
THROUGH POST. THALAMUS

CROSS SECTION
THROUGH MIDBRAIN

CROSS SECTION
THROUGH PONS

CROSS SECTION THROUGH
UPPER MEDULLA

CROSS SECTION THROUGH
LOWER MEDULLA

CENTRAL
PROCESS

PERIPHERAL
PROCESS

CROSS SECTION
THROUGH CERVICAL
SPINAL CORD

TOUCH RECEPTOR$_A$
PRIMARY NEURON$_B$
SECONDARY NEURON$_E$
  ANT. SPINOTHALAMIC
  TRACT$_{E^1}$
  BRANCH TO RETIC. FORM$_{E^2}$
  BRANCH TO LAT.
  RETIC. NUC.$_{E^3}$
RETICULAR FORMATION$_C$
LAT. RETICULAR NUC.$_D$
TERTIARY NEURON$_F$
VENT. POST. LAT. NUC. OF
  THALAMUS$_G$
INTERNAL CAPSULE$_H$
CORONA RADIATA$_I$
POSTCENT. GYRUS OF
  CEREB. CORTEX$_J$

ASCENDING PATHWAYS: POSTERIOR SPINOCEREBELLAR AND CUNEOCEREBELLAR TRACTS

The spinocerebellar tracts conduct impulses related to position and movement of muscles to the cerebellum. This information enables the cerebellum to add smoothness and precision to patterns of movement initiated in the cerebral hemispheres. Spinocerebellar impulses, by definition, never reach the cerebrum directly and therefore have no conscious representation.

Four tracts constitute the spinocerebellar pathway: *posterior spinocerebellar* (E^1) and *cuneocerebellar* (E^3), and anterior and rostral spinocerebellar tracts.

The posterior spinocerebellar tract conveys muscle spindle– or tendon organ–related impulses from the lower half of the body (below the level of the C8 spinal cord segment); the cuneocerebellar tract is concerned with such impulses from the body above C8. The "grain" of information carried in these two tracts is fine, often involving single muscle cells or portions of a muscle-tendon complex.

A much broader representation is carried by the individual fibers of the anterior and rostral spinocerebellar tracts, which will be the subject of the next plate.

Color this plate as you did the previous three plates, using the same color scheme for the neurons and their related pathways and nuclei, where applicable. Start with the heading Posterior Spinocerebellar Tract and titles A through G. Color the related pathway (B, E) in the small diagram at the upper left. Color the lower half of the body (A) at lower left. Then color arrows A and the primary neuron (B) at the S1 spinal segment of the main illustration, and so on. Finally, color the cerebellum (G).

The axons conducting impulses from muscle spindles, tendon organs, and skin in the *lower half of the body* (A) are large Ia, Ib, and II fibers, the cell bodies of which are in the spinal ganglia of spinal nerves below C8.

Primary neurons (B) below L3 send their central processes into the *posterior columns* (C). These processes then bend and ascend in the columns to the L3 level. From L3 up to C8, incoming central processes and those

in the posterior columns project to the medial part of lamina VII (intermediate gray zone), where there is a well-demarcated column of cells, called *Clarke's column* (D). Largely limited to the thoracic cord, Clarke's column can be seen from segments L3 to C8 of the cord. Here the central processes of the primary neurons synapse with *secondary neurons* (E), the axons of which are directed to the lateral funiculi as the *posterior spinocerebellar tracts* (E^1).

The posterior spinocerebellar tracts drift posteriorly as they ascend, and at the upper medullary level they enter the *inferior cerebellar peduncle* (F; also called restiform body) and on into the *cerebellum* (G). Fibers of this tract, among the most rapidly conducting elements of the central nervous system, terminate as mossy fibers on portions of the ipsilateral medial cerebellar cortex (vermis and paramedian lobule; not shown), which represents the hind (lower) limb and trunk areas for muscle and position sense input.

Color the heading Cuneocerebellar Tract, titles A^1 through E^3, and the rest as you did before. Color the related pathway (B, E^2) in the small diagram at the upper left. The primary neuron of this pathway begins at the T6 spinal segment. Note arrow A^1.

Central processes of *primary neurons* (B^1) conducting impulses from muscle spindles, tendon organs, and skin in the *upper half of the body* (A^1) (above C8 enter the *fasciculus cuneatus* (C^1) and ascend to terminate on cells of the *external (accessory) cuneate nucleus* (H) in the most posterior portion of the medulla. This is just lateral to one of the synaptic zones (nucleus cuneatus) for the tracts of the posterior columns (recall Plate 4-4). The axons of the secondary neurons run rostrally as the *cuneocerebellar tract* (E^3). In company with the posterior spinocerebellar tract, it passes through the *inferior cerebellar peduncle* (F) into the *cerebellum* (G). The fibers of this tract also end as mossy fibers on the medial part of the cerebellar cortex, the upper trunk and fore (upper) limb representation area of the cerebellar cortex (not shown).

ASCENDING PATHWAYS: POSTERIOR SPINOCEREBELLAR AND CUNEOCEREBELLAR TRACTS.

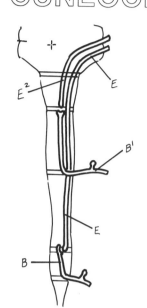

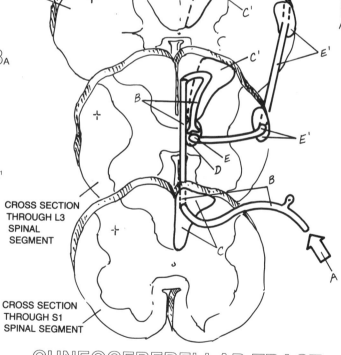

CROSS SECTION THROUGH UPPER MEDULLA

CROSS SECTION THROUGH LOWER MEDULLA

CROSS SECTION THROUGH C7 SPINAL SEGMENT

CROSS SECTION THROUGH L3 SPINAL SEGMENT

CROSS SECTION THROUGH S1 SPINAL SEGMENT

POSTERIOR SPINOCEREBELLAR TRACT ★
POSITION/MOVEMENT SENSATIONS: BELOW C8$_A$
PRIMARY NEURON$_B$
POSTERIOR COLUMN$_C$
CLARKE'S COLUMN$_D$
SECONDARY NEURON$_E$
   POST. SPINOCEREB. TR.$_{E^1}$
INF. CEREBELLAR PEDUNCLE$_F$
CEREBELLUM$_G$

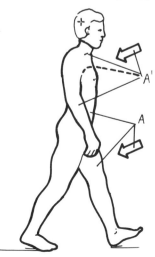

CUNEOCEREBELLAR TRACT ★
POS./MOVE. SENS.: ABOVE C8$_{A^1}$
PRIMARY NEURON$_{B^1}$
FASC. CUNEATUS$_{C^1}$
EXT. CUNEATE NUC.$_H$
SECONDARY NEURON$_{E^2}$
CUNEOCEREB. TR.$_{E^3}$

ASCENDING PATHWAYS: ANTERIOR AND ROSTRAL SPINOCEREBELLAR TRACTS

The anterior and rostral spinocerebellar tracts conduct impulses related to movement and position sense from tendon organs and muscle spindles to the cerebellum. The information traveling in this pathway represents an integration of input from a much broader spectrum than that conducted in the posterior spinocerebellar and cuneocerebellar tracts (recall Plate 4-7). Whereas these latter tracts may conduct postural information about a part of an individual muscle, the anterior and rostral spinocerebellar tracts may convey postural information regarding an entire limb! It is difficult to imagine the amount of convergence of primary neurons on a single secondary neuron necessary to allow the axon of that neuron to conduct information about an entire limb to the cerebellum.

Color this plate as before. Start with titles A and A^1. Color the related structures at lower left. Then color the heading, titles, and structures of the Anterior Spinocerebellar Tract. Note that the subscript D does not appear on this plate. Stop after coloring the cerebellum (G).

Peripheral processes of the *primary neurons* (B) of the anterior spinocerebellar system conduct impulses from *muscle spindles* (A) and *tendon organs* (A^1) and approach their cell bodies in the spinal root ganglia of lumbar and sacral spinal nerves. The central processes of these neurons enter the cord at these levels (up to the first lumbar segment) and synapse with the *secondary neurons* (E), believed to be in the bases of the posterior and anterior horns.

The axons of these secondary neurons cross to the contralateral side via the gray commissure and turn rostrally in the lateral funiculus as the *anterior spinocerebellar tract*

(E^1). This tract ascends the brain stem to the upper pons, where it bends back on itself to enter the *cerebellum* (G) via the ipsilateral *superior cerebellar peduncle* (C; also called *brachium conjunctivum*). About 10 percent of the anterior spinocerebellar fibers recross the midline at the cerebellum, entering the latter over the contralateral superior cerebellar peduncle (not shown). In both cases, the fibers terminate in the medial part of the cerebellar cortex, where hind (lower) limb representation is concentrated (not shown).

Color the heading, titles, and structures of the Rostral Spinocerebellar Tract. Begin with Arrow A at the right of the spinal segment. For simplicity, the primary neurons of both anterior and rostral spinocerebellar tracts are shown entering the same spinal level; in fact, they do not.

The *rostral spinocerebellar tract* (E^3) is the fore (upper) limb equivalent of the anterior tract. Having been investigated only in the cat, the data here, as it applies to humans, is inferential. The central processes of the *primary neuron* (B^1) enter the cervical cord and are believed to synapse there with *secondary neurons* (E^2). The axons of these neurons remain uncrossed and join the *rostral spinocerebellar tract* (E^2). The fibers of this tract may enter the *inferior cerebellar peduncle* (F) in the upper medulla, or they may continue to ascend to the upper pons and enter the superior cerebellar peduncle. The fibers terminate in the medial cerebellar cortex where fore (upper) limb movement and position sense are represented.

The integrative functions of the cerebellum with respect to input as described here are the subjects, in part, of Plates 5-13, 5-14, and 5-15.

ASCENDING PATHWAYS: ANTERIOR AND ROSTRAL SPINOCEREBELLAR TRACTS.

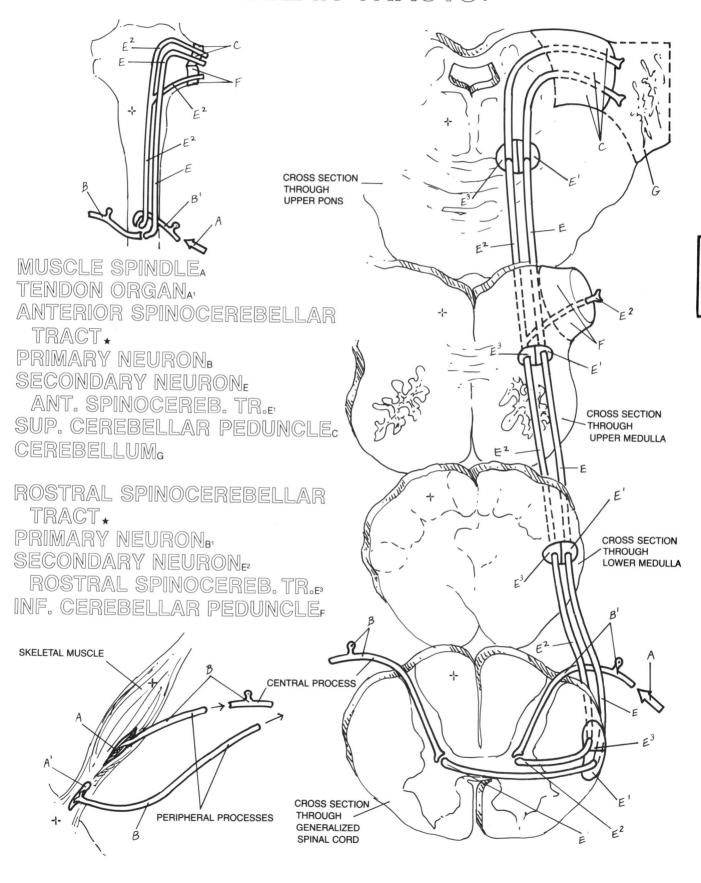

MUSCLE SPINDLE_A
TENDON ORGAN_A'
ANTERIOR SPINOCEREBELLAR
   TRACT. ★
PRIMARY NEURON_B
SECONDARY NEURON_E
   ANT. SPINOCEREB. TR._E'
SUP. CEREBELLAR PEDUNCLE_C
CEREBELLUM_G

ROSTRAL SPINOCEREBELLAR
   TRACT. ★
PRIMARY NEURON_B'
SECONDARY NEURON_E²
   ROSTRAL SPINOCEREB. TR._E³
INF. CEREBELLAR PEDUNCLE_F

CROSS SECTION THROUGH UPPER PONS

CROSS SECTION THROUGH UPPER MEDULLA

CROSS SECTION THROUGH LOWER MEDULLA

SKELETAL MUSCLE

CENTRAL PROCESS

PERIPHERAL PROCESSES

CROSS SECTION THROUGH GENERALIZED SPINAL CORD

DESCENDING PATHWAYS: CORTICOSPINAL TRACT

The corticospinal tract is the major cortically derived descending pathway affecting the motor neurons as well as the sensory interneurons of the spinal cord. Found in most mammals, it reaches its greatest size and importance in humans, where much of its function deals with voluntary control of the upper limbs (manipulation of objects) and lower limbs (locomotion), as well as modifying sensory impulses to regulate ascending information. Like all tracts that descend into the spinal cord, the corticospinal pathway may be termed a suprasegmental or supraspinal tract and is considered a part of the upper motor neuron system.

This plate is the first of four plates on descending pathways, and the sequence of coloring these is reversed from the previous plates on ascending pathways; that is, the coloring of the tracts is initiated at the upper part of the plate and is terminated below. Further, for each tract, there is no sequence of primary and secondary neurons; the neurons arise in the cortex or subcortical nuclei and descend to the lower motor (anterior horn) neurons without synapsing. However, there may be several nuclei that contribute axons to a particular tract.

Color the title and extent of the corticospinal tract (A) in the diagram at the upper right. Color titles B and B^1, the areas of the cortex labeled B and B^1 (with light pastel colors) in the lateral view of the cerebral hemisphere at the upper left, and the area of cortex labeled B^1 in the upper left part of the main illustration. Then color titles A^1 and C through I, the corticospinal tract in its entirety and related structures, the lower motor neuron and its related structures (G through I), and the arrow (I) at the lower left pointing to the figure representing skilled movement.

Approximately one million neurons located in extensive areas on each side of the *cerebral cortex* (B) (see inset of brain at upper left; dot density correlates with neuron density) contribute axons to the *corticospinal tract* (A). Those projecting to the anterior horn are among the cells called upper motor neurons. Many of their axons are unmyelinated, and their function remains uncertain; of those

axons that are myelinated, 90 percent are very small (1–4 μm), and only 2 to 4 percent are large (10–20 μm). These large, rapidly conducting axons are derived from the giant pyramidal cells of Betz located in the *primary motor cortex* (B^1) of the frontal lobe. Their action briefly inhibits the antigravity tone of extensor muscles preceding a motor act.

These axons descend from the cortex to become part of the vast *corona radiata* (C), which narrows just lateral to the diencephalon to become the *internal capsule* (D). Tightly compacted here, these axons are especially vulnerable to a small hemorrhage or thrombosis, which can result in serious neurological consequences. Continuing in their descent, giving off *collaterals* (A^1) and terminals en route, the corticospinal tract traverses the base of the midbrain, making up the middle two-thirds of the *crus cerebri* (E; the remainder of the crus contains corticopontine and corticobulbar or cortex-to-medulla fibers). The tract reaches the anterior pons and is broken up into bundles by clusters of pontine cells. The bundles reassemble caudally as they approach the medulla, giving off collaterals and terminals there and forming *pyramids* (F) on the medullary anterior surface.

At the medullospinal junction, the greatest part of the tract (75 to 90 percent) on each side crosses to the contralateral side and forms the *decussation* ("crossing") *of the pyramids* (F^1). After crossing, each tract takes up a position in the lateral funiculus of the spinal cord as the *lateral corticospinal tract* (A^2). The uncrossed fibers continue caudally in the anterior funiculus as the *anterior corticospinal tract* (A^4), but usually no further than the caudal thoracic segments. These fibers will decussate at the cord segment within which they terminate.

Almost one-half of the corticospinal fibers terminate on interneurons in the base of the posterior horn of the cord (*terminal fiber,* A^3), modifying sensory input. The remainder terminate on the *anterior horn motor neurons* (G) in lamina IX and on adjacent interneurons. The anterior horn motor cell, with its cranial nerve motor nuclei counterparts and their *axons* (G^1), constitutes the final common pathway for the expression of voluntary motor activity (Sherrington, 1906) and terminates at the *neuromuscular junction* (H) of the *muscle* (I).

DESCENDING PATHWAYS: CORTICOSPINAL TRACT.

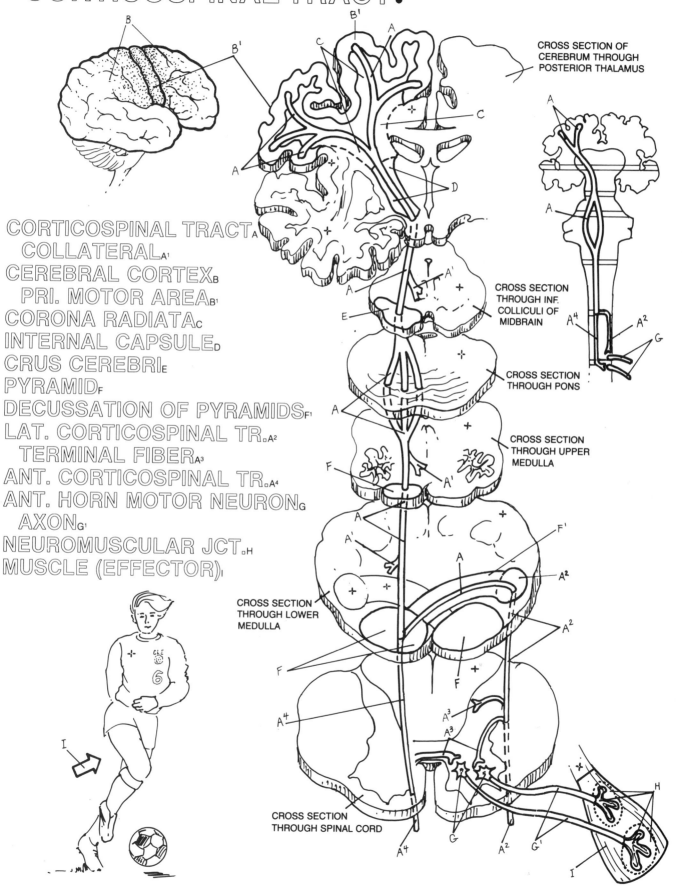

CORTICOSPINAL TRACT$_A$
COLLATERAL$_{A^1}$
CEREBRAL CORTEX$_B$
PRI. MOTOR AREA$_{B^1}$
CORONA RADIATA$_C$
INTERNAL CAPSULE$_D$
CRUS CEREBRI$_E$
PYRAMID$_F$
DECUSSATION OF PYRAMIDS$_{F^1}$
LAT. CORTICOSPINAL TR.$_{A^2}$
TERMINAL FIBER$_{A^3}$
ANT. CORTICOSPINAL TR.$_{A^4}$
ANT. HORN MOTOR NEURON$_G$
AXON$_{G^1}$
NEUROMUSCULAR JCT.$_H$
MUSCLE (EFFECTOR)$_I$

CROSS SECTION OF CEREBRUM THROUGH POSTERIOR THALAMUS

CROSS SECTION THROUGH INF. COLLICULI OF MIDBRAIN

CROSS SECTION THROUGH PONS

CROSS SECTION THROUGH UPPER MEDULLA

CROSS SECTION THROUGH LOWER MEDULLA

CROSS SECTION THROUGH SPINAL CORD

In addition to the corticospinal tract (Plate 4-9), there are several phylogenetically older tracts, elements of the "upper motor neuron pool," that descend to the spinal cord from subcortical centers of the brain. They are known as the extrapyramidal pathways because they do not travel in the medullary pyramids of the corticospinal system. Each of these extrapyramidal tracts helps set the stage for individual motor acts initiated by the corticospinal tract. This complex of descending fibers can thus be conceived as functioning like the various instruments of an orchestra playing on a common theme, the output of the final common pathway (anterior horn motor neuron).

Here we consider two extrapyramidal pathways originating in whole or in part from the vestibular nuclear complex in the caudal pons and rostral medulla.

Color the heading Medial Longitudinal Fasciculus Pathway, title A, and the related pathway in the orientation diagram at the upper right. Color titles A[1] through F[1]. On the right side of the main illustration, color the descending MLF fibers (A[1]) and related arrows, their sources B through E[1], and the termination neuron F and its axon F[1]. Then color titles A[2] through I. On the right side of the main illustration, at the level of the upper medulla, color the ascending fibers of the MLF (A[2]) and related arrows, beginning adjacent to the vestibular nuclei (E), and their destination nuclei G through I.

The *medial longitudinal fasciculus* (A; abbreviated MLF) is a bundle of axons situated near the midline of the brain stem. It is complexly arranged, composed of ascending and descending fibers arising from several sources and terminating in different areas.

The descending fibers arise mainly from the *medial vestibular nucleus* (E[1]) of the upper medulla. Fibers from this nucleus exert inhibitory effects on anterior horn motor neurons of the cervical cord. Descending fibers also arise from the *superior colliculus* (B) of the rostral midbrain (visual reflexes), the *accessory oculomotor nuclei* (C) of the rostral midbrain (visual tracking), the *pontine reticular formation* (D; facilitating extensor muscle tone), and the *vestibular nuclei* (E) of the medulla (balance and equilibrium). The MLF descends ipsilaterally through the anterior funiculus of the spinal cord, with some fibers synapsing directly on the *anterior horn motor neurons* (F) of the

cervical segments. The *axons* (F[1]) of these neurons terminate primarily in neuromuscular junctions of neck muscles (not shown).

Ascending fibers of the MLF arise primarily from the vestibular nuclei in the upper medulla. These fibers terminate in the *oculomotor* (III) (I), *trochlear* (IV) (H), and *abducens* (VI) (G) *cranial nerve nuclei,* the axons of which innervate the extraocular ("tracking") muscles of the eyeball.

The visual tracking of a moving object through coordinated movements of eyes, head, neck, and trunk constitutes a typical example of MLF activity. The corticospinal tract adds a component of voluntary movement to these reflexive activities.

Color the heading Vestibulospinal Pathway, titles J through O[1], the condensed diagram of the pathway (M) at the upper right, and the related components on the left side of the main illustration, starting with afferents J and K.

All vestibular nuclei receive *afferent fibers* (J) from the *vestibular* apparatus of the inner ear (via the vestibular nerve, a part of the VIII cranial nerve) and *afferent fibers* (K) from the *cerebellum,* which control various aspects of balance and coordination. Axons of neurons in the *lateral vestibular nucleus* (L) make up the *vestibulospinal tract* (M). These fibers descend ipsilaterally through the full length of the anterolateral spinal cord. At each cord segment, *terminal fibers* (M[1]) turn into laminae VII and VIII and synapse on *interneurons* (N), the axons of which in turn project on *anterior horn motor neurons* (O). Their *axons* (O[1]) terminate at neuromuscular junctions and muscle spindles of the effectors (not shown).

The vestibulospinal tract facilitates activity in all extensor (antigravity) muscles, thereby providing a basic posture or stance. Maintenance of this activity is briefly inhibited just prior to the development of a willed action and resumed immediately afterward. The powerful antigravity effect of this pathway can be seen in severely injured victims whose brain stem is traumatized just rostral to the vestibular nuclei. In these cases, inhibition of vestibulospinal impulses from more rostral centers in the cerebrum is lost, and a state of continuous extensor rigidity develops (decerebrate rigidity).

MIXED PATHWAYS: MEDIAL LONGITUDINAL FASCICULUS DESCEND. PATHWAYS:VESTIB.-SP. TRACT.

MEDIAL LONGITUDINAL
FASCICULUS PATHWAY ★
MED. LONGITUDINAL FASC.A
DESCENDING FIBERSA¹
SUPERIOR COLLICULUSB
ACCESS. OCULOMOTOR NUC.C
PONTINE RETIC. FORM.D
VESTIBULAR NUCLEIE
MED. VESTIB. NUC.E¹
ANT. HORN MOTOR NEURONF/
AXONF¹

ASCENDING FIBERSA²
VESTIBULAR NUCLEIE
NUCLEUS OF VI CR. N.G
NUCLEUS OF IV CR. N.H
NUCLEUS OF III CR. N.I

SEMICIRCULAR CANALS

CEREBELLUM

VESTIBULOSPINAL PATHWAY ★
VESTIBULAR AFFERENTJ
CEREBELLAR AFFERENTK
LAT. VESTIBULAR NUC.L
VESTIBULOSPINAL TRACTM
TERMINAL FIBERM¹
INTERNEURONN
ANT. HORN MOTOR NEURONO/ AXONO¹

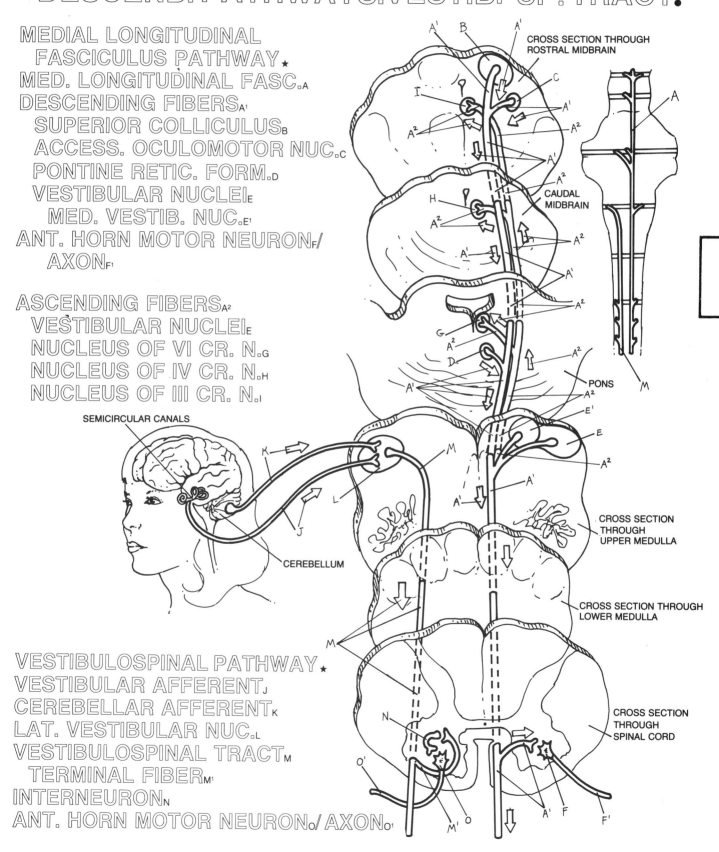

CROSS SECTION THROUGH
ROSTRAL MIDBRAIN

CAUDAL
MIDBRAIN

PONS

CROSS SECTION
THROUGH
UPPER MEDULLA

CROSS SECTION THROUGH
LOWER MEDULLA

CROSS SECTION
THROUGH
SPINAL CORD

The anterior horn cell of the spinal cord is continuously influenced by impulses from long descending tracts, as shown in Plates 4-9 and 4-10. Here are illustrated two other descending tracts originating from the brain stem: the tectospinal tract, arising in the tectum of the midbrain, and the rubrospinal tract, arising in the red nucleus of the same region. Both tracts are included in the upper motor neuron pool.

Color the heading Tectospinal Tract and titles A through G at the upper left. Color B, D, and E in the small diagram at the upper right and the arrow B pointing at the eyes in the figure at the left. Starting with the superior colliculus (A) at the top of the main illustration, color the parts of the tectospinal tract, the interneuron (D), and the anterior horn motor neuron and relations (E through G).

The *tectospinal tract* (B) begins with the *superior colliculus* (A) of the midbrain, an important center for visual-following and eye-centering reflexes. Descending from this nucleus, the fibers circle under the periaqueductal gray, crossing the midline to form the *dorsal tegmental decussation* (C). The tectospinal tract then descends, just anterior to the medial longitudinal fasciculus (MLF, not shown); in the lower brain stem, it actually intermingles with this tract. In the spinal cord, the tectospinal tract lies near the anterior median fissure of the anterior funiculus, running as far caudally as the cervical cord. The *terminal fibers* (B^1) end in layers VI, VII, and VIII on *interneurons* (D), which synapse with *anterior horn motor neurons* (E). The *axons* (E^1) from these cells terminate at the *neuromuscular junctions* (F) and muscle spindles (not shown) of the *effector* (G).

The tectospinal tract probably blends the interaction of visual and auditory stimuli with postural reflex movements, although this function is not well established.

Color the heading Rubrospinal Tract and titles H through G^1 at the lower left. Color I, D^1, and E^2 in the small diagram at the upper right. Color the arrow I pointing to the flexed joints in the figure at the middle left. Starting at the red nucleus (H) at the top of the main illustration, color the rubrospinal tract and terminal fiber, interneuron D^1, and the anterior horn motor neuron and its relations (E^2 through G^1).

Axons from the *red nucleus* (H) of the midbrain cross the midline and descend to the spinal cord, where they are closely intermingled with the corticospinal tract (not shown). The *rubrospinal tract* (I) descends as far as the thoracic level of the cord. Its *terminal fibers* (I^1) end on *interneurons* (D^1) in layers V, VI, and VIII of the anterior horn; they do not terminate directly on the larger motor neurons. The interneurons project to *motor neurons* (E^2; including both alpha and gamma types), the *axons* (E^3) of which terminate on the *neuromuscular junctions* (F^1) and muscle spindles (not shown) of the *effector* (G^1).

The rubrospinal tract is thought to serve as an alternate pathway from cerebral cortex to spinal cord because the red nucleus receives fibers from the descending corticospinal tract. A very important function of the rubrospinal tract is to control the tone of flexor muscle groups in the limbs. The activity of the rubrospinal tract is regulated by the cerebellum and cerebral cortex based on sensory input. For example, the spinocerebellar tract conveys information on posture and muscle movement to the cerebellum, which in turn modifies the activity of the red nucleus.

DESCENDING PATHWAYS: TECTOSPINAL AND RUBROSPINAL TRACTS.

TECTOSPINAL TRACT ★
SUPERIOR COLLICULUS_A
TECTOSPINAL TRACT_B
TERMINAL FIBER_B1
DORS. TEGMENTAL DECUSS._C
INTERNEURON_D
ANT. HORN MOTOR NEURON_E
AXON_E1
NEUROMUSCULAR JCT._F
EFFECTOR_G

RUBROSPINAL TRACT ★
RED NUCLEUS_H
RUBROSPINAL TRACT_I
TERMINAL FIBER_I1
INTERNEURON_D1
ANT. HORN MOTOR NEURON_E2
AXON_E3
NEUROMUSCULAR JCT._F1
EFFECTOR_G1

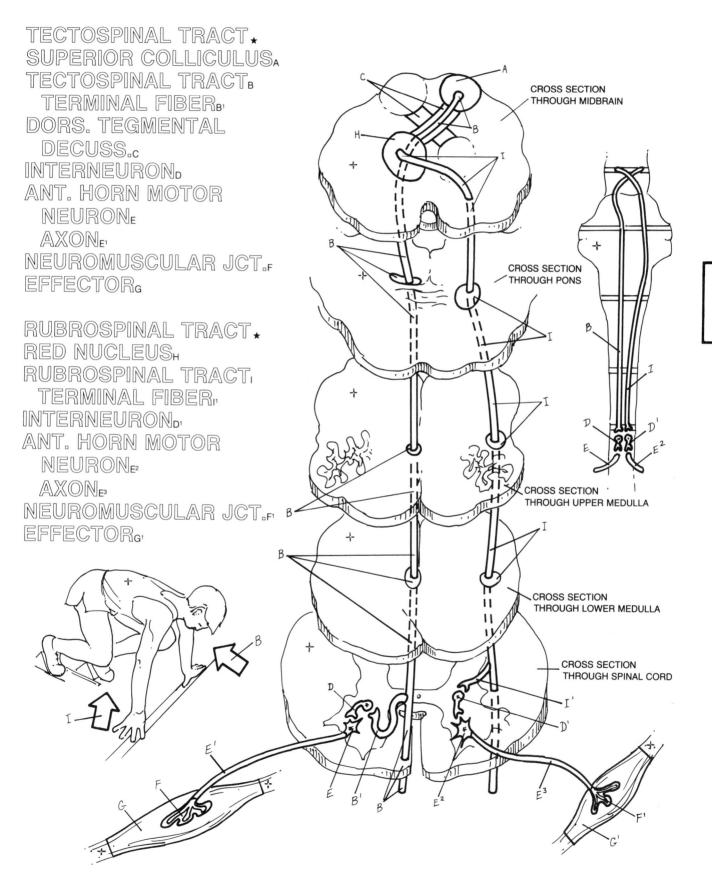

CROSS SECTION THROUGH MIDBRAIN

CROSS SECTION THROUGH PONS

CROSS SECTION THROUGH UPPER MEDULLA

CROSS SECTION THROUGH LOWER MEDULLA

CROSS SECTION THROUGH SPINAL CORD

DESCENDING PATHWAYS: RETICULOSPINAL TRACTS

Here we present another of the suprasegmental tracts of subcortical origin, the reticulospinal tracts. Though subcortical nuclei may give rise to the fibers of these tracts, it is important to recognize the substantial innervation of these subcortical nuclei by descending cortical fibers. In fact, an alternative term coming into current use for such tracts is cortico-subcortico-spinal, emphasizing the cortical contributions.

Color the heading Pontine Reticulospinal Tract and titles A through E^2. Color B and B^1 in the small diagram at the upper left. After coloring the nuclei A^1 and A^2 in the upper part of the main illustration, color the pontine reticulospinal tract (B and B^1), interneuron (C), and alpha and gamma motor neurons and related parts (D through E^2).

The reticulospinal tracts originate from cells at several levels in the brain stem reticular core (presented in Plate 5-12) and modify motor and sensory functions of the spinal cord. Two tracts are generally recognized. The *pontine reticulospinal tract* (B) arises from cells in the *pontine tegmentum* (A), primarily the *nuclei pontis oralis* (A^1) and *caudalis* (A^2). The tract descends through the brain stem and spinal cord as uncrossed bundles in the anterior funiculus, giving off *terminal fibers* (B^1) en route. These terminal fibers end on *interneurons* (C) in laminae VII and VIII of the spinal cord. Axons of the interneurons project onto *anterior horn alpha motor neurons* (D^1), the *axons* (D^2) of which terminate in *neuromuscular junctions* (E^1) of the extrafusal skeletal muscle fibers (*effectors;* E). These interneurons also project axons onto *gamma motor neurons* (D^3) of the anterior horn. The gamma efferent *axons* (D^4) innervate the small intrafusal fibers of the *muscle spindles* (E^2; recall Plate 2-10).

Color the heading Medullary Reticulospinal Tract and titles F through G^1. Color G and G^1 in the small diagram at the upper left. Starting with the nucleus (F^1), color the medullary reticulospinal tract and terminal fiber (G and G^1).

The *medullary reticulospinal tract* (G) originates in the medial two-thirds of the medulla, particularly the large neurons of the *nucleus reticularis magnocellularis* (F^1). The tract descends through the brain stem and spinal cord, like its companion tract, as uncrossed bundles in the anterior funiculus. The tract gives off *terminal fibers* (G^1) to interneurons in laminae VII and VIII of the spinal cord. As in the pontine reticulospinal tract, these interneurons project onto both alpha and gamma motor neurons. Many of the interneurons of the cord receive innervation from several cortico-subcortico-spinal tracts, including rubrospinal and vestibulospinal systems. These interneurons function as subcenters of convergence for a number of influences pouring down from the brain stem. Their axons play on both alpha and gamma motor neurons of the anterior horn.

It is now known that the reticular formation of the brain stem can inhibit or facilitate motor activity and muscle tone, influence the respiratory and circulatory systems, and affect transmission of sensory impulses to higher centers. Although it is still not possible to correlate each of these functions with these two tracts, a few generalizations can be made. The medullary reticulospinal tract appears to be involved in the inhibition of motor activity, depression of cardiovascular (pulse and blood pressure) responses, and stimulation of the inspiratory phase of respiration. Functions of the pontine reticulospinal tract are less clear but undoubtedly include the facilitation of motor activity and cardiovascular responses.

DESCENDING PATHWAYS: RETICULOSPINAL TRACTS.

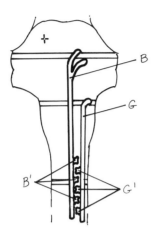

PONTINE RETICULOSPINAL
   TRACT.★
PONTINE RETICULAR
   TEGMENTUM_{A()}
   N. RETIC. PONT. ORALIS_{A^1}
   N. RETIC. PONT. CAUDALIS_{A^2}
PONTINE RETICULOSPINAL
   TRACT_B
   TERMINAL FIBER_{B^1}
INTERNEURON_C
ANT. HORN MOTOR
   NEURONS_{D()}
   ALPHA NEURON_{D^1}/AXON_{D^2}
   GAMMA NEURON_{D^3}/AXON_{D^4}
EFFECTOR_E
   NEUROMUSCULAR JCT._{E^1}
   MUSCLE SPINDLE_{E^2}

MEDULLARY
   RETICULOSPINAL TR.★
MEDULLARY RETICULAR
   FORMATION_{F()}
   NUC. RETICULARIS
      MAGNOCELLULARIS_{F^1}
MEDULLARY
   RETICULOSPINAL TRACT_G
   TERMINAL FIBER_{G^1}

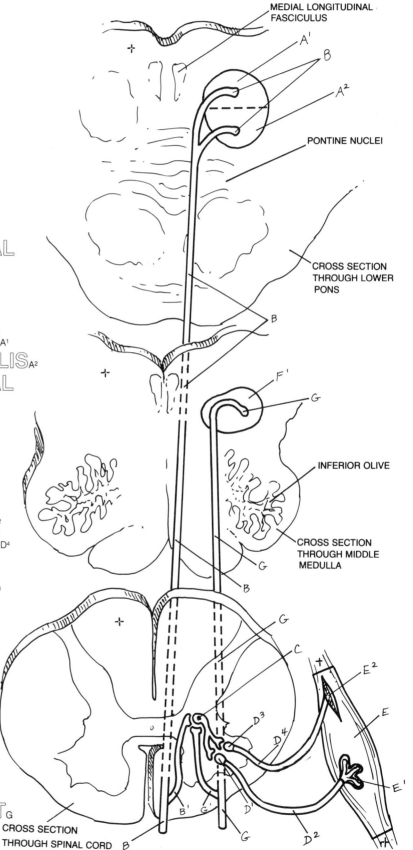

MEDIAL LONGITUDINAL FASCICULUS
PONTINE NUCLEI
CROSS SECTION THROUGH LOWER PONS
INFERIOR OLIVE
CROSS SECTION THROUGH MIDDLE MEDULLA
CROSS SECTION THROUGH SPINAL CORD

This plate provides a review of the relative positions of pathways in the spinal cord. It is assumed that all preceding plates in this unit have been colored. The section of spinal cord shown here is a generalized cervical segment. The coloring of this plate, as a sequel to the plates of individual pathways, will provide an excellent perspective preparatory to working on the plates of the brain in the next unit.

Color the headings, titles, related tracts, and fasciculi A through Q, in the order listed on the illustration. Note that the ascending tracts are shown on the left and descending and mixed tracts on the right. Consider using different shades of the same color for ascending tracts, shades of another color for the association fasciculi, and shades of a third for the descending tracts.

The plates of this unit, which illustrate one or more of the individual pathways in the spinal cord segment shown here, are as follows:

ASCENDING

Fasciculus gracilis (A). . . . . Plate 4-4
Fasciculus cuneatus (B). . . . . Plate 4-4
Posterior spinocerebellar (C). . . . . Plate 4-7
Rostral spinocerebellar (D). . . . . Plate 4-8
Lateral spinothalamic (E) . . . . Plate 4-5
Anterior spinocerebellar (F) . . . . Plate 4-8
Anterior spinothalamic (G). . . . . Plate 4-6
Association tracts (H, I, J) . . . . Plate 4-13

DESCENDING

Lateral corticospinal (K). . . . . Plate 4-9
Anterior corticospinal (K^1). . . . . Plate 4-9
Rubrospinal (L) . . . . Plate 4-11
Reticulospinal (M). . . . . Plate 4-12
Vestibulospinal (N) . . . . Plate 4-10
Tectospinal (O). Plate 4-11

MIXED

Medial longitudinal fasciculus (P) . . . . Plate 4-10
Lissauer's fasciculus (Q) . . . . Plate 4-5

There are short pathways that arise and terminate within the spinal cord that have not been presented previously. These are the spinospinal pathways, commonly known as the *fasciculi proprii* (H; sing. *fasciculus proprius*). These pathways consist of interneurons within the gray matter that receive afferent input from the posterior root and project their axons to other neurons at segments higher or lower than the segment of the interneuron cell body of origin. Their axons travel in the funiculus closest to the cell body of origin; all funiculi contain these fibers, closely surrounding the gray matter, central to the more peripherally situated longer tracts.

Posterior root fibers entering the cord often descend or ascend several segments before synapsing with a secondary neuron. In the cervical and thoracic regions of the cord, bundles of descending posterior root fibers constitute the *fasciculus interfascicularis* (I); in the lumbar region, they constitute the *fasciculus septomarginalis* (J).

SPINAL CORD:
SUMMARY OF TRACTS.

ASCENDING TRACTS ★
FASC. GRACILIS A
FASC. CUNEATUS B
POST. SPINOCEREB. C
ROSTRAL SPINOCEREB. D
LAT. SPINOTHALAMIC E
ANT. SPINOCEREB. F
ANT. SPINOTHALAMIC G

ASSOCIATION TRACTS ★
FASC. PROPRIUS H
FASC. INTERFASCIC. I
FASC. SEPTOMARGIN. J

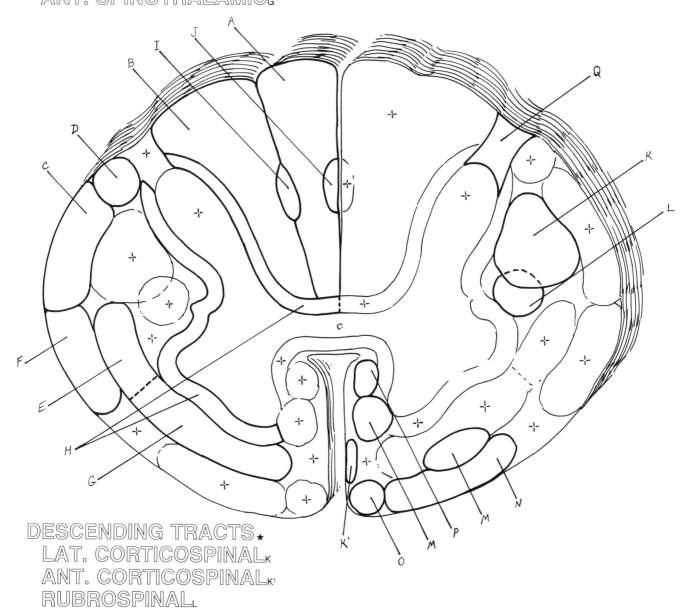

DESCENDING TRACTS ★
LAT. CORTICOSPINAL K
ANT. CORTICOSPINAL K1
RUBROSPINAL L
RETICULOSPINAL M
VESTIBULOSPINAL N
TECTOSPINAL O

MIXED TRACTS ★
MED. LONG. FASC. P
LISSAUER'S FASC. Q

INTRODUCTION: THE BRAIN

Unit Five, the longest in this book, is organized in the following way. Plates 5-1 and 5-2 provide an opportunity to color the entire brain stem from both anterior and posterior aspects and are subscripted for color coordination. Plate 5-3 illustrates the shapes of common brain stem cross sections, which have been seen in Unit Four and will be seen numerous times in this and the following units. Rapid identification of these shapes will prove very helpful when reviewing cross sections or following tracts through the brain stem. Plates 5-4 through 5-11 are cross sections of the brain stem in ascending order. They are subscripted for color coordination. Plates 5-12 through 5-32 illustrate specific regions of the brain stem, cerebellum, and cerebral hemispheres; here the organization of the region is unraveled, the incoming and outgoing fibers are shown, and a functional overview is given. Plate 5-33 is concerned with the organization of white matter in the cerebrum, and Plate 5-34 goes into a subject of current interest and intense research, pain-inhibition pathways. Plates 5-35 through 5-48 make up the Atlas of Brain Sections (see ahead).

CROSS SECTIONS OF THE BRAIN STEM (PLATES 5-4 THROUGH 5-11)

The brain stem is, in a sense, the keystone of the entire central nervous system. On the one hand, it serves as a connection—the physical interface—between the spinal cord and the cerebral hemispheres. On the other hand, it maintains neural control over the functions that are basic to existence, particularly respiration and circulation. In fact, destruction of the brain stem is incompatible with life. It is in every sense the ultimate site of "life's little candle," yet it constitutes barely 10 percent of the central nervous system.

In Plates 5-4 through 5-11, the major tracts are shown in three dimensions on the right side, suggesting passage or movement. On the left side, the principal nuclei are drawn in with stippling (all nuclei throughout the plates of this unit are stippled). Of course, each of the structures shown is in fact bilateral. To visualize a nucleus-tract relationship, it will be necessary for you to bring the nucleus over to the tract side in your mind's eye.

At the upper right of each of Plates 5-4 through 5-10, a median view of the brain indicates the level at which the main cross section is taken. At the lower left of the main illustration in each of these plates and at the lower right in Plate 5-11, there is a smaller, action-oriented diagram of the section. This is used to illustrate fibers in action, crossing the section shown, making synapses, leaving nu-

clei, joining tracts, and so on. As you progress through these plates, you will notice the appearance and disappearance of some structures (and their titles) as they are initially formed or terminate or simply pass into an adjacent area not shown. Other structures may show a change in position from one section to another. You will notice that some structures are characteristic of certain levels and may become defining criteria for them—for example, inferior olive in the medulla and the colliculi in the midbrain. All of these stages of recognition serve as building blocks for your knowledge of the brain stem. Review frequently as you progress, starting several levels below (caudal to) the one you are coloring. This habit not only keeps nudging your learning curve but also prepares a bed for the new material within the more familiar matrix of the old.

The titles in Plates 5-4 through 5-11 are arranged in the following order of headings: Ascending Tracts and Related Nuclei, Descending Tracts and Related Nuclei, Cranial Nerve Nuclei and Related Tracts and Nerves, and Other Tracts and Nuclei. Throughout these plates, structures are color-coordinated to the related heading. As you progress through the series of plates, new structures and titles will be added to each group. Plan your coloring accordingly; select contrasting colors for the four groups. Scan the plates to check the total number of colors required for each group (the title list on Plate 5-11 shows the subscript with the highest exponent for each heading). For structures listed under Other Tracts, for example, 26 shades of one color are needed. In such a case, seek a color with four or five shades; before using a color twice or more, consider using patterns, such as circles, diamonds, ×'s, crosshatching, dots, and dashes.

ATLAS OF BRAIN SECTIONS

Plates 5-35 through 5-48 make up the Atlas of Brain Sections: a series of sections (four or five in each of three different planes) of the brain, subscripted for color coordination. You will find this atlas most helpful in orienting yourself while studying or reviewing the brain stem cross sections or the specific areas of the hemispheres. If you are seeking a less intense study of the brain, the atlas, in conjunction with Plates 5-1 and 5-2, may provide all that you require.

For cross referencing of brain structures, see the compilations opposite the illustrations of the atlas (Plates 5-35 through 5-48) or the index. For definitions, look up the word in the index.

BRAIN STEM: POSTERIOR ASPECT

The brain is organized into a brain stem, cerebral hemispheres, and cerebellum (recall Plates 1-2 and 3-8). This plate illustrates some landmarks on the posterior aspect of the brain stem that will help orient you as you color the cross sections of the brain stem (Plates 5-4 through 5-11).

Color titles and related structures A through D⁵ as well as the plate numbers (5-4, and so on) next to the lines representing cross-sectional planes. It is suggested that different shades of one color be used for each of the brain regions and its parts and related nerves. You may wish to color this and the next plate together, as they share common subscripts.

The brain stem changes continuously as it ascends from its junction with the spinal cord (at the foramen magnum of the skull; recall Plate 4-1) through the length of the medulla, pons, and midbrain and into the diencephalon. Ascending from the spinomedullary junction, the *medulla* (A) of the brain stem widens progressively in its caudal-to-rostral course, opening along its posterior surface to reveal the *floor of the fourth ventricle* (A^3). The *gracile* (A^1) and *cuneate tubercles* (A^2; *tubercle,* "small bump") form two moundlike structures on each side of the midline immediately caudal to the ventricular floor. These tubercles are surface manifestations of the underlying gracile and cuneate nuclei (a cross-sectional view of the tubercles can be seen in Plate 5-5). Within the fourth ventricle (and throughout the brain stem as well), there are numerous such bumps and other surface irregularities that often mark the presence of important structures immediately beneath. The *hypoglossal trigones* (A^4; *trigone,* "triangle") rising from the caudal half of the floor of the fourth ventricle are further examples of such irregularities. They are formed by the underlying hypoglossal nuclei.

The rostral half of the *floor of the fourth ventricle* (B^1) continues up from the medulla through the *pons* (B). On each side of the midline, the *facial colliculus* (B^2; *colliculus,* "hill"; pl. *colliculi*) rises up on the ventricular floor as a small, round structure, marking the curvature of the facial (VII) nerve underneath.

On each side of the fourth ventricle, massive stalks connect the cerebellum to the brain stem. These are the three paired *cerebellar peduncles* ("stemlike bundles of fibers"): *inferior* (A^5), *middle* (B^3), and *superior* (B^4). The inferior cerebellar peduncle *(restiform body)* angles cranially and laterally from the rostral medulla to the cerebellum. The middle cerebellar peduncle *(brachium pontis),* the largest of the three, projects laterally and posteriorly to enter the cerebellum. Each superior cerebellar peduncle *(brachium conjunctivum)* connects the cerebellum to the upper, lateral pons. The rostral apex of the diamond-shaped ventricular wall is formed by the converging superior cerebellar peduncles. It is at this apex that the pons merges with the *midbrain* (C).

The floor of the fourth ventricle narrows at the pontine-midbrain border to form the tunnel-like *cerebral aqueduct* (C^1; also called *aqueduct of Sylvius;* Plate 5-44) that runs through the midbrain. The posterior surface or roof of the midbrain is made up largely of the paired *inferior* (C^2) and *superior colliculi* (C^4). The former continues rostrally and laterally as the *brachium* (C^3; "arm") of the inferior colliculus; it terminates in the medial geniculate body (not shown) of the thalamus. The rostral and lateral continuation of the superior colliculus is its *brachium* (C^5), which enters the lateral geniculate body (not shown) of the thalamus. The *trochlear* (IV) *cranial nerve* (C^6) leaves the midbrain on its posterior surface (the only cranial nerve to do so) just caudal to the inferior colliculus.

Originating from the diencephalon and lying over the posterior surface of the mesencephalon is the *pineal gland* (D^1). Other visible diencephalic structures include the *habenula* (D^2) and the *thalamus* (D^4). The habenular nuclei (Plate 5-23) are just rostral to the pineal gland, flanking the *third ventricle* (D^3). The great mass of the thalamus lies lateral to the habenular nuclei on each side, forming the walls of the third ventricle and making up most of the tissue mass immediately rostral to the midbrain. The massive fiber bundles of the *internal capsule* (D^5; Plate 5-33) pass between the basal ganglia (in the base of the telencephalon) and the diencephalon.

BRAIN STEM: POSTERIOR ASPECT.

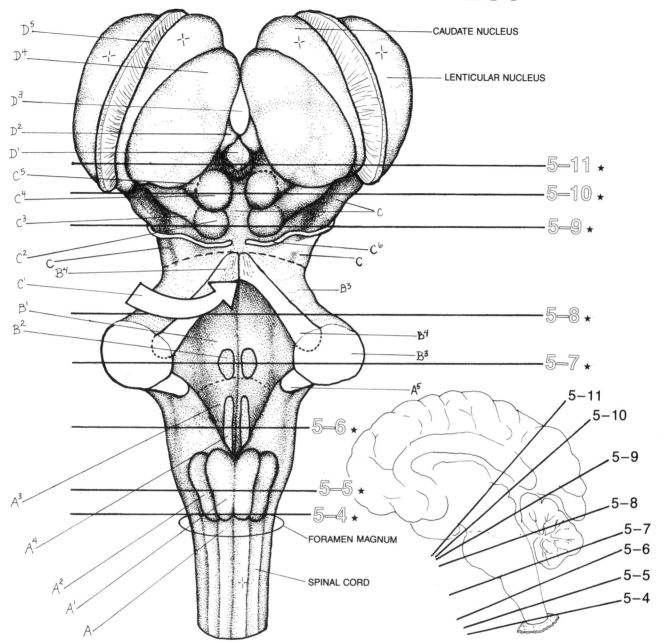

CAUDATE NUCLEUS

LENTICULAR NUCLEUS

5–11 ★
5–10 ★
5–9 ★
5–8 ★
5–7 ★
5–6 ★
5–5 ★
5–4 ★

FORAMEN MAGNUM

SPINAL CORD

5–11
5–10
5–9
5–8
5–7
5–6
5–5
5–4

MEDULLA OBLONGATA_A
  GRACILE TUBERCLE_{A1}
  CUNEATE TUBERCLE_{A2}
  FOURTH VENT. FLOOR_{A3}
    HYPOGLOSS. TRIGONE_{A4}
  INF. CEREBELL. PED._{A5}
PONS_B
  FOURTH VENT. FLOOR_{B1}
    FACIAL COLLICULUS_{B2}
  MID. CEREBELL. PED._{B3}
  SUP. CEREBELL. PED._{B4}

MIDBRAIN_C
  CEREBRAL AQUEDUCT_{C1}
  INF. COLLIC._{C2}/BRACH._{C3}
  SUP. COLLIC._{C4}/BRACH._{C5}
TROCHLEAR (IV) N._{C6}
DIENCEPHALON_{D( )}
  PINEAL GLAND_{D1}
  HABENULA_{D2}
  THIRD VENTRICLE_{D3}
  THALAMUS_{D4}
  INTERNAL CAPSULE_{D5}

Continuing the introduction to the brain stem, the structural landmarks of the anterior–inferior aspect of the brain stem and related, paired cranial nerves (Unit Six) are presented in this plate. The orientation of the brain stem is shown at an angle to illustrate better the roots of the cranial nerves. The cerebral hemispheres have been largely deleted from view. As in Plate 5-1, the horizontal lines running across the brain stem represent cross-sectional planes illustrated in the corresponding plates (5-4, etc.).

Color titles and related structures A through D^{12} as well as the plate numbers next to the lines representing cross-sectional planes as you did in Plate 5-1, using the same color scheme. The subscripts used in this plate and Plate 5-1 *do not* correlate with those in the following plates.

The *medulla oblongata* (A) is characterized on its anterior surface by a pair of parallel ridges on either side of the midline, the *pyramids* (A^6), created by the underlying corticospinal tracts. The pyramids run from the level of the foramen magnum to the massive transverse fiber mass constituting the *pons* (B). Just lateral to each pyramid is the elongated *inferior olive* (A^7). Two groups of cranial nerves can be seen on this surface of the brain. One group consists of fibers of the *hypoglossal* (XII) *nerve* (A^8), which emerges anteromedially between the inferior olive and the pyramid. The other group appears more laterally, just posterior to the inferior olive. This group includes the cranial roots of the *spinal accessory* (XI) *nerve* (A^9), *vagus* (X) *nerve* (A^{10}), and *glossopharyngeal* (IX) *nerve* (A^{11}).

The junction of the medulla and the pons, where the pyramids meet the massive bulk of transverse fibers, is an obvious demarcation. Within this junction, the *abducens* (VI) *nerve* (B^5) emerges anteriorly; the *facial* (VII) *nerve* (B^6) appears anterolaterally; more laterally, in the cerebellopontine angle, the *vestibulocochlear* (VIII) *nerve* (B^7) emerges. The anterior surface of the pons is characterized by a slight median sulcus in which lies the basilar artery (not shown). The roots of the *trigeminal* (V) *nerve* (B^8) project from the lateral surface of the pons, where the pons disappears bilaterally in the substance of the cerebellum as the middle cerebellar peduncles.

Directly above the pons, the large columns of descending cortical fibers, each called the *crus cerebri* (C^7; also called the *cerebral peduncle*), characterize the anterior surface of the midbrain. Situated between the crura is the *interpeduncular fossa* (C^8), through which emerges the *oculomotor* (III) *nerve* (C^9).

The anterior surface of the midbrain merges with that of the *diencephalon* (D). The twin swellings of the *mammillary bodies* (D^7) and the stalk of the pituitary gland, the *infundibulum* (D^8), are part of the *hypothalamus* (D^6) and mark its position. On the anterior surface of the hypothalamus is the *optic chiasm* (D^{10}), formed by the crossing of the *optic* (II) *nerves* (D^9). The *optic tracts* (D^{11}) project posteriorly from the chiasm toward the lateral part of the thalamus. The most rostral portions of the hypothalamus appear to merge with the undersurface of the cerebral hemispheres in the area of the *anterior perforated substance* (D^{12}).

BRAIN STEM: ANTERIOR—INFERIOR ASPECT.

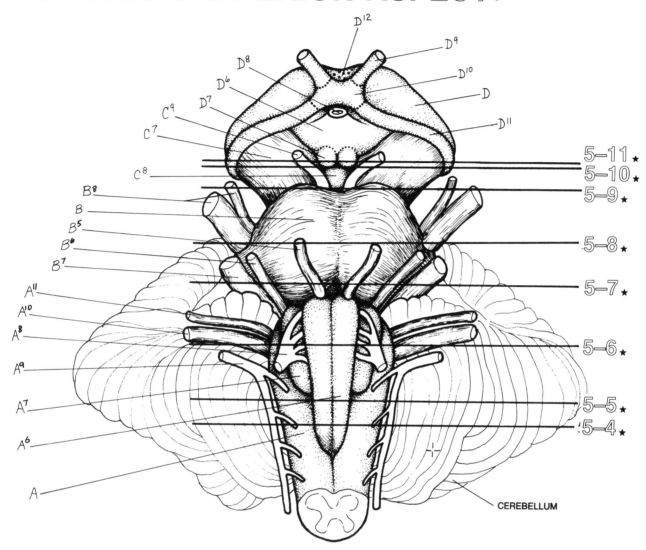

CEREBELLUM

MEDULLA OBLONGATA$_A$
  PYRAMID$_{A6}$
  INFERIOR OLIVE$_{A7}$
HYPOGLOSSAL (XII) N.$_{A8}$
SP. ACCESSORY (XI) N.$_{A9}$
VAGUS (X) N.$_{A10}$
GLOSSOPHARYNGEAL (IX) N.$_{A11}$
PONS$_B$
ABDUCENS (VI) N.$_{B5}$
FACIAL (VII) N.$_{B6}$
VESTIB. COCH. (VIII) N.$_{B7}$
TRIGEMINAL (V) N.$_{B8}$

MIDBRAIN$_{C()}$
  CRUS CEREBRI$_{C7}$
  INTERPEDUNC. FOSSA$_{C8}$
OCULOMOTOR (III) N.$_{C9}$
DIENCEPHALON$_D$
  HYPOTHALAMUS$_{D6}$
   MAMMILLARY BODY$_{D7}$
   INFUNDIBULUM$_{D8}$
OPTIC (II) N.$_{D9}$
OPTIC CHIASM$_{D10}$
OPTIC TRACT$_{D11}$
ANT. PERF. SUBST.$_{D12}$

One of the most common ways to study the brain stem is to look at cross sections at various levels. It is helpful to be able to recognize the brain stem region by simply noting the characteristic shape of the section. To enhance your ability at rapid recognition of brain stem slices, the following common sections are provided here in association with a median view of the whole brain stem.

Start by coloring the bar (A) on the brain stem at upper left; then color the representative cross section and related title the same color. Repeat with B through E. Use light colors to preserve detail.

The lowest part of the *medulla* (A) is similar to the spinal cord in its external appearance. Internally, the decussation (crossing) of the fibers of the pyramids is a distinctive feature. Two sections of the *medulla* (B and C) are characterized by the large bulge of fibers on the anterior aspect, the pyramids. From the middle of the medulla (B) through the pons (D), the fourth ventricle is apparent over the posterior surface of the brain stem. The more rostral section of the medulla (C) is clearly distinguishable by the presence of the inferior olivary nucleus, which, appearing like a shrunken olive without a pit, gives a lateral bulge to the surface.

The *pontine level* (D) is clearly identifiable by the massive transverse arrangement of fibers as they extend laterally toward the cerebellum. The large cerebellar peduncles, seen in sections of the upper medulla and pons (C and D) are also aids to identification by shape. The cerebellum or some part of it may be attached to the peduncles in sections of the upper medulla and pons, giving some extra bulk to the posterior aspects of these sections.

Cross sections of the *midbrain* (E) are quickly identified by the prominent crura cerebri anteriorly, the paired colliculi posteriorly, and the greatly reduced ventricle at this level, the circular (tubular in three dimensions) cerebral aqueduct.

In the following several plates, you will have the opportunity to study the functional structure of the brain stem areas through the medium of cross sections such as you have colored here.

SHAPES OF BRAIN STEM SECTIONS.

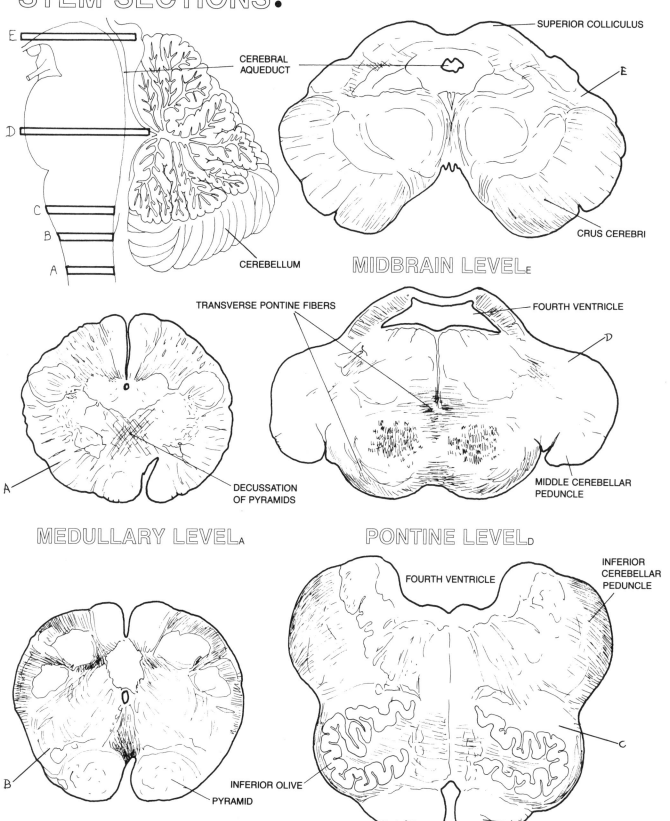

CEREBRAL AQUEDUCT

CEREBELLUM

SUPERIOR COLLICULUS

E

CRUS CEREBRI

MIDBRAIN LEVEL_E

TRANSVERSE PONTINE FIBERS

FOURTH VENTRICLE

D

MIDDLE CEREBELLAR PEDUNCLE

A

DECUSSATION OF PYRAMIDS

MEDULLARY LEVEL_A

PONTINE LEVEL_D

FOURTH VENTRICLE

INFERIOR CEREBELLAR PEDUNCLE

B

INFERIOR OLIVE

PYRAMID

C

PYRAMID

MEDULLARY LEVEL_B

MEDULLARY LEVEL_C

Before beginning this plate, read the Introduction to Unit Five.

This plate illustrates the transition from the spinal cord to the medulla oblongata. A series of dramatic structural changes here alters the familiar configuration of the spinal cord, which was built around an H-shaped central core of gray surrounded by white matter.

Color the heading Ascending Tracts and Related Nuclei (A), titles A^1 through A^9, and the representative structures in the central illustration. Structures A^1 through A^4 in the inset action diagram can also be colored.

Central processes of sensory neurons concerned with two-point discrimination and position and movement sense enter and ascend in the posterior funiculi (columns) of the spinal cord. In the upper thoracic cord to the lower medulla, each column is divided into the *fasciculi gracilis* (A^1) (medially) and *cuneatus* (A^3). Groups of neuronal cell bodies, the *nuclei gracilis* (A^2) and *cuneatus* (A^4), can be seen in the bases of their respective fasciculi. It is in these nuclei that the central processes make their first synapse (recall Plate 4-4). In the next plate, the axons of cells in these nuclei will be seen to stream anteromedially to cross the midline and form the medial lemniscus (not shown here).

The *posterior* (A^5) and *anterior spinocerebellar tracts* (A^6; recall Plates 4-7 and 4-8) convey impulses from muscle spindles and Golgi tendon organs. These tracts are located in the lateral funiculi, as are the *spinothalamic tracts* (A^7 and A^8; recall Plates 4-5 and 4-6), which conduct impulses related to pain, temperature, and touch. Fibers of the *spinoreticular tract* (A^9) synapse on neurons of the reticular core and the adjacent lateral reticular nucleus seen in higher medullary sections.

Color the heading Descending Tracts (B), titles B^1 through B^6, and the representative structures in the central illustration. Structures B^1 through B^3 in the inset action diagram can also be colored.

The *pyramids* (B^1) of the medulla consist of the massive corticospinal tracts, right and left. The majority (85 percent) of the corticospinal fibers of each side are diverted posteriorly and laterally, crossing one another (asymmetrically) in the *decussation of the pyramids* (B^2) to form the *lateral corticospinal tracts* (B^3). The decussation is a prominent structure at this level. The corticospinal tracts convey skilled, voluntary, motor-related impulses to anterior horn motor neurons.

Immediately adjacent (anterior) to the lateral corticospinal tracts are the *rubrospinal tracts* (B^4; recall Plate 4-11). These tracts convey impulses concerned with postural adjustments and run from the red nucleus in the midbrain to spinal interneurons affecting the anterior horn motor neurons. The *vestibulospinal tract* (B^5; recall Plate 4-10) can be seen in the anterior portion of the lateral funiculus. Arising in the lateral vestibular nucleus of the lower pons, the fibers conduct impulses to the spinal cord, where they facilitate extensor muscle tone and spinal reflexes.

The *medial longitudinal fasciculus,* or *MLF* (B^6; recall Plate 4-10), shown here in the anterior funiculus, is largely a motor tract at this level, arising from the vestibular nuclei in the lower pons and medulla and terminating on cervical and thoracic motor neurons for head-eye coordination.

Now color the heading Cranial Nerve Nuclei and Related Tracts (C), titles C^1 through C^4, and the representative structures in the central and inset illustrations.

In the medulla, the *spinal trigeminal nucleus* (C^1) replaces the outermost part of the dorsal horn (laminae I through IV) of the spinal cord. This nucleus extends from the pons (at the level of the trigeminal nerve; Plate 6-12) to the second cervical segment. The *spinal trigeminal tract* (C^2) is a rostral continuation of Lissauer's fasciculus (recall Plate 4-2). The nucleus and tract are concerned with pain and temperature from the face.

One component of the *spinal accessory* (XI) *nucleus* (C^3) and *nerve* (C^4) can be seen at this level (see inset action diagram). This nerve supplies the trapezius and sternocleidomastoid muscles of the neck and superficial back.

MEDULLA OBLONGATA: LOWER LEVEL.

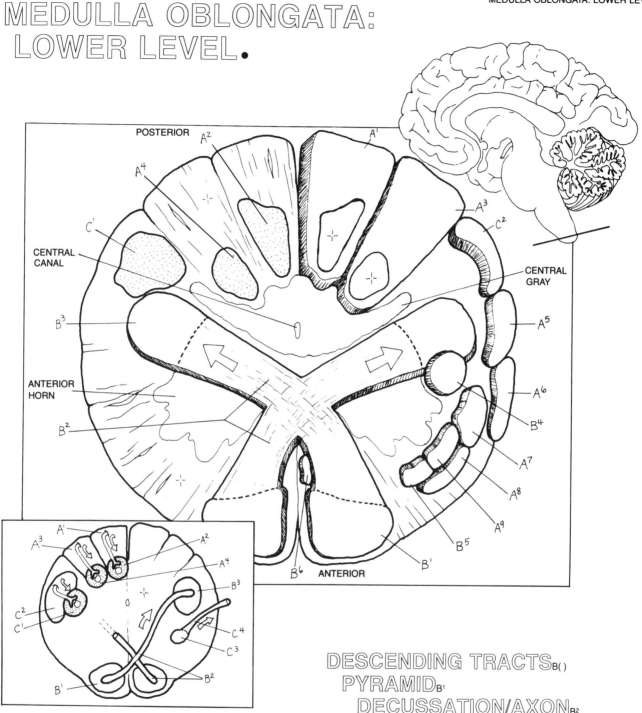

ASCEND. TRACTS/REL. NUC.A( )
FASC. GRACILIS/AXONA1
NUC. GRACILISA2
FASC. CUNEATUS/AXONA3
NUC. CUNEATUSA4
POST.A5/ANT.
   SPINOCEREBELL. TR.A6
LAT.A7/ANT. SPINOTHAL. TR.A8
SPINORETICULAR TR.A9

DESCENDING TRACTSB( )
PYRAMIDB1
   DECUSSATION/AXONB2
LAT. CORTICOSPINAL TR.B3
RUBROSPINAL TR.B4
VESTIBULOSPINAL TR.B5
MED. LONG. FASC.B6

CRANIAL N. NUC./REL. TR.C( )
SPINAL TRIGEM. NUC.C1/TR.C2
SPINAL ACCESS. NUC.C3/
   NERVEC4

The most important feature of the medulla oblongata to be shown at this level is the decussation of fibers from the posterior column nuclei (gracilis and cuneatus) to form the medial lemniscus. The medial lemniscus is the rostral continuation of the important epicritic (well-localized and refined touch) and conscious proprioception (position and movement sense) pathway ascending through the spinal cord in the posterior columns (recall Plates 2-10 and 4-4). The external configuration of this brain stem section resembles the previous one, and most of the tracts and nuclei are familiar.

Color the heading Ascending Tracts and Related Nuclei, titles A^1 through A^{12}, and their representative structures, as before. Color the heading Other Nuclei, titles D^1 and D^2, and their related structures. Where appropriate, use the same colors for the structures and titles as on Plate 5-4.

The ascending fiber tracts within the posterior funiculi are the *fasciculi gracilis* (A^1) and *cuneatus* (A^3), which terminate in the *nuclei gracilis* (A^2) and *cuneatus* (A^4), respectively. The surface swelling produced over the nucleus gracilis and tract is the gracile tubercle (clava); the more lateral swelling over the cuneate nucleus and tract is the cuneate tubercle (recall Plate 5-1). Axons leaving the gracile and cuneate nuclei (see action diagram) run ventrally and curve medially as the *internal arcuate fibers* (A^{11}), which cross the midline and ascend toward the thalamus as the *medial lemniscus* (A^{12}). The *accessory cuneate nucleus* (A^{10}) receives cuneocerebellar fibers originating above the C8 spinal cord segment (recall Plate 4-7). The axons of this nucleus join the fibers of the inferior cerebellar peduncle.

Ascending fibers within the lateral portion of medulla are a continuation of those seen in Plate 5-4. They include the *posterior* (A^5) and *anterior spinocerebellar* (A^6) and the *lateral* (A^7) and *anterior spinothalamic tracts* (A^8). *Spinoreticular fibers* (A^9) continue up the

cord into the medulla, where they synapse in the core of the *reticular formation* (D^1), as well as in the *lateral reticular nucleus* (D^2).

Fibers ascending from the lower brain stem can influence much of the cortex via direct tracts to the thalamus. Other sensory pathways reach the cortex via the reticular formation. The latter route may have an important influence on levels of consciousness. Though much of the reticular formation occupies the central portion of the brain stem (see Plate 5-12), the lateral reticular nucleus is well defined laterally and projects its axons exclusively to the cerebellum.

Color the heading Descending Tracts, titles B^1 through B^7, and representative structures in the central illustration. Color the heading Cranial Nerve Nuclei and Related Tracts, titles C^1 through C^5, and representative structures in the central and inset illustrations, as indicated. Plan your use of colors as suggested before.

The *pyramids* (B^1) and the *rubrospinal* (B^4) and *vestibulospinal tracts* (B^5) continue to be seen at this level of the medulla. The *tecto-bulbo-spinal tract** (B^7) is found near the midline just anterior to the MLF. The tecto-bulbo-spinal tract arises from the tectum of the midbrain and terminates in the brain stem and spinal cord. This tract is concerned with visual-motor correlations. The term *bulbo-* usually refers to the medulla, although in the case of this tract, some fibers terminate in the midbrain and pons as well. The *medial longitudinal fasciculus* (B^6) at this level consists largely of descending fibers; more rostrally, it contains both ascending and descending fibers.

The *spinal trigeminal nucleus* (C^1) and *tract* (C^2) are prominent in the lateral funiculus. *Fibers* (C^1) from the spinal trigeminal nucleus (often written *spinal nucleus of V* or called *spinal nucleus of five*) cross the midline and ascend to the thalamus as the *trigeminothalamic tract* (C^5).

---

*In this unit, a tract of three or more components will be hyphenated in the first plate in which the structure appears; in subsequent plates, it will be spelled conventionally, as one word.

MEDULLA OBLONGATA: LOWER LEVEL.

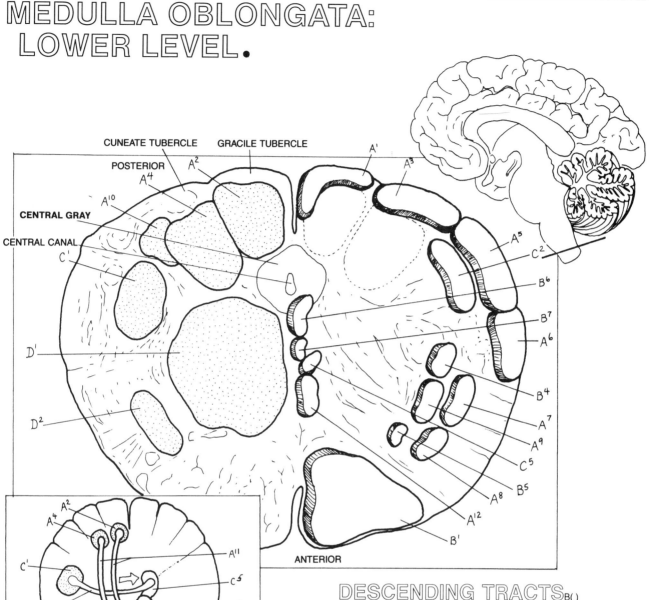

CUNEATE TUBERCLE   GRACILE TUBERCLE

POSTERIOR A^2

A^4

A^{10}

CENTRAL GRAY

CENTRAL CANAL

C^1

D^1

D^2

A^1

A^3

A^5

C^2

B^6

B^7

A^6

B^4

A^7

A^9

C^5

A^8 B^5

A^{12}

B^1

ANTERIOR

A^4 A^2

C^1

c^1

A^{11}

C^5

A^{12}

DESCENDING TRACTS$_{B()}$
    PYRAMID$_{B^1}$
    RUBROSPINAL TR.$_{B^4}$
    VESTIBULOSPINAL TR.$_{B^5}$
    MED. LONG. FASC.$_{B^6}$
    TECTO-BULBO-SPINAL TR.$_{B^7}$

CRANIAL N. NUC./REL. TR.$_{C()}$
    SPINAL TRIGEM. NUC.$_{C^1}$/
        FIBER$_{C^1}$/TR.$_{C^2}$
    TRIGEMINOTHAL. TR.$_{C^5}$

ASCEND. TRACTS/REL. NUC.$_{A()}$
    FASC.$_{A^1}$/NUC. GRACILIS$_{A^2}$
    FASC.$_{A^3}$/NUC. CUNEATUS$_{A^4}$
    ACCESS. CUNEATE NUC.$_{A^{10}}$
    POST.$_{A^5}$/ANT.
        SPINOCEREBELL. TR.$_{A^6}$
    LAT.$_{A^7}$/ANT. SPINOTHAL. TR.$_{A^8}$
    SPINORETICULAR TR.$_{A^9}$
    INT. ARCUATE FIBER$_{A^{11}}$
    MED. LEMNISCUS$_{A^{12}}$

OTHER NUCLEI$_{D()}$
    RETIC. FORM.$_{D^1}$
    LAT. RETIC. NUC.$_{D^2}$

The rostral half of the medulla oblongata is easily identified by the prominent inferior olivary nucleus ("inferior olive") on the anterior surface and the broad fourth ventricle on the posterior surface. The ventricle opens widely and deeply into the medulla, roofed over by the superior and inferior medullary vela (sing. *velum,* "roof") and the cerebellum.

Color the heading, titles, and related structures pertaining to ascending tracts, as you have done on the two preceding plates.

The *posterior* (A^5) and *anterior spinocerebellar tracts* (A^6) ascend near the lateral surface of the medulla as they approach the cerebellum but are here situated more posteriorly. The *lateral* (A^7) and *anterior spinothalamic tracts* (A^8) are somewhat reduced in size and are no longer recognizable as separate entities. As the spinothalamic fibers ascend, they progressively lose some fibers, which turn medially into the medullary reticular formation. The *medial lemniscus* (A^{12}) is on each side of the midline, medial to the inferior olive.

Color the heading, titles, and structures pertaining to the descending tracts as before.

Among the major descending fiber systems, the *pyramids* (B^1), made up of corticospinal axons, and the *rubrospinal* (B^4) and *vestibulospinal tracts* (B^5) are in positions similar to those seen in Plate 5-5. The fiber bundles of the *medial longitudinal fasciculus* (B^6) and the *tectobulbospinal tract* (B^7) flank the midline, anterior to the fourth ventricle. At this level, the MLF continues to carry predominantly descending fibers, although the number of ascending axons from the reticular formation and vestibular nuclei increases at this and progressively rostral levels.

Color the heading, titles, and respective structures pertaining to cranial nerve nuclei and related tracts and nerves as before.

The *spinal trigeminal nucleus* (C^1) and *tract* (C^2) and the *trigeminothalamic tract* (C^5) are in positions similar to those seen at lower levels. Posterolaterally, the *medial* (C^6) and *inferior vestibular nuclei* (C^7) can be seen at this level. These constitute the most caudal of the four vestibular nuclei and are concerned with sensory impulses related to position and balance.

The *dorsal motor nucleus of the vagus* (X) *nerve* (C^8) is situated below (anterior to) the floor of the fourth ventricle. It is a visceral motor center, the axons of which contribute to the innervation of viscera (glands and smooth muscle of the visceral walls and the cardiac pacemaker) via the *vagus nerve* (C^{12}).

The *solitary nucleus* (C^9) and its *tract* (C^{10}), in the posterior part of the medulla, anterolateral to the fourth ventricle, is the major sensory receptive system for all kinds of visceral sensations: sensory stimuli from receptors in the walls of the gastrointestinal tract, from taste receptors in the tongue and pharynx, and so on. Areas receptive to taste are concentrated in the rostral portion, while the areas receptive to more general visceral stimuli are found more caudally.

The *nucleus ambiguus* (C^{11}) can be found somewhat lateral to the reticular formation. Difficulties experienced by early anatomists in specifying its exact position led to its name. The nucleus ambiguus is a motor center sending fibers via cranial nerves IX, X, and XI to the muscles of the pharynx and larynx (swallowing and speech).

The *nucleus of the hypoglossal* (XII) *nerve* (C^{13}) is located beneath the floor of the fourth ventricle near the midline. Its *nerve fibers* (C^{14}) stream anteriorly, leave the medulla just lateral to the pyramids, and innervate the muscles of the tongue.

Color the heading, titles, and structures pertaining to other tracts and nuclei as before.

The *reticular formation* (D^1) is obvious at this level of the medulla. An overview of its extent in the brain stem can be seen in Plate 5-12.

The inferior olives (inferior olivary nuclei), resembling olive-shaped rumpled sacs with partially pulled drawstrings, are made up of convoluted laminae of cell bodies and a central core of myelinated fibers. In addition to the large *principal olive* (D^4), there are thin, platelike *dorsal* (D^5) and *medial accessory olives* (D^6), which are phylogenetically older. Afferents to the olivary complex come from the cerebral cortex, red nucleus, and periaqueductal gray matter of the midbrain. The major efferent projection is to the cerebellum via the *olivocerebellar fibers* (D^7), which form the largest component of the contralateral *inferior cerebellar peduncle* (D^8).

MEDULLA OBLONGATA: UPPER LEVEL.

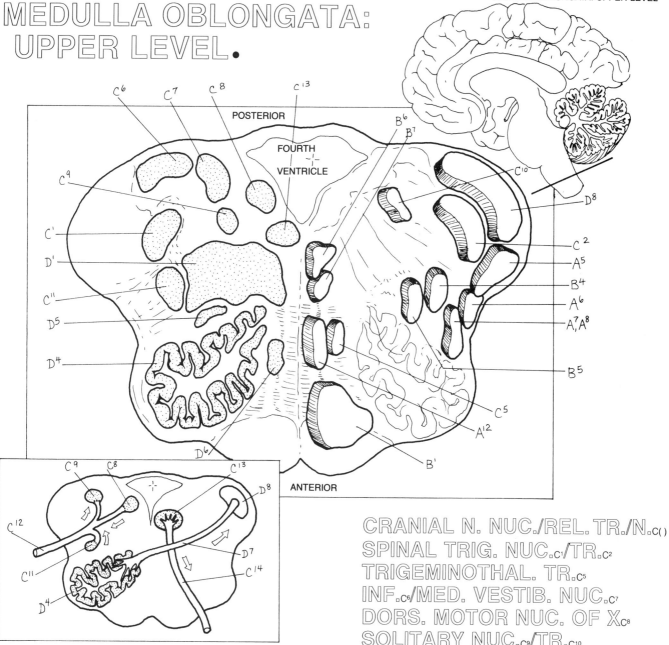

POSTERIOR

FOURTH VENTRICLE

ANTERIOR

ASCENDING TRACTS$_{A(\ )}$
POST.$_{A5}$/ANT.
  SPINOCEREBELL. TR.$_{A6}$
LAT.$_{A7}$/ANT. SPINOTHALAMIC TR.$_{A8}$
MED. LEMNISCUS$_{A12}$

DESCENDING TRACTS$_{B(\ )}$
  PYRAMID$_{B1}$
  RUBROSPINAL TR.$_{B4}$
  VESTIBULOSPINAL TR.$_{B5}$
  MED. LONG. FASC.$_{B6}$
  TECTOBULBOSP. TR.$_{B7}$

CRANIAL N. NUC./REL. TR./N.$_{C(\ )}$
SPINAL TRIG. NUC.$_{C1}$/TR.$_{C2}$
TRIGEMINOTHAL. TR.$_{C5}$
INF.$_{C6}$/MED. VESTIB. NUC.$_{C7}$
DORS. MOTOR NUC. OF X$_{C8}$
SOLITARY NUC.$_{C9}$/TR.$_{C10}$
NUC. AMBIGUUS$_{C11}$
VAGUS (X) NERVE$_{C12}$
HYPOGLOSS. (XII) NUC.$_{C13}$/
  AXON$_{C14}$
OTHER TRACTS AND NUCLEI$_{D(\ )}$
  RETIC. FORM.$_{D1}$
  INFERIOR OLIVE$_{D3(\ )}$
    PRINCIPAL NUC.$_{D4}$
    DORS.$_{D5}$/MED. ACCESS.
      NUC.$_{D6}$
  OLIVOCEREBELL. TR.$_{D7}$
  INF. CEREBELL. PED.$_{D8}$

The pons surrounds the anterior part of the brain stem and extends bilaterally as the middle cerebellar peduncle into the cerebellum. The posterior portion of the pons is the rostral continuation of the medulla oblongata and is called the *tegmentum*. The pons, middle cerebellar peduncles, and cerebellar hemispheres together achieve their greatest size in human beings, due in part to increased use of hands and fingers and, perhaps, to the development of human speech.

Color the heading, titles, and structures pertaining to ascending tracts as before. Also color title D⁸ and its structure.

The axons constituting the posterior spinocerebellar tract have disappeared into the ipsilateral *inferior cerebellar peduncle* (D^8), which ascends to enter the anterior lobe of the cerebellum (Plate 5-15). The *anterior spinocerebellar tract* (A^6) has moved posteriorly and enters the cerebellum at a more rostral level via the superior cerebellar peduncle (not seen at this level). The *spinothalamic tracts* (A^7 and A^8) are further decreased in size at this level and lie lateral to the *medial lemniscus* (A^{12}), which, with the disappearance of the inferior olives, has drifted laterally near the anterior border of the tegmentum. Lateral to the spinothalamics are the newly formed *lateral lemnisci* (A^{13}). These fibers originate from several structures of the auditory pathway (Plate 6-18), run rostrally while drifting posteriorly, and terminate in more rostral auditory processing centers. These centers include the inferior colliculus of the midbrain and the medial geniculate body of the thalamus.

Color the heading, titles, and structures pertaining to descending tracts as before.

The descending tracts here include the *corticobulbospinal* (B^1), *rubrospinal* (B^4), and *tectobulbospinal tracts* (B^7). Many ascending fibers join the descending fibers of the *medial longitudinal fasciculus* (B^6) in this area. Note that the descending corticospinal fibers run through the midst of the pons, where they are separated widely by the cell masses of the pontine nuclei (D^9; see ahead). The vestibulospinal tract begins at this level (see ahead to vestibular nucleus).

Color the heading, titles, and structures pertaining to cranial nerve nuclei and related tracts and nerves as before.

The *spinal trigeminal nucleus* (C^1) and *tract* (C^2) can still be found in the posterolateral tegmentum of the lower pons. The *trigeminothalamic tract* (C^5) is posterolateral to the medial lemniscus at this level. The *nucleus of the abducens* (VI) *nerve* (C^{15}) protrudes into the floor of the fourth ventricle under the facial colliculus. The *abducens nerve* (C^{16}) innervates the lateral rectus muscle of the eyeball. Between the nucleus of VI and the ventricular floor run the arching fibers (*genu*) of the *facial* (VII) *nerve* (C^{18}). They arise from their *nucleus* (C^{17}) in the tegmentum and arc medially around the nucleus of VI, emerging from the brain stem at the cerebellopontine angle. The facial nerve innervates the muscles of facial expression as well as other structures.

Several components of the auditory system are visible at this level, including the *trapezoid body* (C^{19}) and the *superior olivary nucleus* (C^{20}). The trapezoid body (discussed in Plate 6-18) is one of the more prominent bundles of horizontal crossing fibers in the pontine tegmentum. Many of the trapezoid fibers enter and ascend in the lateral lemniscus. The superior olivary nucleus appears to represent the earliest auditory processing level, at which direction of the source of an auditory stimulus (lateralization) is established. Components of the vestibular system include the *lateral* (C^{21}) and *superior vestibular nuclei* (C^{22}). The former is the source of the vestibulospinal tract (recall Plate 4-10). The superior vestibular nucleus sends most of its axons to the cerebellum via the inferior cerebellar peduncle (Plate 5-15).

Color the heading, titles, and structures pertaining to other tracts and nuclei as before.

The *reticular formation* (D^1) occupies its usual position in the central portion of the tegmentum (see Plate 5-12). The *central tegmental tract* (D^{12}) runs through the center of the reticular formation, connecting the cerebral cortex and the upper brain stem with the inferior olive and medulla. It is not seen caudal to this level.

Cells of the *pontine nuclei* (D^9), located anterior to the tegmentum, receive the massive descending corticopontine projections (not shown), which run with the corticobulbospinal tract to this level of the brain stem. The axons of these pontine cells form the *pontocerebellar projections* (D^{10}), which form the *middle cerebellar peduncles* (D^{11}).

PONS: LOWER LEVEL.

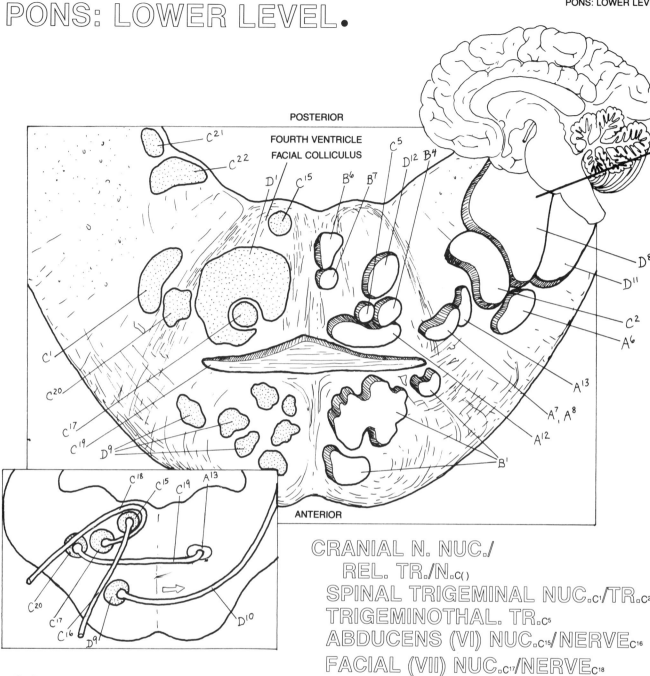

POSTERIOR

FOURTH VENTRICLE
FACIAL COLLICULUS

ANTERIOR

CRANIAL N. NUC./
REL. TR./N.$_{C()}$
SPINAL TRIGEMINAL NUC.$_{C1}$/TR.$_{C2}$
TRIGEMINOTHAL. TR.$_{C5}$
ABDUCENS (VI) NUC.$_{C15}$/NERVE$_{C16}$
FACIAL (VII) NUC.$_{C17}$/NERVE$_{C18}$
TRAPEZOID BODY$_{C19}$
SUP. OLIVARY NUC.$_{C20}$
LAT.$_{C21}$/SUP. VESTIB. NUC.$_{C22}$

OTHER TRACTS/NUCLEI$_{D()}$
RETIC. FORM.$_{D1}$
CENT. TEGMENTAL TR.$_{D12}$
INF. CEREBELL. PED.$_{D8}$
PONTINE NUC.$_{D9}$
PONTOCEREBELL. PROJ.$_{D10}$
MID. CEREBELL. PED.$_{D11}$

ASCENDING TRACTS$_{A()}$
ANT. SPINOCEREBELL. TR.$_{A6}$
SPINOTHALAMIC TR.$_{A7, A8}$
MED. LEMNISCUS$_{A12}$
LAT. LEMNISCUS$_{A13}$

DESCENDING TRACTS$_{B()}$
CORTICOBULBOSP. TR.$_{B1}$
RUBROSPINAL TR.$_{B4}$
MED. LONG. FASC.$_{B6}$
TECTOBULBOSP. TR.$_{B7}$

The major landmarks of this level of the pons include a somewhat smaller fourth ventricle, its rostral part closed in by the tentlike cover of the superior medullary velum; the posterolateral superior cerebellar peduncles on either side of the superior medullary velum; and the pontine tegmentum, just anterior to the fourth ventricle. The mass of the pons proper lies anterior to the tegmentum and constitutes about half of the total area of this part of the brain stem.

Color the heading, titles, and structures of the ascending tracts as before.

The *anterior spinocerebellar tract* (A^6) ascends to this level and turns laterally and posteriorly about 140 degrees to join the superior cerebellar peduncle. The *spinothalamic tracts* (A^7 and A^8) and the *medial* (A^{12}) and *lateral lemnisci* (A^{13}) are in positions similar to those seen in the previous plate.

Color the heading, titles, and structures pertaining to descending tracts as before, as well as title and structure D^{14}, B^6.

The *corticobulbospinal tract* (B^1) is seen at this level as before, broken up into bundles spread apart by the broadly dispersed pontine nuclei. The *rubrospinal tract* (B^4) and *tectobulbospinal tract* (B^7) are in positions similar to those seen in the lower segment of the pons. The *medial longitudinal fasciculus* (D^{14}, B^6) is a fully mixed tract at this level and is therefore now listed under that heading (Other Tracts and Nuclei) with both old and new subscripts.

Color the heading, titles, and structures pertaining to cranial nerve nuclei and related tracts and nerves as before.

Three of the components of the trigeminal (V) nerve nuclei and related fibers are seen at this level for the first time.

The *main sensory nucleus* (C^{23}) receives touch and pressure sensation from the face and part of the head via the three divisions of the *trigeminal nerve* (C^{26}).

The *mesencephalic nucleus of the fifth nerve* (C^{24}) is in the wall of the fourth ventricle medial to the superior cerebellar peduncle and reaches rostrally from this level into the mesencephalon. It receives proprioceptive impulses from the muscles of mastication (moving the lower jaw), establishing a pathway for the reflex control of biting and chewing. It is unique among sensory nuclei (inside the CNS) in having only pseudounipolar neurons such as those found in the spinal and cranial ganglia (outside the CNS).

The axons of the *motor nucleus of V* (C^{25}) innervate the muscles of mastication and function in concert with the mesencephalic nucleus.

Impulses related to pain, temperature, and certain aspects of tactile sensibility from the face also enter via the trigeminal nerve. The fibers conducting such impulses enter the pons and turn caudally to form the spinal trigeminal tract seen in lower sections. The *trigeminothalamic tract* (C^5), you may recall, conveys impulses from the spinal nucleus of V (trigeminal) to the thalamus and maintains a position at this level of the pons similar to that seen in lower brain stem levels.

Color the heading, titles, and structures pertaining to other tracts and nuclei as before.

The *central tegmental tract* (D^{12}) continues to be seen at this level as a rather poorly defined bundle running through the *reticular formation* (D^1) carrying fibers from midbrain to inferior olive and from lower brain stem to thalamus. The pontine nuclei have been discussed with the descending tracts. As was true in the lower section (seen in the previous plate), axons of the *pontine nuclei* (D^9) form *pontocerebellar projections* (D^{10}) at this level as well. These projections (see inset action diagram) form the *middle cerebellar peduncle* (D^{11}).

The *superior cerebellar peduncle* (D^{13}) and its relation to the anterior spinocerebellar tract have been discussed with ascending tracts.

The *locus ceruleus* (D^{15}) is a nucleus of approximately 30,000 neurons found bilaterally at this level of the pons. In fresh, unstained cross sections, the locus ceruleus shows up as an intense blue dot in the posterolateral tegmentum near the fourth ventricle and represents the most important source of the neurotransmitter norepinephrine in the central nervous system. The axons from the neurons in the locus ceruleus spread widely through the cerebral cortex, subcortical centers, brain stem, cerebellum, and spinal cord. This tiny cell population and its enormous norepinephrine-bearing axon system appears to be involved in many functions including sleep, wakefulness, and the control of mood. It is also apparently essential in embryological development for the laminar organization of the cerebral cortex (recall Plate 3-11).

PONS: UPPER LEVEL.

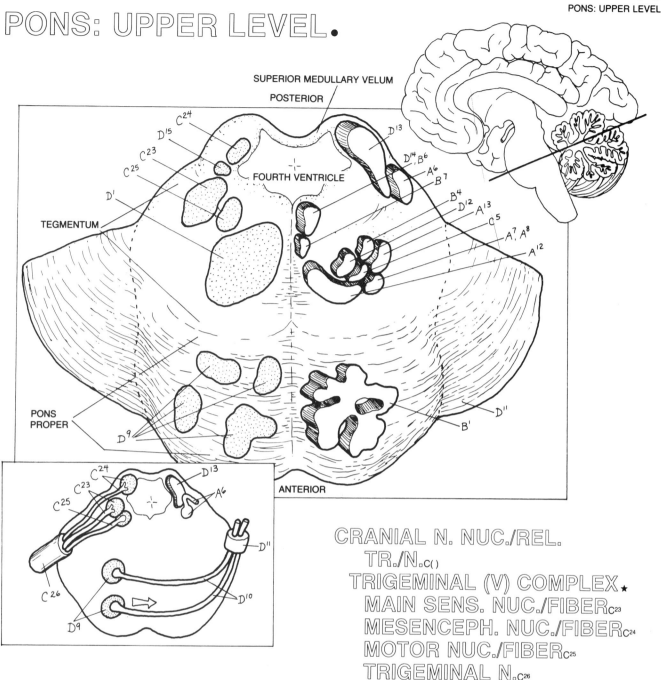

SUPERIOR MEDULLARY VELUM

POSTERIOR

FOURTH VENTRICLE

TEGMENTUM

PONS PROPER

ANTERIOR

CRANIAL N. NUC./REL. TR./N.$_{C()}$
  TRIGEMINAL (V) COMPLEX ★
    MAIN SENS. NUC./FIBER$_{C23}$
    MESENCEPH. NUC./FIBER$_{C24}$
    MOTOR NUC./FIBER$_{C25}$
    TRIGEMINAL N.$_{C26}$
    TRIGEMINOTHALAMIC TR.$_{C5}$

ASCENDING TRACTS$_{A()}$
  ANT. SPINOCEREBELL. TR.$_{A6}$
  SPINOTHALAMIC TR.$_{A7, A8}$
  MED. LEMNISCUS$_{A12}$
  LAT. LEMNISCUS$_{A13}$

OTHER TRACTS/NUCLEI$_{D()}$
  RETIC. FORM.$_{D1}$
    CENT. TEGMENTAL TR.$_{D12}$
  PONTINE NUC.$_{D9}$
  PONTOCEREBELL. PROJ.$_{D10}$
  MID. CEREBELL. PED.$_{D11}$
  SUP. CEREBELL. PED.$_{D13}$
  MED. LONG. FASC.$_{D14, B6}$
  LOCUS CERULEUS$_{D15}$

DESCENDING TRACTS$_{B()}$
  CORTICOBULBOSP. TR.$_{B1}$
  RUBROSPINAL TR.$_{B4}$
  TECTOBULBOSP. TR.$_{B7}$

A section taken at this level includes the most rostral part of the pons (bulge of the pontine transverse fibers, pontine nuclei, and related descending tracts) anteriorly and the most caudal part of the midbrain (midbrain tegmentum, cerebral aqueduct and its circumscribed periaqueductal gray matter, and inferior colliculi) posteriorly.

Color the headings, titles, and related structures pertaining to both ascending and descending tracts as before, as well as titles and structures D⁹ and D¹⁰.

The *spinothalamic tracts* (A⁷ and A⁸) and *medial lemnisci* (A¹²) continue through the midbrain. It is at this level that the *lateral lemniscus* (A¹³) disappears into its target nucleus in the inferior colliculus (see ahead).

At this level, the *corticobulbospinal tract* (B¹) includes *corticopontine fibers* (B¹¹), one of which is shown in the inset action diagram synapsing with one neuron of the *pontine nuclei* (D⁹). The axons of the pontine cells project to the cerebellum (*pontocerebellar projection,* D¹⁰) via the middle cerebellar peduncle (not shown). The *rubrospinal* (B⁴) and *tectobulbospinal tracts* (B⁷) continue in their descent as shown.

Color the heading, titles, and structures pertaining to cranial nerve nuclei and related tracts and nerves as before.

The *mesencephalic nucleus of the fifth nerve* (C²⁴) and its related *tract* (C²⁷) are seen most clearly at this level just lateral to the periaqueductal gray matter (see ahead). The *trigeminothalamic tract* (C⁵) continues here in its ascent to the thalamus. The cells of the *nucleus of the trochlear (IV) nerve* (C²⁸), at the base of the periaqueductal gray, project their axons (*nerve,* C²⁹) in a unique course posterolaterally and caudally around the periaqueductal gray. They decussate in the pontine roof of the fourth ventricle (superior medullary velum, see Plate 5-8) and exit from the posterior surface of the brain just caudal to the inferior colliculus.

Color the heading, titles, and structures pertaining to other tracts and nuclei as before.

The *reticular formation* (D¹) of the midbrain takes up considerable space in the tegmentum as part of a long column of neurons running through the brain stem (see Plate 5-12). A number of overlapping *raphe nuclei* (D¹⁶), specialized components of the reticular formation, lie along the midline of the tegmentum. The *central tegmental tract* (D¹²) continues to run through the reticular core.

The *superior cerebellar peduncles* (D¹³), shown in the previous plate to be in the posterolateral pons, at this level swing anteriorly and medially into the substance of the tegmentum and *decussate* in the midline (see inset action diagram). The crossed fibers turn rostrally and project toward the red nucleus (*cerebellodentatorubral fibers,* not shown) and ventrolateral nucleus of the thalamus (*cerebellodentatothalamic fibers,* not shown; see Plate 5-11).

The *medial longitudinal fasciculus* (D¹⁴, B⁶), consisting of both ascending and descending fibers, continues to be seen at this level.

Within the inferior colliculi, located on the posterior surface of the caudal midbrain, are large *nuclei of the inferior colliculi* (D¹⁷). They receive auditory information from the lateral lemniscus and serve as centers for auditory reflex responses, such as jumping in response to a loud noise. These nuclei also receive afferents (not shown) from the opposite inferior colliculus, the ipsilateral medial geniculate body (nucleus) of the thalamus, and the auditory cortex (cerebral cortex related to auditory input). The most important efferent fibers from the inferior colliculus project to the medial geniculate body via the brachium of the inferior colliculus (recall Plate 5-1). Other efferents project to the contralateral inferior colliculus and to more caudally situated auditory nuclei in the brain stem, such as the nucleus of the lateral lemniscus (Plate 6–18).

The *periaqueductal gray* (D¹⁸), discussed with cranial nerve nuclei, is rich in small neurons and is a significant repository of the naturally occurring opioid (morphine-like) peptide *β* (beta) endorphin. Electrical stimulation in this area has been shown dramatically to reduce the awareness of pain (the subject of Plate 5-34).

The *dorsal longitudinal fasciculus* (D¹⁹) is a compact column of fibers passing through the periaqueductal gray. It contains both ascending and descending fibers between hypothalamus and midbrain and is believed to be related to visceral reflex activity.

MIDBRAIN: LOWER LEVEL.

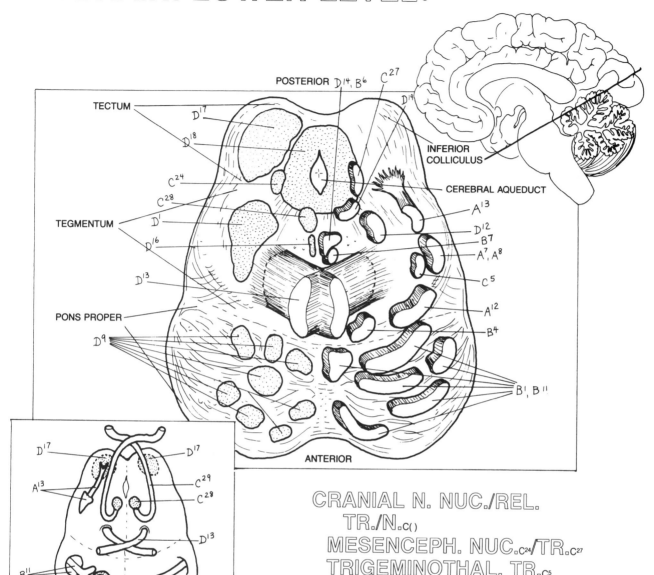

POSTERIOR D^{14}, B^6 C^{27}

D^{19}

TECTUM

D^{17}

D^{18}

INFERIOR
COLLICULUS

CEREBRAL AQUEDUCT

C^{24}

C^{28}

TEGMENTUM

D^1

D^{16}

D^{13}

A^{13}

D^{12}

B^7

A^7, A^8

C^5

A^{12}

PONS PROPER

B^4

D^9

B^1, B^{11}

ANTERIOR

D^{17} D^{17}

A^{13}

C^{29}

C^{28}

D^{13}

B^{11}

D^{10}

D^9

CRANIAL N. NUC./REL.
    TR./N.$_{C(\ )}$
    MESENCEPH. NUC.$_{C^{24}}$/TR.$_{C^{27}}$
    TRIGEMINOTHAL. TR.$_{C^5}$
    TROCHLEAR NUC.$_{C^{28}}$/N.$_{C^{29}}$

OTHER TRACTS/NUCLEI$_{D(\ )}$
    RETIC. FORM.$_{D^1}$
    RAPHE NUC.$_{D^{16}}$
    CENT. TEGMENTAL TR.$_{D^{12}}$
    PONTINE NUC.$_{D^9}$
    PONTOCEREBELL. PROJ.$_{D^{10}}$
    DECUSS. FIBERS OF
        SUP. CEREBELL. PED.$_{D^{13}}$
    MED. LONG. FASC.$_{D^{14}, B^6}$
    NUC. INF. COLLICULUS$_{D^{17}}$
    PERIAQUED. GRAY$_{D^{18}}$
    DORSAL LONG. FASC.$_{D^{19}}$

ASCENDING TRACTS$_{A(\ )}$
    SPINOTHALAMIC TR.$_{A^7, A^8}$
    MED. LEMNISCUS$_{A^{12}}$
    LAT. LEMNISCUS/FIBER$_{A^{13}}$

DESCENDING TRACTS$_{B(\ )}$
    CORTICOBULBOSP. TR.$_{B^1}$
    CORTICOPONT. TR.$_{B^{11}}$
    RUBROSPINAL TR.$_{B^4}$
    TECTOBULBOSP. TR.$_{B^7}$

At this level of the midbrain, the superior colliculi can be seen posteriorly and the great crura cerebri anteriorly, giving the characteristic shape you colored in Plate 5-3.

Color the heading, titles, and structures pertaining to both ascending tracts and descending tracts as before.

The *spinothalamic tract* (A^7, A^8) and the *medial lemniscus* (A^{12}) continue to be seen at this level, although the former is smaller as fibers are continually lost to nuclei in the brain stem along the way. Ascending from the decussation of the superior cerebellar peduncle, the *cerebello-dentato-rubral* (A^{14}) and *cerebello-dentato-thalamic tracts* (A^{15}) are seen here adjacent to the red nucleus (see ahead). The former tract terminates in the red nucleus (next plate), while the latter reaches for the thalamus.

The most prominent mass of descending fibers at this level is the *crus cerebri* (B^{12}). Of the approximately 20 million fibers making up each of the bilateral crura, the corticospinal component (not shown) of the *corticobulbospinal tract* (B^1) takes up only about 5 percent of the total; the bulk of the remainder are corticopontine fibers. These axons are further delineated into *frontopontine* (B^{13}) and *parietopontine, temporopontine, and occipitopontine tracts* (B^{14}).

The fibers of the *rubrospinal tract* (B^4) originate at this level as axons from cells of the red nucleus. The *tectobulbospinal tract* (B^{10}) is formed from efferents of the superior colliculus (see ahead).

Color the heading, titles, and structures pertaining to cranial nerve nuclei and related tracts and nerves as before.

The *mesencephalic nucleus* (C^{24}) and *tract* (C^{27}) of the fifth nerve can still be seen at this level, while the *trigeminothalamic tract* (C^5) continues on to the thalamus. The *nucleus of the oculomotor nerve* (C^{30}) lies on each side of the midline, anterior to the periaqueductal gray. The *oculomotor nerve* (C^{31}) projects from these nuclei to four of the six extrinsic muscles of the eye, muscle of the eyelid, and the intrinsic (smooth) muscles of the eye associated with accommodation and light reflex responses. Lateral and posterior to the oculomotor nucleus are the accessory oculomotor nuclei, the *interstitial nucleus of Cajal* (C^{32}) and the *nucleus of Darkschewitsch* (C^{33}).

These two nuclei are involved in visual tracking reflex activity.

Color the heading, titles, and structures pertaining to other tracts and nuclei as before.

The *reticular formation* (D^1) and related *central tegmental tract* (D^{12}) continue to occupy a central position. The *medial longitudinal fasciculus* (D^{14}, B^6) has fibers of origin and termination connecting to the accessory oculomotor nuclei (of Cajal and Darkschewitsch) and to a lesser degree the superior colliculus; it is seen here at its most rostral extent (recall Plate 4-10). The *periaqueductal gray* (D^{18}) can be seen surrounding the rostral cerebral aqueduct. The *interpeduncular nuclei* (D^{30}) are seen at this level, possibly relaying impulses from the limbic system.

The *superior colliculi* (D^{20}) constitute the rostral half of the posterior midbrain (tectum) and are concerned with visual activity. They function as reflex centers influencing the position of eyes and head in response to visual, auditory, and somatic stimuli. Afferent fibers come in from the optic and other pathways (not shown). Efferent *axons* (D^{21}) project anteriorly and medially from the superior colliculus, cross the midline below the MLF, and form the tectobulbospinal tract.

The *red nucleus* (D^{22}) is a large, round cell mass in the midbrain tegmentum that has a faintly pink cast in the fresh state. It receives afferents (cerebello-dentato-rubral tract) from the cerebellum via the superior cerebellar peduncle and from the cerebral cortex via the crura cerebri. It projects *axons* (D^{23}) to the spinal cord via the rubrospinal tract as well as a more diffuse set of rubrobulbar fibers to the inferior olive and a number of cranial nerve nuclei (not shown).

The *substantia nigra* (D^{24}; *nigra,* "black"), the largest nucleus in the midbrain, is characterized by compactly arranged, melanin pigment–rich neurons. Afferent fibers enter from the basal ganglia and reticular formation, and efferents are sent in return. These fibers are associated with several neurotransmitters, such as dopamine, substance P, and GABA. Reduction of dopamine synthesis in nigral cells leads to depletion of dopamine in their terminals located in the basal ganglia, resulting in the progressively crippling affliction known as Parkinson's disease (paralysis agitans).

MIDBRAIN: UPPER LEVEL.

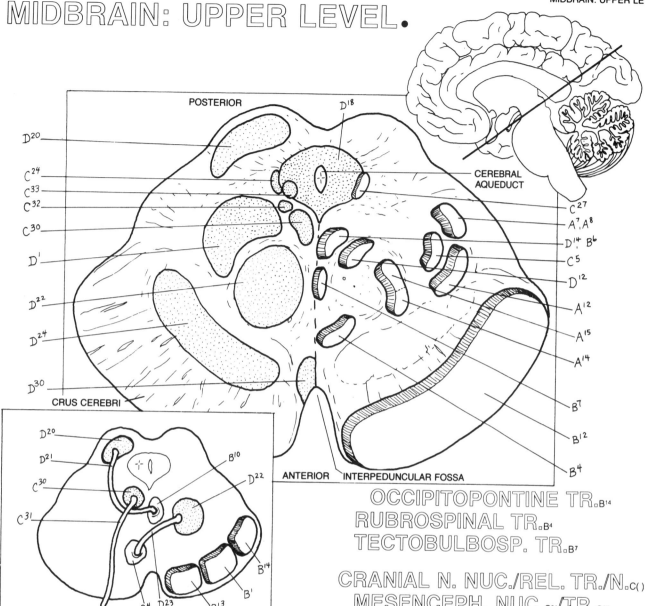

POSTERIOR

D¹⁸

D²⁰
C²⁴
C³³
C³²
C³⁰
D¹
D²²
D²⁴
D³⁰

CRUS CEREBRI

CEREBRAL AQUEDUCT

C²⁷
A⁷, A⁸
D¹⁴, B⁶
C⁵
D¹²
A¹²
A¹⁵
A¹⁴
B⁷
B¹²
B⁴

ANTERIOR   INTERPEDUNCULAR FOSSA

D²⁰
D²¹
C³⁰
C³¹
B¹⁰
D²²
B¹⁴
B⁴ D²³ B¹³ B¹

ASCENDING TRACTS_A( )
  SPINOTHALAMIC TR._A⁷, A⁸
  MED. LEMNISCUS_A¹²
  CEREBELLO-DENTATO-
    RUBRAL TR._A¹⁴
  CEREBELLO-DENTATO-
    THAL. TR._A¹⁵
DESCENDING TRACTS_B( )
  CRUS CEREBRI_B¹²
    CORTICOBULBOSP. TR._B¹
    FRONTOPONTINE TR._B¹³
    PARIETOPONTINE TR._₉
    TEMPOROPONTINE TR._₉

OCCIPITOPONTINE TR._B¹⁴
RUBROSPINAL TR._B⁴
TECTOBULBOSP. TR._B⁷

CRANIAL N. NUC./REL. TR./N._C( )
  MESENCEPH. NUC._C²⁴/TR._C²⁷
  TRIGEMINOTHAL. TR._C⁵
  OCULOMOTOR NUC._C³⁰/N._C³¹
  INTERSTIT. NUC. CAJAL_C³²
  NUC. DARKSCHEWITSCH_C³³

OTHER TRACTS/NUCLEI_D( )
  RETIC. FORM._D¹
  CENTRAL TEGMENTAL TR._D¹²
  MED. LONG. FASC._D¹⁴, B⁶
  PERIAQUED. GRAY_D¹⁸
  SUP. COLLICULUS_D²⁰/AXONS_D²¹
  RED NUCLEUS_D²²/AXONS_D²³
  SUBSTANTIA NIGRA_D²⁴
  INTERPEDUNC. NUC._D³⁰

The brain stem widens dramatically at the junction of the mesencephalon and the diencephalon as a number of structures characteristic of the thalamus first appear. Most obvious is the large posterolateral mass called the pulvinar. You will also note that some nuclei and tracts with which you have become familiar in midbrain sections continue into this level.

This plate is the last of a series, beginning with Plate 5-4, of cross sections through the brain stem that were subscripted for color coordination. You may also wish to color-coordinate structures seen in the cross sections with the coronal, sagittal, and horizontal sections seen in the atlas (Plates 5-35 through 5-48).

Color the heading Mesencephalon and the subheadings, titles, and structures pertaining to the mesencephalon (A through D^{26}) as before. The subscripts E and F here apply to this plate only.

The *spinothalamic tract* (A^7, A^8) and *medial lemniscus* (A^{12}) are among the ascending fibers (en route to the thalamus) that continue to be seen at this level. The *cerebellodentatorubral tract* (A^{14}) terminates in the red nucleus. The *cerebellodentatothalamic tract* (A^{15}) continues rostrally to the thalamus.

The descending fibers of cortical origin (*corticobulbospinal*, B^1; *corticopontine*, B^{11}) traverse the *crus cerebri* (B^{12}). The crus appears to have shifted laterally from its position in the lower section. It will become the internal capsule in the diencephalon and telencephalon rostrally.

The *red nucleus* (D^{22}) receives the fibers of the cerebellodentatorubral tract here. The *substantia nigra* (D^{24}) continues to be seen at this level. The *cerebral aqueduct* (D^{25}) deepens to form the most caudal part of the third ventricle (not shown) of the diencephalon. A modified part of the ependymal lining of the rostral cerebral aqueduct is called the *subcommissural organ* (D^{26}). It lies just anterior to the posterior commissure (see ahead) and is concerned with thirst and water intake.

Color the heading Transitional Zone (E), titles E^1 and E^2, and the related structures in the two illustrations.

The *pretectal area* (E^1) is situated rostral to the tectum (colliculi) of the midbrain. As a visual reflex integrative center, it receives *afferents* from the optic tract (not shown), the lateral geniculate body (F^3), the contralateral pretectum via the posterior commissure (E^2), the pulvinar of the thalamus (F^5), and areas of the cerebral cortex (not shown) that process visual information. Some pretectal efferents project to the oculomotor nucleus to control pupillary constriction to light (pupillary light reflex; see Plate 6-7).

The *posterior commissure* (E^2), bridging the midline, carries pretectal fibers to the contralateral pretectum and oculomotor nucleus. Interruption of this pathway reduces (but does not abolish) the consensual pupillary light reflex (whereby a beam of light brought to one eye causes a reflex constriction in the opposite eye).

Color the heading Diencephalon (F), titles F^1 through F^6, and related structures.

The *pineal gland* (F^1; discussed more fully in Plate 5-23) is an outgrowth of the roof of the diencephalon. It consists of modified secretory glial cells called *pinealocytes* that are light sensitive and function, in part, as a biological clock.

The *medial* (F^2) and *lateral geniculate bodies* (F^3; nuclei) are thalamic processing stations for auditory and visual impulses, respectively. Each of the nuclei projects fibers to and receives fibers from its related midbrain colliculus via the respective inferior and superior brachium (recall Plate 5-2). The geniculates project efferent fibers to the related auditory and visual parts of the cerebral cortex. The *optic radiation* (F^4) arises as *efferent fibers* (F^3) from the lateral geniculate body.

The posterior thalamic mass, called the *pulvinar* (F^5), overhangs the posterolateral surface of the midbrain and the geniculate bodies. It is known to have reciprocal relations with the occipital and temporal cortices and appears to be concerned with visual associative functions. It also supplies *efferent fibers* (F^5) to the pretectal area.

The *posterior thalamic nucleus* (F^6), medial to the medial geniculate body, is a diffuse group of cells and fibers (often abbreviated as PO) where most spinothalamic fibers terminate.

At this level, the midbrain reticular formation (not shown) becomes continuous with a group of cells, the zona incerta, in the subthalamus (discussed in Plate 5-23).

MIDBRAIN AND DIENCEPHALON: JUNCTION.

MESENCEPHALON.★
ASCENDING TRACTS_A( )
    SPINOTHALAMIC TR._A7, A8
    MED. LEMNISCUS_A12
    CEREBELLODENTATO-
        RUBRAL TR._A14
    CEREBELLODENTATO-
        THALAMIC TR._A15

DESCENDING TRACTS_B( )
    CRUS CEREBRI_B12
        CORTICOBULBOSP. TR._B1
        CORTICOPONT. TR._B11

OTHER TRACTS/NUCLEI_D( )
    RED NUCLEUS_D22
    SUBSTANTIA NIGRA_D24
    CEREBRAL AQUEDUCT_D25
    SUBCOMMISS. ORGAN_D26

TRANSITIONAL ZONE_E( )
PRETECTAL AREA_E1
POST. COMMISSURE/FIBER_E2

DIENCEPHALON_F( )
PINEAL GLAND_F1
MED._F2/LAT. GENICULATE
    BODY/EFF. FIBER_F3
OPTIC RADIATION_F4
PULVINAR/EFF. FIBER_F5
POST. THAL. NUC._F6

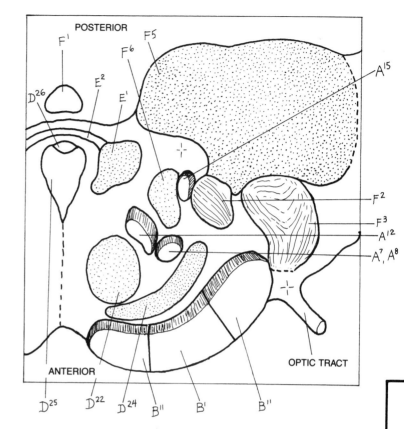

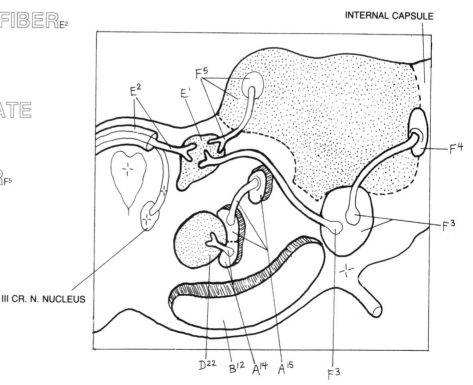

The central core of the brain stem is made up of a complex system of nerve cells and fibers called the reticular ("net-like") formation or reticular core. To earlier anatomists, the area resembled a diffuse net of neurons and fibers, a kind of "neural excelsior," providing unspecified integrative functions for the surrounding cranial nerve nuclei. More recent research has shown conclusively the importance of this area in controlling critical body functions, such as respiration and circulation, and monitoring and adjusting all informational and outgoing command signals, ranging from maximal interaction with the environment (alertness) through relaxed wakefulness to sleep and coma. In fact, the brain stem reticular core is the only intracranial neural structure without which our life is impossible.

Color the headings and titles A through C^5 and the related structures in the upper illustration. Different shades of the same color should be used for structures sharing the same subscript.

The reticular core varies at different levels of the brain stem, due to the diversity of its nuclei and their different chemical properties, as well as variations in the structure of neuronal processes and their connections. Generally, three major cell groupings can be seen: (1) nuclei clustered along the midline or raphe ("seam"), called the *raphe cell groups* (A); (2) *lateral reticular nuclei* (B) located along the periphery of the brain stem; and (3) *central cell groups* (C), including the largest reticular nuclei, both in cell size and cell numbers, located within the central portions of left and right halves of the brain stem.

There are at least seven discrete raphe nuclei, including the *nuclei raphe pallidus* (A^1) and *obscurus* (A^2) in the medulla, the *nuclei raphe magnus* (A^3; *magnus,* "large") and *pontis* (A^4) in the pons, and the *dorsal* (A^5) and *medial raphe nuclei* (A^6) and the *nucleus linearis* (A^7) in the midbrain. Most of these neurons are characterized by a high content of serotonin, a neurotransmitter, and a close relationship between their dendrites and the small blood vessels intertwining among them. It is conceivable that serotonin synthesis may be controlled or triggered (or both) by substances circulating in the blood and "sensed" by the perivascular dendrites of these raphe group neurons.

The principal lateral cell group is called the *lateral reticular nucleus* (B) and receives input from the inner surface of the spinothalamic tracts.

Many of the *central cell groups* (C) have been delineated on the basis of cell size. The *nucleus reticularis parvocellularis* (C^1; *parvo,* "little") in the caudal medulla and the *nucleus reticularis magnocellularis* (C^2) in the rostral medulla are cases in point. The *nuclei reticularis pontis caudalis* (C^3) and *oralis* (C^4; *oral,* "rostral") are located in the caudal and rostral pons, respectively. Neurons of the mesencephalic reticular core are called the *nucleus cuneiformis* (C^5; "wedge-shaped") or midbrain tegmental complex. This very narrow area is known as the "wasp's waist" of the reticular core. Experimental lesions here destroy the functional integrity of the entire formation. Experiments such as these in the early 1950s helped establish the role of the reticular formation in the control of wakefulness and sleep.

Color the heading Action Diagram, titles A^8 through H^1, and related structures in the lower illustration. Cells are shown on the right side of the section and are highly magnified; some of the fibers that project onto these cells are shown on the left, and these are greatly enlarged. Note that H^1 is in the upper drawing.

The dendritic structure and position of the brain stem reticular core neurons reflect the nature of the dendritic input. *Raphe cells* (A^8) remain close to the midline and synapse with several pathways in the area, such as the MLF. Dendrites of the larger *central cells* (C^6) radiate outward for maximum exposure. Such "dedicated dendrites" seem to place themselves in the path of incoming fibers, such as the *afferents* from *vestibular* (D) nuclei and tracts, the *pyramidal tract* (E), the *spinothalamic tract* (F), and the *medial longitudinal fasciculus,* or *MLF* (G). The axonal outflow of reticular cells may be very extensive. Some project to the spinal cord as reticulospinal tract fibers (Plate 4-12), while others project to the diencephalon and even to the cerebral cortex. Some *reticular neurons* (H) project both upstream and downstream via *bifurcating axons* (H^1), influencing nuclei along the way by means of collateral branches, constantly retuning the brain to the needs of the internal and external environment.

BRAIN STEM RETICULAR FORMATION.

RAPHE CELL GROUPS$_{A(\ )}$
  NUC. RAPHE PALLIDUS$_{A^1}$
  NUC. RAPHE OBSCURUS$_{A^2}$
  NUC. RAPHE MAGNUS$_{A^3}$
  NUC. RAPHE PONTIS$_{A^4}$
  NUC. OF DORSAL RAPHE$_{A^5}$
  NUC. OF MEDIAL RAPHE$_{A^6}$
  NUC. LINEARIS$_{A^7}$

LATERAL RETICULAR NUC.$_B$

CENTRAL CELL GROUPS$_{C(\ )}$
  NUC. RET.
    PARVOCELLULARIS$_{C^1}$
  NUC. RET.
    MAGNOCELLULARIS$_{C^2}$
  NUC. RET. PONTIS
    CAUDALIS$_{C^3}$
  NUC. RET. PONTIS ORALIS$_{C^4}$
  NUC. CUNEIFORMIS$_{C^5}$

ACTION DIAGRAM ★
RAPHE CELL$_{A^8}$
CENTRAL CELL$_{C^6}$
VESTIBULAR AFFERENT$_D$
PYRAMIDAL TR. AFFERENT$_E$
SPINOTHAL. TR. AFFERENT$_F$
MLF AFFERENT$_G$
RETIC. NEURON$_H$
  BIFURCATING AXON$_{H^1}$

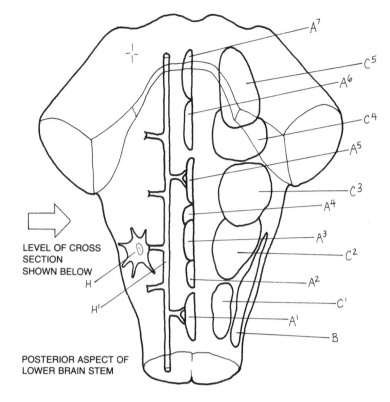

LEVEL OF CROSS SECTION SHOWN BELOW

POSTERIOR ASPECT OF LOWER BRAIN STEM

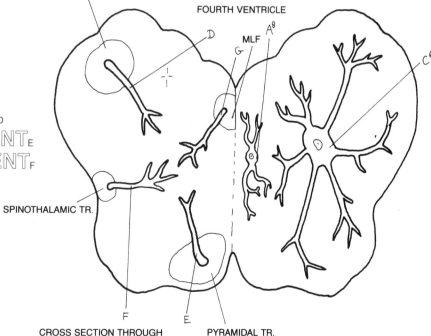

VESTIBULAR NUCLEI

FOURTH VENTRICLE

MLF

SPINOTHALAMIC TR.

CROSS SECTION THROUGH UPPER MEDULLA (CELLS/FIBERS HIGHLY MAGNIFIED)

PYRAMIDAL TR.

The cerebellum is a derivative of the metencephalon. It is situated posterior to the pons and medulla and occupies the posterior cranial fossa. Like the cerebral hemispheres, the cerebellum is convoluted; the folds (folia) are far more finely fissured, however. For this reason, perhaps, the cerebellum has been given a name that means "little cerebrum." But there the similarity ends. The cerebellum is attached to the brain stem by the superior, middle, and inferior cerebellar peduncles (recall Plate 5-1) and is essentially concerned with coordinated movements and maintenance of muscle tone and of equilibrium, although there is evidence that its function exceeds this.

Color the heading Cerebellum and titles A and B. Color A in the small drawing at the upper left and B in the lower two illustrations. Color title C and the related fissure in the upper illustration. Color the heading Archicerebellum (D), titles D^1 through D^3, and the related structures in the upper and lower illustrations.

The cerebellum consists of two *cerebellar hemispheres* (A) flanking the midline *vermis* (B; "worm"). Phylogenetically, the cerebellum (both hemispheres and vermis) consists of an archicerebellum ("oldest"), paleocerebellum ("old") and neocerebellum ("new").

The archicerebellum, separated from the other two regions by the *posterolateral fissure* (C), consists of the *flocculonodular lobe* (D^1). The *nodule* (D^2) occupies the most inferior portion of the vermis, and the two *flocculi* (D^3) extend laterally from the nodule (see lowest illustration). The flocculonodular lobe receives fibers from the inferior and medial vestibular nuclei (not shown) via the inferior cerebellar peduncle. Lesions of this lobe induce an uncoordinated walk with a broad base, not unlike that of an intoxicated person.

Color the heading Paleocerebellum (E), title E^1, and the related structure in each of the three illustrations.

The paleocerebellum is represented by the *anterior lobe* (E^1). This lobe receives the posterior and anterior spinocerebellar tracts (not shown) via the inferior and superior cerebellar peduncles, respectively. These fibers convey primarily proprioceptive-related impulses concerned with muscle tone. Lesions in the anterior lobe produce severe disturbances in extensor muscle tone and posture.

Color title F and the related fissure in the upper two illustrations. Color the heading Neocerebellum (G), titles G^1 and G^2, and the related structures in each of the three illustrations, as applicable.

The neocerebellum, separated from the other two lobes by the *primary* (F) and posterolateral *fissures*, consists of the *posterior lobe* (G^1) and the *tonsil* (G^2). The posterior lobe is closely related to the development of the cerebral cortex through the corticopontine fibers from the frontal, parietal, occipital, and temporal lobes. These fibers descend to synapse on the pontine nuclei. The pontocerebellar fibers then decussate to enter the posterior lobe via the middle cerebellar peduncle.

The tonsil is sometimes forced down into the foramen magnum (tentorial herniation) by increased intracranial pressure created by a tumor, compressing the caudal medulla and obstructing the flow of cerebrospinal fluid through the fourth ventricle. In such a case, hydrocephalus (enlargement of the ventricles) and interruption of medullary activity (producing severe respiratory and cardiac distress) may result.

Lesions of the neocerebellum affect skilled voluntary movements. For example, a rapid shaking or series of oscillations (intention tremor) may accompany voluntary movements of the limbs. Skeletal muscles are easily tired and lose their tone, and coordinated movement is profoundly affected. Normal neocerebellar function makes possible the coordinated finger movement of the pianist or machinist. To observe your own cerebellum at work, close your eyes, extend your arm out to the side, then bring the tip of the index finger of that hand quickly to the tip of your nose.

CEREBELLUM: EXTERNAL STRUCTURE.

INFERIOR VIEW

A — A

MIDBRAIN

PONS

MEDULLA

LINGULA

CULMEN

E'

MEDIAN SECTION THROUGH VERMIS

F

DECLIVE

ARBOR VITAE

G'

TUBER

PYRAMIS

UVULA

D² C

CEREBELLUM ★
  CEREBELLAR HEMISPHERE A
  VERMIS B
  POSTEROLATERAL FISSURE C

ARCHICEREBELLUM D( )
  FLOCCULONOD. LOBE D'
  NODULE D²
  FLOCCULUS D³

ANTERIOR SURFACE

B + E'

E'

F

G'

SUPERIOR VIEW

HORIZONTAL FISSURE

POSTERIOR SURFACE
B + G'

SUPERIOR ASPECT

LINGULA

B + E'

D²

E'

SUPERIOR CEREBELLAR PEDUNCLE

MIDDLE CEREBELLAR PEDUNCLE

HORIZONTAL FISSURE

G'

G'

D³

D³

G²

INFERIOR ASPECT

G²

D³

INFERIOR CEREBELLAR PEDUNCLE

ANTERIOR VIEW

PALEOCEREBELLUM E( )
  ANTERIOR LOBE E'
  PRIMARY FISSURE F

NEOCEREBELLUM G( )
  POSTERIOR LOBE G'
  TONSIL G²

The *cerebellar cortex* (A) is made up of three well-defined layers, from the surface of the cortex to the underlying white matter: the *molecular* (B), *Purkinje* (C), and *granule layers* (D).

Color the title Cerebellar Cortex (A) and its structure in Figure 1. Color the heading Cortical Layers, titles B through D, and the related layers in Figure 2. Color the heading Cell Types, titles C^1 and D^1, and the related cells in Figure 3. Note that each cell is shown twice, once in the coronal plane and once in the sagittal plane.

The cerebellar cortex is dominated by the single layer of *Purkinje neurons* (C^1), each neuron characterized by its unique two-dimensional dendritic tree (arbor). In the coronal plane, only a thin edge of the arbor can be seen; in the sagittal plane, the arbor spread can be appreciated (see Figure 2 for orientation and Figure 3 for the two views). These neurons receive, directly or indirectly, the two major cerebellar afferents and generate, by their axons, the only efferent pathway from the cortex. For this reason, the Purkinje cell is the protagonist of cerebellar cortical activity, facilitated and inhibited by the neurons discussed below.

The granule layer consists of enormous numbers (approximately 10 billion) of tightly packed *granule cells* (D^1) characterized, in part, by several short dendrites with clawlike terminals. The granule cell axons ascend to the molecular layer, then bifurcate (divide) into branches that run parallel to the cortical (folial) surface. These parallel fibers conduct impulses to and synapse on spines of the smallest dendrites (not shown) of the Purkinje cells.

Color titles B^1, B^2, and D^2 and their structures in Figure 3. The basket cell is shown close to the Purkinje layer in the sagittal plane; the stellate cell is in the molecular layer in the sagittal plane; the Golgi II cell is shown on the edge of the sagittal and coronal planes.

The *basket cells* (B^1) belong to a family of cells in the molecular layer. The axons of these cells encircle the Purkinje neuron cell bodies and axon hillocks, exerting inhibitory effects on them. The *stellate cells* (B^2) are small neurons superficially placed in the molecular layer. They are seen to make synaptic contact with the Purkinje cell dendrites. The *Golgi II cells* (D^2) are located in the granule layer and spread their dendritic arbor into the molecular layer in a three-dimensional array (unlike the Purkinje neurons with two-dimensional arbors). Their short axons break up in the granule layer, forming many synapses with granule cell dendrites and other structures to be mentioned below.

Color the heading Intracerebellar Afferents of Major Tracts, titles H through J, and the related structures and arrow in Figure 3. Start the coloring of H and J at the bottom of the plate, along with the facilitation sign (+). The arrow I, pointing to the glomerulus, can be found at the terminal of H. Color titles K through K^5 and related structures in Figures 1 and 4. Color the inhibition sign (−), labeled C^1, and the related cell (K^2) at the bottom of the plate.

There are two major types of facilitatory (+) cerebellar afferent fibers. Of these, the large-diameter, rapidly conducting *mossy fibers* (H) represent the intracerebellar (*intra-,* "within") terminations of several major tracts including the spinocerebellar, pontocerebellar, and vestibulocerebellar tracts, among others. The enlarged, mossy, tuftlike terminals of these axons enter into complex synaptic arrangements, called *glomeruli* (I), with granule cell dendritic expansions and Golgi II cell axon terminals. These glomeruli, involving several types of presynaptic fibers and surrounded by a glial capsule (dotted line, Figure 3), constitute a significant unit for information processing.

The *climbing fiber* (J), the second major axon type entering the cerebellum, appears to represent the intracerebellar continuation of olivocerebellar and reticulocerebellar fibers. This type of axon, distributed on a one-to-one basis to the Purkinje cells, literally wraps itself around the branches of the Purkinje dendritic arbor like an ivy stalk about a tree, establishing numerous synapses. Climbing fibers are powerful facilitators of Purkinje cell activity. The mossy fiber—granule cell—parallel fiber system is also facilitatory, although the effects of individual parallel fibers are limited to the small area of each Purkinje dendrite arbor that they traverse.

Virtually the entire output of the cerebellar cortex provides an *inhibitory influence* (C^1) on the *cells* (K^2) of the cerebellar (roof) nuclei, located in the trunk of the cerebellar white matter at the roof of the fourth ventricle (Figure 4). These nuclei include the *dentate* (K^1; the largest), the *emboliform* (K^3), the *globose* (K^4), and the *fastigial* (K^5). The axons projecting from these nuclei in turn enter the brain stem.

CEREBELLAR CORTEX.

CEREBELLAR CORTEX$_A$
CORTICAL LAYERS ★
  MOLECULAR$_B$
  PURKINJE$_C$
  GRANULE$_D$

CELL TYPES ★
  PURKINJE(−)$_{C^1}$
  GRANULE$_{D^1}$
  BASKET$_{B^1}$
  STELLATE$_{B^2}$
  GOLGI II$_{D^2}$

INTRACEREBELL. AFF.
  OF MAJOR TRACTS ★
MOSSY FIBERS(+)$_H$
GLOMERULUS$_I$
CLIMBING FIBER(+)$_J$

CEREBELLAR
NUCLEI$_{K(\ )}$
DENTATE
  NUC.$_{K^1}$/CELL$_{K^2}$
EMBOLIFORM
  NUC.$_{K^3}$
GLOBOSE
  NUC.$_{K^4}$
FASTIGIAL
  NUC.$_{K^5}$

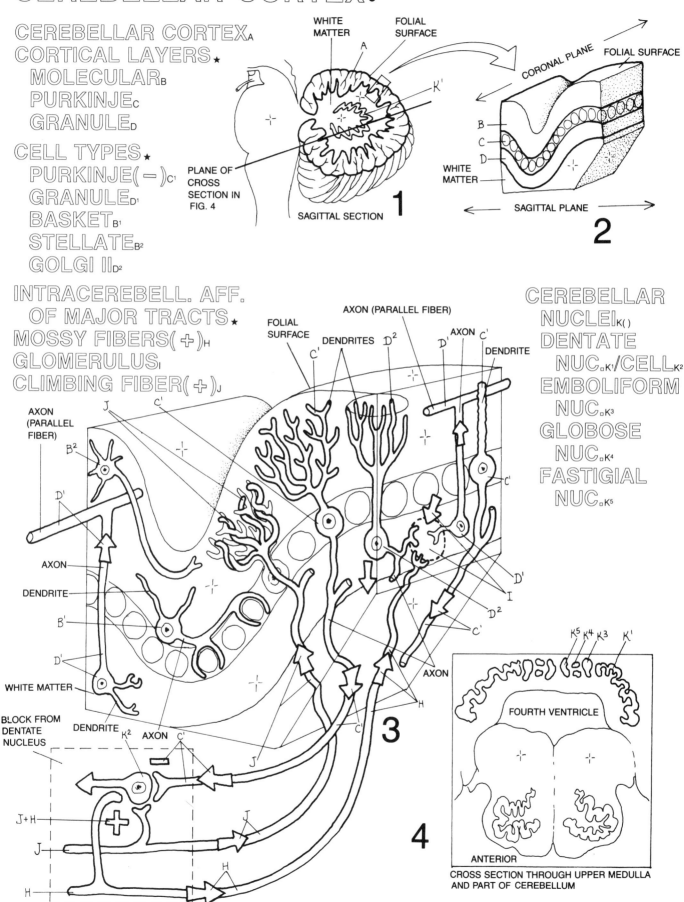

WHITE MATTER
FOLIAL SURFACE
A
K'
PLANE OF CROSS SECTION IN FIG. 4
SAGITTAL SECTION
1

CORONAL PLANE
FOLIAL SURFACE
B
C
D
WHITE MATTER
SAGITTAL PLANE
2

AXON (PARALLEL FIBER)
FOLIAL SURFACE
DENDRITES
D^2
D^1
AXON
C'
DENDRITE
C'
AXON (PARALLEL FIBER)
B^2
D^1
AXON
DENDRITE
B'
D^1
WHITE MATTER
BLOCK FROM DENTATE NUCLEUS
DENDRITE
K^2
AXON
C'
C'
D'
I
D^2
C'
AXON
H
C'
J
J
3

J+H
J
H
H

FOURTH VENTRICLE
K^5 K^4 K^3 K^1
ANTERIOR
4
CROSS SECTION THROUGH UPPER MEDULLA AND PART OF CEREBELLUM

Traditionally thought to be concerned only with muscle tone, sensorimotor coordination, and balance, the cerebellum has been shown in recent studies to be involved with almost every brain system including the limbic lobe (recall Plate 1-3). In testimony to the enormous amount of cerebellar input and output, the cerebellum is connected to the brain stem by three massive fiber tract systems, the *cerebellar peduncles,* which encompass the vast majority of the axons entering and leaving the cerebellum.

There are several "ground rules" about communication between brain stem and cerebellum that seem to apply to virtually all of the fiber systems involved: (1) All fibers entering the cerebellum terminate in specified portions of the *cerebellar cortex* (A); (2) entering fibers give collaterals to one or more of the *cerebellar nuclei* (B) en route; (3) all fibers exiting the cerebellar cortex are axons of Purkinje neurons; (4) all of these Purkinje axons terminate in the cerebellar nuclei, with one exception (a remarkably short trip for so stout a company of fibers!); and (5) all fibers leaving the cerebellum are axons of cells of cerebellar nuclei, with the same exception (cerebellovestibular fibers; see ahead).

Color titles A and B and their related structures in the lower illustration. Color the heading Inferior Cerebellar Peduncle and Related Nuclei, titles C through C⁵, including D, E, and F, and related structures, as applicable, in both illustrations.

The *inferior cerebellar peduncle* (C) consists of at least four afferent tracts and one efferent tract. The *posterior spinocerebellar tract* (C^1; recall Plate 4-7), and its analogue for the upper extremity, the cuneocerebellar tract (not shown), conduct proprioceptive information from the spinal cord to the anterior lobe and vermis (paleocerebellum). The *lateral vestibular nucleus* (D) and other vestibular nuclei (not shown) project *vestibulocerebellar fibers* (C^2) to the vermis and flocculonodular lobe (archicerebellum), transmitting information about the position and direction of movement of head and body. Fibers of primary sensory neurons of the vestibular apparatus (not shown) are also included in this bundle. *Olivocerebellar fibers* (C^3), projecting from the contralateral *inferior olive* (E), make up a large portion of the peduncle and appear to project to all parts of the cerebellum, where they terminate as climbing fibers (see Plate 5-14). *Reticulocerebellar fibers* (C^4) project from the *lateral reticular nucleus* (F) widely

upon the cerebellar cortex, conducting integrated inputs from cerebral cortex, brain stem, and spinal cord (not shown).

The inferior cerebellar peduncle also carries the efferent *cerebellovestibular tract* (C^5), composed of Purkinje axons that directly inhibit the vestibular nuclei without synapsing in the cerebellar nuclei. Proprioceptive fibers from the head, particularly the face, enter the cerebellum via the trigeminocerebellar tract (not shown), which employs this peduncle.

Color the heading Middle Cerebellar Peduncle and Related Nuclei, titles G, G¹, and H, and related structures in the upper and lower illustrations. Color the heading Superior Cerebellar Peduncle and Related Nuclei, titles I through K, and related structures in the upper and lower illustrations.

The *middle cerebellar peduncle* (G), the largest of the three peduncles, carries only afferent fibers from the *pontine nuclei* (H) to the posterior lobe (neocerebellum) as the *pontocerebellar tract* (G^1). This tract is the most important structure for introducing information from sensory and motor areas of the cerebral cortex into the cerebellum and appears largely concerned with skilled activities of the extremities (e.g., hands and fingers).

The *superior cerebellar peduncle* (I) carries the fibers of the *anterior spinocerebellar tract* (I^1; recall Plate 4-8) to the anterior lobe (paleocerebellum) from the spinal cord. In addition, the norepinephrine-rich cells of the locus ceruleus (recall Plate 5-8) send axons (not shown) into the cerebellum through this peduncle. Their precise destination and function remain unclear. The efferent fibers of the superior cerebellar peduncle arise exclusively from the cerebellar nuclei (which receive Purkinje axons) and project, as *cerebellodentatorubral fibers* (I^2) to the *red nucleus* (J), *cerebellodentatothalamic fibers* (I^3) to the *ventrolateral nucleus of the thalamus* (K), and *fastigiobulbar fibers* (I^4) to the medulla. After synapsing, the thalamic contingent continues on to the cerebral cortex, completing a great cerebro-ponto-cerebello-thalamo-cortical loop. This pathway is believed to constitute a feedback mechanism for fine tuning of cerebral output. The fiber contingent that synapses in the red nucleus exerts effects on spinal cord mechanisms via the rubrospinal tract (recall Plate 5-11).

CEREBELLUM: PEDUNCLES.

CEREBELLAR CORTEX_A

CEREBELLAR NUCLEI_B

INF. CEREBELL. PED./REL. NUC. ★

INF. CEREBELL. PED._C
   POST. SPINOCEREBELL. TR._{C1}
   VESTIBULOCEREBELL. TR._{C2}

LAT. VESTIB. NUC._D
   OLIVOCEREBELLAR TR._{C3}

INFERIOR OLIVE_E
   RETICULOCEREBELL. TR._{C4}

LAT. RETICULAR NUC._F

CEREBELLOVESTIB. TR._{C5}

MID. CEREBELL. PED./REL. NUC. ★

MID. CEREBELL. PED._G
   PONTOCEREBELL. TR._{G1}

PONTINE NUC._H

SUP. CEREBELL. PED./REL. NUC. ★

SUP. CEREBELL. PED._I
   ANT. SPINOCEREB. TR._{I1}
   CEREBELLODENTATO-
     RUBRAL TR._{I2}
   CEREBELLODENTATO-
     THALAMIC TR._{I3}
   FASTIGIOBULBAR TR._{I4}

RED NUCLEUS_J

VENT. LAT. NUC. THAL._K

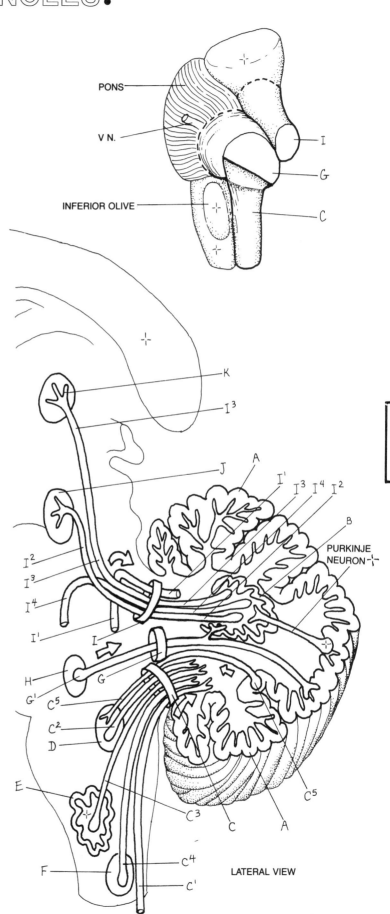

PONS

V N.

INFERIOR OLIVE

I

G

C

K

I³

J

A

I¹

I³ I⁴ I²

B

PURKINJE NEURON

I²

I³

I⁴

I¹

I

H

G

G¹

C⁵

C²

D

E

C³

C

A

C⁵

F

C⁴

C¹

LATERAL VIEW

The thalamus ("inner chamber") of the diencephalon consists of a group of nuclei, 3 cm long anteroposteriorly, 1.5 cm vertically, and 1.5 cm mediolaterally, located at the base of the cerebral hemispheres on each side of the third ventricle. As a probable embryological derivative of the alar plate of the developing diencephalon (Plate 3-8), the thalamus functions as a processing station for all sensory pathways (except the olfactory) en route to the cerebral cortex.

The purpose of this plate is to learn the terminology associated with the thalamus and the relationships among its various nuclei.

Color title A, the heading Orientation, titles B through G, and the related structures and arrows in Figures 1 and 2.

In Figure 1, note the orientation of the left *thalamus* (A). Unlike the spinal cord, the long axis of this structure is oriented from front to rear (anterior to posterior), rather than up and down (superior/rostral to inferior/caudal). Because of the 90 degree change in orientation, *dorsal* becomes synonymous with *superior* and *ventral* with *inferior*. As shown in Figure 1, the terms *dorsal* (E) and *ventral* (F) are used in conjunction with and are *not* synonymous with *posterior* (G) and *anterior* (B) in the naming of thalamic (and hypothalamic) nuclei. A "life size," dimensional block (Figure 2) of the left thalamus, seen from a posterior lateral aspect, illustrates the relationship of *anterior* (B) and *posterior* (G) to *medial* (C) and *lateral* (D).

Color the thalamic shape (Figure 3), which demonstrates the relative position of segments named according to the six terms of orientation just colored. Color the heading Thalamic Nuclei, titles B^1 through H^2, and the nuclei in Figure 4.

The thalamus has a number of nuclei, over 30 by some counts, 13 of which are shown here. They are named according to their positions using the six terms of orientation just introduced. Coloring the basic reference areas in the thalamic shape illustration will help you get your bearings before encountering the "real thing" in the lower illustration.

The *internal medullary lamina* (H) traverses the long axis of the thalamus, splitting anteriorly to enclose the *anterior nucleus* (B^1). The length of the lamina forms a partition between the medial and lateral groups of nuclei. The medial group is dominated by the *dorsomedial nucleus* (C^2). A thin layer of *midline nuclei* (C^3) lines the medial thalamic wall facing the third ventricle.

The lateral group of thalamic nuclei can be divided into dorsal and ventral divisions, each of which contains several important nuclei. The dorsal division includes three nuclei, from anterior to posterior: *lateral dorsal* (E^2; abbreviated LD), *lateral posterior* (E^3; abbreviated LP), and *pulvinar* (E^4). The last dominates the posterior third of the thalamus and overhangs the metathalamus made up of the *medial* and *lateral geniculate bodies* (G^2 and G^3; abbreviated MGB and LGB, respectively).

The ventral division of the lateral group includes four nuclei, from anterior to posterior: *ventral anterior* (F^2; abbreviated VA), *ventral lateral* (F^3; abbreviated VL), *ventral posterior medial* (F^4; abbreviated VPM), and *ventral posterior lateral* (F^5; abbreviated VPL). The VPM and VPL are known collectively as the ventrobasal complex (VB).

The internal medullary lamina consists of myelinated axons interspersed with small, discontinuous cell groups known as the intralaminar nuclei (H^1; the subject of Plate 5-19). The largest of these, the *centromedian* (H^2; abbreviated Cm), is located quite centrally and medially in the posterior third of the thalamic mass.

The connections and functional significance of these nuclei can be learned in the three following plates.

THALAMUS: NUCLEAR ORIENTATION.

THALAMUS$_A$
ORIENTATION ★
  ANTERIOR$_B$
  MEDIAL$_C$
  LATERAL$_D$
  DORSAL$_E$
  VENTRAL$_F$
  POSTERIOR$_G$

THALAMIC NUCLEI ★
ANTERIOR$_{B^1}$
MEDIAL GROUP$_{C^1()}$
  DORSOMEDIAL$_{C^2}$
  MIDLINE$_{C^3}$
LAT. GROUP:$_{D^1()}$ DORS. DIV.$_{E^1()}$
  LAT. DORS.$_{E^2}$/LAT. POST.$_{E^3}$
  PULVINAR$_{E^4}$
LAT. GROUP:$_{D^1()}$ VENT. DIV.$_{F^1()}$
  VENT. ANT.$_{F^2}$/VENT. LAT.$_{F^3}$
  VENT. POST. MED.$_{F^4}$/
    VENT. POST. LAT.$_{F^5}$
METATHALAMUS$_{G^1()}$
  MED.$_{G^2}$/LAT.
    GENICULATE BODY$_{G^3}$
INT. MEDULLARY
  LAMINA$_H$
INTRALAMINAR$_{H^1()}$
  CENTROMEDIAN$_{H^2}$

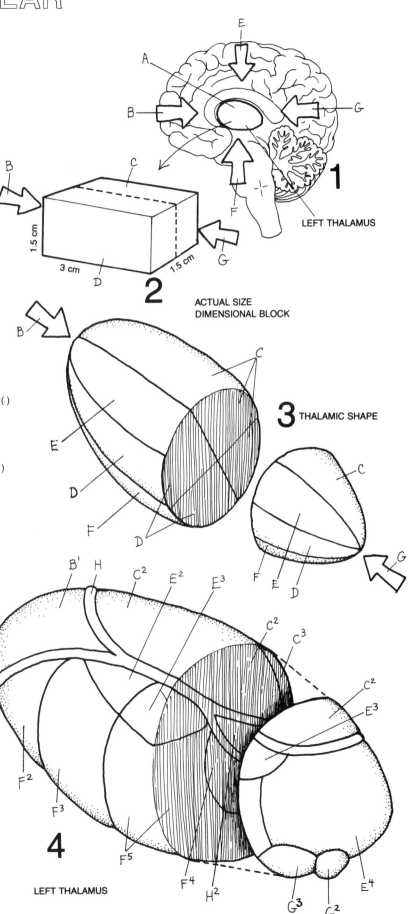

1 LEFT THALAMUS

2 ACTUAL SIZE DIMENSIONAL BLOCK

1.5 cm   3 cm   1.5 cm

3 THALAMIC SHAPE

4 LEFT THALAMUS

The thalamus is currently believed to represent the level in the central nervous system at which sensations are first consciously experienced. Sensory and motor-related pathways passing up the brain stem synapse in the thalamus before proceeding on to the cerebral cortex for more elaborate integration and analysis.

In this plate, the principal afferent connections to the major nuclei of the thalamus are considered. Many afferents other than the ones shown reach the thalamus, and these are complemented by intricate intrathalamic connections.

In this and certain following plates, reference will be made to numbered areas of the cerebral cortex, for example, areas 4 and 6. This system of numbering allows greater specificity in delineation of cortical areas. A more complete assignment of numbers to cortical areas can be seen in Plate 5-29.

The subscripts on this plate relate to those of the preceding and following plate; for this reason you may wish to color this and the next plate together.

Color the heading Target Nuclei and Source of Afferent Projections, all of the titles (B^1 through H^6), and the related structures. The subscripts A and D are not used on this plate. Use the colors you used for thalamic nuclei on the previous plate for the same nuclei here. The hypothalamus, prefrontal cortex, basal ganglia, and occipital cortex are each the source of two projections here, and each receives two titles and subscripts as well as two colors.

The *anterior nucleus* (B^1) receives afferents primarily from the *mammillary bodies* (B^3) of the *hypothalamus* (B^2) via the mammillothalamic tract (not shown; see Plate 5-22). This pathway is an important part of the circuit connecting the hypothalamus, the thalamus, and the limbic lobe.

Of the medial nuclear group, the *dorsomedial nucleus* (C^2) constitutes the largest element. Most of its afferents come from the *hypothalamus* (C^3) and the *prefrontal cortex* (C^4; anterior two-thirds of the frontal lobe). Direct stimulation of the dorsomedial nucleus produces feelings of anxiety and dread.

The dorsal nuclei of the lateral nuclear group consist of the lateral dorsal nucleus, the lateral posterior nucleus, and the pulvinar. Afferents to the *lateral dorsal* (E^2) are believed to include projections from the *cingulate gyrus* (E^5), a part of the limbic system, and from association areas of the *parietal cortex* (E^6). Afferents to the *lateral posterior* (E^3) nucleus include those from the *occipital (visual) cortex* (E^7). The two nuclei are probably involved in synthesis of higher-order sensory perceptions.

The *pulvinar* (E^4), largest of the lateral group of nuclei, receives afferents from all areas of the *occipital cortex* (E^8) and adjacent areas of the parietal and temporal lobes. It is undoubtedly concerned with visual associative functions.

The *ventral anterior* (F^2) nucleus receives large numbers of afferents from the *basal ganglia* (F^6). The *ventral lateral nucleus* (F^3) receives fibers from the *cerebellar nuclei* (F^7) via the superior cerebellar peduncle and the cerebellodentatothalamic tract (not shown; recall Plate 5-11), and it shares the afferents from the basal ganglia, most of which project to the ventral anterior nucleus. Between them, the ventral anterior and ventral lateral nuclei process input from these two areas (basal ganglia and cerebellum), which are important in motor activity.

The ventral posterior nuclei are subdivided into medial and lateral nuclei, *ventral posterior medial* (F^4) and *ventral posterior lateral* (F^5). These nuclei constitute the main thalamic processing center for general sensory input. The ventral posterior medial nucleus receives sensory input from the *face* and the *oral and nasal cavities* (F^8) via the trigeminothalamic tract (not shown). The ventral posterior lateral nucleus acquires similar input from the *extremities and trunk* (F^9) via the spinothalamics and the medial lemniscus (not shown).

The *medial geniculate body* (G^2) receives afferents carrying auditory-related impulses from the *inner ear* (G^4). The *lateral geniculate body* (G^3) obtains visual-related impulses from the *retina* (G^5).

Interposed between the medial and lateral nuclear groups, within the internal medullary lamina, are thin plates of *intralaminar nuclei* (H^1). These nuclei represent a part of the reticular formation. They receive afferents from the *basal ganglia* (H^3), the *midbrain* (H^4), *motor areas 4 and 6 of the frontal lobe* (H^5), and the *prefrontal cortex* (H^6). This heterogeneous input is essential to intralaminar control of levels of cerebral cortical activity and fine tuning of conscious states.

THALAMUS: AFFERENT PROJECTIONS.

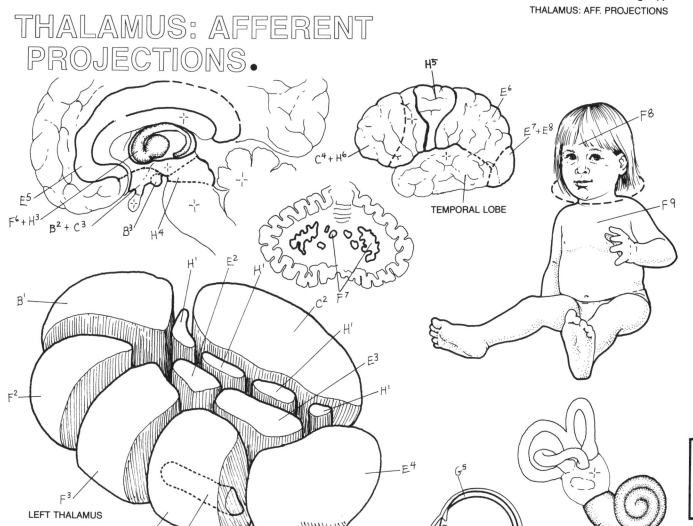

TEMPORAL LOBE

LEFT THALAMUS

TARGET NUCLEI AND
SOURCES OF AFF.
PROJECTIONS★
ANTERIOR NUC.$_{B^1}$
HYPOTHAL.$_{B^2}$/MAMM. BODY$_{B^3}$
DORSOMEDIAL NUC.$_{C^2}$
HYPOTHAL.$_{C^3}$/PREFRNT.
CORTEX$_{C^4}$
LAT. DORSAL NUC.$_{E^2}$
CINGUL. G.$_{E^5}$/PAR. CORTEX.$_{E^6}$
LAT. POSTERIOR NUC.$_{E^3}$
OCCIPITAL CORTEX$_{E^7}$
PULVINAR$_{E^4}$
OCCIPITAL CORTEX$_{E^8}$
VENT. ANTERIOR NUC.$_{F^2}$

BASAL GANGLIA$_{F^6}$
VENT. LATERAL NUC.$_{F^3}$
CEREBELLAR NUCLEI$_{F^7}$
VENT. POST. MED. NUC.$_{F^4}$
FACE/ORAL, NASAL CAV.$_{F^8}$
VENT. POST. LAT. NUC.$_{F^5}$
EXTREMITIES/TRUNK$_{F^9}$
MED. GENICULATE BODY$_{G^2}$
INNER EAR$_{G^4}$
LAT. GENICULATE BODY$_{G^3}$
RETINA$_{G^5}$
INTRALAMINAR NUC.$_{H^1}$
BASAL GANG.$_{H^3}$/MIDBRAIN$_{H^4}$
FRONT. CORTEX 4, 6$_{H^5}$
PREFRONTAL CORTEX$_{H^6}$

The thalamus is the great portal to the cerebral cortex in that almost all of the major projections from the thalamic nuclei are directed to the cortex. As you color these connections, note that it is possible to develop a veritable thalamocortical map in which almost every area of the cortex has a corresponding thalamic source nucleus.

Color the heading Source Nuclei and Target Areas, the titles of each thalamic nucleus, the corresponding target(s) for its efferent fibers, and the respective representations of the nuclei and their targets. In cases where a target area receives more than one efferent, blend or pattern the colors used for the two titles on the related structure. In Association Areas (H^4), use a constant color throughout, and crosshatch over it with the second color where required.

The most important projection of the *anterior nucleus* (B^1) goes to the *cingulate gyrus* (B^4) on the medial aspect of the hemisphere, providing another link in the hypothalamic-limbic circuit (Plates 5-22 and 5-26).

The *dorsomedial nucleus* (C^2) sends its largest fiber projections to the *prefrontal cortex* (C^5). In the now seldom-used procedure known as prefrontal lobotomy, various proportions of these fibers were severed. The profound personality changes (such as disregard for personal care) that frequently followed provide some clues to the significance of the projection in human behavior.

The efferents of the *lateral dorsal nucleus* (E^2) reach primarily the *cingulate gyrus* (E^9) and the overlying parts of the parietal lobe. Fibers from the *lateral posterior nucleus* (E^3) are directed to the *association areas* (areas 5 and 7) of the *parietal cortex* (E^{10}). Cortical association areas combine information received by cortical sensory areas to produce more complex levels of integration.

The *pulvinar* (E^4) projects its efferents widely upon the *visual areas* (E^{11}; areas 17, 18, and 19) of the occipital cortex as well as *adjacent areas* (E^{12}) of the temporal and parietal cortices.

The *ventral anterior nucleus* (F^2) projects many of its fibers to the *premotor area* (F^{10}; area 6) of the frontal cortex. The *ventral lateral nucleus* (F^3) sends many of its efferent fibers to a strip of the frontal cortex called the *motor area* (F^{11}; area 4). Between them, these two nuclei ensure that cortical motor mechanisms are continuously updated by inputs from the cerebellum and basal ganglia.

Both *ventral posterior medial* (F^4) and *ventral posterior lateral* (F^5) *nuclei* project fibers to a strip of parietal cortex known as the *primary somesthetic receptive area* (F^{12} and F^{13}; areas 3, 1, and 2). The parts of the body are represented quite precisely along this strip in the form of a sensory homunculus (not shown). The ventral posterior medial nucleus projects its efferents (facial sensations) to the lower part of this somesthetic strip, while the ventral posterior lateral nucleus projects its fibers (trunk and extremities) much more broadly along this cortical area.

The *medial geniculate body* (G^2) projects almost all of its axons to the *primary auditory area* (G^6; areas 41 and 42) of the superior surface of the temporal lobe and to a narrow band of association cortex surrounding it.

The *lateral geniculate body* (G^3) projects most of its efferents to the *primary visual area* (G^7; area 17), with much less intensive projections to the adjacent visual association areas (18 and 19). In some ways, the pulvinar and the lateral geniculate projections can be thought of as parallel systems, even though the former receives no direct input from the optic tract. The significance of this "parallel system" is not yet known.

The *intralaminar nuclei* (H^1) send fibers to the *basal ganglia* (H^3) and, via collaterals, widely upon the *association areas* (H^4) of the cerebral cortex.

THALAMUS: EFFERENT PROJECTIONS.

SOURCE NUCLEI AND
TARGET AREAS.★
ANTERIOR NUC.$_{B^1}$
CINGULATE GYRUS$_{B^4}$
DORSOMEDIAL NUC.$_{C^2}$
PREFRONT. CORTEX$_{C^5}$
LAT. DORS. NUC.$_{E^2}$
CINGULATE GYRUS$_{E^9}$
LAT. POST. NUC.$_{E^3}$
PAR. ASSOC. AREAS$_{E^{10}}$
PULVINAR$_{E^4}$
VISUAL AREA$_{E^{11}}$
ADJACENT AREA$_{E^{12}}$
VENT. ANT. NUC.$_{F^2}$
PREMOTOR AREA$_{F^{10}}$

VENT. LAT. NUC.$_{F^3}$
MOTOR AREA$_{F^{11}}$
VENT. POST. MED. NUC.$_{F^4}$
PRI. SOMESTH. AREA$_{F^{12}}$
VENT. POST. LAT. NUC.$_{F^5}$
PRI. SOMESTH. AREA$_{F^{13}}$
MED. GENICULATE BODY$_{G^2}$
PRI. AUDITORY AREA$_{G^6}$
LAT. GENICULATE BODY$_{G^3}$
PRI. VISUAL AREA$_{G^7}$
INTRALAMINAR NUC.$_{H^1}$
BASAL GANGLIA$_{H^3}$
ASSOC. AREA$_{H^4}$

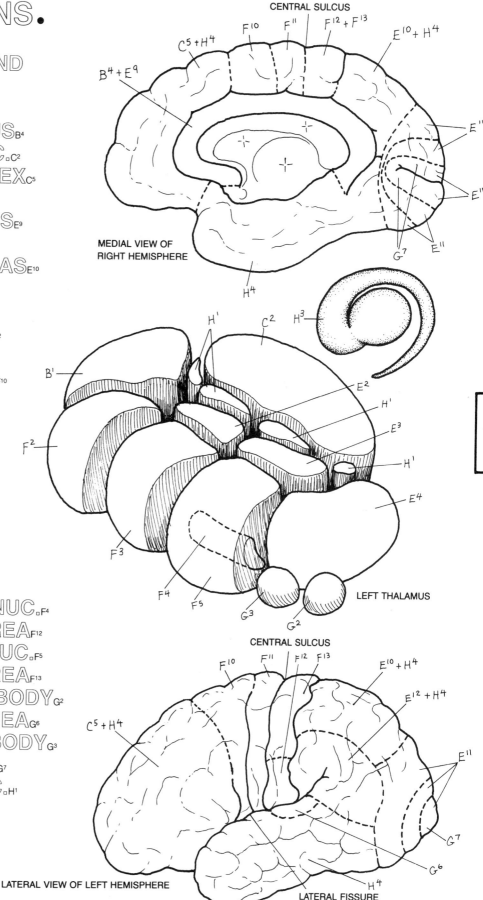

MEDIAL VIEW OF
RIGHT HEMISPHERE

LEFT THALAMUS

LATERAL VIEW OF LEFT HEMISPHERE

Significant masses of reticular-like cells are found in the internal medullary lamina of each thalamus. Starting out in the medial thalamus near the third ventricle (see inset drawing at the upper right), the lamina continues dorsally and laterally to form a thin extension, which curves upward and outward. The cells within constitute a system known as the thalamic intralaminar system or thalamic "nonspecific" system. The latter name is derived from the fact that the axons of these cells are not limited to specific sensory areas but are spread more diffusely over the cerebral cortex. The other thalamic neurons are termed "specific" because of their known cortical connections.

Color titles A through C and the related nuclei in the upper illustration.

The most prominent components of the intralaminar system are the *centromedian,* or Cm (A^1), and *parafascicular* (A^2; abbreviated Pf) nuclei located just rostral to the mesodiencephalic junction. The name of the first reflects the central and medial position of the nucleus in the thalamus; the name of the second (*para-,* "alongside"; *fasciculus,* "bundle") relates to its proximity to the habenulointerpeduncular tract (not shown). Rostral to the Cm-Pf complex, within the extension of the lamina, are small groups of central nuclei, *paracentral* (A^4), *central lateral* (A^5), and *central medial* (A^6). More medial, along the walls of the third ventricle, are small aggregates of neurons making up the *midline nuclei* (B).

A thin plate of reticular-like cells closely invests the sides and front of the thalamus. This capping layer constitutes the *nucleus reticularis thalami* (C; here the Latin form is used to differentiate these neurons from the intralaminar reticular cells). Through this nucleus pass most of the thalamocortical and corticothalamic fibers.

Color titles D through E^4 and the related arrows representing the direction of fiber projection in the middle illustration. Color the other structures of the middle diagram as well.

The importance of the intralaminar system is indicated by the remarkable convergence of heterogeneous fiber systems upon the Cm-Pf complex and more rostral intralaminar nuclei.

Afferent fibers originate from the *motor areas* (D^1) and *prefrontal lobe* (D^2) of the cerebral cortex, *globus pallidus* (D^3) of the basal ganglia, *substantia nigra* (D^4),

vestibular (D^5) and *reticular nuclei* (D^6) of the brain stem, the *spinothalamic tract* (D^7), the *nucleus reticularis thalami* (D^8), and the *hippocampus* (D^9) via the fornix.

Efferent fibers from the Cm-Pf complex (E) pass to the *putamen* (E^1) and *caudate nucleus* (E^2) of the basal ganglia, the *association cortices* (E^3) of the cerebral cortex, and the *nucleus reticularis thalami* (E^4). The reticularis neurons apparently occupy a special relationship to thalamocortical interactions.

Color the heading Nucleus Reticularis Thalami Gate Hypothesis, titles C^1 through H^3, and the related structures and signs in the lower diagram. Color C and D^1 in the lower diagram as well.

The nucleus reticularis (C) lies across many lines of transmission that pass between cortex and thalamus. *Axons* (F) en route to the cortex from the midbrain tegmentum (not shown) send *collaterals* (F^1) to the *reticularis neuron* (C^1) and have an *inhibitory* (F^2) effect on its impulse transmission. The *axons* (G^1 and H^1) of *corticothalamic* (G) and *thalamocortical neurons* (H) also provide *collaterals* (G^2 and H^2) for synapse with reticular cells, exerting a *facilitatory* (G^3, H^3) effect. Note that the *axon* (G^1) of the corticothalamic neuron terminates on the thalamocortical cell, having a *facilitatory* (G^4) effect. The *axons* (C^2) of the GABA (neurotransmitter)-rich reticularis cells project back on the specific thalamic neurons, continuously modulating (by *inhibition,* C^3) the ascending flow of thalamocortical impulses.

The circuit just described has been compared to an ensemble of tiny "gates" that control access to various kinds of information to the cortex. In the case shown, the "gate" seems to be closed by a volley ascending in a thalamocortical axon from a specific thalamic nucleus, the collateral of which facilitates the firing of the inhibitory reticularis neuron. In turn, the reticularis neuron casts an inhibitory influence on the continued firing of the specific thalamocortical neuron. The "gate" may be opened by inhibitory influences brought to the reticularis neuron by the midbrain tegmental tract. It is possible that the maintenance of selective or focused attention relates to this mechanism.

Among the range of functions suggested for the thalamic nonspecific nuclei are: (1) pacemaker for electrical rhythm of the cerebral cortex, (2) fine tuning of levels of alertness, and (3) modulation of sensory and motor activities.

THALAMUS: NONSPECIFIC NEURONAL SYSTEMS.

INTRALAMINAR NUCLEI$_{A(\ )}$
  CENTROMEDIAN$_{A1}$
  PARAFASCICULAR$_{A2}$
  CENTRAL$_{A3(\ )}$
    PARA.$_{A4}$/LAT.$_{A5}$/MED.$_{A6}$
MIDLINE NUCLEI$_B$
NUC. RETICULARIS THAL.$_C$
AFFERENTS TO
  INTRALAMINAR NUC.$_{D(\ )}$
  MOTOR CORTEX$_{D1}$
  PREFRONTAL CORTEX$_{D2}$
  GLOBUS PALLIDUS$_{D3}$
  SUBSTANTIA NIGRA$_{D4}$
  VESTIBULAR NUC.$_{D5}$
  RETICULAR FORM.$_{D6}$
  SPINOTHALAMIC TR.$_{D7}$
  NUC. RETIC. THAL.$_{D8}$
  HIPPOCAMPUS$_{D9}$
EFFERENTS FROM
  INTRALAMINAR NUC.$_E$
  PUTAMEN$_{E1}$
  CAUDATE NUC.$_{E2}$
  ASSOCIATION CORTEX$_{E3}$
  NUC. RETIC. THAL.$_{E4}$

NUC. RETIC. THAL. GATE
  HYPOTHESIS ★
RETICULARIS NEURON$_{C1}$/
AXON$_{C2}$/INHIB. (−)$_{C3}$
MIDBRAIN TEG. AXON$_F$/
COLL.$_{F1}$/INHIB. (−)$_{F2}$
CORTICOTHAL. NEUR.$_G$/
AXON$_{G1}$/COLL.$_{G2}$/
FACIL. (+)$_{G3}$/FACIL. (+)$_{G4}$
THALAMOCORT. NEUR.$_H$/
AXON$_{H1}$/COLL.$_{H2}$/
FACIL.(+)$_{H3}$

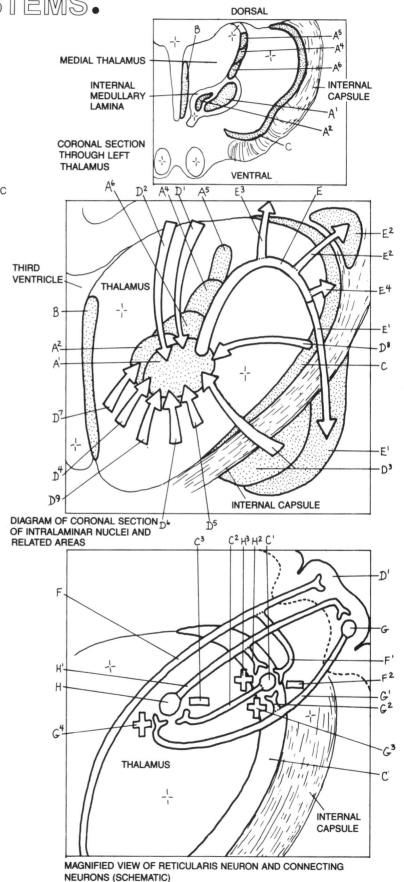

DORSAL

MEDIAL THALAMUS

INTERNAL
MEDULLARY
LAMINA

INTERNAL
CAPSULE

CORONAL SECTION
THROUGH LEFT
THALAMUS

VENTRAL

THIRD
VENTRICLE

THALAMUS

INTERNAL CAPSULE

DIAGRAM OF CORONAL SECTION
OF INTRALAMINAR NUCLEI AND
RELATED AREAS

THALAMUS

INTERNAL
CAPSULE

MAGNIFIED VIEW OF RETICULARIS NEURON AND CONNECTING
NEURONS (SCHEMATIC)

The hypothalamus is without peer in its authority over body adjustments to our external and internal environments. This region, located just under the thalamus (*hypo-,* "under"), weighing 4 grams and taking up about 0.5 percent of the volume of the entire brain, regulates body temperature, hunger, thirst, sexual activity, goal-seeking behavior, endocrine functions, affective (emotional) behavior, and the activity of the visceral nervous system.

Color the heading Landmarks, titles A through I, and the related structures in both illustrations. Save four contrasting light colors for J through M.

The hypothalamus makes up the base of the diencephalon (see Plate 5-37). It extends from the *lamina terminalis* (A) anteriorly to the *midbrain tegmentum* (B) posteriorly. On its medial surface, the wall of the third ventricle (not shown; see Plate 5-37), the hypothalamus is demarcated from the overlying *thalamus* (C) by the hypothalamic sulcus (recall Plate 3-8). Laterally it is bordered by the subthalamus and the internal capsule (not visible in this median section, but see Plate 5-38). Along its inferior border are found, from anterior to posterior, the *optic chiasm* (D), the *pituitary gland* (E; also called *hypophysis*) and its supporting *stalk* (E¹), and the *tuber cinereum* (H). The stalk of the pituitary gland is attached by way of a funnel-like base (*infundibulum,* F) to the highly vascularized floor (*median eminence,* G) of the hypothalamus. The *fornix* (I) is an excellent landmark (see ahead).

Color the heading Regions and Nuclei, titles J through M², and the regions of hypothalamic nuclei in the upper illustration. Then color the individual nuclei in the lower illustration.

The hypothalamus consists of nuclear masses that can be separated into five regions (one of which, the *lateral,* is not shown). The *preoptic region* (J) is tucked behind the lamina terminalis in the periventricular gray matter surrounding the third ventricle. The neurons of the *preoptic nuclei* (J¹) produce gonadotropin-releasing hormones, which stimulate the secretion of gonadotrophic (gonad-stimulating) hormones from the anterior pituitary gland. Within the preoptic region is the sexually dimorphic nucleus (not shown; *di-,* "two"; *morph,* "structure"). Its

function is unknown; it is known to be larger in males and is dependent on the male sex hormone (testosterone) for its development.

The *supraoptic region* (K) incorporates four nuclei. The *supraoptic nucleus* (K¹), dorsal to the optic chiasm, and the *paraventricular nucleus* (K²), located even more dorsally in the walls of the third ventricle, contain secretory neurons that produce vasopressin (antidiuretic hormone) and oxytocin (uterine muscle stimulant). These hormones are transported by axons into the posterior lobe of the pituitary gland and stored in those axons until released into the local capillaries.

A third component of the supraoptic region is the *anterior hypothalamic nucleus* (K³), which, when stimulated, produces parasympathetic (see Plate 8-2) responses such as reduced heart rate and enhanced secretomotor activity of the gastrointestinal tract. Another group of cells in the supraoptic region is the small *suprachiasmatic nucleus* (K⁴), which lies over the optic chiasm rostral to the supraoptic nucleus. Damage to this vasopressin-rich nucleus alters the light-stimulated circadean rhythm ("biological clock").

The *tuberal region* (L), characterized by the ventral tuber cinereum, is divided into a medial and lateral division (not shown) by the fornix en route to the more posterior mammillary bodies. Three pairs of nuclei are shown in the walls of the ventricles in the tuberal region. The *ventromedial nucleus* (L¹) is concerned with control of the balance between hunger and satiety. The *dorsomedial nucleus* (L²), along with the ventromedial nucleus, is involved in emotional behavior; stimulation of the former and destruction of the latter brings about a rage response in the cat. The *arcuate nucleus* (L³) of the tuberal region contributes neurosecretory fibers to the vascular portal system of the anterior pituitary (next plate).

The *mammillary region* (M) includes the *mammillary bodies* (M¹) and the *posterior hypothalamic nuclei* (M²). Each mammillary body consists of medial and lateral (not shown) cell groups, which integrate information coming from the limbic system via the fornix and from the midbrain tegmentum. The posterior nuclei, when stimulated, produce sympathetic responses (see Plate 8-4), such as increased heart rate and inhibition of secretomotor activity in the gastrointestinal tract. Contrary to previous concepts, the posterior hypothalamus is not now thought to influence temperature regulation.

HYPOTHALAMUS: NUCLEAR ORGANIZATION. ●

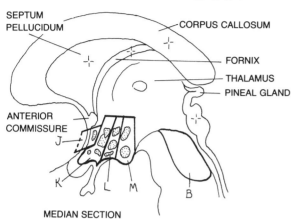

SEPTUM
PELLUCIDUM

CORPUS CALLOSUM

FORNIX

THALAMUS

PINEAL GLAND

ANTERIOR
COMMISSURE

J

K   L   M   B

MEDIAN SECTION

LANDMARKS ★
LAMINA TERMINALIS$_A$
MIDBRAIN TEGMENTUM$_B$
THALAMUS$_C$
OPTIC CHIASM$_D$
PITUITARY GLAND$_E$/STALK$_{E^1}$
INFUNDIBULUM$_F$
MEDIAN EMINENCE$_G$
TUBER CINEREUM$_H$
FORNIX$_I$

REGIONS AND NUCLEI ★
PREOPTIC$_J$
　PREOPTIC$_{J^1}$
SUPRAOPTIC$_K$
　SUPRAOPTIC$_{K^1}$
　PARAVENTRIC.$_{K^2}$
　ANT. HYPOTHAL.$_{K^3}$
　SUPRACHIASMATIC$_{K^4}$
TUBERAL$_L$
　VENTROMEDIAL$_{L^1}$
　DORSOMEDIAL$_{L^2}$
　ARCUATE$_{L^3}$
MAMMILLARY$_M$
　MAMMILLARY BODY$_{M^1}$
　POST. HYPOTHAL.$_{M^2}$
LATERAL$_{N.S.}$

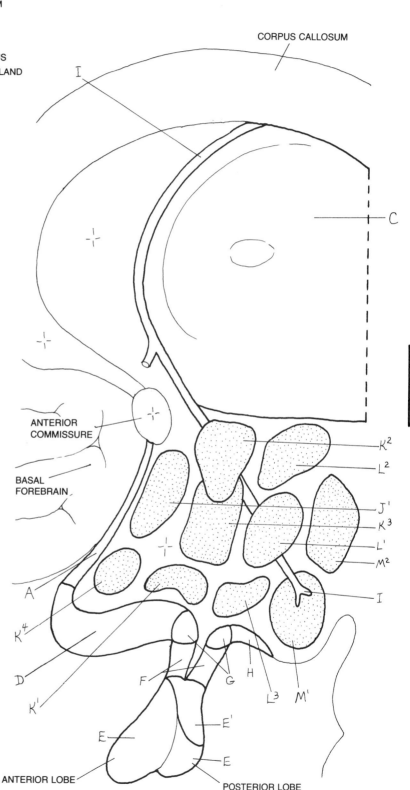

CORPUS CALLOSUM

I

C

K^2

L^2

ANTERIOR
COMMISSURE

J^1

K^3

BASAL
FOREBRAIN

L^1

M^2

A

I

K^4

D

K^1

F   G   H

L^3 M^1

E'

E

E

ANTERIOR LOBE

POSTERIOR LOBE

The hypothalamus receives several well-defined afferent pathways and more diffusely arranged fibers from the forebrain and limbic system, the upper brain stem and thalamus, and the visual pathways. Many of the afferent fibers are part of a two-way system projecting between the midbrain and the limbic lobe and related areas. This two-way path, called the septo-hypothalamo-midbrain continuum by Nauta (1972), is seen as at least part of the neural mechanism for the expression of emotions. The evidence linking precise roles in emotional behavior to specific nuclei or cell-fiber complexes is, however, incomplete.

Color the heading Tracts and Connections, titles A through B[11], and related tracts and nuclei in the upper illustration. Note that the septal nuclei representation receives two colors.

The *medial forebrain bundle* (A) is a significant part of the septo-hypothalamo-midbrain system. The medial forebrain bundle originates in the olfactory portions of the basal forebrain area and in the *septal nuclei* (A[1]), a diffuse group of cells (see Plate 5-26) rostral to the lamina terminalis. The median forebrain bundle runs through the hypothalamus, giving off fibers to the *lateral hypothalamic nuclei* (A[2]), en route to the *midbrain tegmentum* (A[3]). The olfactory-derived hypothalamic afferents are probably related to basic emotional drives associated with olfaction. The septal nuclei–derived fibers represent an important limbic input to the hypothalamus. Fibers continuing to the midbrain are believed to influence somatic motor as well as visceral centers in the brain stem. Considering the role of the hypothalamus in regulation of visceral functions, it would appear that the hypothalamus mediates visceral reactions (as in fear or compulsive eating) via both visceral and somatic motor centers in response to limbic, emotion-related input. In this same context, it is worth noting that some fibers from the locus ceruleus (not shown; recall Plate 5-8) in the upper pons occupy the medial forebrain bundle, delivering the neurotransmitter norepinephrine into hypothalamic nuclei.

The hippocampal-hypothalamic tract was first proposed by Papez (1937) as part of a major circuit connecting hippocampus, hypothalamus, thalamus, and cingulate gyrus, providing an anatomical basis for experiencing emotions. The progressive expansion of the Papez circuit into the concept of the limbic lobe (Plate 5-26) brings with it suggestions of subtle interactions of emotions, memory processing, and motivation. Fibers from the *hippocampus*

(B[1]; a limbic structure of the temporal lobe) form the *fimbria* (B[2]), which continues dorsally as the *fornix* (B[3]; "arch"). Arching over the thalamus, it sends off *collaterals* (B[4]) to the *anterior nucleus of the thalamus* (B[5]) and turns ventrally as the *column of the fornix* (B[6]). As the column approaches the anterior commissure, its fibers bifurcate into *precommissural fibers* (B[7]; in front of or rostral to the commissure) and *postcommissural fibers* (B[8]) posterior to the commissure. The precommissural fibers terminate in the *septal nuclei* (B[9]); the postcommissural fibers reach the *mammillary bodies* (B[10]). A few fibers from the hippocampus reach the septal nuclei via the *supracallosal gyrus* (B[11]; also called *induseum griseum,* "enveloping gray"). These fibers follow the dorsal surface of the corpus callosum and project to the septal area.

Color titles and structures C through D[1], as well as structure A, in the lower illustration.

The amygdalo-hypothalamic tract forms another link between the limbic system and the hypothalamus. Fibers leaving the *amygdaloid nucleus* (C[1]) form the *stria terminalis* (C[2]), which arches over the thalamus, lateral to the fornix. Its principal termination is the *nuclei of the stria terminalis* (C[3]), immediately dorsal to the anterior commissure. Collaterals of the stria terminate in the *preoptic area* (C[4]), *tuberal nuclei* (C[5]), and anterior hypothalamic nucleus (not shown). Some fibers merge with the medial forebrain bundle. Stimulated electrically, the stria terminalis brings on a defense reaction in experimental animals (arching of the back, erect hair, etc.). The multiple nuclei of the amygdala are believed to play a key role in the formation and processing of emotional content, and their connections with the hypothalamus provide yet another input to what seems to be the grand mediator of emotional expression.

The *retino-hypothalamic tract* (D), which indirectly affects the pineal gland, is concerned with light influences on the circadian rhythm. The fibers of this tract arise in the ganglion cells of the retina (not shown; see Plate 6-6) and project to the *suprachiasmatic nucleus* (D[1]) as collaterals of the optic tract.

Recently, direct neocortical input to the hypothalamus, in the form of fine corticohypothalamic fibers, has been reported. These fibers have been shown to originate from the posterior part of the orbital gyrus of the frontal lobe. The functional significance of these fibers is not yet clear.

HYPOTHALAMUS: AFFERENT PROJECTIONS.

TRACTS AND
 CONNECTIONS.★
MEDIAL FOREBRAIN
 BUNDLE A
 SEPTAL NUCLEI A1
 LAT. HYPOTHAL. NUC. A2
 MIDBRAIN TEGMENT. A3

HIPPOCAMP.-
 HYPOTHAL. TR. B( )
 HIPPOCAMPUS B1
  FIMBRIA B2
 FORNIX B3
  COLLATERAL B4
 ANT. NUC. THALAMUS B5
 COLUMN OF FORNIX B6
  PRECOMM. FIBER B7
  POSTCOMM. FIBER B8
 SEPTAL NUCLEI B9
 MAMMILLARY BODY B10
 SUPRACALLOSAL G. B11

AMYGDALO-
 HYPOTHAL. TR. C( )
 AMYGDALOID NUC. C1
 STRIA TERMINALIS C2
 NUC. STRIA TERM. C3
 PREOPTIC AREA C4
 TUBERAL NUCLEI C5

RETINO-
 HYPOTHALAMIC TR. D
 SUPRACHIASMATIC NUC. D1

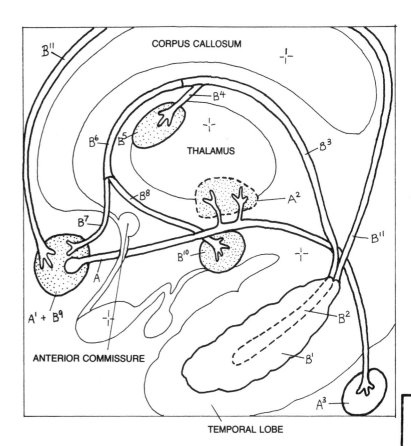

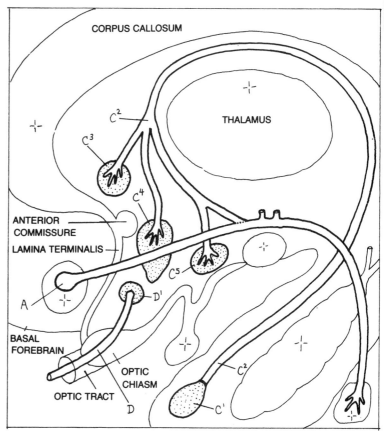

The hypothalamus sends efferents to many regions including the forebrain, the pituitary gland, the midbrain, the hindbrain, and the spinal cord. Major efferent paths shown here include the median forebrain bundle, the hypothalamic-hypophyseal tract, and the mammillothalamic and mammillotegmental tracts. In fact, many efferent fibers follow in opposite directions the paths of the afferent fibers seen in the preceding plate. If you have not already done so, consider briefly scanning Plate 5-26 (introduction to the limbic system) before coloring this plate.

Color the heading Tracts and Connections, titles A through B^3, and the related pathways and connecting points in both illustrations, as applicable.

The *medial forebrain bundle* (A) and its role in the septal-hypothalamic-midbrain axis have been discussed in Plate 5-21. *Fibers* (A^2) from the *lateral hypothalamic nuclei* (A^1) travel via this bundle to the *septal nuclei* (A^3), probably integrating visceral with olfactory functions. Fibers from the lateral hypothalamic nuclei also project to the *midbrain tegmentum* (A^4) via the medial forebrain bundle.

Descending fibers from hypothalamic nuclei around the third ventricle (periventricular nuclei) contribute to the two-way dorsal longitudinal fasciculus (not shown; recall Plate 5-9) between the hypothalamus and the midbrain tegmentum. It has been conventionally held that descending impulses of hypothalamic origin probably percolate through multiple synapses within the reticular core to reach visceral and somatic motor neurons. However, hypothalamic fibers have been found in the lower brain stem and spinal cord, supporting speculation that the hypothalamus may influence the activity of these motor cells directly.

The *hypothalamic-hypophyseal tract* (B; also called *supraopticohypophyseal tract*) originates in both *supraoptic* (B^1) and *paraventricular nuclei* (B^2) and projects to the *posterior lobe of the pituitary gland* (B^3). These axons transport vasopressin and oxytocin to the posterior lobe for release directly into capillaries (E^2; see ahead).

Color titles and related structures C through D^2. Note that the midbrain tegmentum (A^4 and C^3) requires two colors, one of which can be patterned over the other.

The *principal mammillary fasciculus* (C) is a well-defined bundle of fibers that extends dorsally from the nuclei of the *mammillary body* (C^1) a short distance before dividing into the *mammillotegmental* (C^2) and *mammillothalamic tracts* (C^4). The mammillotegmental tract curves caudally toward the *midbrain tegmentum* (C^3), providing another descending pathway for hypothalamic output. The mammillothalamic tract ascends through the hypothalamus to synapse in the *anterior nucleus of the thalamus* (C^5). *Axons* (C^6) from the anterior thalamic nucleus project to the *cingulate gyrus* (C^7). The mammillothalamic-cingulate pathway represents a portion of the Papez (hippocampal-hypothalamic-thalamic-cingulate-hippocampal) circuit, which is now believed to be involved in memory processing (recall Plate 5-21).

The *stria terminalis* (D) carries fibers from the *ventromedial hypothalamic nucleus* (D^1) to the *amygdaloid nucleus* (D^2) and reciprocal fibers as well (see Plate 5-21).

After coloring these pathways, you can begin to appreciate the dense interconnections between the hypothalamus and the limbic system and why it is so difficult to separate the activities belonging to one from those belonging to the other.

The impact of the hypothalamus in involuntary behavior can be exemplified in the actions of its fibers, which descend through the brain stem reticular formation to terminate on visceral motor neurons. Normal hypothalamic output tunes the production of gastric acid to the food load presented for digestion. In the case of the person under severe continued stress (e.g., the worried business executive), long-term hypothalamic overdischarge may cause stomach cramping, oversecretion of acid, and the eventual development of an ulcer.

Color titles and structures E through E^3.

The *tuberoinfundibular tract* (E) arises primarily from the *arcuate nucleus* (E^1) and terminates near the *hypophyseal portal system* (E^2), a plexus of small blood vessels between the hypothalamus and the *anterior lobe of the pituitary* (E^3). Neurosecretions (releasing hormones) from the axons of this tract diffuse into the vessels of the portal system to enter the pituitary and stimulate the release of the anterior lobe hormones.

HYPOTHALAMUS: EFFERENT PROJECTIONS.

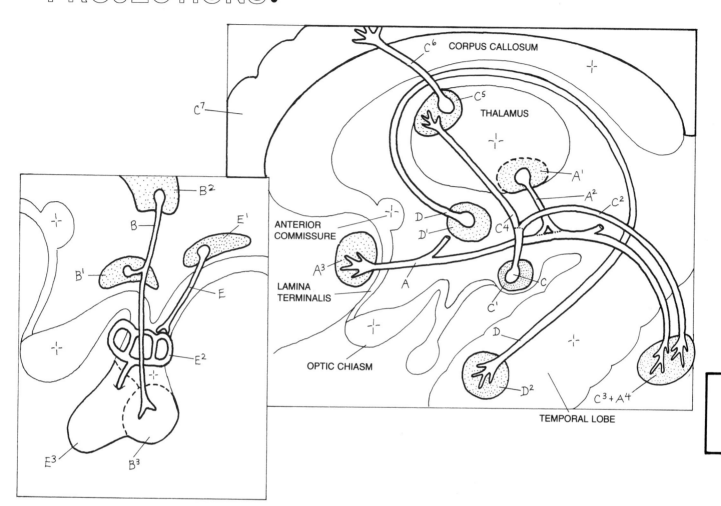

TRACTS AND CONNECTIONS. ★

MED. FOREBRAIN BUNDLE A
  LAT. HYPOTHAL. NUC. A1 /
    AXON A2
  SEPTAL NUC. A3
  MIDBRAIN TEGMENT. A4
HYPOTHAL.-HYPOPH. TR. B
  SUPRAOPTIC NUC. B1
  PARAVENTRIC. NUC. B2
  POST. PITUITARY B3
PRINC. MAMMILL. FASC. C
  MAMMILLARY BODY C1
  MAMMILLOTEG. TR. C2

MIDBRAIN TEGMENT. C3
MAMMILLOTHAL. TR. C4
ANT. NUC. THAL. C5
  AXON C6
CINGULATE G. C7
STRIA TERMINALIS D
VENTROMED. HYPOTHAL.
  NUC. D1
AMYGDALOID NUC. D2
TUBEROINFUNDIB. TR. E
ARCUATE NUC. E1
HYPOPH. PORT. SYS. E2
ANT. PITUITARY E3

The epithalamus (*epi-*, "upon") lies, in part, over the dorsal aspect of the thalamus and consists of the medial and lateral habenular nuclei, the pineal gland and stalk, and the stria medullaris.

Color the heading Epithalamus, titles A through B¹ and D, and related structures in the upper illustration.

The *medial habenular nucleus* (A) is situated anterior (rostral) to the pineal gland in the posterolateral wall of the third ventricle. The *lateral habenular nucleus* (A¹) is lateral and posterior to the medial nucleus on either side of the *habenular commissure* (A²; see Plate 5-47). Axons of the lateral habenular nucleus cross via this commissure to the contralateral nucleus. The role of the habenula will be considered with its related pathways (see ahead).

The *pineal gland* (B) is a small (7 mm by 5 mm) neuro-endocrine organ attached by a *stalk* (B¹) to the posterior, dorsal aspect of the diencephalon. The third ventricle extends into this stalk, creating a pineal recess. In the dorsal arm of the stalk are the fibers of the habenular commissure; the *posterior commissure* (D) is found in the ventral (inferior) arm. The posterior commissure marks the dorsal part of the midbrain-diencephalon junction, carries fibers from one hemisphere to the next, and is associated with the oculomotor and other nuclei concerned with visual tracking movements.

The pineal has a variety of functions. It synthesizes melatonin, a pigment-enhancing hormone, from serotonin. Fluctuations in melatonin synthesis follow the diurnal (daylight) cycle. Pineal extracts containing melatonin have an inhibitory effect on the gonads, delaying the onset of puberty. Calcium and magnesium salts begin to accumulate in the pineal after puberty. These sometimes provide useful landmarks in establishing the position of the pineal in X-ray studies.

The *stria medullaris* (C) is a tract running on the dorsal-medial border of the thalamus. Its constitution is considered with pathways.

Color the heading Pathways and Related Nuclei, titles C through E⁴, and the related structures in the upper illustration.

The habenular nuclei (habenula) receive afferents via the stria medullaris. Some of these afferents arise from the *dorsal septal area* (C¹; discussed fully in Plate 5-26), which projects *axons* (C²) to the medial habenular nucleus. Some *axons* (C⁴) springing from the *preoptic area* (C³) of the hypothalamus project to the lateral habenular nucleus. The *globus pallidus* (C⁵) of the basal ganglion also projects *axons* (C⁶) to the lateral habenular nucleus.

The habenular nuclei disburse efferents by way of the *habenulo-interpeduncular tract* (E) in the following manner: From the lateral habenular nucleus, *axons* (E¹) pass to the *interpeduncular nucleus* (E²) between the cerebral peduncles or crura cerebri and to the basal ganglia (not shown); from the medial habenular nucleus, *axons* (E³) pass to the *raphe nucleus* (E⁴) of the pontine reticular formation. In addition, olfactory-related information (not shown) may pass from the dorsal septal area via the stria medullaris.

The habenula serves as an important link among the basal ganglia (globus pallidus), the limbic system (septal nuclei), the hypothalamus (preoptic nuclei), and the midbrain (raphe and interpeduncular nuclei).

Color the heading Subthalamus, titles F through K, and the related structures in the lower illustration of the right side of a coronal section through the thalamus (upper part) and a cross section through the midbrain (lower part).

The subthalamus consists of the *subthalamic nuclei* (F), *zona incerta* (G), and the *field of Forel II* (H; a cell-fiber mass containing pallidothalamic fibers; see Plate 5-25). This region lies ventral to the thalamus and medial to the internal capsule (see Plate 5-38). The subthalamic nuclei receive *afferents* (I¹, J¹) from *cortical area 4* (I; motor cortex) and the *globus pallidus* (J) and sends *efferents* (F¹ and F²) across the internal capsule to the globus pallidus and the more caudal *substantia nigra* (K). The subthalamic nuclei are concerned with motor control; disturbances in these nuclei bring on violent, uncontrolled movements characterized by strong, rapid arm or leg flailings and jerking of the torso. The aberrant movements are often limited to one side of the body, giving rise to the name of the condition, *hemiballismus* (*hemi-*, "half"; *ballismus*, "throwing or jumping").

EPITHALAMUS AND SUBTHALAMUS.

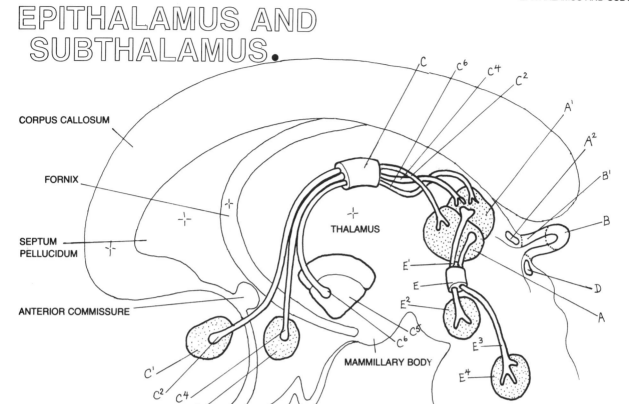

CORPUS CALLOSUM

FORNIX

SEPTUM PELLUCIDUM

ANTERIOR COMMISSURE

THALAMUS

MAMMILLARY BODY

BRAIN STEM

EPITHALAMUS ★
MED. HABENULAR NUC. A
LAT. HABENULAR NUC. A¹
HABENULAR COMMISS. A²
PINEAL GLAND B
STALK B¹
POSTERIOR COMMISSURE D

SUBTHALAMUS ★
SUBTHALAMIC NUC. F
ZONA INCERTA G
FIELD OF FOREL II H
CORTICAL AREA 4 I/
AFFERENT I¹
GLOB. PALLIDUS J/
AFFERENT J¹
EFFERENT F¹/
GLOB. PALLIDUS J
EFFERENT F²/
SUBSTANTIA NIGRA K

PATHWAYS AND RELATED NUCLEI ★
STRIA MEDULLARIS C
DORS. SEPTAL NUC. C¹/
AXON C²
PREOPTIC AREA C³/AXON C⁴
GLOB. PALLIDUS C⁵/AXON C⁶
HABENULO-INTERPED. TR. E
AXON E¹/INTERPEDUNC. N. E²
AXON E³/RAPHE NUC. E⁴

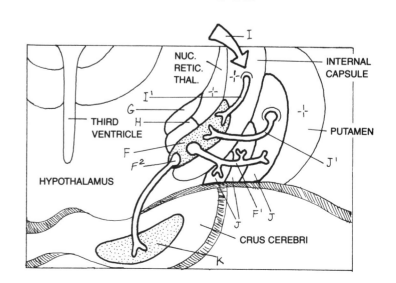

NUC. RETIC. THAL.

INTERNAL CAPSULE

THIRD VENTRICLE

PUTAMEN

HYPOTHALAMUS

CRUS CEREBRI

The basal ganglia are large, rounded masses of neural tissue that develop in the wall of the early telencephalic vesicle (recall Plate 3-9) and eventually surround and overhang the thalamus and internal capsule. Although we still know little about the roles and modes of action of the basal ganglia, it has become increasingly clear that they are responsible not only for the integration of motor activity but probably also for the programming, inception, and termination of such activity. One has only to watch a person with a typical basal ganglion affliction, such as Parkinson's disease, characterized by a masklike face, "zombielike" shuffling gait, and difficulty in starting or stopping the walking sequence, to realize how profoundly these nuclei are involved in daily life.

Color titles A through C^5 and the related components of the basal ganglia. Select shades of the same color for structures with the same subscript but different exponents. Next, color the heading Landmarks. Of the remaining titles, only F and I, with their related structures, are to be colored.

Some flexibility exists in the definition of the term *basal ganglia.* Here we will use the term to include the *archistriatum* (A), the paleostriatum, and the neostriatum. The archistriatum consists primarily of the *amygdala* (A^1; "almond"), a compact, almond-shaped and almond-sized mass of many nuclei (hence, it is also referred to as the amygdaloid nucleus, nuclei, or complex) buried near the tip of the temporal lobe. Due to its connections, the amygdala is considered with the limbic system (Plate 5-26).

The globus pallidus (*pallidus,* "pale") is the main component of the *paleostriatum* (B). Lying medial to and contiguous with the *putamen* (C^5), the globus pallidus consists of *medial* (B^2) and *lateral segments* (B^3) separated by a thin lamina of white matter.

The *neostriatum* (C) consists of the *caudate nucleus* (C^1) and putamen, together called the *corpus striatum* or simply *striatum.* Microscopically, these two structures are identical. The striatum is named after the striated appearance of fibers and cell islands that make up these nuclei. The globus pallidus contains more myelinated fibers than the adjacent striatum (putamen) and is, accordingly, lighter in color. The globus pallidus and the putamen together form a lens-shaped mass called the *lenticular* or *lentiform nucleus* (*lentil,* "lens").

The caudate nucleus is an elongated C-shaped nuclear mass (see lower drawing) consisting of a *head* (C^2), *body* (C^3), and *tail* (C^4). The caudate (*cauda,* "tail") is separated from the thalamus (D) and lentiform nucleus by the fiber mass of the internal capsule (E). The head of the caudate lies anterior to the thalamus and bulges into the *lateral ventricle* (F). The more slender body of the caudate arches over, around, and behind the thalamus; the narrowed tail extends forward in the roof of the inferior horn of the lateral ventricle (see Plate 9-11) within the temporal lobe, where it terminates against the caudal edge of the amygdala.

The *putamen* (C^5), the largest part of the striatum, makes up the outer portion of the lenticular nucleus and is separated from the more laterally situated insular cortex (G; recall Plate 3-9) by two thin sheets of myelinated fibers, the external and extreme capsules (H, J) separated from one another by a thin cell mass called the *claustrum* (I). In effect, the internal and external capsules "encapsulate" the lenticular nucleus, and the external and extreme capsules encapsulate the claustrum. The putamen is continuous with the head of the caudate rostrally (also see Plate 5-35).

The following plate considers the connections of the basal ganglia.

BASAL GANGLIA: NUCLEI.

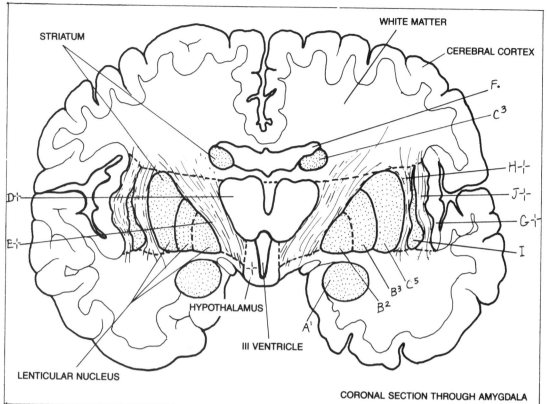

STRIATUM

WHITE MATTER

CEREBRAL CORTEX

F.

C³

H ‐|‐

J ‐|‐

G ‐|‐

I

D ‐|‐

E ‐|‐

B³ C⁵

B²

A¹

HYPOTHALAMUS

III VENTRICLE

LENTICULAR NUCLEUS

CORONAL SECTION THROUGH AMYGDALA

ARCHISTRIATUM A( )
  AMYGDALA A¹
PALEOSTRIATUM B( )
  GLOBUS PALLIDUS B¹( )
    MED. SEGMENT B²
    LAT. SEGMENT B³
NEOSTRIATUM/STRIATUM C( )
  CAUDATE NUC. C¹( )
    HEAD C²
    BODY C³
    TAIL C⁴
  PUTAMEN C⁵

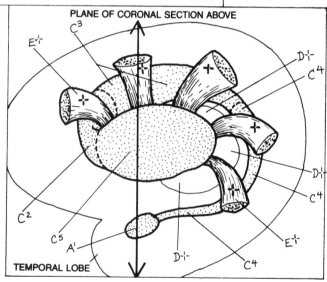

PLANE OF CORONAL SECTION ABOVE

C³

E ‐|‐

D ‐|‐

C⁴

C²

C⁵

A¹

D ‐|‐

C⁴

D ‐|‐

C⁴

E ‐|‐

TEMPORAL LOBE

LANDMARKS ★
THALAMUS D ‐|‐
INTERNAL CAPSULE E ‐|‐
LAT. VENTRICLE F●
INSULAR CORTEX G ‐|‐
EXTERNAL CAPSULE H ‐|‐
CLAUSTRUM I
EXTREME CAPSULE J ‐|‐

In considering the connections of the basal ganglia, you might think of the caudate nucleus and putamen as a great funneling system receiving fibers from virtually every portion of the cerebral cortex in precise topographic fashion and passing them on to the globus pallidus. From the latter, fibers reach for the thalamus and brain stem nuclei. By virtue of these pathways, the basal ganglia carry out their responsibility for the programming, inception, integration, and termination of motor activity.

Color the heading Nuclei, titles A through G, and related nuclei, using the same color scheme for B², B³, C¹, and C⁵ as on Plate 5-24. Color the heading Connections, titles H through K, and the related pathways. Color the heading Landmarks, titles L and M, and the ventricles. Plan dark, contrasting colors for I, K, and the two groups of fibers (H and J), and use similar or identical colors within each group.

The mass of axons (here represented by one fiber) projecting from the *cerebral cortex* (A) on to the *caudate nucleus* (C^1) and the *putamen* (C^5) constitute the *corticostriate projection* (H^1). From these nuclei, a series of short, *intrabasal ganglionar fibers* (I) project to the *medial* (B^2) and *lateral segments of the globus pallidus* (B^3); such fibers also provide communication between the pallidal medial and lateral segments and between caudate and putamen as well. The medial segment of the globus pallidus serves as a major source of efferent axons from the basal ganglia complex, with large numbers (*pallidotegmental fibers*, J^1) projecting caudally toward the *midbrain tegmentum* (D; shown on one side only). Other fibers from the medial pallidal segment project rostrally to the thalamus as pallidothalamic fibers. Specifically, fibers from the globus pallidus project to the *intralaminar* (E), *ventral lateral* (F), and *ventral anterior nuclei* (not shown) via several well-defined bundles of the pallidothalamic complex. One such bundle is the *lenticular fasciculus* (J^3) crossing the internal capsule; another is the *ansa lenticularis* (J^4; *ansa*, "loop"), which "loops" around the internal capsule. From these nuclei of the thalamus, *thalamocortical fibers* (K; intralaminar fibers not shown) project back to the cerebral cortex, especially the premotor area (area 6) of the fron-

tal lobe. In this manner, an important cortico-striato-thalamo-cortical loop is established.

A significant *thalamostriate* (H^2) connection exists between the intralaminar nuclei of the thalamus (recall Plate 5-19) and the striatum (recall Plate 5-24; only the connection to the caudate is shown). Impulses can transfer from the striatum to the globus pallidus via the intrabasal ganglionar fibers and on to the intralaminar nuclei via the pallidothalamic fibers, thereby demonstrating another significant closed loop of pathways.

The *pallidonigral* (J^5), *strionigral* (not shown), and *nigrostriatal projections* (H^3) establish extremely important two-way connections between the basal ganglia and the *substantia nigra* (G) of the midbrain. The striatum has remarkably high concentrations of a number of neurotransmitters, including acetylcholine, dopamine, serotonin, and GABA. Tracts conveying impulses from the globus pallidus and striatum to the substantia nigra contain GABA, while tracts carrying impulses from the substantia nigra to the caudate and putamen store dopamine in their terminals. This represents the most important source of dopamine in the striatum. Failure of dopamine synthesis in the substantia nigra results in progressive depletion of this critical neurotransmitter in the caudate and putamen, with a consequent development of Parkinson's disease. The characteristic signs of this crippling illness (tremor at rest, muscle rigidity, and abnormal gait) are to some extent reversible upon administration of the dopamine precursor, L-dopa.

In addition to Parkinson's disease, pathology in the basal ganglia may lead to one of a number of motor dysfunctions known as dyskinesias (uncontrolled, purposeless movements) and dystonias (abnormal changes in muscular tone). Such dysfunctions include Sydenham's chorea (the dreaded "St. Vitus dance" of medieval Europe) characterized by involuntary, abrupt, jerking movements of arms and legs, and athetosis, which is manifested by continuous writhing movements of the extremities, head, and trunk. Selective surgical destruction of parts of the globus pallidus or ventral lateral nucleus of the thalamus often have significant ameliorative effects on these motor-related diseases, perhaps by breaking into the cortico-ganglionar-thalamo-cortical loops just considered.

BASAL GANGLIA: CONNECTIONS.

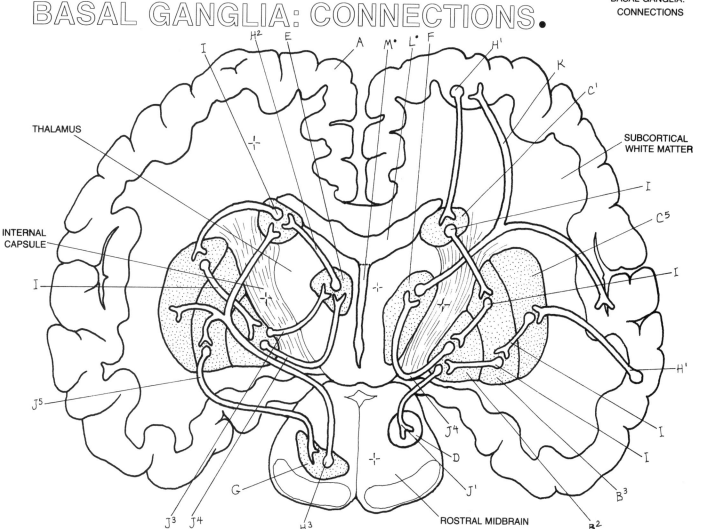

THALAMUS

INTERNAL
CAPSULE

SUBCORTICAL
WHITE MATTER

ROSTRAL MIDBRAIN

NUCLEI ★
CEREBRAL CORTEX_A
GLOB. PALL.: MED. SEG.□B²
GLOB. PALL.: LAT. SEG.□B³
CAUDATE NUC.□C¹
PUTAMEN_{C⁵}
MIDBRAIN TEGMENTUM_D
INTRALAMINAR NUC. THAL._E
VENT. LAT. NUC. THAL.□F
SUBSTANTIA NIGRA_G

THALAMOSTRIATE_{H²}
NIGROSTRIATAL_{H³}
INTRABASAL GANG. FIBER_I
EFFERENTS_{J( )}
PALLIDOTEGMENTAL_{J¹}
PALLIDOTHALAMIC_{J²( )}
LENTIC. FASC.□J³
ANSA LENTIC.□J⁴
PALLIDONIGRAL_{J⁵}
THALAMOCORTICAL_K

CONNECTIONS ★
AFFERENTS_{H( )}
    CORTICOSTRIATE_{H¹}

LANDMARKS ●
LAT. VENTRICLE_{L●}
THIRD VENTRICLE_{M●}

The limbic system, also known as the visceral or emotional brain, is concerned with behavioral and emotional expression. It appears to include within its repertoire most of those strategies necessary to the preservation of the organism, such as feeding behavior, fight, and flight, as well as those vital to the continuance of the species, such as mating, reproduction, and care of the young. In addition, it is centrally involved in memory processing and in relating the organism to its environment, both in the immediate sense and over time. The limbic system receives continuous samples of all incoming sensory information, while its output, directly or indirectly, affects all endocrine, visceral motor, and somatic motor effectors.

Color all headings, titles, and related structures in all three drawings. Note the legends explaining the orientation of each illustration.

The precise limits of this system remain arguable, but the building blocks most generally agreed on include a group of cortical (transitional archipallial and neopallial in origin; recall Plates 3-9 and 3-10) and subcortical structures on the medial and inferior surfaces of each hemisphere and several of their projections into the diencephalon.

The system gains its name (*limbus,* "border, edge") from the arc of cortical structures that surround the borders of the rostral brain stem, the interhemispheric *corpus callosum* (A), and the *anterior commissure* (B).

Beginning anteriorly, a ring of cortex reaches from below and in front of the *rostrum* (A[1]) of the corpus callosum, arcs over the corpus callosum to one side of the median plane, and terminates on the anterior part of the medial surface of the temporal lobe. This ring of cortex includes the *subcallosal* (C), *cingulate* (D), and *parahippocampal gyri* (E), seen in the upper illustration, as well as the small *paraterminal gyrus* (K) seen in the middle illustration.

Moving laterally (or deeper into the right hemisphere; see lowest illustration), one sees another partial ring of cortex (of archipallial origin) composed of the *hippocampal-dentate complex* (F) and the *supracallosal gyrus* (G). Although this constitutes a complete arc surrounding the corpus callosum in most mammals, it is reduced in human beings for the most part to a lobulated form (hippocampal-dentate) hidden deep to the medial border of the temporal lobe. The superior remnant of this arc of cortex is a vestigial, thin plate of tissue (supracallosal gyrus) lying on the superior surface of the corpus callosum beneath the overlying cingulate gyrus.

Projecting from the *fimbria* (L[1]) at the posterior aspect of the hippocampal-dentate complex (middle and lowest illustrations), the *fornix* (L) describes a tighter arc than the supracallosal gyrus, remaining under the corpus callosum, to reach the septal nuclei and hypothalamus (recall Plate 5-22). In the rostral portion of its trajectory, the fornix appears suspended in a sheet of the septum pellucidum, a thin translucent membrane that forms part of the medial boundary of the lateral ventricle. By virtue of such pathways as the fornix, areas of the hypothalamus fall within the domain of the limbic system.

Appearing more deeply in the hemisphere (lowest drawing), at the rostral tip of the temporal lobe, anterior to the hippocampal-dentate complex, are the *corticomedial* (H[1]) and *basolateral* (H[2]) *divisions* of the amygdala. They seem to control access to rage, aggression, and sexuality—the veritable Picasso of our emotional color. The principal efferent pathway from the amygdala is the *stria terminalis* (I; recall Plate 5-21; only a portion of the tract is shown).

The *septal nuclei* (J; not related to septum pellucidum) constitute the anterior linchpin of the limbic system. They are dispersed deep (internal) to the subcallosal and paraterminal gyri, anterior to the anterior commissure, and caudal to the rostrum of the corpus callosum. The subcallosal and paraterminal gyri collectively constitute the septal area, distinct from but adjacent to the septal nuclei. The septal nuclei are divided into medial and lateral components (only the medial is shown) and have significant connections with the hippocampal-dentate complex and amygdala via the *diagonal band of Broca* (M), the fornix, and the *olfactory tract* (N[1]).

The *olfactory bulb* (N) and tract are components of cranial nerve I (olfactory; see Plate 6-5) and feed into the "front end" of the limbic system via the *medial* (N[2]) and *lateral olfactory stria* (N[3]). The medial olfactory stria conducts olfactory fibers (not shown) to the septal nuclei. The lateral olfactory stria directs olfactory fibers to the amygdala and surrounding periamygdaloid (consisting of the anterior end of the parahippocampal gyrus) and prepyriform (lateral to the olfactory stria) cortex.

These anatomical connections between olfactory areas and the "visceral brain" bear witness to a formerly powerful and unique relationship. Although the primacy of these connections has long since been diluted in human beings, it may help explain why scents, such as perfumes or an old leather-bound book, remain so powerfully evocative of mood or memory.

LIMBIC SYSTEM: NUCLEI AND CONNECTIONS.

LANDMARKS★
CORPUS CALLOSUM$_A$
  ROSTRUM$_{A^1}$
ANT. COMMISSURE$_B$

NUCLEI/GYRI/CELL-FIBER COMPLEXES★
SUBCALLOSAL GYRUS$_C$
CINGULATE GYRUS$_D$
PARAHIPPOCAMP. GYRUS$_E$
HIPPOCAMP.-DENT. CPLX$_F$
SUPRACALLOSAL GYRUS$_G$
AMYGDALA$_{H(\ )}$
  CORTICOMED. DIV.$_{H^1}$
  BASOLAT. DIV.$_{H^2}$
STRIA TERMINALIS$_I$
SEPTAL NUC.$_J$
PARATERMINAL GYRUS$_K$

CONNECTIONS★
FORNIX$_L$/FIMBRIA$_{L^1}$
DIAGONAL BAND OF BROCA$_M$
OLFACT. BULB$_N$/TRACT$_{N^1}$
  MED. OLFACT. STRIA$_{N^2}$
  LAT. OLFACT. STRIA$_{N^3}$

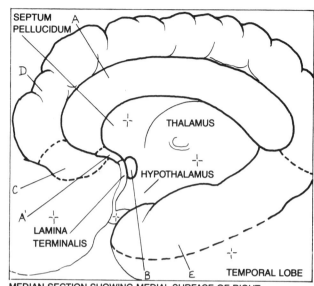

MEDIAN SECTION SHOWING MEDIAL SURFACE OF RIGHT HEMISPHERE

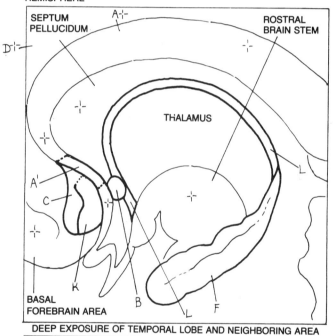

DEEP EXPOSURE OF TEMPORAL LOBE AND NEIGHBORING AREA

DEEPER EXPOSURE OF TEMPORAL LOBE AND NEIGHBORING AREA

The hippocampus ("sea horse"), named for its fancied similarity to the sea creature, is found curled within the medial border of the temporal lobe. It interlocks with the dentate gyrus like two capital C's facing each other; hence the name hippocampal-dentate complex. As the oldest cortical portion of the limbic system, this complex contains only three recognizable layers, instead of the more usual six layers of the neocortex.

Color titles A through F^5 and B through B^4 at the upper left and related structures in the upper right and middle illustrations. Contrasting colors for B and C are recommended. As before, shades of the same color are recommended for structures with the same subscript but differing exponents.

The *hippocampus* (B) and *dentate* (C; also called *dentate gyrus*) are demarcated from the adjacent temporal cortex (*parahippocampal gyrus,* F) by the *hippocampal fissure* (D). The parahippocampal gyrus is in turn demarcated from the rest of the *temporal lobe* (A) by the *collateral sulcus* (E). The parahippocampal gyrus is the zone of transition between the six-layered neocortex (recall Plate 3-11) and the three-layered archicortex or hippocampal-dentate complex (following plate).

The parahippocampal gyrus is divided into the *entorhinal cortex* (F^1; *ento-,* "within"; *rhinal,* "of the nose"; referring to the "nosebrain," an early term for this part of the brain, once thought to be concerned with olfaction) and the *subicular* ("lifting, supporting") *cortex* (F^2). Proceeding medially from the entorhinal cortex, the subicular cortex is organized into *presubiculum* (F^3), *subiculum* (F^4), and *prosubiculum* (F^5), which last is continuous with the hippocampus. In continuation of this same progression, the hippocampus is divided into four sections: CA_1, CA_2, CA_3, and CA_4 (B^1 through B^4; *CA* stands for *cornis Ammonis,* from the coiled horn of Ammon, an Egyptian god). Sections CA_1 through CA_3 of the hippocampus exhibit an organized laminar structure, which can be seen in the following plate (inset); this pattern is lost in CA_4.

Color the headings Afferent Pathway and Efferent Pathway, titles G through J^5, and related structures in the middle illustration (for afferent pathways) and lower illustration (for efferent pathways). Note also I in the uppermost illustration. Color titles K through N and related nuclei at the lower right.

Afferent fibers to the hippocampus approach from three sources: the parahippocampal gyrus, the septal-hippocampal pathway (not shown, but part of the K–G^1 pathway shown at the lower right) of the fornix, and the contralateral hippocampus via the hippocampal commissure (not shown). The entorhinal neocortex constitutes an important site of convergence for fibers from many sensory systems. Shown here are two slightly different paths, *alvear fibers* (G; *alveus,* "trench") and *perforant fibers* (H), running through the transitional subicular areas to enter the hippocampal-dentate complex. The fornix (see lower right illustration) brings afferent fibers (not shown) from the septal area, the basal forebrain area, and the diencephalon (recall Plate 5-21). The afferent septal-hippocampal pathway in the fornix is now believed to serve as the pacemaker for hippocampal electrical activity (hippocampal activity recorded by electrical patterns or waves produced on the electroencephalogram, or EEG).

The largest proportion of efferent fibers leave the hippocampus and subiculum as the *alveus* (G^1) and *fimbria* (I). On each side, the fibers of the fimbria become the *crus* (J^1) of the fornix. Each crus arches superiorly and medially to become the *body* (J^2) of the fornix and curves inferiorly to form the *column* (J^3) of the fornix. About half of these fornical fibers project in front of the anterior commissure to become *precommissural fibers* (J^4). These pass to the *septal nuclei* (K), anterior hypothalamus (not labeled), and the nuclei of the diagonal band of Broca (not shown; recall Plate 5-26). The *postcommissural fibers* (J^5) project to the *mammillary body* (L) and other areas of the hypothalamus, the anterior and *intralaminar nuclei of the thalamus* (M), and the *midbrain tegmentum* (N). In addition, some efferents (not shown) cross with the anterior commissure to reach the contralateral hippocampus, while others project to the subiculum and entorhinal cortex.

The precise functional role of the hippocampus remains ill defined. However, present information suggests that it is involved in learning and memory processing, emotional reactions, and sexual behavior.

LIMBIC SYSTEM: HIPPOCAMPUS.

TEMPORAL LOBE$_A$
HIPPOCAMPUS$_B$/DENTATE$_C$
HIPPOCAMPAL FISSURE$_D$
COLLATERAL SULCUS$_E$
PARAHIPPOCAMPAL GYRUS$_F$
   ENTORHINAL CORTEX$_{F^1}$
   SUBICULAR CORTEX$_{F^2( )}$
      PRE.$_{F^3}$/SUB.$_{F^4}$/PRO.$_{F^5}$
HIPPOCAMPUS
   SECTORS:$_{B( )}$ CA$_{1_{B^1}}$
   CA$_{2_{B^2}}$, CA$_{3_{B^3}}$
   CA$_{4_{B^4}}$

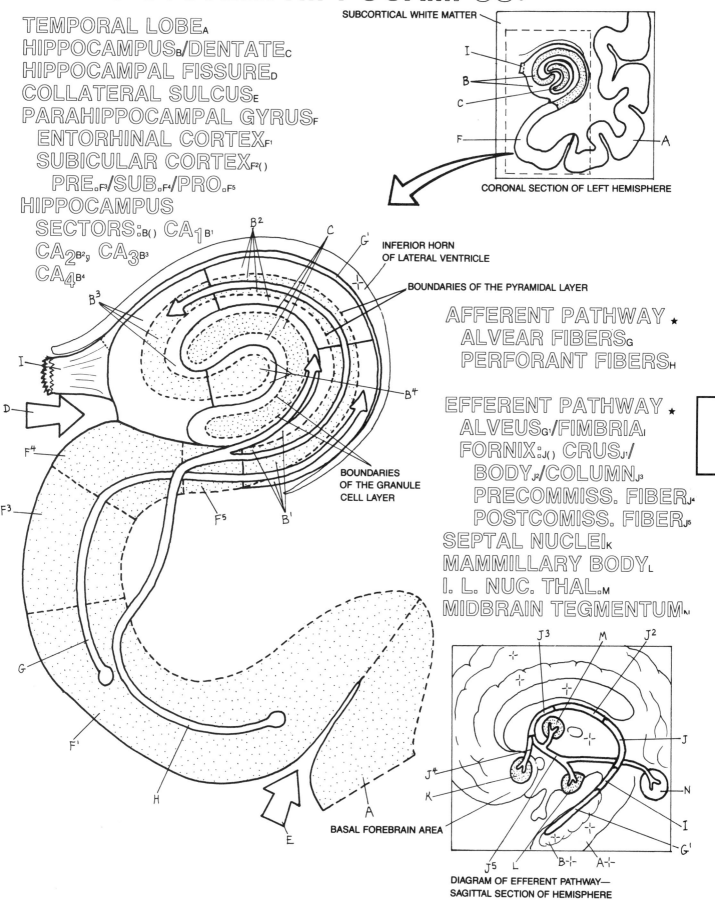

SUBCORTICAL WHITE MATTER

CORONAL SECTION OF LEFT HEMISPHERE

INFERIOR HORN
OF LATERAL VENTRICLE

BOUNDARIES OF THE PYRAMIDAL LAYER

AFFERENT PATHWAY ★
   ALVEAR FIBERS$_G$
   PERFORANT FIBERS$_H$

EFFERENT PATHWAY ★
   ALVEUS$_{G^1}$/FIMBRIA$_I$
   FORNIX:$_{J( )}$ CRUS$_{J^1}$/
      BODY$_{J^2}$/COLUMN$_{J^3}$
      PRECOMMISS. FIBER$_{J^4}$
      POSTCOMISS. FIBER$_{J^5}$
SEPTAL NUCLEI$_K$
MAMMILLARY BODY$_L$
I. L. NUC. THAL.$_M$
MIDBRAIN TEGMENTUM$_N$

BOUNDARIES
OF THE GRANULE
CELL LAYER

BASAL FOREBRAIN AREA

DIAGRAM OF EFFERENT PATHWAY—
SAGITTAL SECTION OF HEMISPHERE

Each sector of the hippocampus is distinguished by its own idiosyncratic mixture of afferent and efferent fibers, yet the overall pattern is generally similar. In this plate, the microscopic arrangement of the hippocampal-dentate complex is presented.

Color titles A through D^6 and the related layers and cells in the cross section through the hippocampus at the upper right. Color layer D^2 and the cell or cell parts (D^4 through D^6) in the large illustration. Consider using here the same colors as on the previous plate for applicable structures. Light shades of the same color for the layers and a contrasting dark color for the pyramidal cell and its parts are recommended. Use a very light color (such as yellow) for A.

The hippocampal sectors CA_1 through CA_3 are characterized by an outer layer of myelinated fibers called the *alveus* (C), separated from the overlying inferior horn of the *lateral ventricle* (A) by a single layer of *ependymal glia* (B). Deep to the alveus are the layers of the hippocampus: *polymorph* (D^1), *pyramidal* (D^2), and *molecular* (D^3). The primary neurons of the hippocampus are *pyramidal cells* (D^4), lined up two to four rows deep in the pyramidal layer. The major (apical) *dendrites* (D^5) of these cells extend down into the molecular layer; the *axons* (D^6) reach up through the polymorph layer to the alveus.

Color the heading Afferent Fibers and Related Cells, titles E through H^3, and related structures in the larger illustration, including D^4, D^5, and D^6.

The *alvear* (E) and *perforant fibers* (F) (presented in Plate 5-27) and *fornical fibers* (G) are among the afferent pathways approaching the hippocampus and *dentate gyrus* (H). In addition, axons of the *dentate granule cells* (H^1) comprise a powerful "intrinsic" source of afferents to the pyramidal cells of the hippocampus. These axons, which encircle virtually the entire hippocampus, generate a system of enlarged, saclike synaptic terminals called *mossy tufts* (H^2), which synapse on the initial portions of the hippocampal apical dendrites and provide powerful *facilitative* (H^3) drive to the hippocampal cells.

Color the heading Efferent Fibers and Related Cells, titles I through K^2, and associated structures.

The axons of the pyramidal cells carry all efferent impulses from the hippocampus. These axons ascend into the alveus and, in the case of CA_1 and CA_2 cells at least (recall Plate 5-27), each bifurcates into two major branches. One branch is directed toward and into the *fimbria* (I) to form the *fornix* (I). The second major branch projects in an opposite direction, toward the adjacent transitional cortical areas, that is, the subicular and entorhinal cortices and beyond.

Before entering the alveus, the axons of most hippocampal pyramidal cells give rise to collaterals that activate small cells in the polymorph layer. These small cells are called *basket cells* (J) and, reminiscent of the cerebellar basket cells (recall Plate 5-14), play back on the pyramidal neurons with basketlike terminals (*axons*, J^1) that enfold the cell body and *inhibit* (J^2) pyramidal cell firing activity.

Before entering the fimbria and fornix, the axons of pyramidal cells in CA_3 give off *Schaffer collaterals* (K), which project back on the pyramidal cells of CA_2 and CA_3. As is the case with most other input systems to the hippocampus, the sites of termination of these collaterals are expressed with a high degree of precision. Here the *terminals* (K^1) of the collaterals are clustered on a very small zone of the pyramidal apical dendritic shaft about halfway between the cell body and the developing apical arbor (treelike expansion). Impulses in these fibers produce powerful local depolarizing (*facilitatory*, K^2) potentials in the shafts and may account for the presence of dendritic spiking (action potential) phenomena described in these dendrite systems.

It is possible that this may, in turn, be partly responsible for the fact that the hippocampus has the lowest threshold for electrical seizures (not synonymous with epilepsy) of any area in the central nervous system. Some data suggest that the increased electrical instability that accompanies this low seizure threshold may conceivably be necessary to the process of memory formation.

LIMBIC SYSTEM: HIPPOCAMPAL-
DENTATE MICROSTRUCTURE.

LATERAL VENTRICLE.A
EPENDYMAL GLIA.B
ALVEUS.C
HIPPOCAMPAL LAYERS.D( )
   POLYMORPH.D1/PYRAMID.D2/
     MOLEC.D3
PYRAMIDAL CELL.D4
   DEND.D5/AXON.D6

AFFERENT FIBERS AND
   RELATED CELLS ★
ALVEAR FIBER.E
PERFORANT FIBER.F
FORNICAL FIBER.G
DENTATE GYRUS.H-|-
DENTATE GRAN. CELL.H1
   MOSSY TUFT.H2/FACIL.H3

EFFERENT FIBERS AND
   RELATED CELLS ★
FIMBRIA-FORNIX.I
BASKET CELL.J/AXON.J1/INHIB.J2
SCHAFFER COLLATERAL.K
   TERMINAL.K1/FACIL.K2

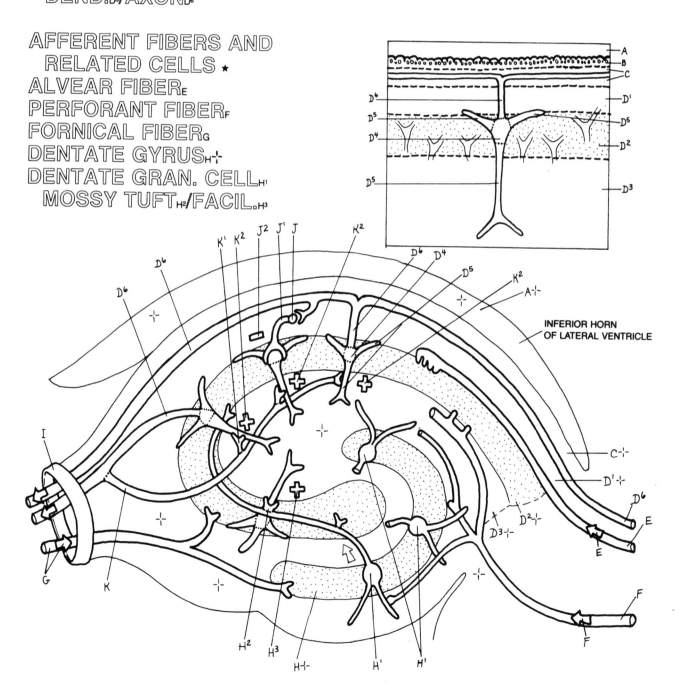

INFERIOR HORN
OF LATERAL VENTRICLE

The surface of each cerebral hemisphere consists of a highly convoluted cerebral cortex divided into regions or lobes, each with its specific gyri (folds or convolutions) and sulci (clefts or fissures). The cortical surfaces of the two hemispheres are not mirror images of each other, and there is increasing evidence of unilateral hemispheric specialization. You should color this and the next plate as a set.

Color titles A through H⁶ and the related structures in the upper illustration as follows: (1) Pick four contrasting colors, each with dark and light shades, for the four lobes; (2) color one lobe at a time, using dark colors for the sulci or fissures and light colors for the gyri. Consider coloring all the gyri of each lobe the same color.

The frontal lobe consists of the cortex rostral to the *central sulcus* (B). The *precentral sulcus* (A¹) separates the more vertically oriented *precentral gyrus* (A⁴) from the more horizontally oriented frontal gyri (A⁵). The *superior* (A²) and *inferior frontal sulci*(A³) delineate the *superior* (A⁶), *middle* (A⁷), and *inferior frontal gyri* (A⁸). The inferior frontal gyrus is partitioned into smaller gyri (see ahead).

The parietal lobe is demarcated by the central sulcus rostrally and the *lateral fissure* (C) inferiorly, extended to an imaginary line posteriorly, drawn between the *parieto-occipital fissure* (E) and the *preoccipital notch* (F). The *postcentral sulcus* (D¹) separates the more rostral *postcentral gyrus* (D³) from the *superior* (D⁵) and *inferior parietal lobules* (D⁶), which are separated from each other by the *intraparietal sulcus* (D²). The inferior parietal lobule is subdivided into smaller gyri, one of which is discussed in the next section.

The *occipital lobe* (G) is posterior to the imaginary line representing the posterior border of the parietal lobe. It is subdivided into smaller areas (discussed in the next section). The temporal lobe is subdivided by the *superior* (H¹) and *inferior temporal sulci* (H²) into the *superior* (H⁴), *middle* (H⁵), and *inferior temporal gyri* (H⁶).

Color the heading Major Cytoarchitectonic Areas, titles A⁹ through H⁹, and related areas in the lower illustration, following the same coloring scheme as in the upper illustration.

The cerebral cortex has been described by many investigators on the basis of cellular organization (cytoarchitecton-

ics). Here we use the numerical designations devised by Brodmann (1909). There are over 200 such designated areas of the cortex; we have illustrated only a representative sample.

Area 4 (A⁹), corresponding to the precentral gyrus, is the primary source for the origin of discrete voluntary movements. The muscles of the body are represented on the surface of area 4 in great detail (motor homunculus, not shown). *Area 6* (A¹⁰) is the premotor cortex. Stimulation of this area organizes the individual motor responses characteristic of area 4 into larger entities, creating more generalized movements. *Area 8* (A¹¹) controls voluntary, conjugate (bilateral) eye movements. *Area 44* (A¹²) and *areas 45 and 47* (A¹³) correspond to the opercular and triangular gyri, respectively. They constitute the motor speech area (of Broca) in the left hemisphere in the majority of people. *Areas 9, 10, 11 and 46* (A¹⁴), constituting most of the prefrontal cortex rostral to the premotor area, have no obvious role in motor activity but are concerned with more complex functions such as foresight and judgment.

Areas 3, 1, and 2 (D⁷) correspond to the postcentral gyrus and constitute the primary sensory area (or S I) receiving general sensations from the body. The sensory areas of the body are represented in areas 3, 1, and 2 in great detail (sensory homunculus, not shown). The *secondary somatic sensory area* (D⁸; also called *somatic sensory area II*, or SS II) is seen at the base of the postcentral gyrus and seems to be involved in emotionally meaningful sensations, such as pain. *Areas 39* (D⁹) and *40* (D¹⁰) are the angular and supramarginal gyri, respectively. These areas are concerned with language, mathematical operations, and body imaging.

Area 17 (G¹) is the primary visual area (also called the *striate cortex*) and is located largely on the medial surface of the occipital lobe. It extends laterally over the occipital pole, where precise daylight vision is represented. The visual image, retinally dissected (see Plate 6-6) for transmission to the brain, begins to be reassembled in area 17, a process that is continued in adjacent association areas (*areas 18 and 19*, G²) and in the inferior temporal cortex (areas 20, 21, and 37; not shown).

Areas 41 (H⁷) and *42* (H⁸) are the primary auditory areas. The *posterior portion of area 22* (H⁹), called Wernicke's area, is associated with the interpretation of language; if this area is damaged, a person cannot understand the meaning of spoken words.

CEREBRAL HEMISPHERE: LATERAL SURFACE.

FRONTAL LOBE $_{A()}$
 PRECENTRAL S. $_{A^1}$
 SUP. FRONT. S. $_{A^2}$
 INF. FRONT. S. $_{A^3}$
 PRECENTRAL G. $_{A^4}$
 FRONT. G. $_{A^5()}$: SUP. $_{A^6}$
 MID. $_{A^7}$/INF. $_{A^8}$
CENTRAL SULCUS $_B$
LATERAL FISSURE $_C$

PARIETAL LOBE $_{D()}$
 POSTCENTRAL S. $_{D^1}$
 INTRAPARIETAL S. $_{D^2}$
 POSTCENTRAL G. $_{D^3}$
 PARIETAL LOBULE $_{D^4()}$:
 SUP. $_{D^5}$/INF. $_{D^6}$
PARIETO-OCCIPITAL F. $_E$
PREOCCIPITAL NOTCH $_F$

OCCIPITAL LOBE $_G$

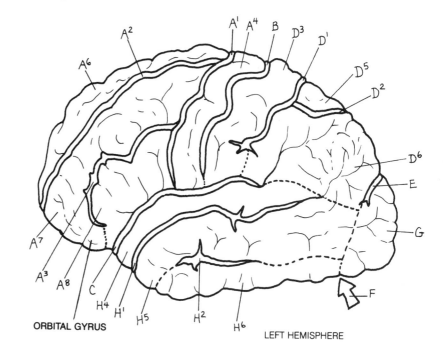

ORBITAL GYRUS

LEFT HEMISPHERE

TEMPORAL LOBE $_{H()}$
 SUP. TEMP. S. $_{H^1}$
 INF. TEMP. S. $_{H^2}$
 TEMP. G. $_{H^3()}$: SUP. $_{H^4}$
 MID. $_{H^5}$/INF. $_{H^6}$

MAJOR CYTOARCHI-
TECTONIC AREAS ★
AREAS 4 $_{A^9}$/6 $_{A^{10}}$/8 $_{A^{11}}$
AREA 44 $_{A^{12}}$
AREAS 45, 47 $_{A^{13}}$
AREAS 9, 10, 11, 46 $_{A^{14}}$
AREAS 3, 2, 1 $_{D^7}$
SEC. SENS. AREA $_{D^8}$
AREA 39 $_{D^9}$
AREA 40 $_{D^{10}}$
AREAS 17 $_{G^1}$/18, 19 $_{G^2}$
AREAS 41 $_{H^7}$/42 $_{H^8}$
POST. PART AREA 22 $_{H^9}$

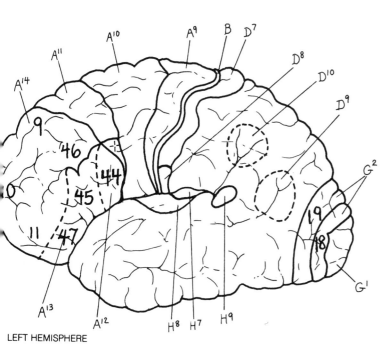

LEFT HEMISPHERE

This plate and the preceding plate have been organized as a set and should be colored together. The subscripts on this plate are a continuation of those used on the previous plate.

Color titles A through H¹² and the related structures using the coloring scheme of the previous plate.

The *superior frontal gyrus* (A^6) continues on to the medial surface of the hemisphere. This gyrus extends forward from the *central sulcus* (B), curving along the superior surface of the cingulate gyrus and sulcus and downward along the anterior surfaces of the subcallosal and paraterminal gyri to the *gyrus rectus* (A^{15}). On either side of the central sulcus are the *paracentral* (A^{16}) and *marginal sulci* (D^{11}). These sulci embrace the *paracentral lobule* (A^{17}, D^{10}), shared by both frontal and parietal lobes and representing the medial continuations of the precentral and postcentral gyri. The *precuneus lobule* (D^{12}) is bordered anteriorly by the marginal sulcus and posteriorly by the *parieto-occipital fissure* (E).

The occipital lobe is more extensive on its medial surface, represented by the *cuneus* (G^3) and *lingual gyri* (G^5), which are separated by the *calcarine fissure* (G^4). Both sides of this fissure are occupied by the primary visual area (area 17; not shown). The visual association areas (areas 18 and 19) surround area 17 (not shown; recall Plate 5-29). The cortex of the inferolateral occipital surface is shared with the temporal lobe as the *medial* and *lateral occipitotemporal gyri* (G^6; H^{10}).

The *rhinal sulcus* (H^{11}) and the more posterior *collateral sulcus* (H^{12}) separate the medial occipitotemporal gyrus from the more medial lingual gyrus and parahippocampal gyrus, respectively.

Color all remaining titles and related structures, using the coloring scheme as before.

The *cingulate* (I) and *callosal sulci* (J) delimit the superior and inferior boundaries of the cingulate gyrus, a prominent part of the limbic lobe. Originally called *le grand lobe limbique* by the French neurologist Paul Broca, this lobe includes the *paraterminal* (K^1) and *subcallosal gyri* (K^2); the *cingulate gyrus* (K^3); the *isthmus of the cingulate* (K^4), consisting of a cortical strip beneath the splenium; and the *parahippocampal gyrus* (K^5) with its anteromedial hooklike protrusion, the *uncus* (K^6). The limbic lobe has been examined in Plates 5-26 through 5-28. The subcallosal and paraterminal gyri constitute the cortical zone called the septal area (recall Plate 5-26).

The posterior superior part of the cingulate gyrus is related to sexual behavior. Tumors in this area may lead to satyriasis (perpetual penile erection) in the male and nymphomania (continuous sexual desire) in the female.

The cingulate gyrus is also concerned with another behavioral abnormality called obsessive-compulsive neurosis. The neurosurgical procedure found to be best suited for this condition is cingulotomy. The same operation has been performed on patients with severe chronic depressive illness or anxiety states, with good results reported. Few major personality changes and little reduction in intellectual functions have yet been observed as a consequence of these operations.

CEREBRAL HEMISPHERE: MEDIAL SURFACE.

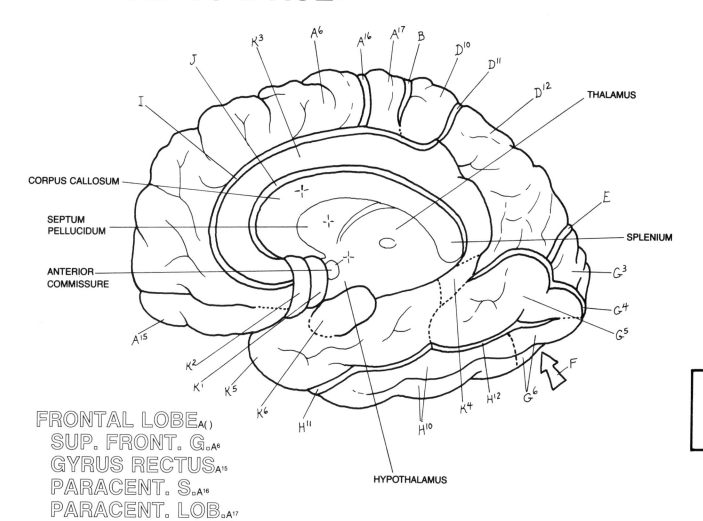

CORPUS CALLOSUM

SEPTUM PELLUCIDUM

ANTERIOR COMMISSURE

THALAMUS

SPLENIUM

HYPOTHALAMUS

FRONTAL LOBE_A( )
  SUP. FRONT. G._A6
  GYRUS RECTUS_A15
  PARACENT. S._A16
  PARACENT. LOB._A17
CENTRAL SULCUS_B

PARIETAL LOBE_D( )
  PARACENT. LOB._D10
  MARGINAL S._D11
  PRECUNEUS LOB._D12
PARIETO-OCCIPITAL F._E
PREOCCIPITAL NOTCH_F

OCCIPITAL LOBE_G( )
  CUNEUS_G3
  CALCARINE F._G4
  LINGUAL G._G5
  MED./LAT. OCCIP.-
    TEMP. G._G6

TEMPORAL LOBE_H( )
  MED./LAT. O-T G._H10
  RHINAL S._H11
  COLLATERAL S._H12

CINGULATE S._I
CALLOSAL S._J

LIMBIC LOBE_K( )
  PARATERM. G._K1
  SUBCALLOSAL G._K2
  CINGULATE G._K3
    ISTHMUS_K4
  PARAHIPPOCAMP. G._K5
  UNCUS_K6

CEREBRAL CORTEX: CELLULAR ORGANIZATION

The cerebral cortex, ranging in thickness from 1.5 to 4.0 mm, provides the circuitry and connections that support our highest level of cognitive functions. The neuron types and the six cortical layers in which they are arranged are presented in this plate.

Color the heading Cortical Layers, titles A through F, and the related cortical laminations in the illustration at the upper right, using light pastel colors. Color the Roman numerals and vertical bars to the left of the main illustration. Then color the heading Cell Types, titles G through K², and the related neurons in the main illustration. This plate and the next share many of the same structures and subscripts; you may wish to color them together.

The *pyramidal* (G) and *stellate* (H; granule) cells are the most numerous neuron types in the cerebral cortex. The pyramidal cell is characterized by an *apical dendrite* (G^2) extending toward the cortical surface with *oblique dendrites* (G^3) directed laterally from the shaft. *Basal dendrites* (G^4) leave the lower (basal) angles of the cell body. The largest pyramidal cell in the cortex is the *Betz cell* (G^1; 60–100 μm in diameter) of layer V, found only in the precentral gyrus. All pyramidal cells are Golgi I (long-axoned) cells with *axons* (G^5) terminating in the adjacent gyrus, the opposite hemisphere, the brain stem, or as far away as the lumbosacral spinal cord!

Stellate cells are located in all layers except layer I. They are in greatest concentration in layer IV. Their *dendrite* (H^1) systems, which may or may not be covered with dendritic spines, usually surround the cell bodies like a halo. The short *axons* (H^2) of these cells (hence their Golgi II classification) do not leave the cortex. Dense networks of interwoven dendritic and axonal processes (called *neuropil*) become increasingly complex in higher vertebrates; in the final analysis, it is through the wealth of these connections that cerebral processing power develops.

The *fusiform cell* (I) is a spindle-shaped neuron lying within the deeper lamina of the cortex, usually layer VI. It is characterized by vertically oriented *dendrites* (I^1). Its *axon* (I^2) enters the subcortical white matter as a commissural, association, or projection fiber (discussed in Plate 5-33).

The *cells of Martinotti* (J) are found in all layers of the cortex except layer I. The *dendrites* (J^1) are small, and the *axon* (J^2) of each cell is usually directed toward layer I, often arborizing in that layer.

The *horizontal cells of Cajal* (K) are found within layer I. Their *dendrites* (K^1) and *axons* (K^2) run parallel to the cortical surface and remain in the same layer.

In general, the six layers of the cerebral cortex can fit into a common scheme:

Layer I (A). The molecular layer, rich in axons and dendrites, lies beneath the pial-glial membrane. The astrocytes of this layer contribute to this protective and supportive membrane. Only a few scattered neurons, such as the horizontal cells of Cajal, are present.

Layer II (B). The external granular layer consists of rounded, small pyramidal cells of which the dendrites extend into layer I and the axons project to deeper cortical layers.

Layer III (C). The external pyramidal layer consists of medium to large pyramidal cells of which the apical dendrites reach layer I and the axons may project to cortical or subcortical targets.

Layer IV (D). The internal granular layer consists largely of stellate cells with an admixture of small pyramidal cells. Their branching systems have been described with the stellate cells.

Layer V (E). The internal pyramidal layer is composed primarily of medium to large pyramidal cells with some stellate neurons and cells of Martinotti. It is within this layer that the large Betz cells, numbering only about 30,000 per hemisphere, are distributed within the motor strip of the frontal cortex (area 4).

Layer VI (F). The multiform layer contains an abundant number of fusiform cells in addition to other neurons of various shapes. The great mass of descending and ascending fibers contributes to the indistinct boundary between layer VI and the subadjacent white matter of the cerebral hemisphere.

A number of variations of this scheme are actually found in the cerebral cortex, depending on the site and functional role of the area. For example, motor cortices (such as areas 4 and 6; not shown) are characterized by a predominance of pyramidal cells and a diminution of granule-rich layer IV and are referred to as the *agranular cortices*. Sensory receptive cortices (not shown), such as areas 3, 1, and 2, have dense concentrations of granule cells, and even the pyramidal cells have somewhat rounded contours, giving rise to the term *granular cortex* for these areas. Association areas share some features of both of these extreme types and more closely resemble the cortex illustrated.

CEREBRAL CORTEX: CELLULAR ORGANIZATION.

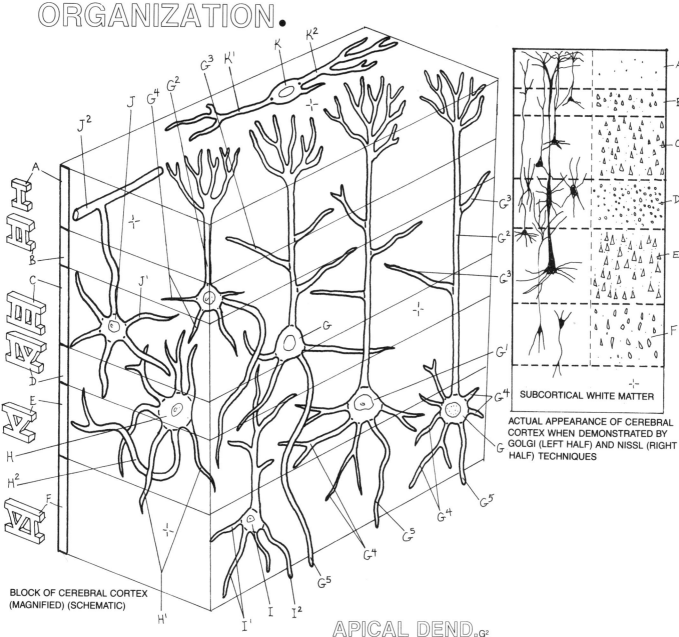

ACTUAL APPEARANCE OF CEREBRAL CORTEX WHEN DEMONSTRATED BY GOLGI (LEFT HALF) AND NISSL (RIGHT HALF) TECHNIQUES

SUBCORTICAL WHITE MATTER

BLOCK OF CEREBRAL CORTEX (MAGNIFIED) (SCHEMATIC)

CORTICAL LAYERS ★
LAYER I$_A$
LAYER II$_B$
LAYER III$_C$
LAYER IV$_D$
LAYER V$_E$
LAYER VI$_F$

CELL TYPES ★
PYRAMIDAL CELL$_G$/
   BETZ CELL$_{G^1}$

APICAL DEND.$_{G^2}$
OBLIQ. DEND.$_{G^3}$
BASAL DEND.$_{G^4}$
AXON$_{G^5}$
STELLATE CELL$_H$
   DEND.$_{H^1}$/AXON$_{H^2}$
FUSIFORM CELL$_I$
   DEND.$_{I^1}$/AXON$_{I^2}$
MARTINOTTI CELL$_J$
   DEND.$_{J^1}$/AXON$_{J^2}$
HORIZ. CELL CAJAL$_K$
   DEND.$_{K^1}$/AXON$_{K^2}$

CEREBRAL CORTEX: INTRACORTICAL CIRCUITS, INPUT AND OUTPUT

One of the most consistent features of organization throughout the cerebral cortex is the basic plan of axonal and dendritic branching. Regardless of the source of afferent fibers or the destination of efferents, the overall configuration of input and output systems and intracortical circuits remains similar.

Color the title Cortical Layers a mixture of colors used for A through F on the preceding plate, and color the related vertical bars and Roman numerals I through VI. Color the heading Afferents, titles L and M, and related fibers. Then color the heading Intracortical Cells and Efferents, titles G through N^2, and related cells, using the same colors as on Plate 5-31. Note that the subscripts are carried over from the previous plate. Subscript J is not used on this plate.

Afferent fibers to the cortex originate from the brain stem, the thalamus, and distant and adjacent cortical areas, including commissural fibers from the opposite cortex. In fact, afferents of ipsilateral and contralateral cortical origin outnumber those from subcortical stations by more than 10 to 1! *Specific thalamocortical fibers* (L) ascend to *layer IV* (D), where they branch and synapse among the *dendrites* (N^1, H^1) of the stellate basket cells and stellate cells. Some of the terminals of these thalamocortical fibers reach the neurons of *layer III* (C). A single stellate cell may receive as many as 60,000 terminals from a cluster of overlapping thalamocortical afferents. *Nonspecific thalamocortical axons* (M; recall Plate 5-19) terminate in all layers, usually ascending along and synapsing with the *apical dendrites* (G^2) of *pyramidal cells* (G), constantly readjusting levels of cortical excitability.

Fibers of cortical origin show widespread patterns of intracortical distribution, often synapsing along the *basal* (G^4) and *oblique dendrites* (G^3) of the pyramidal cells. These axons and their receptive dendrites may be the most capable of reshaping in response to novel stimuli or challenge throughout life. The shortest *axons* (H^2) of intracortical origin arise from *stellate cells* (H) and terminate in the immediate area, usually layer IV. Many such cells, inhibitory in function, are called *stellate basket cells* (N) because the terminal collaterals of their *axons* (N^2) surround the cell bodies of nearby pyramidal cells.

Efferent axonal systems also show a recognizable pattern, although the details vary. In a general way, the pattern of axon organization among intracortical cells changes from a horizontal to a vertical orientation as one proceeds from *layer I* (A) to *layer VI* (F). The *horizontal cells of Cajal* (K) of layer I produce *dendrites* (K^1) and arbors of *axons* (K^2) that synapse almost exclusively on the terminal branches of apical dendrites (of deeper cells) in layer I. The pyramidal cells in the deeper portions of *layers II* (B) and III have axons of varying length with both horizontal and vertical branching patterns. These axons usually terminate in intracortical or contiguous subcortical areas, respectively.

In contrast, *axons* (G^5) of *layer V* (E) pyramidal cells tend to enter the subcortical white matter (not shown) and project to the brain stem or spinal cord. En route, these axons, along with those from layers II and III, form intracortical *recurrent collaterals* (G^6), which reverse course and ascend obliquely for varying distances through the cortex. Such branches contribute the single richest source of axon terminals in the cortex and document the enormous importance of information feedback in cortical circuitry. The *dendrites* (I^1) of *fusiform cells* (I) found in layer VI project up to either layer I or layer IV. The *axons* (I^2) of these cells descend to leave the cortex.

Color titles O through Q in the upper part of the plate and the related structures in the adjacent magnified cortical block. Select colors that contrast O from P and Q.

The predominant pattern of cortical organization appears to consist of horizontal layers of cells and processes traversed perpendicularly by the apical dendrites and axons of cell bodies in other laminae, all within the laminar organization previously discussed. Particularly heavy bundles of horizontal fibers in layers IV and V are known, respectively, as *external* (O) and *internal bands of Baillarger* (P); in the primary visual area, a quite prominent version of the former is known as the *strip of Gennari* (not shown).

In addition to laminar organization, cortical neurons are also arranged in *vertical columns* (Q) that extend through the full thickness of the cortex. The cells in each column appear to "code" for a particular aspect of sensory input. The progressive integration of the discrete information in these columns by intracortical circuitry is responsible for the reassembly of the total sensory perception.

CEREBRAL CORTEX: INTRACORTICAL CIRCUITS, INPUT AND OUTPUT.

SCHEMATIC BLOCK
OF CELL COLUMNS
COMPOSING CEREBRAL
CORTEX (MAGNIFIED)

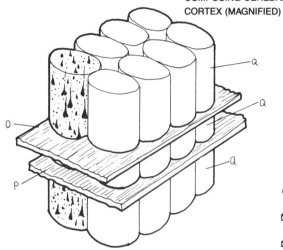

EXT. BANDS BAILLARGER$_O$
INT. BANDS BAILLARGER$_P$
VERTICAL COLUMNS$_Q$

CORTICAL LAYERS$_{A-F}$
AFFERENTS ★
SPEC. THAL-CORT. AXON$_L$
NONSPEC. THAL-CORT.
AXON$_M$

INTRACORT. CELLS AND
EFFERENTS ★
PYRAMIDAL CELL$_G$
APICAL DEND.$_{G^2}$
OBLIQUE DEND.$_{G^3}$
BASAL DEND.$_{G^4}$
AXON$_{G^5}$
RECURRENT COLLAT.$_{G^6}$
STELLATE CELL$_H$
DEND.$_{H^1}$/AXON$_{H^2}$
FUSIFORM CELL$_I$
DEND.$_{I^1}$/AXON$_{I^2}$
HORIZ. CELL CAJAL$_K$
DEND.$_{K^1}$/AXON$_{K^2}$
STELL. BASKET CELL$_N$
DEND.$_{N^1}$/AXON$_{N^2}$

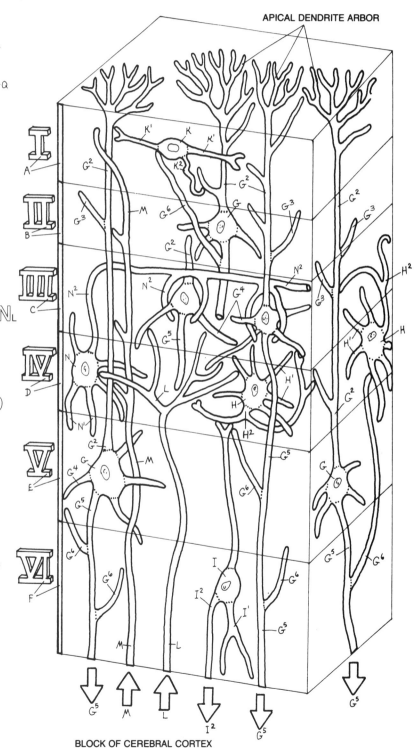

APICAL DENDRITE ARBOR

BLOCK OF CEREBRAL CORTEX
(SCHEMATIC)

The billions of fibers carrying information to and from the cortex make up the white matter of the cerebral hemispheres. This great mass of subcortical myelinated fibers can be arranged into families, including fibers interconnecting one hemisphere with the other (commissures), long and short fibers interconnecting cortical areas of the same hemisphere (association tracts), and fibers connecting the cortex with subcortical centers (projection fibers).

The anterior commissure is not shown here, but see Plates 5-36, 5-47, and 6-5.

Color the heading Association Tracts, titles A through A⁶, and related fiber bundles.

The *short association fibers* (A) connect adjacent gyri and are often called *U fibers*. The long association tracts (A¹) consist of three major bundles, the *cingulum* (A²), *uncinate fasciculus* (A³; *uncus,* "hook"), and *arcuate fasciculus* (A⁵). The cingulum lies within the white matter of the cingulate gyrus and connects frontal and parietal lobes with the ipsilateral parahippocampal gyrus and other parts of the temporal lobe and is therefore considered part of the limbic lobe. The curved uncinate fasciculus forms a connection between the orbital gyrus (of the frontal lobe; see Plate 5-29) and parts of the middle and inferior frontal gyri with the anterior region of the temporal lobe. The deeper fibers of this bundle (*inferior occipitofrontal fasciculus,* A⁴) reach to the occipital lobe. The arcuate fasciculus connects the superior and middle frontal gyri with parts of the temporal lobe; its uppermost fibers constitute the *superior longitudinal fasciculus* (A⁶).

Color the heading Commissures, titles B through B⁵, and related fiber bundles.

The two main commissural fiber connections of the cerebral hemispheres are the corpus callosum and the anterior commissure (not shown here); these can be seen from different perspectives in the Atlas of Brain Sections, Plates 5-35 through 5-46. The corpus callosum, a broad band of myelinated fibers, interconnects cortical regions in one lobe with homotopic ("similarly placed") regions in the opposite lobe. There are approximately 300 million fibers in the average corpus callosum, but the size differs among individuals of the same sex and between the sexes; the splenium may be larger in the female.

At the rostral end (rostrum) of the corpus callosum, the callosal fibers curve (*genu,* B¹) anteriorly to form the *anterior forceps* (B²; referring to its fanciful appearance to the two-bladed instrument), which connects regions of the frontal lobes. Posterior to the genu, fibers of the massive callosal *body* (B³) connect regions of the parietal and frontal lobes. At the posterior aspect of the corpus callosum, the callosal fibers (*splenium,* B⁴) radiate caudally as the *posterior forceps* (B⁵).

The cerebral commissures are concerned with short-term memory and with transferring learned tasks from one hemisphere to the other. Transection of the corpus callosum prevents communication between the hemispheres and is used to control severe cases of epilepsy. This surgical procedure has allowed investigators to study "split-brain" patients and note significant differences in behavior between the two hemispheres.

Color the heading Projection Tracts, titles C through C⁶, and the related fiber bundles.

The radiating masses of subcortical white fibers are called the *corona radiata* (C). Caudally, the corona condenses to form the internal capsule (C¹; see Plates 5-46 and 5-47). This V-shaped band of fibers descends between the lenticular nucleus laterally and the caudate nucleus and thalamus medially, continuing into the midbrain as the crus cerebri. Ascending fibers within the capsule arise primarily from the thalamus; descending fibers originate from all areas of the cortex.

The internal capsule is divided into five components. The *anterior limb* (C²) lies between the head of the caudate and the lentiform nucleus and carries frontopontine fibers as well as fibers interconnecting the thalamus with the frontal cortex. The *genu* (C³), between the anterior and posterior limbs, conveys corticobulbar fibers. The largest of the components, though not apparent as shown, is the *posterior limb* (C⁴), which is made up of the corticospinal and parieto-occipito-temporo-pontine fibers. The *retrolenticular* (C⁵; *retro-,* "back") fibers, largely of lateral geniculate origin, pass behind the lentiform nucleus to form the optic radiation component of the corona radiata. The *sublenticular fibers* (C⁶), largely of medial geniculate origin, are directed horizontally as the auditory radiation (not shown) en route to the auditory areas of the temporal lobe.

FIBER SYSTEMS OF THE CEREBRAL HEMISPHERES.

ASSOCIATION TRACTS ★
SHORT ASSOC. FIBERS$_A$
LONG ASSOC. FIBERS$_{A^1()}$
CINGULUM$_{A^2}$
UNCINATE FASC.$_{A^3}$
INF. O-F FASC.$_{A^4}$
ARCUATE FASC.$_{A^5}$
SUP. LONG. FASC.$_{A^6}$

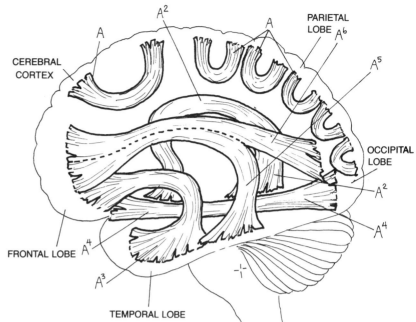

CEREBRAL CORTEX
PARIETAL LOBE
OCCIPITAL LOBE
FRONTAL LOBE
TEMPORAL LOBE

COMMISSURES ★
CORPUS CALLOSUM$_{B()}$
GENU$_{B^1}$
ANTERIOR FORCEPS$_{B^2}$
BODY$_{B^3}$
SPLENIUM$_{B^4}$
POSTERIOR FORCEPS$_{B^5}$

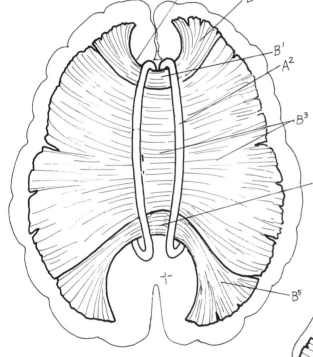

ROSTRUM

PROJECTION TRACTS ★
CORONA RADIATA$_C$
INTERNAL CAPSULE$_{C^1()}$
ANTERIOR LIMB$_{C^2}$
GENU$_{C^3}$
POSTERIOR LIMB$_{C^4}$
RETROLENT. FIBERS$_{C^5}$
SUBLENT. FIBERS$_{C^6}$

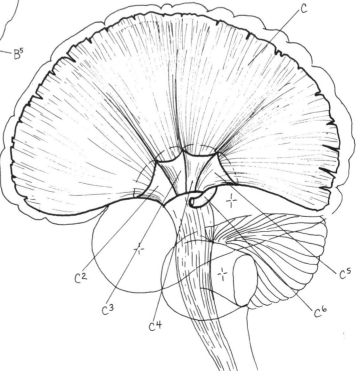

MAJOR PAIN-INHIBITORY PATHWAYS

Evidence for the presence of the brain's own pain inhibition or analgesic system began to emerge in the 1970s. This system involves descending inhibitory pathways and a brainwide distribution of opiate receptors and opiate-containing neurons. The functional interrelationships of these elements are not yet clear; it is evident, however, that all parts of the basic divisions of the neural tube are included in the perception and processing of pain input.

Color the heading Ascending Pain Pathway, titles A through B^1, and the related structures, starting at the lower right of the spinal cord section.

Pain impulses begin in free nerve endings (recall Plate 2-9). These endings are called *nociceptors.* Sharp pain is conducted via *A delta fibers* (A), which terminate in laminae I and V of the spinal cord (recall Plate 4-2). Prolonged, often burning pain is conducted via *C fibers* (A^1), which terminate in laminae II and V of the cord. The neurotransmitter of these pain afferent endings is called *substance P.* The neurons in these laminae contribute to the formation of the *lateral spinothalamic tract* (B; recall Plate 4-5). This pathway not only projects fibers directly to the thalamus but also provides *collaterals* (B^1) at every level of the spinal cord and brain stem. Synaptic interaction of these collaterals at the mesencephalic level results in an enhanced state of readiness without conscious awareness of the pain stimulus. Consciousness of nonlocalized pain probably begins in the thalamus. The intensity of the pain input and the state of alertness created in the midbrain awaken more rostral levels all the way to the cerebral cortex.

Color the headings Descending Inhibitory Pathway, Forebrain, Midbrain, and Hindbrain, titles C through G, and related structures, beginning with the uppermost drawing. Then color the titles H through H^3 and related structures in the two lower drawings. F^1 is exaggerated in size to accommodate its connections.

It is within the cerebral cortex that descending pain-inhibitory pathways begin. Electrical stimulation of cells in the medial *prefrontal cortex* (C^1) has identified inhibitory *fibers* (C^2) descending to the *periaqueductal gray* (E) of the midbrain. Though not well established, it has been suggested that the *periventricular* (midline) (D^1) and *paraventricular nuclei* (D^2) in the thalamus contribute *fibers* (D^3) to this midbrain region.

Fibers from both *posterior* (E^1) and *anterior* (E^2) parts of the periaqueductal gray project to the *nucleus raphe magnus* (F^1) of the reticular formation (F; recall Plate 5-12). Some *fibers* (F^2) of this nucleus feed back on the *spinal trigeminal nucleus* (G), which receives facial pain input, thus closing the inhibitory reflex arc there. The reticular formation allows a mixing of other systems and changes of neurotransmitters to enhance and refine the degree of inhibition that will play on primary pain afferents.

Fibers from the nucleus raphe magnus descend bilaterally in the *posterolateral funiculus* (H^1; shown on the right side only) of the *spinal cord* (H). Fibers from this same nucleus are also joined ipsilaterally by *fibers* (F^4) from *large cell nuclei* (F^3) of the reticular formation; these descend, unilaterally and bilaterally (shown on the left side only), in the *anterior and anteriolateral funiculi* (H^2) of the spinal cord. Here, in laminae I, II, and V, these descending inhibitory fibers synapse with *interneurons* (H^3). The axons of these interneurons synapse with both incoming primary pain afferents and the cells whose axons form the lateral spinothalamic tract, closing the inhibitory reflex arc.

All of the areas involved in the descending inhibitory pathway, and other parts of the brain as well, are rich in opiate receptors. These receptors are responsive to both exogenous (from a source outside the body) and endogenous analgesic (*an-*, "without"; *algesia,* "pain") substances. Such substances include morphine, codeine, and meperidine (Demerol) as well as the very potent endogenous opiates known as enkephalins and endorphins. The enkephalins (made up of five amino acid units called peptides) have a wider distribution than the 31 amino-acid endorphins. The enkephalins and endorphins have been found throughout the brain stem, including the periaqueductal gray. The neurons in laminae I and II of the spinal cord have a high affinity for these substances as well. The mechanism by which these descending pathways, opiate receptors, and analgesic substances interact with incoming pain signals is not yet clear. However, there is some indication that enkephalins may alter the degree to which the calcium channels of synaptic zones (recall Plate 2-5) permit the release of substance P.

Ongoing and future investigations will hopefully provide us with an ability to manipulate and amplify these pain-controlling elements.

MAJOR PAIN-INHIBITORY PATHWAYS.

ASCENDING PAIN PATHWAY★
PRI. PAIN A DELTA FIBER$_{A}$
PRI. PAIN C FIBER$_{A^1}$
LAT. SPINOTHAL. TR.$_{B}$
COLLATERAL$_{B^1}$

DESCENDING INHIB. PATHWAY★

FOREBRAIN★
CEREBRAL CORTEX$_{C()}$
MED. PREFRONTAL CORTEX$_{C^1}$/FIBER$_{C^2}$
THALAMUS$_{D}$
PERIVENTRIC. NUC.$_{D^1}$
PARAVENTRIC. NUC.$_{D^2}$/FIBER$_{D^3}$

MIDBRAIN★
PERIAQUEDUCTAL GRAY$_{E()}$
POST.$_{E^1}$/ANT.$_{E^2}$/FIBER$_{E^3}$

HINDBRAIN★
RETICULAR FORMATION$_{F()}$
N. RAPHE MAGNUS$_{F^1}$/FIBER$_{F^2}$
LARGE CELL NUC.$_{F^3}$/FIBER$_{F^4}$
SPINAL TRIG. NUC.$_{G}$

SPINAL CORD$_{H()}$
POST. LAT. FUNICULUS$_{H^1}$
ANT-LAT./ANT. FUNIC.$_{H^2}$
INTERNEURON$_{H^3}$

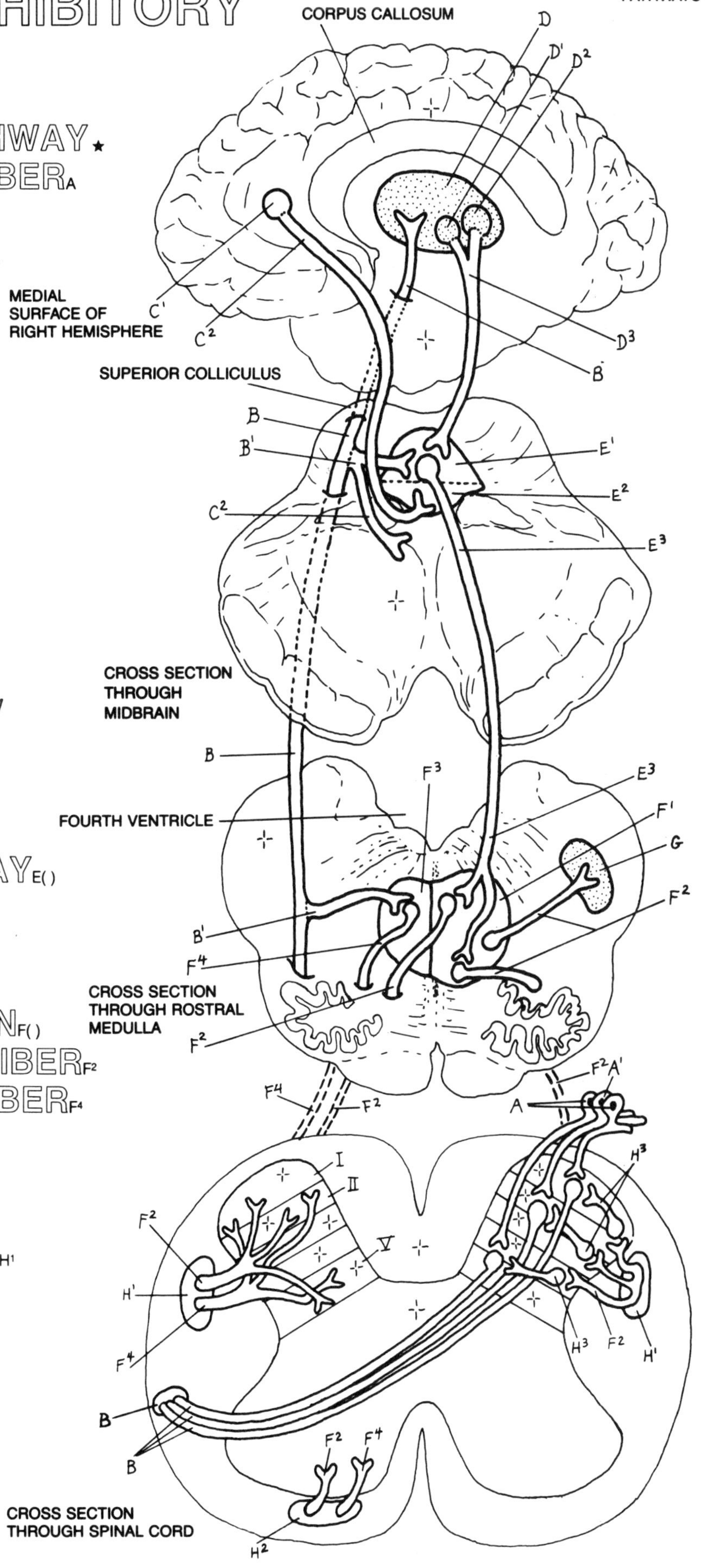

CORPUS CALLOSUM
D
D'
D²
MEDIAL SURFACE OF RIGHT HEMISPHERE
C'
C²
D³
B'
SUPERIOR COLLICULUS
B
B'
E'
E²
C²
E³
CROSS SECTION THROUGH MIDBRAIN
B
F³
E³
FOURTH VENTRICLE
F'
G
F²
B'
F⁴
CROSS SECTION THROUGH ROSTRAL MEDULLA
F²
F⁴
F²
F² A'
A
I
II
V
H³
F²
H'
F⁴
H³
F²
H'
B
B
F²
F⁴
CROSS SECTION THROUGH SPINAL CORD
H²

In this and each of the following plates of the Atlas, the base subscripts of brain structure for the purposes of color coordination are as follows:

gyrus (A)   tract/nerve (D)
sulcus/fissure (B)   ventricle (E)
nucleus (C)   landmark/other (F)

The exponents of these subscripts will be added cumulatively, beginning with this plate and continuing through Plate 5-48. These subscripts are not related to those of any plates other than these. As you progress through the plates, note that titles of a structure (on the art plate) seen in a continuous sequence may be dropped after the first or second section even though the subscript may be retained on the plate to identify the structure. In all such cases, the left page will list the structure and its applicable references. The circles adjacent to each structure title can be used for the related color.

You are invited to color-coordinate as you wish, subscripts notwithstanding. For example, you may wish to color-coordinate these 14 plates with the anterior and posterior views of the brain stem (Plates 5-1 and 5-2), the plates on the lateral and medial surfaces of the cerebral hemispheres (Plates 5-28 and 5-29), the cross sections of the brain stem (Plates 5-4 through 5-11), and so on. There are many imaginative possibilities for color coordination that can greatly enhance the learning of the structures. Recall that lighter colors are best for larger structures; dark colors tend to obscure detail within the color boundaries. Degrees of the same color can be achieved by using different background patterns (dots, stripes, crosshatching, circles, triangles, diamonds, and so on).

We recommend that you color the sulci and fissures gray ($\star$) and ventricles black ($\bullet$). A number of large fiber masses (corona radiata, etc.) are designated ($-\frac{}{|}-$; no color) to prevent color confusion when reviewing. For the same reason, use a very light, pale color (such as yellow) for the corpus callosum (D^1, D^2) and the internal capsule (D^5).

On this and the following plates of the Atlas, each of the structures illustrated will be referenced to plates in which that structure has been explained, discussed, or illustrated in a helpful manner.

○ cingulate gyrus (A^1): 5-26
○ superior frontal gyrus (A^2): 3-9, 5-29, 5-30
○ middle frontal gyrus (A^3): 3-9, 5-29
○ inferior frontal gyrus (A^4): 3-9, 5-29
○ orbital gyrus (A^5): 5-29
○ rectus gyrus (A^6): 5-30
⊛ longitudinal cerebral fissure (B^1): 1-2
⊛ lateral fissure (B^2): 5-29
⊛ cingulate sulcus (B^3): 5-30
○ caudate nucleus (C^1): 3-10, 5-24, 5-25
○ putamen (C^2): 3-10, 5-24, 5-25
○ corpus callosum: rostrum (D^1): 5-33
○ corpus callosum: body (D^2): 5-33
⊙ corona radiata (D^3): 5-33
○ olfactory tract (D^4): 3-9, 6-5
○ internal capsule (D^5): 5-33
⊙ superior longitudinal fasciculus (D^6): 5-33
◉ lateral ventricle (E^1): 9-11
○ septum pellucidum (F^1): 5-26

CORONAL SECTION THROUGH FRONTAL LOBES: LEVEL OF HEAD OF THE CAUDATE NUCLEUS.

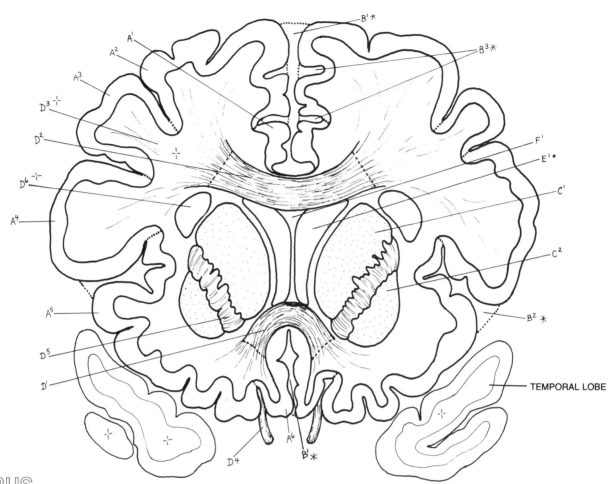

TEMPORAL LOBE

GYRUS$_{A(\ )}$
   CINGULATE$_{A^1}$
   SUP. FRONTAL$_{A^2}$
   MID. FRONTAL$_{A^3}$
   INF. FRONTAL$_{A^4}$
   ORBITAL$_{A^5}$
   RECTUS$_{A^6}$

SULCUS/FISSURE$_{B(\ )}$★
   LONG. CEREB. F.$_{B^1}$★
   LATERAL F.$_{B^2}$★
   CINGULATE S.$_{B^3}$★

NUCLEUS$_{C(\ )}$
   CAUDATE NUC.: HEAD$_{C^1}$
   PUTAMEN$_{C^2}$

TRACT/NERVE$_{D(\ )}$
   C. CALLOSUM: ROSTRUM$_{D^1}$
   C. CALLOSUM: BODY$_{D^2}$
   C. RADIATA$_{D^3}$-¦-
   OLFACTORY TR.$_{D^4}$
   INT. CAPSULE: ANT. LIMB$_{D^5}$
   SUP. LONG. FASC.$_{D^6}$-¦-

VENTRICLE$_{E(\ )}$●
   LAT. VENTRICLE: ANT.
   HORN$_{E^1}$●

LANDMARK$_{F(\ )}$
   SEPTUM PELLUCIDUM$_{F^1}$

○ cingulate gyrus (A^1): 5-26
○ superior frontal gyrus (A^2): 3-9, 5-29, 5-30
○ middle frontal gyrus (A^3): 3-9, 5-29
○ inferior frontal gyrus (A^4): 3-9, 5-29
○ insular gyrus (A^7): 3-9, 3-10
⊛ longitudinal cerebral fissure (B^1): 1-2
⊛ lateral fissure (B^2): 5-29
⊛ cingulate sulcus (B^3): 5-30
○ caudate nucleus (C^1): 3-10, 5-24, 5-25
○ putamen (C^2): 3-10, 5-24, 5-25
○ globus pallidus (C^3): 3-10, 5-24, 5-25
○ claustrum (C^4): 5-24
○ septal nucleus (C^5): 5-21, 5-22, 5-26

○ amygdaloid nucleus (C^6): 3-10, 5-26
○ corpus callosum (D^2): 5-33
⊕ corona radiata (D^3): 5-33
○ internal capsule (D^5): 5-33
⊕ superior longitudinal fasciculus (D^6): 5-33
⊕ uncinate fasciculus (D^7): 5-33
⊕ external capsule (D^8): 5-24
⊕ extreme capsule (D^9): 5-24
○ optic chiasm (D^{10}): 5-2, 6-7, 6-8
○ optic tract (D^{11}): 3-7, 5-2, 6-7, 6-8
○ anterior commissure (D^{12}): 6-5
● lateral ventricle (E^2): 9-11
○ septum pellucidum (F^1): 5-26

CORONAL SECTION THROUGH FRONTAL LOBES: LEVEL OF THE ANTERIOR COMMISSURE.

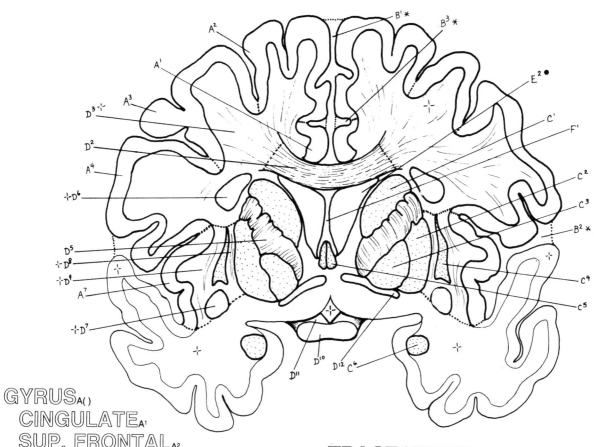

GYRUS$_{A(\ )}$
   CINGULATE$_{A^1}$
   SUP. FRONTAL$_{A^2}$
   MID. FRONTAL$_{A^3}$
   INF. FRONTAL$_{A^4}$
   INSULAR$_{A^7}$

SULCUS/FISSURE$_{B(\ )}$★
   LONG. CEREB. F.$_{B^1}$★
   LATERAL F.$_{B^2}$★
   CINGULATE S.$_{B^3}$★

NUCLEUS$_{C(\ )}$
   CAUDATE NUC.: HEAD$_{C^1}$
   PUTAMEN$_{C^2}$
   GLOB. PALLIDUS$_{C^3}$
   CLAUSTRUM$_{C^4}$
   SEPTAL NUC.$_{C^5}$
   AMYGDALOID NUC.$_{C^6}$

TRACT/NERVE$_{D(\ )}$
   C. CALLOSUM: BODY$_{D^2}$
   C. RADIATA$_{D^3}$⊹
   INT. CAPSULE: ANT. LIMB$_{D^5}$
   SUP. LONG. FASC.$_{D^6}$⊹/UNC.
     FASC.$_{D^7}$⊹
   EXT. CAPSULE$_{D^8}$⊹
   EXTR. CAPSULE$_{D^9}$⊹
   OPTIC CHIASM$_{D^{10}}$
   OPTIC TRACT$_{D^{11}}$
   ANT. COMMISSURE$_{D^{12}}$

VENTRICLE$_{E(\ )}$●
   LAT. VENTRICLE: BODY$_{E^2}$●
LANDMARK$_{F(\ )}$
   SEPTUM PELLUCIDUM$_{F^1}$

CORONAL SECTION THROUGH FRONTAL/TEMPORAL LOBES: LEVEL OF THE INFUNDIBULUM

- ○ cingulate gyrus (A^1): 5-26
- ○ superior frontal gyrus (A^2): 3-9, 5-29, 5-30
- ○ middle frontal gyrus (A^3): 3-9, 5-29
- ○ inferior frontal gyrus (A^4): 3-9, 5-29
- ○ insular gyrus (A^7): 3-9, 3-10
- ○ superior temporal gyrus (A^8): 3-9, 5-29
- ○ middle temporal gyrus (A^9): 3-9, 5-29
- ○ inferior temporal gyrus (A^{10}): 3-9, 5-29
- ○ occipitotemporal gyrus (A^{11}): 5-29, 5-30
- ○ parahippocampal gyrus (A^{12}): 5-26, 5-27, 5-30
- ★ longitudinal cerebral fissure (B^1): 1-2
- ★ lateral fissure (B^2): 5-29
- ★ cingulate sulcus (B^3): 5-30
- ○ caudate nucleus (C^1): 3-10, 5-24, 5-25
- ○ putamen (C^2): 3-10, 5-24, 5-25
- ○ globus pallidus (C^3): 3-10, 5-24, 5-25
- ○ claustrum (C^4): 5-24
- ○ amygdaloid nucleus (C^6): 3-10, 5-26
- ○ hypothalamus (C^7): 3-8, 5-20, 5-21, 5-22
- ○ tuber cinereum (C^8): 5-20
- ○ infundibulum (C^9): 5-20
- ○ corpus callosum (D^2): 5-33
- ⊙ corona radiata (D^3): 5-33
- ○ internal capsule (D^5): 5-33
- ⊙ external capsule (D^8): 5-24
- ⊙ extreme capsule (D^9): 5-24
- ○ optic tract (D^{11}): 3-7, 5-2, 6-7, 6-8
- ○ anterior commissure (D^{12}): 6-5
- ○ fornix (D^{13}): 3-10, 5-21, 5-26, 5-27
- ● lateral ventricle (E^2): 9-11
- ● third ventricle (E^3): 9-11
- ○ septum pellucidum (F^1): 5-26

CORONAL SECTION THROUGH FRONTAL/TEMPORAL LOBES: LEVEL OF THE INFUNDIBULUM.

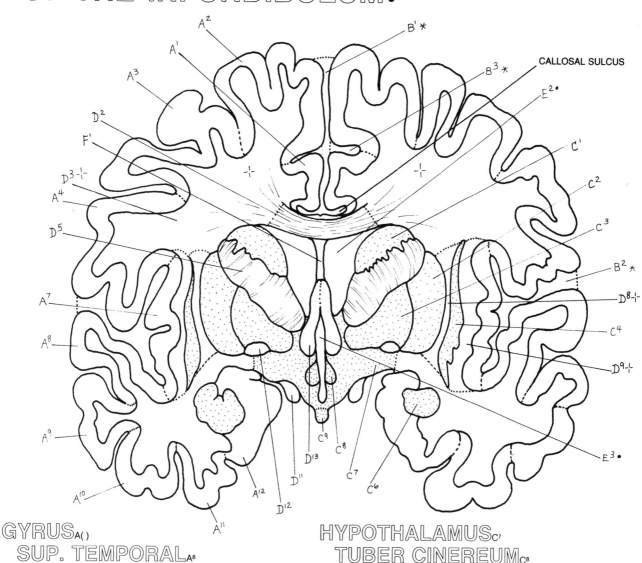

CALLOSAL SULCUS

GYRUS$_{A(\ )}$
SUP. TEMPORAL$_{A8}$
MID. TEMPORAL$_{A9}$
INF. TEMPORAL$_{A10}$
OCCIPITOTEMP.$_{A11}$
PARAHIPPOCAMP.$_{A12}$

SULCUS/FISSURE$_{B(\ )}$★
LONG. CEREB. F.$_{B1}$★
LATERAL F.$_{B2}$★

NUCLEUS$_{C(\ )}$
AMYGDALOID NUC.$_{C6}$

HYPOTHALAMUS$_{C7}$
TUBER CINEREUM$_{C8}$
INFUNDIBULUM$_{C9}$

TRACT/NERVE$_{D(\ )}$
C. RADIATA$_{D3}$-¦-
INT. CAPSULE: ANT. LIMB$_{D5}$
OPTIC TR.$_{D11}$
ANT. COMMISSURE$_{D12}$
FORNIX: COLUMN$_{D13}$

VENTRICLE$_{E(\ )}$●
LAT. VENTRICLE: BODY$_{E2}$●
THIRD VENTRICLE$_{E3}$●

CORONAL SECTION THROUGH FRONTAL/TEMPORAL LOBES: LEVEL OF THE MAMMILLARY BODIES

- ○ cingulate gyrus (A^1): 5-26
- ○ superior frontal gyrus (A^2): 3-9, 5-29, 5-30
- ○ middle frontal gyrus (A^3): 3-9, 5-29
- ○ inferior frontal gyrus (A^4): 3-9, 5-29
- ○ insular gyrus (A^7): 3-9, 3-10
- ○ superior temporal gyrus (A^8): 3-9, 5-29
- ○ middle temporal gyrus (A^9): 3-9, 5-29
- ○ inferior temporal gyrus (A^{10}): 3-9, 5-29
- ○ occipitotemporal gyrus (A^{11}): 5-29, 5-30
- ○ parahippocampal gyrus (A^{12}): 5-26, 5-27, 5-30
- ⊛ longitudinal cerebral fissure (B^1): 1-2
- ⊛ lateral fissure (B^2): 5-29
- ⊛ cingulate sulcus (B^3): 5-30
- ⊛ collateral sulcus (B^4): 5-27
- ○ caudate nucleus (C^1): 3-10, 5-24, 5-25
- ○ putamen (C^2): 3-10, 5-24, 5-25
- ○ globus pallidus (C^3): 3-10, 5-24, 5-25
- ○ claustrum (C^4): 5-24
- ○ anterior nucleus of the thalamus (C^{10}): 5-16, 5-17, 5-18
- ○ medial nucleus of the thalamus (C^{11}): 5-16, 5-17, 5-18
- ○ ventral posterior lateral nucleus of the thalamus (C^{12}): 5-16, 5-17, 5-18
- ○ hippocampus-dentate (C^{13}): 3-10, 5-26, 5-27, 5-28
- ○ mammillary body (C^{14}): 5-20, 5-21, 5-22
- ○ subthalamic region (C^{15}): 5-23
- ○ corpus callosum (D^2): 5-33
- ⊙ corona radiata (D^3): 5-33
- ○ internal capsule (D^5): 5-33
- ⊙ external capsule (D^8): 5-24
- ⊙ extreme capsule (D^9): 5-24
- ○ optic tract (D^{11}): 3-7, 5-2, 6-7, 6-8
- ○ fornix (D^{13}): 3-10, 5-21, 5-26, 5-27
- ○ mammillothalamic tract (D^{14}): 5-22
- ◉ lateral ventricle (E^2, E^4): 9-11
- ◉ third ventricle (E^3): 9-11

CORONAL SECTION THROUGH FRONTAL/TEMPORAL LOBES: LEVEL OF THE MAMMILLARY BODIES.

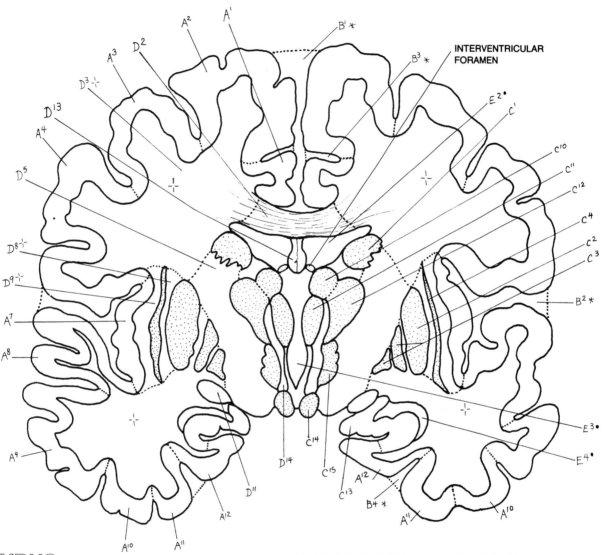

INTERVENTRICULAR FORAMEN

GYRUS$_{A(\,)}$
    PARAHIPPOCAMP.$_{□A^{12}}$

SULCUS/FISSURE$_{B(\,)}$ ★
    COLLATERAL S.$_{□B^4}$ ★

NUCLEUS$_{C(\,)}$
    ANT. NUC. THAL.$_{□C^{10}}$
    MED. NUC. THAL.$_{□C^{11}}$
    VENT. POST. LAT. NUC.
        THAL.$_{□C^{12}}$

HIPPOCAMP.-DENTATE$_{C^{13}}$
MAMMILLARY BODY$_{C^{14}}$
SUBTHALAMIC REGION$_{C^{15}}$

TRACT/NERVE$_{D(\,)}$
INT. CAPSULE: POST. LIMB$_{D^5}$
FORNIX: BODY$_{D^{13}}$
MAMMILLOTHALAMIC TR.$_{□D^{14}}$

VENTRICLE$_{E(\,)}$●
LAT. VENTRICLE: INF. HORN$_{E^4}$●

○ cingulate gyrus (A^1): 5-26
○ insular gyrus (A^7): 3-9, 3-10
○ superior temporal gyrus (A^8): 3-9, 5-29
○ middle temporal gyrus (A^9): 3-9, 5-29
○ inferior temporal gyrus (A^{10}): 3-9, 5-29
○ occipitotemporal gyrus (A^{11}): 5-29, 5-30
○ parahippocampal gyrus (A^{12}): 5-26, 5-27, 5-30
○ superior parietal lobule (A^{13}): 3-9, 5-29
○ inferior parietal lobule (A^{14}): 3-9, 5-29
⊛ longitudinal cerebral fissure (B^1): 1-2
⊛ lateral fissure (B^2): 5-29
⊛ cingulate sulcus (B^3): 5-30
⊛ collateral sulcus (B^4): 5-27
⊛ hippocampal fissure (B^5): 5-27
○ caudate nucleus (C^1): 3-10, 5-24, 5-25
○ putamen (C^2): 3-10, 5-24, 5-25
○ globus pallidus (C^3): 3-10, 5-24, 5-25
○ claustrum (C^4): 5-24
○ anterior nucleus of thalamus (C^{10}): 5-16, 5-17, 5-18

○ medial nucleus of the thalamus (C^{11}): 5-16, 5-17, 5-18
○ ventral posterior lateral nucleus of the thalamus (C^{12}): 5-16, 5-17, 5-18
○ hippocampus-dentate (C^{13}): 3-10, 5-26, 5-27, 5-28
○ lateral dorsal nucleus of the thalamus (C^{16}): 5-16, 5-17, 5-18
○ red nucleus (C^{17}): 5-10, 5-11, 5-15
○ substantia nigra (C^{18}): 5-10, 5-11, 5-23, 5-25
○ corpus callosum (D^2): 5-33
⊙ corona radiata (D^3): 5-33
○ internal capsule (D^5): 5-33
⊙ external capsule (D^8): 5-24
⊙ extreme capsule (D^9): 5-24
○ optic tract (D^{11}): 3-7, 5-2, 6-7, 6-8
○ fornix (D^{13}): 3-10, 5-21, 5-26, 5-27
○ crus cerebri (D^{15}): 5-2, 5-10, 5-11
◉ lateral ventricle (E^2, E^4): 9-11
◉ third ventricle (E^3): 9-11
○ pons (F^2): 3-8, 5-2, 5-7, 5-8

CORONAL SECTION THROUGH PARIETAL/TEMPORAL LOBES: LEVEL OF THE RED NUCLEUS.

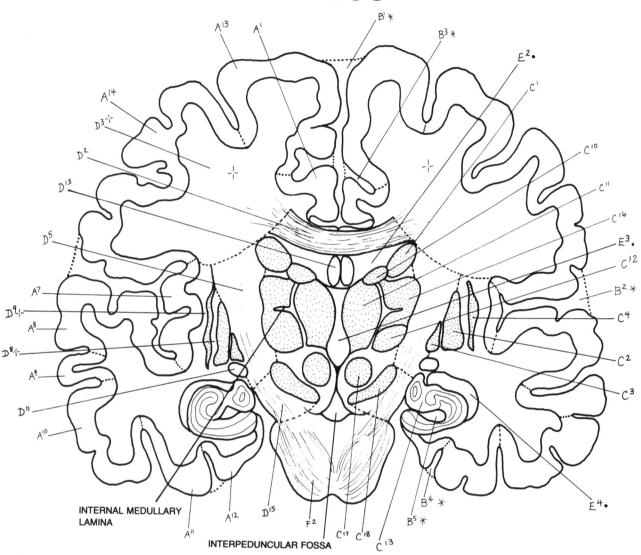

INTERNAL MEDULLARY LAMINA

INTERPEDUNCULAR FOSSA

GYRUS$_{A()}$
  SUP. PARIETAL$_{A^{13}}$
  INF. PARIETAL$_{A^{14}}$

SULCUS/FISSURE$_{B()}$ ★
  COLLATERAL S.$_{B^4}$ ★
  HIPPOCAMPAL F.$_{B^5}$ ★

NUCLEUS$_{C()}$
  ANT. NUC. THAL.$_{C^{10}}$
  MED. NUC. THAL.$_{C^{11}}$
  HIPPOCAMP.-DENTATE$_{C^{13}}$

VENT. POST. LAT. NUC. THAL.$_{C^{16}}$
RED NUC.$_{C^{17}}$
SUBSTANTIA NIGRA$_{C^{18}}$

TRACT/NERVE$_{D()}$
  INT. CAPSULE: POST. LIMB$_{D^5}$
  FORNIX: BODY$_{D^{13}}$
  CRUS CEREBRI$_{D^{15}}$

LANDMARK$_{F()}$
  PONS$_{F^2}$

5–40

CORONAL SECTION THROUGH PARIETAL/TEMPORAL LOBES: LEVEL OF THE PINEAL GLAND

- cingulate gyrus (A^1): 5-26
- superior temporal gyrus (A^8): 3-9, 5-29
- middle temporal gyrus (A^9): 3-9, 5-29
- inferior temporal gyrus (A^{10}): 3-9, 5-29
- occipitotemporal gyrus (A^{11}): 5-29, 5-30
- parahippocampal gyrus (A^{12}): 5-26, 5-27, 5-30
- paracentral lobule (A^{15}): 5-30
- postcentral gyrus (A^{16}): 4-4, 4-5, 5-29
- supramarginal gyrus (A^{17}): 5-29
- longitudinal cerebral fissure (B^1): 1-2
- lateral fissure (B^2): 5-29
- cingulate sulcus (B^3): 5-30
- collateral sulcus (B^4): 5-27
- central sulcus (B^6): 5-29, 5-30
- hippocampus-dentate (C^{13}): 3-10, 5-26, 5-27, 5-28
- pulvinar (C^{19}): 5-11, 5-16, 5-17, 5-18
- superior colliculus (C^{20}): 5-1, 5-10, 6-7
- corpus callosum (D^2): 5-33
- corona radiata (D^3): 5-33
- internal capsule (D^5): 5-33
- fornix (D^{13}): 3-10, 5-21, 5-26, 5-27
- fimbria hippocampus (D^{16}): 5-27, 5-28
- superior cerebellar peduncle (D^{17}): 5-1, 5-8, 5-9, 5-10, 5-15
- middle cerebellar peduncle (D^{18}): 5-1, 5-7, 5-8, 5-15
- inferior cerebellar peduncle (D^{19}): 5-1, 5-6, 5-7, 5-15
- lateral ventricle (E^1, E^4): 9-11
- fourth ventricle (E^5): 9-11
- pineal gland (F^3): 5-11, 5-23
- cerebellar cortex (F^4): 3-8, 5-13, 5-14, 5-15
- medulla oblongata (F^5): 3-8, 5-1, 5-2, 5-4, 5-5, 5-6
- arbor vitae (F^6): 5-13, 5-14

CORONAL SECTION THROUGH PARIETAL/TEMPORAL LOBES: LEVEL OF THE PINEAL GLAND.

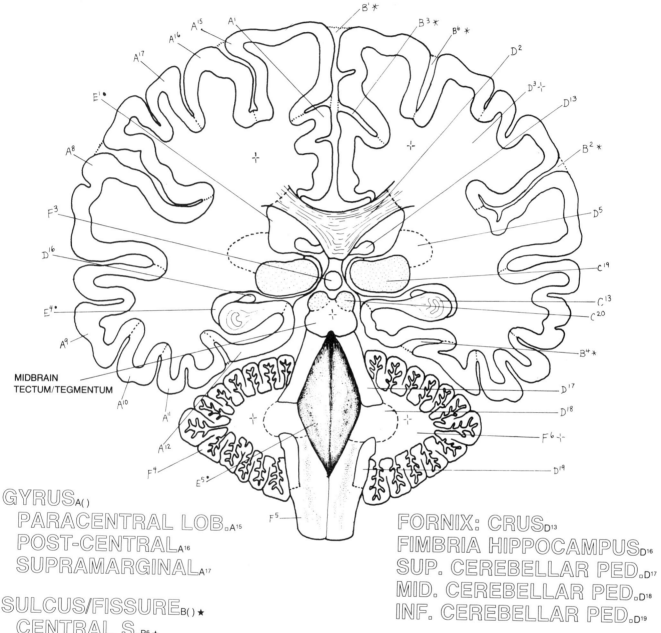

MIDBRAIN
TECTUM/TEGMENTUM

GYRUS A( )
PARACENTRAL LOB. A15
POST-CENTRAL A16
SUPRAMARGINAL A17

SULCUS/FISSURE B( ) ★
CENTRAL S. B6 ★

NUCLEUS C( )
PULVINAR C19
SUP. COLLICULUS C20

TRACT/NERVE D( )
C. CALLOSUM: SPLENIUM D2
INT. CAPSULE: RETROLENT. D5

FORNIX: CRUS D13
FIMBRIA HIPPOCAMPUS D16
SUP. CEREBELLAR PED. D17
MID. CEREBELLAR PED. D18
INF. CEREBELLAR PED. D19

VENTRICLE E( )●
FOURTH VENTRICLE E5●

LANDMARK F( )
PINEAL GLAND F3
CEREBELLAR CORTEX F4
MEDULLA OBLONG. F5
ARBOR VITAE F6⊹

SAGITTAL SECTION THROUGH THE PUTAMEN

○ occipitotemporal gyrus (A^{11}): 5-29, 5-30
○ parahippocampal gyrus (A^{12}): 5-26, 5-27, 5-30
★ lateral fissure (B^2): 5-29
○ putamen (C^2): 3-10, 5-24, 5-25
○ amygdaloid nucleus (C^6): 3-10, 5-26
○ hippocampus-dentate (C^{13}): 3-10, 5-26, 5-27, 5-28

⊙ corona radiata (D^3): 5-33
○ internal capsule (D^5): 5-33
○ anterior commissure (D^{12}): 6-5
● lateral ventricle (E^4, E^6): 9-11
○ cerebellar cortex (F^4): 3-8, 5-13, 5-14, 5-15
○ arbor vitae (F^6): 5-13, 5-14

SAGITTAL SECTION THROUGH THE PUTAMEN.

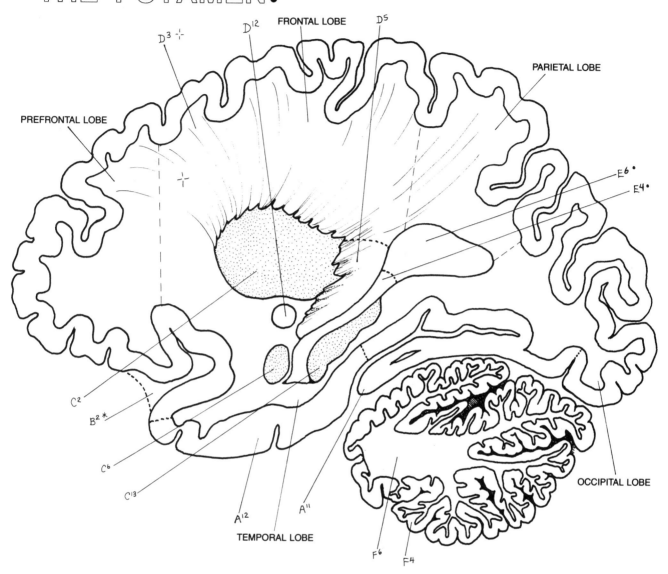

PREFRONTAL LOBE

D^3

D^{12}

FRONTAL LOBE

D^5

PARIETAL LOBE

E^6

E^4

C^2

B^2 ★

C^6

C^{13}

A^{12}

A^{11}

TEMPORAL LOBE

F^6

F^4

OCCIPITAL LOBE

GYRUS$_{A(\ )}$
  OCCIPITOTEMP.$_{\square A^{11}}$
  PARAHIPPOCAMP.$_{\square A^{12}}$

SULCUS/FISSURE$_{B(\ )}$ ★
  LATERAL F.$_{\square B^2}$ ★

NUCLEUS$_{C(\ )}$
  PUTAMEN$_{C^2}$
  AMYGDALOID NUC.$_{\square C^6}$
  HIPPOCAMP.-DENTATE$_{C^{13}}$

TRACT/NERVE$_{D(\ )}$
  C. RADIATA$_{D^3}$

INT. CAPSULE$_{D^5}$
ANT. COMMISSURE$_{D^{12}}$

VENTRICLE$_{E(\ )\bullet}$
  LAT. VENTRICLE: INF.
    HORN$_{E^4\bullet}$
  LAT. VENTRICLE: POST.
    HORN$_{E^6\bullet}$

LANDMARK$_{F(\ )}$
  CEREBELLAR CORTEX$_{F^4}$
  ARBOR VITAE$_{F^6}$

SAGITTAL SECTION THROUGH THE PULVINAR

- ⊛ lateral fissure (B^2): 5-29
- ○ caudate nucleus (C^1): 3-10, 5-24, 5-25
- ○ putamen (C^2): 3-10, 5-24, 5-25
- ○ globus pallidus (C^3): 3-10, 5-24, 5-25
- ○ amygdaloid nucleus (C^6): 3-10, 5-26
- ○ hippocampus-dentate (C^{13}): 3-10, 5-26, 5-27, 5-28
- ○ ventral posterior lateral nucleus of the thalamus (C^{16}): 5-16, 5-17, 5-18
- ○ pulvinar (C^{19}): 5-11, 5-16, 5-17, 5-18
- ○ lateral geniculate body (C^{21}): 5-16, 5-17, 5-18, 6-7, 6-8
- ○ cerebellar nuclei (C^{22}): 5-14, 5-15
- ⊙ corona radiata (D^3): 5-33
- ○ anterior commissure (D^{12}): 6-5
- ○ crus cerebri (D^{15}): 5-2, 5-10, 5-11
- ○ superior cerebellar peduncle (D^{17}): 5-1, 5-8, 5-9, 5-10, 5-15
- ○ middle cerebellar peduncle (D^{18}): 5-1, 5-7, 5-8, 5-15
- ○ inferior cerebellar peduncle (D^{19}): 5-1, 5-6, 5-7, 5-15
- ○ internal capsule (D^{20}, D^{21}, D^{22}): 5-33
- ○ frontopontine tract (D^{23}): 5-10, 5-11
- ○ corticospinal tract (D^{24}): 4-9, 5-4 through 5-11
- ○ parietotemporoccipitopontine tract (D^{25}): 5-10, 5-11
- ◉ lateral ventricle (E^2, E^6, E^7): 9-11
- ○ cerebellar cortex (F^4): 3-8, 5-13, 5-14, 5-15
- ○ arbor vitae (F^6): 5-13, 5-14

SAGITTAL SECTION THROUGH THE PULVINAR.

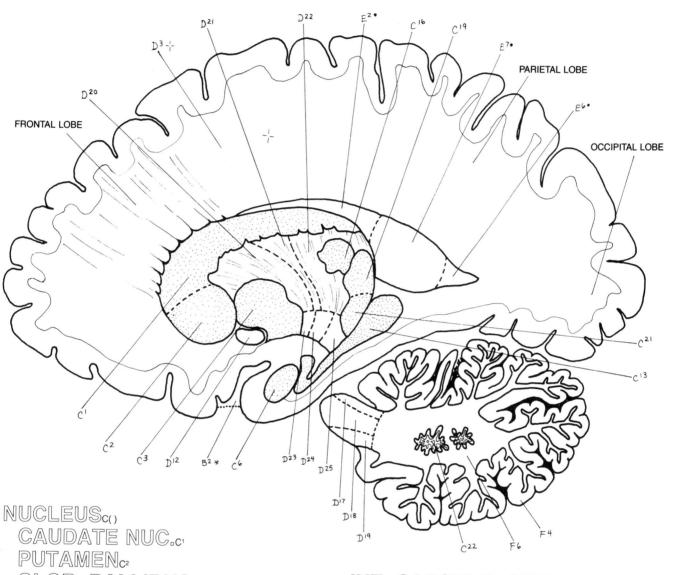

FRONTAL LOBE

PARIETAL LOBE

OCCIPITAL LOBE

NUCLEUS$_{C( )}$
  CAUDATE NUC.$_{C^1}$
  PUTAMEN$_{C^2}$
  GLOB. PALLIDUS$_{C^3}$
  AMYGDALOID NUC.$_{C^6}$
  VENT. POST. LAT. NUC.
    THAL.$_{C^{16}}$
  PULVINAR$_{C^{19}}$
  LAT. GENIC. BODY$_{C^{21}}$
  CEREBELLAR NUC.$_{C^{22}}$

INT. CAPSULE: GENU$_{D^{21}}$
INT. CAPSULE: POST. LIMB$_{D^{22}}$
CRUS CEREBRI$_{D^{15}( )}$
  FRONTOPONT. TR.$_{D^{23}}$
  CORTICOSPINAL TR.$_{D^{24}}$
  PAR-TEMP-OCCIP-PONT.
    TR.$_{D^{25}}$

TRACT/NERVE$_{D( )}$
  INT. CAPSULE: ANT. LIMB$_{D^{20}}$

VENTRICLE$_{E( )}$●
  LAT. VENTRICLE: ATRIUM$_{E^7}$●

- ⊛ calcarine fissure (B⁷): 5-30, 6-7
- ○ caudate nucleus (C¹): 3-10, 5-24, 5-25
- ○ anterior nucleus of the thalamus (C¹⁰): 5-16, 5-17, 5-18
- ○ medial nucleus of the thalamus (C¹¹): 5-16, 5-17, 5-18
- ○ subthalamic region (C¹⁵): 5-23
- ○ red nucleus (C¹⁷): 5-10, 5-11, 5-15
- ○ substantia nigra (C¹⁸): 5-10, 5-11, 5-23, 5-25
- ○ pulvinar (C¹⁹): 5-11, 5-16, 5-17, 5-18
- ○ cerebellar nuclei (C²²): 5-14, 5-15
- ○ pretectum (C²³): 5-11, 6-7
- ○ corpus callosum (D²): 5-33
- ⊙ corona radiata (D³): 5-33

- ○ optic tract (D¹¹): 3-7, 5-2, 6-7, 6-8
- ○ anterior commissure (D¹²): 6-5
- ○ mammillothalamic tract (D¹⁴): 5-22
- ○ superior cerebellar peduncle (D¹⁷): 5-1, 5-8, 5-9, 5-10, 5-15
- ○ corticospinal tract (D²⁴): 4-9, 5-4 through 5-11
- ○ medial lemniscus (D²⁶): 4-4, 5-5 through 5-11, 5-17
- ○ lateral lemniscus (D²⁷): 5-7, 5-8, 5-9, 6-18
- ● lateral ventricle (E²): 9-11
- ○ cerebellar cortex (F⁴): 3-7, 3-8, 5-13, 5-14, 5-15
- ⊙ arbor vitae (F⁶): 5-13, 5-14

SAGITTAL SECTION THROUGH MEDIAL SURFACE OF HEAD OF THE CAUDATE.●

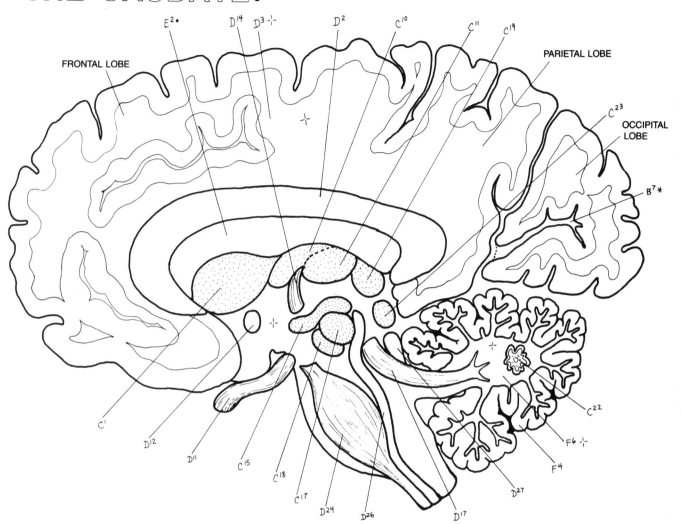

FRONTAL LOBE

PARIETAL LOBE

OCCIPITAL LOBE

SULCUS/FISSURE$_{B()}$ ★
CALCARINE F.$_{□B7}$ ★

NUCLEUS$_{C()}$
CAUDATE NUC.: HEAD$_{C1}$
ANT. NUC. THAL.$_{□C10}$
MED. NUC. THAL.$_{□C11}$
SUBTHALAMIC REG.$_{□C15}$
RED NUC.$_{□C17}$
SUBSTANTIA NIGRA$_{C18}$
PULVINAR$_{C19}$
CEREBELLAR NUC.$_{□C22}$
PRETECTUM$_{C23}$

TRACT/NERVE$_{D()}$
OPTIC TR.$_{□D11}$
MAMMILLOTHALAMIC TR.$_{□D14}$
SUP. CEREBELLAR PED.$_{□D17}$
CORTICOSPINAL TR.$_{□D24}$
MED. LEMNISCUS$_{D26}$
LAT. LEMNISCUS$_{D27}$

VENTRICLE$_{E()}$●
LAT. VENTRICLE: BODY$_{E2}$●

LANDMARK$_{F()}$
CEREBELLAR CORTEX$_{F4}$

○ cingulate gyrus (A^1): 5-26
○ hypothalamus (C^7): 3-8, 5-20, 5-21, 5-22
○ infundibulum (C^9): 5-20
○ medial nucleus of the thalamus (C^{11}): 5-16, 5-17, 5-18
○ mammillary body (C^{14}): 5-20, 5-21, 5-22
○ superior colliculus (C^{20}): 5-1, 5-10, 6-7
○ inferior colliculus (C^{24}): 5-1, 5-9, 6-18
○ midbrain tegmentum (C^{25}): 5-9 through 5-12, 5-23
○ reticular formation (C^{26}): 5-5 through 5-12, 5-19
○ corpus callosum (D^2): 5-33
○ optic tract (D^{11}): 5-2, 6-7, 6-8
○ anterior commissure (D^{12}): 6-5

○ fornix (D^{13}): 3-10, 5-21, 5-26, 5-27
○ stria medullaris (D^{28}): 5-23
◉ fourth ventricle (E^5): 9-11
◉ interventricular foramen (E^8): 3-10, 9-11
◉ cerebral aqueduct (E^9): 5-9, 5-10, 9-11
⊙ septum pellucidum (F^1): 5-26
○ pons (F^2): 3-8, 5-2, 5-7, 5-8
○ pineal gland (F^3): 5-11, 5-23
○ cerebellar cortex (F^4): 5-13, 5-14, 5-15
○ medulla oblongata (F^5): 5-1, 5-2, 5-4, 5-5, 5-6
○ arbor vitae (F^6): 5-13, 5-14
○ superior medullary velum (F^7): 5-8

MEDIAN SECTION.

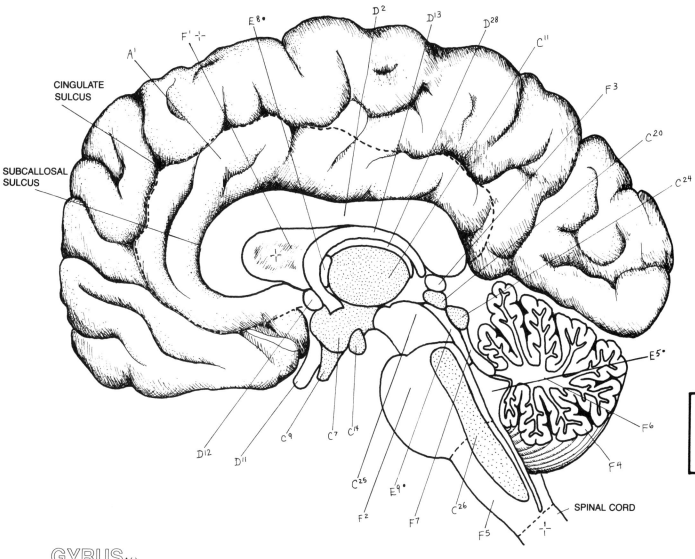

CINGULATE SULCUS

SUBCALLOSAL SULCUS

SPINAL CORD

GYRUS$_{A(\ )}$
   CINGULATE$_{A^1}$

NUCLEUS$_{C(\ )}$
   HYPOTHALAMUS$_{C7}$
   INFUNDIBULUM$_{C9}$
   MAMMILLARY BODY$_{C14}$
   MED. NUC. THAL.$_{C11}$
   SUP. COLLICULUS$_{C20}$
   INF. COLLICULUS$_{C24}$
   MIDBRAIN TEGMENTUM$_{C25}$
   RETIC. FORM.$_{C26}$

TRACT/NERVE$_{D(\ )}$
   OPTIC TR.$_{D11}$

STRIA MEDULLARIS$_{D28}$

VENTRICLE$_{E(\ )\bullet}$
   FOURTH VENTRICLE$_{E5\bullet}$
   INTERVENTRIC. FOR.$_{E8\bullet}$
   CEREB. AQUEDUCT$_{E9\bullet}$

LANDMARKS$_{F(\ )}$
   PONS$_{F2}$
   PINEAL GLAND$_{F3}$
   CEREBELLAR CORTEX$_{F4}$
   MEDULLA OBLONG.$_{F5}$
   SUP. MEDULLARY VELUM$_{F7}$

○ cingulate gyrus (A^1): 5-26
○ postcentral gyrus (A^{16}): 4-4, 4-5, 4-6, 5-29
○ precentral gyrus (A^{18}): 4-9, 5-29
⊛ longitudinal cerebral fissure (B^1): 1-2
⊛ lateral fissure (B^2): 5-29
⊛ central sulcus (B^6): 5-29, 5-30

○ caudate nucleus (C^1): 3-10, 5-24, 5-25
○ corpus callosum (D^2): 5-33
⊙ corona radiata (D^3): 5-33
○ fornix (D^{13}): 3-10, 5-21, 5-26, 5-27
◉ lateral ventricle (E^2): 9-11

HORIZONTAL SECTION THROUGH HEAD OF THE CAUDATE NUCLEUS.

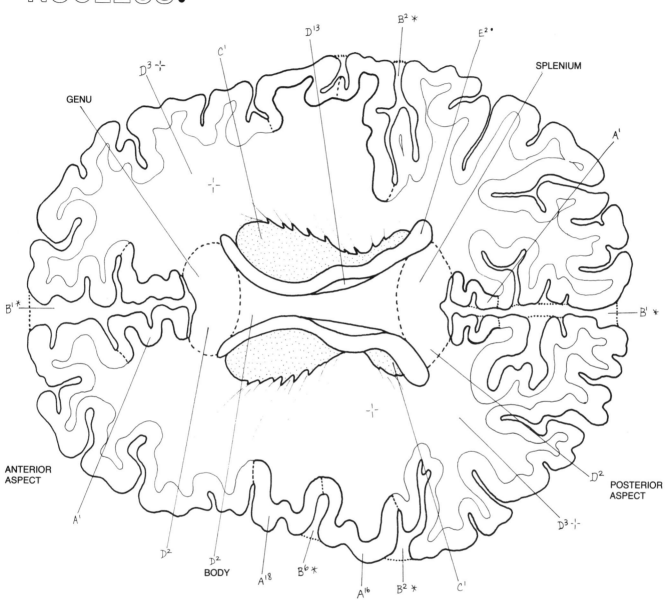

GENU

D³ -¦-

D¹³

C¹

B² *

E² •

SPLENIUM

A¹

B¹ *

B¹ *

ANTERIOR
ASPECT

A¹

D²

D²

BODY

A¹⁸

B⁶ *

A¹⁶

B² *

C¹

D²

POSTERIOR
ASPECT

D³ -¦-

GYRUS_A( )
   CINGULATE_A¹
   POSTCENTRAL_A¹⁶
   PRECENTRAL_A¹⁸

SULCUS/FISSURE_B( ) ★
   LONG. CEREB. F._B¹ ★
   LATERAL F._B² ★
   CENTRAL S._B⁶ ★

NUCLEUS_C( )
   CAUDATE NUC.: HEAD/TAIL_C¹

TRACT/NERVE_D( )
   C. CALLOSUM_D²
   FORNIX_D¹³

VENTRICLE_E( ) •
   LAT. VENTRICLE: BODY_E² •

○ cingulate gyrus (A^1): 5-26
○ insular gyrus (A^7): 3-9, 3-10
○ opercular gyrus (A^{19}): 5-29
⊛ longitudinal cerebral fissure (B^1): 1-2
⊛ calcarine fissure (B^7): 5-30, 6-7
○ caudate nucleus (C^1): 3-10, 5-24, 5-25
○ putamen (C^2): 3-10, 5-24, 5-25
○ anterior nucleus of the thalamus (C^{10}): 5-16, 5-17, 5-18
○ medial nucleus of the thalamus (C^{11}): 5-16, 5-17, 5-18
○ lateral nucleus of the thalamus (C^{12}): 5-16, 5-17, 5-18

○ pulvinar (C^{19}): 5-11, 5-16, 5-17, 5-18
○ corpus callosum (D^2): 5-33
⊙ corona radiata (D^3): 5-33
○ fornix (D^{13}): 3-10, 5-21, 5-26, 5-27
○ internal capsule (D^{20}, D^{21}, D^{22}): 5-33
◉ lateral ventricle (E^1, E^7): 9-11
◉ third ventricle (E^3): 9-11
◉ interventricular foramen (E^8): 3-10, 9-11
⊙ septum pellucidum (F^1): 5-26

HORIZONTAL SECTION THROUGH ANTERIOR NUCLEUS OF THE THALAMUS.

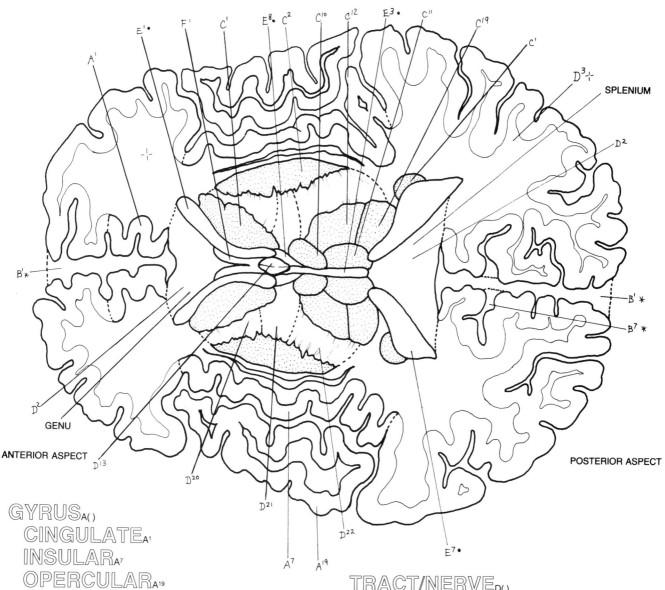

SPLENIUM

ANTERIOR ASPECT

POSTERIOR ASPECT

GENU

GYRUS$_{A(\ )}$
   CINGULATE$_{A1}$
   INSULAR$_{A7}$
   OPERCULAR$_{A19}$

SULCUS/FISSURE$_{B(\ )}$★
   CALCARINE F.$_{B7}$★

NUCLEUS$_{C(\ )}$
   CAUDATE NUC.: HEAD/TAIL$_{C1}$
   PUTAMEN$_{C2}$
   ANT. NUC. THAL.$_{C10}$
   MED. NUC. THAL.$_{C11}$
   LAT. NUC. THAL.$_{C12}$
   PULVINAR$_{C19}$

TRACT/NERVE$_{D(\ )}$
   C. CALLOSUM$_{D2}$
   FORNIX$_{D13}$
   INT. CAPSULE: ANT. LIMB$_{D20}$
   INT. CAPSULE: GENU$_{D21}$
   INT. CAPSULE: POST. LIMB$_{D22}$

VENTRICLE$_{E(\ )}$●
   LAT. VENTRICLE: ANT.
      HORN$_{E1}$●
   LAT. VENTRICLE: ATRIUM$_{E7}$●

○ insular gyrus (A^7): 3-9, 3-10
★ longitudinal cerebral fissure (B^1): 1-2
○ caudate nucleus (C^1): 3-10, 5-24, 5-25
○ putamen (C^2): 3-10, 5-24, 5-25
○ globus pallidus (C^3): 3-10, 5-24, 5-25
○ claustrum (C^4): 5-24
○ ventral posterior lateral nucleus of the thalamus (C^{16}): 5-16, 5-17, 5-18
○ pulvinar (C^{19}): 5-11, 5-16, 5-17, 5-18
○ ventral posterior medial nucleus of the thalamus (C^{27}): 5-16, 5-17, 5-18
○ intralaminar nucleus of the thalamus (C^{28}): 4-5, 5-16 through 5-19, 5-34

○ medial/lateral habenular nucleus (C^{29}): 5-23
⊙ corona radiata (D^3): 5-33
○ internal capsule (D^5): 5-33
⊙ external capsule (D^8): 5-24
⊙ extreme capsule (D^9): 5-24
○ anterior commissure (D^{12}): 6-5
○ mammillothalamic tract (D^{14}): 5-22
○ habenular commissure (D^{29}): 5-23
◉ third ventricle (E^3): 9-11
◉ lateral ventricle (E^6): 9-11
○ pineal gland (F^3): 5-11, 5-23

HORIZONTAL SECTION THROUGH THE PINEAL GLAND.

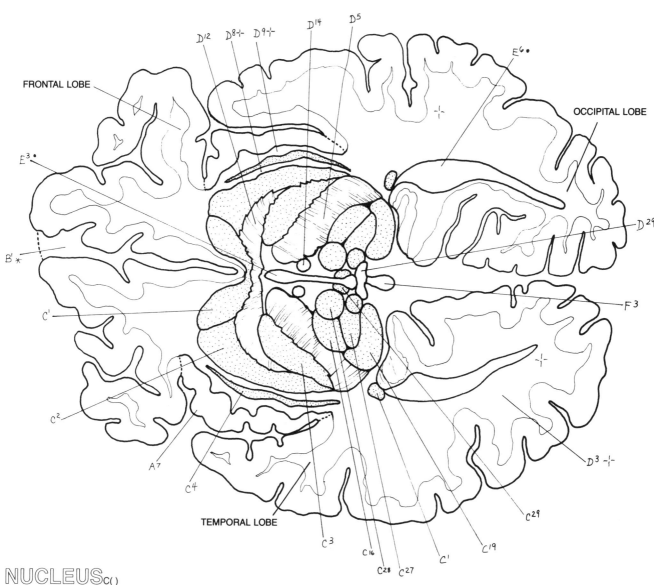

FRONTAL LOBE

OCCIPITAL LOBE

TEMPORAL LOBE

D^{12} D^{8} D^{9} D^{14} D^{5} E^{6}

E^{3}

B'

C^{1}

C^{2}

A^{7}

C^{4}

C^{3}

C^{16} C^{28} C^{27} C^{1} C^{19}

C^{29}

D^{3}

F^{3}

D^{29}

NUCLEUS $_{C( )}$
   CAUDATE NUC.: HEAD/TAIL $_{C^1}$
   PUTAMEN $_{C^2}$
   GLOB. PALLIDUS $_{C^3}$
   CLAUSTRUM $_{C^4}$
   VENT. POST. LAT. NUC.
     THAL. $_{C^{16}}$
   PULVINAR $_{C^{19}}$
   VENT. POST. MED. NUC.
     THAL. $_{C^{27}}$
   INTRALAMINAR NUC. THAL. $_{C^{28}}$
   MED./LAT. HABENULAR NUC. $_{C^{29}}$

TRACT/NERVE $_{D( )}$
   INT. CAPSULE: POST. LIMB $_{D^5}$
   ANT. COMMISSURE $_{D^{12}}$
   MAMMILLOTHALAMIC TR. $_{D^{14}}$
   HABENULAR COMMISSURE $_{D^{29}}$

VENTRICLE $_{E( )}$
   THIRD VENTRICLE $_{E^3}$
   LAT. VENTRICLE: POST. HORN $_{E^6}$

LANDMARK $_{F( )}$
   PINEAL GLAND $_{F^3}$

○ amygdaloid nucleus (C^6): 3-10, 5-26
○ infundibulum (C^9): 5-20
○ hippocampus-dentate (C^{13}): 3-10, 5-26, 5-27, 5-28
○ mammillary body (C^{14}): 5-20, 5-21, 5-22
○ substantia nigra (C^{18}): 5-10, 5-11, 5-23, 5-25
○ inferior colliculus (C^{24}): 5-9, 6-18
○ periaqueductal gray (C^{30}): 4-5, 5-9, 5-10, 5-34
⊙ corona radiata (D^3): 5-33
○ optic chiasm (D^{10}): 5-2, 6-7, 6-8

○ optic tract (D^{11}): 3-7, 5-2, 6-7, 6-8
○ crus cerebri (D^{15}): 5-2, 5-10, 5-11
○ frontopontine tract (D^{23}): 5-10, 5-11
○ corticospinal tract (D^{24}): 4-9, 5-4 through 5-11
○ parietotemporoccipitopontine tract (D^{25}): 5-10, 5-11
● third ventricle (E^3): 9-11
● cerebral aqueduct (E^9): 5-9, 5-10, 9-11
○ cerebellum (F^4): 3-7, 3-8, 5-13, 5-14, 5-15

HORIZONTAL SECTION THROUGH THE MAMMILLARY BODIES.

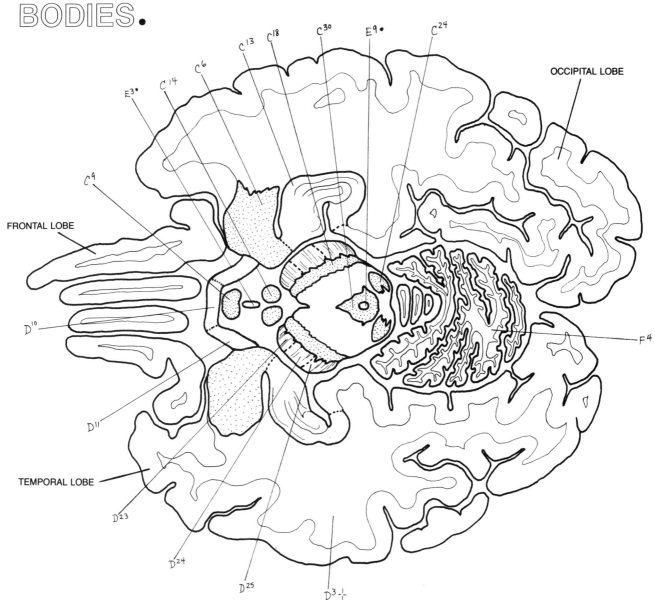

C¹³ C¹⁸ C³⁰ E⁹• C²⁴

C⁶

E³• C¹⁴

OCCIPITAL LOBE

C⁹

FRONTAL LOBE

D¹⁰

D¹¹

F⁴

TEMPORAL LOBE

D²³

D²⁴

D²⁵

D³-⊦

NUCLEUS_C( )
  AMYGDALOID NUC._C⁶
  INFUNDIBULUM_C⁹
  HIPPOCAMP.-DENTATE_C¹³
  MAMMILLARY BODY_C¹⁴
  SUBSTANTIA NIGRA_C¹⁸
  INF. COLLICULUS_C²⁴
  PERIAQUED. GRAY_C³⁰

TRACT/NERVE_D( )
  CRUS CEREBRI_D¹⁵( )

FRONTOPONT. TR._D²³
CORTICOSPINAL TR._D²⁴
PAR-TEMP-OCCIP-PONT.
  TR._D²⁵

VENTRICLE_E( )•
  CEREB. AQUEDUCT_E⁹•

LANDMARK_F( )
  CEREBELLUM_F⁴

Twelve pairs of cranial nerves transmit information to and commands from the brain. The complex receptor organs associated with these nerves in the head and neck are not found in the rest of the body.

Cranial nerves are referred to in Roman numerical order (I through XII), with I at the rostral end of the brain and XII at the caudal end near the medulla–spinal cord junction. The name of a cranial nerve may be written in three ways: for example, cranial nerve II, second (cranial) nerve, or optic nerve.

Color the heading -Encephalon gray (★), titles A through E, and the related representative brain divisions in the left illustration. Use contrasting colors. Color the heading Cranial Nerves, titles A^1 through E^6, and the nerves and numerals related to the brain divisions at the left. Match the color of the nerve and its numeral with the related brain division; for multiple nerves of one brain division (such as E^1 through E^5), use different shades of the color chosen for the division.

Cranial nerves are each associated with a specific region of the embryonic brain. Thus cranial nerve I arises from the telencephalon, cranial nerve II from the diencephalon, and so on. Note that the majority of cranial nerves (V through XII) are related to the hindbrain and that cranial nerve XI has both cranial and spinal origins.

Beginning with A^1, color the paired cranial nerves on the anterior-inferior surface of the brain and the semicircular arrangement of effectors, receptors, and numerals, using the same colors as those of titles A^1 through E^6.

The *olfactory* (I) *nerve* (A^1) consists of short, fine fibers in the olfactory mucous membrane at the roof of the nasal cavity and are receptive to smell (olfaction). These fibers pass through a perforated bony plate to enter the olfactory bulb. The bulb and contiguous olfactory tract are extended parts of the telencephalon; they are not olfactory nerves and therefore are not colored.

The *optic* (II) *nerve* (B^1) arises in the retina (visual photoreceptor layer) in the posterior aspect of the eyeball. The fibers leave the eyeball and surrounding orbit to enter the middle cranial fossa of the skull and merge with contralateral fibers at the optic chiasm. The optic chiasm and contiguous tract are extended parts of the diencephalon and therefore are not colored.

The *oculomotor* (III) *nerve* (C^1) projects from the midbrain, enters the orbit, and innervates four of the six extrinsic eye muscles as well as the intrinsic eye muscles (not shown) and the levator muscle of the upper eyelid.

The *trochlear* (IV) *nerve* (C^2) projects from the midbrain, arising from the posterior surface (the only one to do so), and enters the orbit close to the oculomotor nerve to innervate one (the superior oblique) of the six extrinsic eye muscles.

The *trigeminal* (V) *nerve* (D^1) arises from the pons as three large branches (V_1, V_2, and V_3), each of which passes through different skull foramina to provide sensory fibers to the face, nose, and mouth. The V_3 branch contains a motor component to the muscles of mastication and the tensor tympani muscle (not shown) in the middle ear.

The *abducens* (VI) *nerve* (D^2) arises at the pontine-medullary junction and enters the orbit with the oculomotor and trochlear nerves to innervate one (the lateral rectus) of the six extrinsic eye muscles.

The *facial* (VII) *nerve* (E^1) consists of two branches (one is shown) as it leaves the cerebellopontine angle and divides complexly. It supplies the muscles of facial expression, the stapedius muscle in the middle ear (not shown), two pairs of salivary glands, the soft palate, and the taste buds on the anterior two-thirds of the tongue.

The *vestibulocochlear* (VIII) *nerve* (E^2) leaves the medulla at the cerebellopontine angle to enter the inner ear as two parts, the cochlear division for hearing and the vestibular division for maintenance of equilibrium.

The *glossopharyngeal* (IX) *nerve* (E^3) leaves the medulla and skull to supply the taste buds of the posterior third of the tongue, the parotid salivary gland, and the muscles of the pharynx; it is sensory to the posterior mouth and the pharynx.

The *vagus* (X) *nerve* (E^4) leaves the medulla and skull to supply motor and sensory innervation to the pharynx, larynx, and thoracic and abdominal viscera, as well as part of the ear.

The *accessory* (XI) *nerve* (E^5) has both a spinal (C1–C5) component and a cranial component, of which the cranial part is associated with (accessory to) the vagus nerve. The spinal part (root) supplies the large neck muscles, sternocleidomastoid (laterally), and trapezius (posteriorly).

The *hypoglossal* (XII) *nerve* (E^6) leaves the medulla and skull to supply the muscles of the tongue.

OVERVIEW OF THE CRANIAL NERVES.

-ENCEPHALON.★
TEL-A
DI-B
MES-C
MET-D
MYEL-E

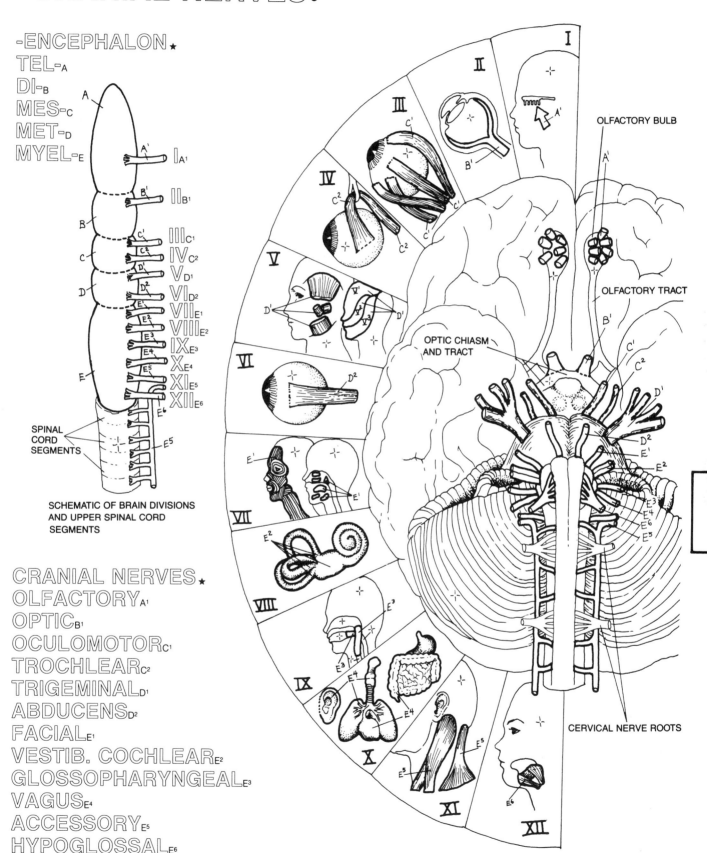

I_{A^1}
II_{B^1}
III_{C^1}
IV_{C^2}
V_{D^1}
VI_{D^2}
VII_{E^1}
VIII_{E^2}
IX_{E^3}
X_{E^4}
XI_{E^5}
XII_{E^6}

SPINAL
CORD
SEGMENTS

SCHEMATIC OF BRAIN DIVISIONS
AND UPPER SPINAL CORD
SEGMENTS

CRANIAL NERVES.★
OLFACTORY$_{A^1}$
OPTIC$_{B^1}$
OCULOMOTOR$_{C^1}$
TROCHLEAR$_{C^2}$
TRIGEMINAL$_{D^1}$
ABDUCENS$_{D^2}$
FACIAL$_{E^1}$
VESTIB. COCHLEAR$_{E^2}$
GLOSSOPHARYNGEAL$_{E^3}$
VAGUS$_{E^4}$
ACCESSORY$_{E^5}$
HYPOGLOSSAL$_{E^6}$

OLFACTORY BULB

OLFACTORY TRACT

OPTIC CHIASM
AND TRACT

CERVICAL NERVE ROOTS

I
II
III
IV
V
VI
VII
VIII
IX
X
XI
XII

The brain reposes in and is protected by the cranial vault of the skull. The fibers of the cranial nerves must enter and exit this enclosed cavity through a series of openings or foramina (sing. *foramen,* "opening, passage") in the base of the skull. Terms generally synonymous with *foramen* (for the purposes of this plate) include *fissure, canal,* and *meatus.* Knowledge of the location of these foramina can help in determining the ultimate destinations of the cranial nerves within. Under certain conditions of trauma or disease, these foramina become potential sites of nerve compression, the symptoms or signs of which will be expressed by the receptors or effectors associated with the respective nerves.

Color the titles of each foramen, canal, and meatus, their respective cranial nerves, and the related nerve (on the left) and foramen (on the right) in the illustration.

The frontal lobes of the cerebral hemispheres fit in the anterior cranial fossae. On each side of the midline, between the fossae, *cribriform* (perforated) *plates of the ethmoid bone* (A) transmit the fibers of the *olfactory nerves* (A^1) ascending from the mucous membrane (surface lining) of the upper nasal cavity. The olfactory bulb and tract lie adjacent to these plates. Trauma to the nose and upper nasal cavity can injure the tiny olfactory fibers in the cribriform plate, resulting in loss of smell (anosmia).

The *optic canal* (B) transmits the *optic nerve* (B^1) in company with the ophthalmic artery to the orbital cavity (orbit) and, in the case of the optic nerve, directly to the eyeball. The central artery of the retina passes within the dural sheath enclosing the optic fibers. Trauma to the head can cause swelling in the sheath of the optic nerve within the optic canal, compressing the nerve fibers and vessel and causing blindness.

The *superior orbital fissure* (C) conducts the *oculomotor* (C^1), *trochlear* (C^2), *ophthalmic* (first) *division of the trigeminal* (C^3), and the *abducens nerves* (C^4). This open-

ing is just under the edge of the anterior cranial fossa and receives these nerves as they project anteriorly into the orbital cavity.

The *foramen rotundum* (D) conducts the *maxillary* (second) *division of the trigeminal nerve* (D^1) in an anterior direction as it proceeds toward the upper teeth, nasal cavity, and face. The *foramen ovale* (E) transmits the *mandibular* (third) *division of the trigeminal nerve* (E^1) in a caudal direction as it enters the infratemporal fossa (in front of and below the ear, deep to the mandible), containing several of the muscles of mastication.

The *internal auditory meatus* (F), located on the lateral wall of the posterior cranial fossa (petrous portion of the temporal bone), receives the fibers of the *facial* (F^1) and *vestibulocochlear nerves* (F^2). Tumors associated with the sheath of cranial nerve VIII (acoustic pseudoneuroma) may grow into the internal auditory meatus, compressing these nerves and resulting in deafness, vestibular problems, or both.

The *jugular foramen* (G), located inferior to the internal auditory meatus, transmits the *glossopharyngeal* (G^1), *vagus* (G^2), and cranial and spinal roots of the *accessory nerves* (G^3). These nerves share the foramen with the jugular vein (not shown; see Plate 9-9), which emerges at this point from the sigmoid sinus. The jugular vein is one of the main vessels draining blood from the brain and conducting it (indirectly) to the heart.

The *hypoglossal canal* (H), located on each side of the foramen magnum, conducts the *hypoglossal nerve* (H^1) en route to the base of the tongue. The internal auditory, jugular, and hypoglossal foramina just described are arranged along the lateral aspects of the lower brain stem and receive their nerves along a descending line.

The *foramen magnum* (I), the largest of all the skull foramina, contains the spinal cord, vertebral arteries and their anterior and posterior spinal branches (not shown), and the *spinal roots of the accessory nerve* (I^1) as they enter or leave the skull.

CRANIAL NERVES AND RESPECTIVE SKULL FORAMINA.

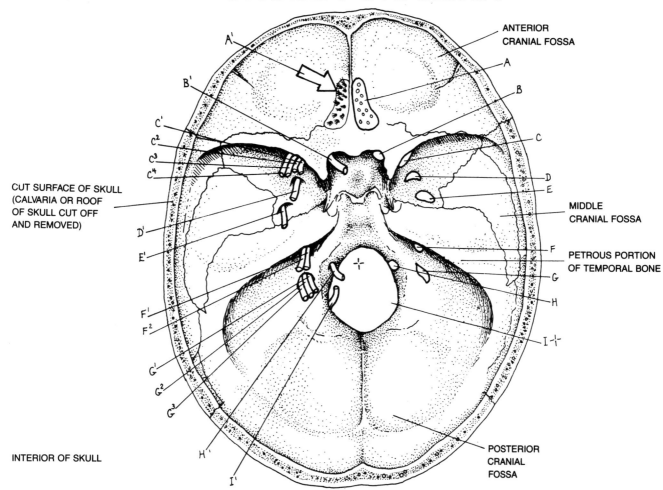

ANTERIOR CRANIAL FOSSA

MIDDLE CRANIAL FOSSA

PETROUS PORTION OF TEMPORAL BONE

CUT SURFACE OF SKULL (CALVARIA OR ROOF OF SKULL CUT OFF AND REMOVED)

INTERIOR OF SKULL

POSTERIOR CRANIAL FOSSA

CRIBRIFORM PLATE OF THE ETHMOID BONE$_A$
OLFACTORY N.$_{A^1}$

OPTIC CANAL$_B$/OPTIC N.$_{B^1}$

SUPERIOR ORBITAL FISSURE$_C$
OCULOMOTOR N.$_{C^1}$
TROCHLEAR N.$_{C^2}$
OPHTHALMIC DIV. TRIGEM. N.$_{C^3}$
ABDUCENS N.$_{C^4}$

FORAMEN ROTUNDUM$_D$
MAXILLARY DIV. TRIGEM. N.$_{D^1}$

FORAMEN OVALE$_E$
MANDIBULAR DIV. TRIGEM. N.$_{E^1}$

INT. AUDITORY MEATUS$_F$
FACIAL N.$_{F^1}$
VESTIBULOCOCHLEAR N.$_{F^2}$

JUGULAR FORAMEN$_G$
GLOSSOPHARYNGEAL N.$_{G^1}$
VAGUS N.$_{G^2}$
CRANIAL/SP. ROOTS ACCESS. N.$_{G^3}$

HYPOGLOSSAL CANAL$_H$
HYPOGLOSSAL N.$_{H^1}$

FORAMEN MAGNUM$_{+}$
SPINAL ROOT ACCESS. N.$_{I^1}$

The adult position and organization of the cranial nerve nuclei reflect their embryological source and development in the brain stem. The three cross sections in this plate represent progressive stages in the evolution of the neural tube from its primitive state in the early embryo (upper) through the stage of ventricular expansion in the rhombencephalon (middle) to the stage of a more mature brain stem configuration (lower). The circles represent cross-sectional views of columns of neurons, the organization of which is the subject of this plate.

Color titles A through G and related areas and arrows in each of the three illustrations. A dark color for A and light colors for B and C are recommended.

The *sulcus limitans* (A) of the embryonic neural tube divides the tube into the *basal* (B) and *alar plates* (C; recall Plate 3-6). The cells in the basal plate are primarily related to motor functions, those in the alar plate to sensory functions. The terms used in this plate for grouping cells into a functional organization are as follows:

afferent = sensory *somatic* = skin, skeletal muscle
efferent = motor *visceral* = hollow organs

The cell bodies in the alar plate receive afferent fibers (largely central processes of primary sensory neurons); the cell bodies in the basal plate give rise to efferent fibers. The efferent neurons and fibers that supply skeletal muscle and related connective tissue and skin are termed *somatic efferent*. The efferent neurons and fibers that supply the smooth muscle in the walls of hollow organs, cardiac muscle, or glands (viscera) are classified as *visceral*. Because both cranial and spinal nerves contain such categories of axons, the terms are preceded by the descriptive term *general*.

Cranial nerves III, IV, VI, and XII are *general somatic efferent* (D) neurons. These neurons are characteristically arranged in a column on each side of the midline anterior to the ventricle in their respective divisions of the brain stem. Throughout brain stem development, this GSE column remains close to the midline of the brain stem.

Cranial nerves VII, IX and X contain, in part, axons of *general visceral efferent* (E) neurons. This column of neurons is at first located more posteriorly than the general somatic efferent column. As the ventricle widens, the visceral efferent column of neurons moves to an adult position lateral to the somatic efferent column, still separated from the afferent neurons by an imaginary line extending inward from the sulcus limitans.

Cranial nerves VII, IX, and X contain axons of *general visceral afferent* (F) neurons. These neurons form a column posterior to the sulcus limitans in the alar plate. Cranial nerves V, VII, IX, and X also contain axons of *general somatic afferent* (G) neurons, which form in the alar plate posterior to the visceral afferent column. With widening of the ventricle (see lowest illustration), the somatic afferent neurons assume a position in the posteriolateral aspect of the brain stem.

Color titles H through J and related areas in the section of the medulla oblongata of the newborn.

The term *special* is used to designate certain afferent and efferent neurons that have no counterpart among the spinal nerves and are special with respect to the muscles they supply or the receptors with which they are associated.

Cranial nerves V, VII, IX, X, and XI contain axons of *special visceral efferent* (H) neurons. These axons innervate muscles that are derived from the embryonic gill arches (branchiomeric muscles). These develop into skeletal (voluntary) muscles of the jaw, mouth, face, pharynx, and larynx. Note that the column of these neurons is located anterior to those of the two general efferent columns.

Cranial nerves VII, IX, and X contain axons of the *special visceral afferent* (I) column located anterior to the general afferent column. These fibers conduct impulses from the taste-bud receptors on the tongue and pharynx.

Cranial nerve VIII contains fibers of *special somatic afferent* (J) neurons, which are located between the two general afferent columns. These fibers conduct impulses concerned with hearing and balance.

CRANIAL NERVE NUCLEI FUNCTIONAL ORGANIZATION.

SULCUS LIMITANS_A
ALAR PLATE_B
BASAL PLATE_C
GENERAL SOMATIC
    EFFERENT (GSE)_D
GENERAL VISCERAL
    EFFERENT (GVE)_E
GENERAL VISCERAL
    AFFERENT (GVA)_F
GENERAL SOMATIC
    AFFERENT (GSA)_G
SPECIAL VISCERAL
    EFFERENT (SVE)_H
SPECIAL VISCERAL
    AFFERENT (SVA)_I
SPECIAL SOMATIC
    AFFERENT (SSA)_J

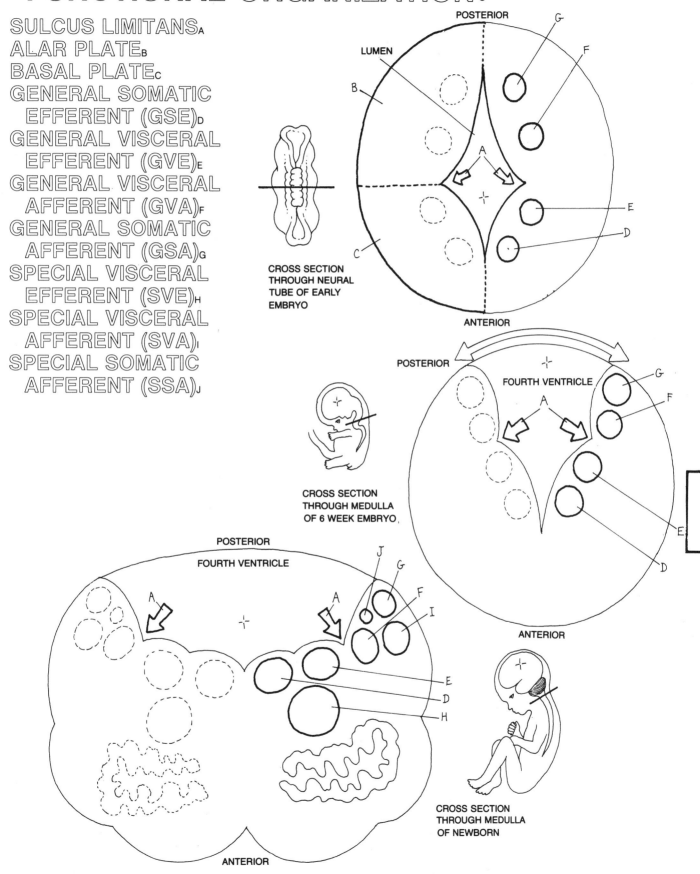

CROSS SECTION
THROUGH NEURAL
TUBE OF EARLY
EMBRYO

CROSS SECTION
THROUGH MEDULLA
OF 6 WEEK EMBRYO

CROSS SECTION
THROUGH MEDULLA
OF NEWBORN

Cranial nerves may contain sensory axons, motor axons, or a combination of both. For the most part, the cell bodies of sensory axons (primary sensory neurons) are located in ganglia outside the brain stem; such ganglia are not shown in this plate. However, the cell bodies of a part of the fifth cranial nerve are located in the brain stem and are included here along with secondary sensory nuclei—nuclei of the fifth nerve, vestibular and cochlear nuclei, and nucleus solitarius. Cranial nerves I and II are not shown.

Color the heading Sensory, titles A through F, and the related nuclei and fibers on the left side of the illustration. Color the fibers the same color as their related nuclei except for C, D, E, and F. Do not color the motor components yet.

The largest of the cranial nerves, the trigeminal (V) has four nuclei in the brain stem, of which three are sensory. The *mesencephalic nucleus of the trigeminal nerve* (A), ascending from upper pons to the level of the superior colliculus, consists of cell bodies receiving proprioceptive impulses from afferents (*fibers,* A^1) located in the muscles of mastication. The *main sensory nucleus of the trigeminal nerve* (A^2), at the level of the pons, receives the central processes (*fibers,* A^3) of the sensory neurons concerned with position sense, touch and two-point discrimination from the face and nasal and oral cavities. The *spinal trigeminal nucleus* (A^4) runs from the mid pons to the cervical spinal cord, receiving pain and temperature sensations from processes (*fibers,* A^5) making up the tract of the spinal trigeminal nucleus.

The *vestibular nuclei* (B) consist of four cell masses that receive the central processes (*fibers,* B^1) of cell bodies in the vestibular ganglion of nerve VIII, relating to balance and equilibrium. The *cochlear nuclei* (B^2) consist of two cell groups that receive the central processes (*fibers,* B^3) of cell bodies in the cochlear (spiral) ganglion of nerve VIII, carrying auditory impulses.

The *nucleus solitarius* (C) receives central processes (*fibers*) from *nerves VII* (D), *IX* (E), and *X* (F) relating to special visceral (taste) and general visceral sensations. These processes form the tractus solitarius.

Color the heading Motor, titles G through N^1, and related nuclei and fibers on the right side of the illustration, using the coloring scheme described be-fore. **Color the title Foramen Magnum (O ⋆) and its representation at the spinal cord–medulla boundary.**

The oculomotor nuclear complex lies anterior to the cerebral aqueduct at the level of the superior colliculus in the midbrain. There are two principal components of this nuclear complex. The smaller, more rostral *nucleus of Edinger Westphal* (G^1) sends visceral motor efferents (not shown) to the intrinsic muscles of the eye. The larger, more caudal *oculomotor nucleus* (G) innervates four of the six extrinsic muscles of the eye as well as the skeletal muscle of the upper eyelid. The *trochlear nucleus* (H) lies caudal to the nuclei just presented, in the same general somatic efferent column, at the level of the inferior colliculi of the midbrain. Its *fibers* (H^1) cross caudal to the nucleus to emerge from the brain stem posteriorly. They wrap around the crus cerebri and exit through the superior orbital fissure to innervate the superior oblique eye muscle.

The *motor nucleus of the trigeminal nerve* (A^6) sends fibers (A^7) with the mandibular division of this nerve to innervate the muscles of mastication. The *abducens nucleus* (I) of nerve VI is in the floor of the fourth ventricle; its *fibers* (I^1) exit anteriorly at the pontine-medullary junction on their way to the lateral rectus muscle of the eye. The *facial nucleus* (D^1) lies lateral and anterior to the nucleus of nerve VI. Its special visceral efferent *fibers* (D^2) follow an unusual course, ascending in the brain stem and sweeping around the nucleus of nerve VI to exit at the pontocerebellar junction and project to the muscles of facial expression.

The *superior salivatory nucleus* (J) contributes general visceral efferent fibers (not shown) to nerve VII; these axons supply secretomotor fibers to the submandibular and sublingual salivary glands. The *inferior salivatory nucleus* (K) sends secretomotor fibers (not shown), via nerve IX, to the parotid salivary gland.

The *nucleus ambiguus* (L) contributes *fibers* to nerves *IX* (E^1), *X* (F^1), and the cranial root of nerve *XI* (M). These special visceral efferents innervate the muscles of the pharynx and larynx. The *dorsal motor nucleus of the vagus nerve* (F^2) sends general visceral efferent *fibers* (F^3) to thoracic and abdominal viscera.

The *nucleus of the spinal accessory nerve* (M^1) in the *anterior horn* of the upper cervical segments of the spinal cord projects its *fibers* (M^2) up through the foramen magnum and jugular foramen to innervate the muscles of the neck and upper back. The *hypoglossal nucleus* (N) lies medial to the dorsal motor nucleus of the vagus; its *fibers* (N^1) project to the muscles of the tongue.

BRAIN STEM CRANIAL NERVES AND THEIR NUCLEI.

SENSORY ★
MESENCEPH. NUC. TRIGEM. A
　FIBERS $_{A^1}$
MAIN SENS. NUC. TRIGEM. $_{A^2}$
　FIBERS $_{A^3}$
SPINAL TRIGEM. NUC. $_{A^4}$
　FIBERS $_{A^5}$
VESTIBULAR NUC. B/FIBERS $_{B^1}$
COCHLEAR NUC. $_{B^2}$/FIBERS $_{B^3}$
NUC. SOLITARIUS C
　VII FIBERS D
　IX FIBERS E
　X FIBERS F

MOTOR ★
OCULOMOTOR NUC. G
NUC. EDINGER WESTPHAL $_{G^1}$
TROCHLEAR NUC. H/FIBERS $_{H^1}$
MOTOR NUC. TRIGEM. $_{A^6}$
　FIBERS $_{A^7}$
ABDUCENS NUC. I/FIBERS $_{I^1}$
　FACIAL NUC. $_{D^1}$/FIBERS $_{D^2}$
SUP. SALIVATORY NUC. J
INF. SALIVATORY NUC. K
NUC. AMBIGUUS L
　IX FIBERS $_{E^1}$
　X FIBERS $_{F^1}$
　XI FIBERS M
DORSAL MOTOR NUC.
　VAGUS $_{F^2}$/FIBERS $_{F^3}$
ANT. HORN NUC. SP.
　ACCESS. $_{M^1}$/FIBERS $_{M^2}$
HYPOGLOSSAL NUC. N/
　FIBERS $_{N^1}$
FORAMEN MAGNUM O ★

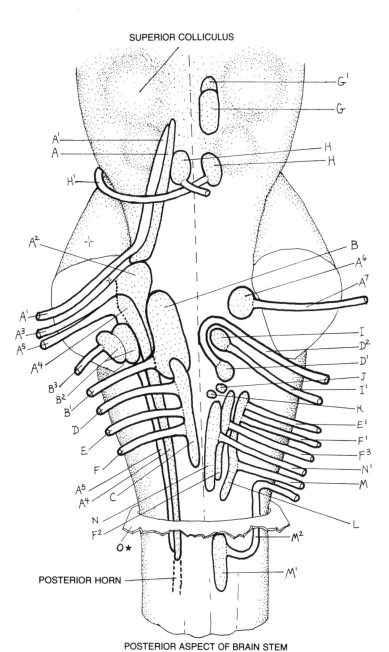

POSTERIOR ASPECT OF BRAIN STEM

The olfactory or first cranial nerve, derived embryologically from the telencephalon, is the most rostral of the cranial nerves. It is composed of unmyelinated axons only a few millimeters in length, making it the shortest of the cranial nerves. As one of our most primitive senses, olfaction is associated with some of our most important instinctual activities, including eating, premating behavior, and procreation.

Color titles A through F. Color arrow E and structures A, B, and F in the upper illustration. Then color structures A through F in the middle illustration.

The sense of smell depends on a pair of small (2.5 to 4.0 cm^2), brownish patches of specialized *(olfactory) epithelia* (A) in the roof of the nasal cavity on either side of the nasal septum, which divides the nasal cavity into left and right parts. Each patch contains about 50 million bipolar *receptor neurons* (B) supported metabolically by at least as many pigmented *sustentacular cells* (C). The peripheral process of each receptor cell terminates in a tuft of six to eight *olfactory cilia* (B^1) surrounded by smaller microvilli (undulating extensions of the cell membrane; not shown). These processes and microvilli are immersed in a *mucous layer* (D). The membrane surfaces of these cilia and microvilli contain receptor sites (not shown) for *inhaled molecules* (E) trapped in the mucous layer. Through processes still poorly understood, the bombardment of receptor sites by such molecules is transduced into a receptor potential that, if large enough, triggers a propagated action potential. The signal is transferred to the olfactory bulb via the *cribriform plate of the ethmoid bone* (F) by the *axons* (B^2; collectively called the olfactory nerve) of receptor neurons.

Color titles G through K and the related structures in the three main illustrations and the inset drawing at the bottom of the plate.

The olfactory axons synapse in the *olfactory bulb* (G) in large, tangled neuropil spheres called *glomeruli.* These glomeruli are made up largely of dendritic processes of second-order neurons: the small *tufted cells* (H) and the larger *mitral cells* (I). Due to a high ratio of primary to second-order neurons in the olfactory bulb, a good deal of selective processing of information must occur here. An unusual feature of the olfactory bulb is the population of *granule cells* (J), which have no axons. These neurons establish dendrodendritic contacts (recall Plate 2-4) with tufted cells, as well as mitral cells, the *axons* (I^1) of which proceed centrally in the *olfactory tract* (K).

Color titles L through U and the related structures in all illustrations. Begin with L in the middle illustration.

Axons of the second-order neurons make synaptic contacts with a number of scattered cells, *olfactory nuclei* (L), along the olfactory tract. The *axons* (L^1) of these nuclei cross the midline in the *anterior commissure* (M) to reach the contralateral olfactory bulb (not shown; note the *contralateral olfactory axon,* L^2, synapsing with the granule cell). The axons (I^1) of the second-order neurons (mitral and tufted cells) continue centrally into the three divisions of the olfactory tract: the *medial* (O), *lateral* (Q), and intermediate (U) *olfactory striae*.

The fibers of the medial olfactory stria project to the *septal area* (P; recall Plate 5-26) from whence they continue to the hippocampus, hypothalamus, and upper brain stem (not shown). The lateral olfactory stria projects to the *amygdaloid complex* (R) and adjacent cortical zones, especially the *prepyriform* (S; *pyriform,* "pear-shaped"; referring to the shape of the temporal lobe; also called *lateral olfactory gyrus*) and *periamygdaloid cortices* (T) on the medial portion of the anterior temporal lobe. From this "primary olfactory cortex" and portions of the amygdala, fibers project throughout the diencephalon and upper brain stem.

The small intermediate olfactory stria projects into the anterior perforated substance, through which many arteries enter the hemisphere (hence the term *perforated*). In animals in which smell is a critical sensory modality, this area, located in the base of the frontal lobes, includes the olfactory tubercle (not shown).

The olfactory system is the only sensory system that reaches the cerebral cortex without first synapsing in the thalamus.

OLFACTORY (I) NERVE AND SYSTEM.

OLFACTORY EPITHELIUM$_A$
RECEPTOR NEURON$_B$
  OLFACT. CILIA$_{B^1}$
  OLFACT. AXON$_{B^2}$
SUSTENTACULAR CELL$_C$
MUCOUS LAYER$_D$
INHALED MOLECULE$_E$
CRIB. PLATE ETHMOID B.$_F$
OLFACTORY BULB$_G$
  TUFTED CELL$_H$
  MITRAL CELL/AXON$_I$
  GRANULE CELL$_J$
OLFACTORY TRACT$_K$
  OLFACT. NUC.$_L$/AXON$_{L^1}$
  CONTRALATERAL AXON$_{L^2}$
ANT. COMMISSURE$_M$
ANT. PERFORATED SUBST.$_N$
MED. OLFACT. STRIA$_O$
SEPTAL AREA$_P$
LAT. OLFACT. STRIA$_Q$
AMYGDALOID COMPLEX$_R$
PRIMARY OLFACT. CORTEX ★
  PREPYRIFORM CORTEX$_S$
  PERIAMYGDALOID CORTEX$_T$
INTERMED. OLFACT. STRIA$_U$

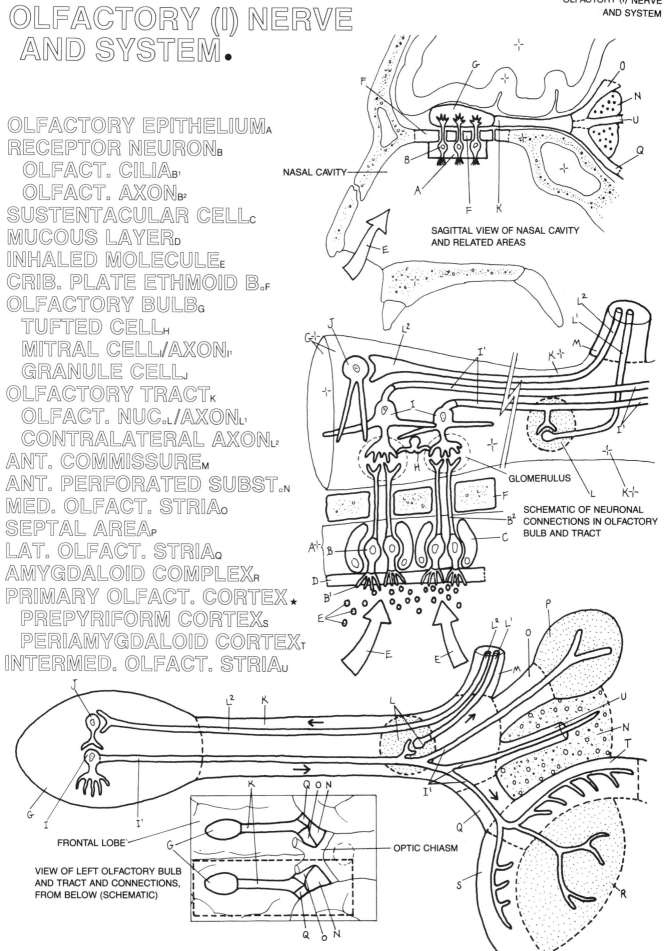

NASAL CAVITY

SAGITTAL VIEW OF NASAL CAVITY
AND RELATED AREAS

GLOMERULUS

SCHEMATIC OF NEURONAL
CONNECTIONS IN OLFACTORY
BULB AND TRACT

FRONTAL LOBE

OPTIC CHIASM

VIEW OF LEFT OLFACTORY BULB
AND TRACT AND CONNECTIONS,
FROM BELOW (SCHEMATIC)

Processing of the visual image begins in the eye, where light waves are focused onto the neural retina. The resulting neural impulses are transmitted from the eye along the visual pathways through the brain to the visual cortex on the medial surface of the occipital lobe. The nonneural structures of the eyeball set the stage for retinal function and offer it support and protection.

Color the heading Eyeball, titles A through M¹, and the related structures and arrow in the upper illustration. Light, pastel colors are recommended for C, D, and L. Structures B and K can also be colored in the lower illustration.

Light rays entering the eyeball first encounter the convex *cornea* (A), which consists of condensed layers of transparent, collagenous, connective-tissue fibers. The cornea is covered externally and internally by layers of epithelium. The cornea is the most refractive (bending and focusing light rays) structure in the eyeball. The lateral continuation of the cornea is the *sclera* (B), the white, nontransparent outer layer of the eyeball.

Upon passing through the cornea, light penetrates the *anterior chamber* (C) of the eye to enter the pupil (F–¦–), which is circumscribed by the *iris* (E). The anterior and *posterior chambers* (D) are filled with the watery aqueous humor (not shown), which is secreted by the *ciliary body* (I) and returned to the venous circulation through the *canals of Schlemm* (G) at the corneal-scleral junction. Obstruction of these canals results in excessive accumulation of fluid in the anterior and posterior chambers and an increase in intraocular pressure, which can cause injury to the delicate retina and optic nerve fibers (glaucoma), resulting in blindness. The iris is a round, disclike structure with smooth muscle to control the size of its aperture, the pupil, in response to the presence or absence of light.

The rounded *lens* (H) consists of compressed layers of epithelial cells that have a capacity for stretching and contracting in response to tension from the circumferential, radially arranged, supportive *suspensory ligaments* (J). These ligaments extend from the ciliary processes of the ciliary body. Contraction of the ciliary muscle within the cilary body alters (reduces) the tension on the suspensory ligaments; this in turn increases the convexity of the lens and its refractive capacity. The elasticity of the lens diminishes with age. The lateral continuation of the ciliary

body is the *choroid* (K), a vascular layer between sclera and retina. Light leaves the lens to traverse the *vitreous body* (L), a semigelatinous mass, and comes to focus on the *retina* (M), the multiple-layered nerve tissue. The retina is characterized by photoreceptor cells that initiate the processing of the visual image imposed on them by the light waves. The area of greatest visual acuity (fovea centralis) is in the *macula lutea* (M¹; "yellow spot") located slightly lateral to the origin of the optic nerve.

Color the heading Retina, titles N through V, and the related structures in the lower illustration. Structures T¹, U, and V can also be colored in the upper illustration.

The retina consists of three basic cell layers: from the outermost to innermost (adjacent to the vitreous body), photoreceptor cells (O and P), *bipolar cells* (Q), and *ganglion cells* (T). Among these three cell layers, *horizontal* (R) and *amacrine cells* (S) provide varying degrees of lateral linkages. Through what appears to be a backward arrangement, the photoreceptors are located on the posterior surface of the retina; light must pass through the ganglion and bipolar layers before reaching the light receptors.

The photoreceptors are of two types, named according to their shape as seen under the light microscope. *Rods* (O) are the most numerous photoreceptors (about 100 million), although they are absent from the fovea centralis. Sensitive to low-intensity illumination, rods are capable of entering the *pigment layer* (N) when exposed to strong light. *Cones* (P) number about 7 million and are most highly concentrated in the fovea centralis. Cones are maximally effective for acute and color vision.

Rods can synapse with many bipolar cells, whereas cones usually have a one-to-one relationship with these cells. Ganglion cells receive their input from bipolar and amacrine cells. The *axons* (T¹) of the ganglion cells run along the inner surface of the retina, then turn outward, projecting through the sclera, to form the *optic nerve* (U; see footnote next page). The sclera is continuous with the connective tissue or *optic sheath* (V) covering the optic nerve. The retinal site of formation of the optic nerve is the optic disc, a functional blind spot. When approaching an intersection while driving a car, it is wise to turn your head at least twice in each direction, as an oncoming vehicle may have been in your "blind spot" with the first look.

VISUAL SYSTEM: THE EYE.

EYEBALL ★
CORNEA_A
SCLERA_B
ANT._C/POST. CHAMBER_D
IRIS_E
  PUPIL_F-'-
CANALS OF SCHLEMM_G
LENS_H
CILIARY BODY_I
  SUSPENSORY LIGAMENTS_J
CHOROID_K
VITREOUS BODY_L
RETINA_M
  MACULA LUTEA_{M¹}

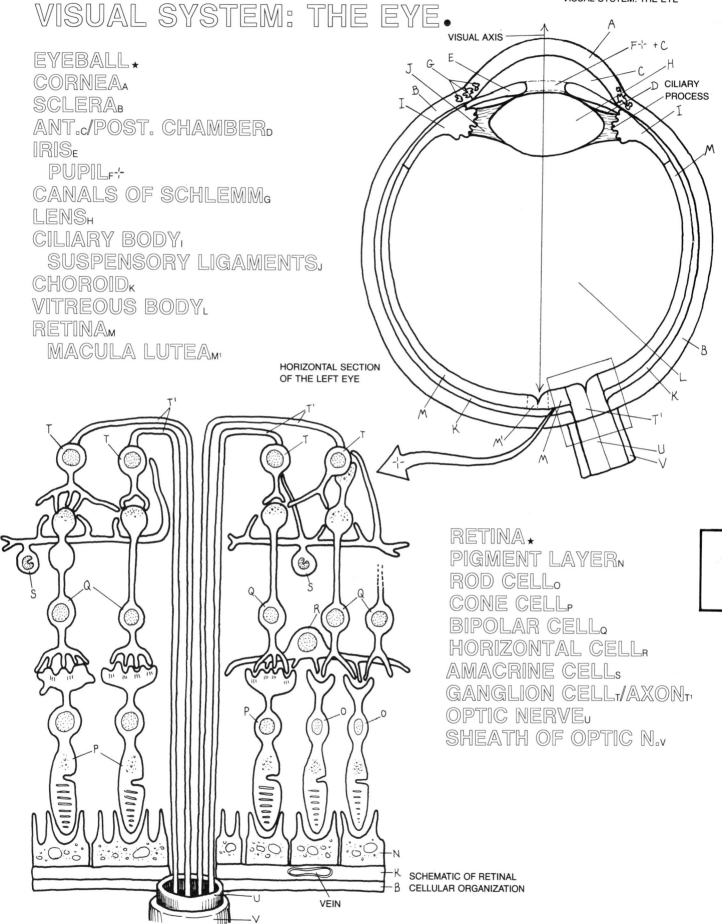

HORIZONTAL SECTION
OF THE LEFT EYE

VISUAL AXIS

CILIARY
PROCESS

RETINA ★
PIGMENT LAYER_N
ROD CELL_O
CONE CELL_P
BIPOLAR CELL_Q
HORIZONTAL CELL_R
AMACRINE CELL_S
GANGLION CELL_T/AXON_{T¹}
OPTIC NERVE_U
SHEATH OF OPTIC N._V

SCHEMATIC OF RETINAL
CELLULAR ORGANIZATION

VEIN

The visual pathway begins with the peripheral receptor organ (retina), which sends visually related impulses to the thalamus and on to the cerebral cortex.

Color the heading Primary Visual Pathway, titles A through G, and related structures. Use distinctly different shades of the same color for B¹ and B². Color the heading Pupillary Light Reflex Pathway, titles H through M, and related structures.

The *optic nerve* (B), formed by the axons of the ganglion cells of the *retina* (A), emerges from the posterior surface of the eyeball to enter the cranial cavity via the optic canal (recall Plate 6-2). The *medial (nasal) fibers* (B¹) of the optic nerve cross in the *optic chiasm* (C; "crossing") to join the contralateral *optic tract* (D).* The *lateral (temporal) fibers* (B²) continue through the chiasm uncrossed to enter the ipsilateral tract. Diverging around the hypothalamus, the fibers of the optic tract follow one of several courses.

The primary visual pathway consists of the majority of optic tract fibers that synapse in the *lateral geniculate body* (E) of the thalamus. Fibers leaving the lateral geniculate body may follow different courses as they form the *optic radiation* (F) or geniculocalcarine tract to the *visual (striate) cortex* (G), where they create both banks of the calcarine fissure of the occipital lobe. Some of these geniculocalcarine fibers run anteriorly and inferiorly into the temporal lobe to loop posteriorly (*Meyer's loop,* F¹), continuing to the calcarine fissure. Meyer's loop carries visual impulses from the upper and outer part of the visual field.

Fibers associated with the pupillary light reflex pathway leave the optic tract as *pretectal afferents* (H). These enter the *pretectal nucleus* (H¹), located between the rostral border of the mesencephalon and the caudal border of the epithalamus (not shown; see Plate 5-43). *Pretectal efferents* (H²) also pass via the *posterior commissure* (I) to *interneurons* (J) of the contralateral pretectal nucleus. The axons of these interneurons project anteriorly to the *nucleus of Edinger Westphal* (K; recall Plate 6-4). From this site, *preganglionic fibers* (K¹) accompany the oculomotor (III) nerve (not shown) to the orbital cavity and synapse in the *ciliary ganglion* (L; a motor ganglion associated with the parasympathetic division of the visceral nervous

system). *Postganglionic fibers* (L¹) leave the ciliary ganglion to innervate the *ciliary muscle* (P) of the ciliary body as well as the constrictor muscle of the iris (*constrictor pupillae,* M). By this pupillary light reflex pathway, the eye can constrict the pupil in response to bright light. By virtue of the fibers crossing in the posterior commissure, a light reflex initiated in one eye will generate a bilateral response (consensual reflex). Pupillary dilatation in response to dim light, distant vision, anger, or fear is induced by sympathetic fibers (pathway not shown; see Plate 8-4).

Color the heading Accommodation Reflex Pathway, titles N, O, and P, and related structures. The afferent limb of this reflex (F) has been colored and should be reviewed. Color the heading Visual Startle/Tracking Reflex Pathway, titles Q and Q¹, and related fibers.

The accommodation reflex, involving flattening or rounding of the lens in association with distant or near vision, respectively, includes primary visual (optic radiation) fibers as the afferent (input) limb of the reflex, unlike the pupillary light reflex, which occurs independent of the cortex. *Corticocollicular* (N) and corticopretectal (not shown) fibers project anteriorly from area 19 of the visual cortex to the *superior colliculus* (O), pretectal nuclei, or both. In association with multiple synapses among several groups of interneurons there, impulses are conducted to the nucleus of Edinger Westphal and beyond, in a course similar to that of the efferent part (limb) of the pupillary light reflex. The effector of this reflex is the ciliary muscle (P), the contraction of which induces rounding of the lens. In this manner, near vision is facilitated.

Some *optic tract–collicular fibers* (Q) leave the optic tract to enter the superior colliculus directly. *Colliculogeniculate fibers* (Q¹) feed back upon incoming visual impulses. Additional collicular axons (not shown) project caudally through the brain stem and spinal cord, controlling eye and head movements associated with visual tracking of moving objects (recall Plate 4-10). This pathway is at least partly responsible for visual startling and visual tracking reflexes.

---

*You will recall that the entire optic system develops as a projection of the diencephalon (Plate 3-7). Accordingly, in the purest sense, the entire optic nerve–chiasm–tract complex is really an externalized tract of the brain.

VISUAL SYSTEM: VISUAL PATHWAYS.

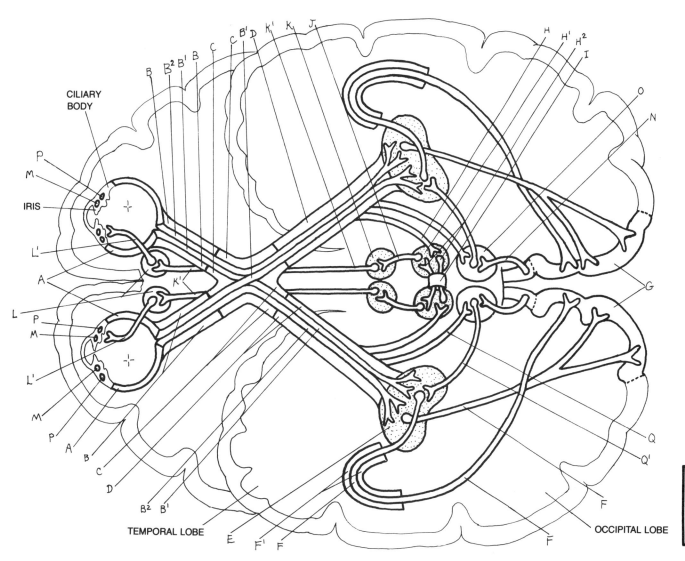

PRIMARY VISUAL PATHWAY ★
RETINA$_A$
OPTIC NERVE$_B$
   NASAL FIBER$_{B^1}$
   TEMP. FIBER$_{B^2}$
OPTIC CHIASM$_C$/TRACT$_D$
LAT. GENIC. BODY$_E$
OPTIC RADIATION$_F$
   MEYER'S LOOP$_{F^1}$
VIS. CORTEX/AREA 17$_G$
PUPILLARY LIGHT REFLEX
      PATHWAY ★
PRETECT. AFF.$_H$/NUC.$_{H^1}$/EFF.$_{H^2}$
POST. COMMISSURE$_I$
INTERNEURON$_J$

NUC. EDINGER WESTPHAL$_K$
PREGANGLIONIC FIBER$_{K^1}$
CILIARY GANGLION$_L$
POSTGANGLIONIC FIBER$_{L^1}$
CONSTRICTOR PUPILLAE$_M$
ACCOMMODATION REFLEX
      PATHWAY ★
CORT.-COLLIC. FIBER$_N$
SUPERIOR COLLICULUS$_O$
CILIARY MUSCLE$_P$
VISUAL STARTLE/TRACKING
      REFLEX PATHWAY ★
OPTIC TR.-COLLIC. FIBER$_Q$
COLLIC-GENICULATE FIBER$_{Q^1}$

Disease of or injury to the visual pathway often produces rather specific complaints of visual defects. This plate deals with typical signs of visual abnormalities associated with interruption of impulse conduction in certain areas of the visual pathway. The circles on the left of the plate represent the visual field on the left side, and the circles on the right represent the right visual field. The visual field of each eye has both temporal (lateral) and nasal (medial) sectors; the nasal sector is projected onto the temporal portion of the retina of the eye, and the temporal sector is projected onto the nasal portion of the retina. The nasal sectors of both left and right visual fields overlap to produce binocular vision. Since a portion of each optic nerve crosses to the contralateral side at the chiasm, lesions posterior to the chiasm usually involve both fields of vision.

Color the headings Left and Right Visual Field/ Retina and titles A, A¹, B, and B¹, using contrasting pastel colors for A and B and different shades of the same colors for the titles with exponents. Color the visual fields above each eye and the binocular visual field at the top center of the plate. Color the parts of the retina of each eye and the corresponding fibers of the optic nerve, chiasma, optic tract, and optic radiation. Color the headings Left Side and Right Side. Color the bar labeled C black, representing a lesion or defect. Then color the related pair of titles (Normal Vision and Anopsia) and the left and right visual fields (uppermost circles), which would develop after a lesion was placed at site C. Repeat with each of the portrayed defects (D through G), related titles and names, and disturbed and normal visual fields, as indicated.

A specific defect of the visual pathway may result in predictable unilateral or bilateral visual-field defects. In the case of a lesion within the retina or optic nerve anterior to the optic chiasm, the resultant loss of a visual field is restricted to one eye. If the lesion is at the chiasm or along the optic radiation, the result is a partial loss of visual field in both eyes. If the lesion occurs at the visual cortex, the visual loss may range from visual aberrations in specific quadrants (quadrantic defects) to total blindness.

Injury to the optic nerve (direct trauma, swelling in the optic sheath, interruption of blood supply, etc.), if complete, as shown at bar C, results in total blindness or *anopsia* (C; *an-*, "without"; *opsia,* "vision") in the affected eye. A partial defect of the optic nerve (bar D) interrupts the nasal retinal fibers on the affected side, resulting in a loss of vision in the temporal field of the same side (*left temporal hemianopsia* (D; *hemi-*, "half"). If a pituitary tumor compresses the optic chiasm (represented by bar E), bilateral nasal retinal components of the optic nerves are affected, resulting in *bitemporal* (*heteronymous*) *hemianopsia* (E; *heteronymous,* "of the opposite side"), in which the temporal fields of both eyes are affected or lost.

Interruption of the optic tract or optic radiation on one side (represented by either bar F) causes *homonymous hemianopsia* (F; *homonymous,* "of the same side"), in which the visual field affected is the same for each eye.

Lesions such as tumors may develop deep within the temporal lobe for some time without symptoms. Their eventual impingement on the optic radiation fibers making up Meyer's loop (bar G; recall Plate 6-7) can be the first sign of temporal lobe disease. The characteristic loss is an upper outer-quadrantic defect, often called a "pie-in-the-sky defect" or *homonymous superior quadrantanopsia* (G).

The defects shown here are only a few examples of a broad range of visual defects that can occur in the visual system.

LESIONS OF THE VISUAL PATHWAY.

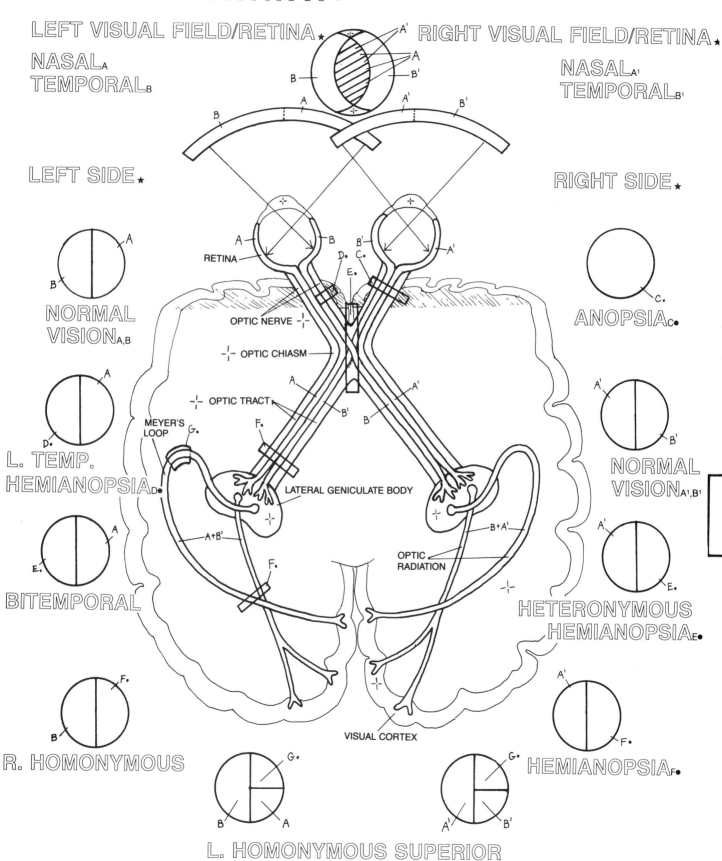

LEFT VISUAL FIELD/RETINA ★

NASAL_A
TEMPORAL_B

RIGHT VISUAL FIELD/RETINA ★

NASAL_{A^1}
TEMPORAL_{B^1}

LEFT SIDE ★

RIGHT SIDE ★

NORMAL VISION_{A,B}

ANOPSIA_C

L. TEMP. HEMIANOPSIA_D

NORMAL VISION_{A^1,B^1}

BITEMPORAL

HETERONYMOUS HEMIANOPSIA_E

R. HOMONYMOUS

HEMIANOPSIA_F

L. HOMONYMOUS SUPERIOR QUADRANTANOPSIA_G

RETINA
OPTIC NERVE
OPTIC CHIASM
OPTIC TRACT
MEYER'S LOOP
LATERAL GENICULATE BODY
OPTIC RADIATION
VISUAL CORTEX

The oculomotor (third) cranial nerve is a mixed nerve, containing both general somatic and visceral efferent (parasympathetic) fibers that supply a number of extrinsic and intrinsic muscles of the eye. In several plates of this unit, the cranial nerves and their nuclei are shown in views of the skull interior, seen from above. In appropriate cases, the cavity housing the eye (orbit) is opened by removing its roof. The brain stem is shown in its anatomical location, magnified, and seen from above. It is sectioned transversely (cross section) at the level of the nucleus or nerve under discussion.

Color titles A, B, and B¹ and related structures in the cross section through the rostral midbrain and in the orbit and B¹ in the lower schematic illustration. Then color the heading General Somatic Efferent Pathway, titles C through E², and the specific nuclei, fibers, and effectors in all illustrations. Shades of the same color are recommended for structures with the same subscript but different exponents.

The *oculomotor nuclei* (A; exclusive of the accessory nuclei) form a longitudinal group of cells in the periaqueductal gray anterior to the cerebral aqueduct at the level of the superior colliculus of the midbrain. The *axons* (B) making up the *oculomotor nerve* (B¹) project through the midbrain tegmentum, with some passing through the red nucleus, to emerge from the brain stem between the crura cerebri (interpeduncular fossa). The nerve then proceeds anteriorly to enter the superior orbital fissure and the orbital cavity, breaking up into its individual components, which innervate their respective effectors.

The complex of nuclei (see lower illustration) are organized bilaterally, with one exception. The *lateral nuclei* (C) project their *axons* (C¹) to the *inferior rectus* (C²), *medial rectus* (C³), and *inferior oblique* (C⁴) extrinsic (extraocular) muscles. The *medial nucleus* (D) projects its *axons* (D¹) to the *superior rectus* (D²) muscle. The *unpaired nucleus* (E) sends its *axons* (E¹) to the *levator palpebrae* (superioris) *muscle* (E²; *palpebra*, "eyelid"), a muscle of the upper eyelid, not an extraocular muscle. Note that the fibers from these three nuclear groups are both crossed and uncrossed. The specific action of the extraocular muscles can be inferred from their attach-

ments to the sclera of the eyeball. However, they function synergistically in moving the eye; no one muscle acts alone. On the other hand, lesions of the third nerve are often indicated by specific abnormal movements or positions of the eyeball with respect to the contralateral eyeball (see ahead).

Color the heading General Visceral Efferent Pathway, titles F through F⁴, and related structures in the lower illustration. Select colors for the titles that contrast sharply with those of the adjacent structures.

The *nucleus of Edinger Westphal* (F) is located in the rostral portion of the third nerve nuclear complex. Associated with the visual system and the parasympathetic division of the visceral nervous system, it is discussed in Plates 6-7 and 8-2. Fibers from this nucleus constitute *preganglionic* (F¹) visceral efferents; that is, they proceed in the company of general somatic efferents of the third nerve to the *ciliary ganglion* (F²) in the orbital cavity and synapse there. *Postganglionic fibers* (F³; also called short ciliary nerves) leave the ciliary ganglion to pierce the posterior surface of the eyeball and pass anteriorly adjacent to the choroid layer to the ciliary muscle and the *sphincter pupillae muscle* (F⁴) of the iris. Recent studies indicate that some fibers of the nucleus of Edinger Westphal may project down the brain stem and spinal cord as far as the lumbar segment. The meaning of this surprising discovery remains unknown.

Lesions to the oculomotor nuclei or nerve create rather well defined symptoms or signs. The upper eyelid droops (ptosis) due to loss of innervation to the levator palpebrae superioris muscle. A condition called lateral strabismus (walleye, in contrast to crosseye) ensues after oculomotor nerve damage. This defect is due to a partially or fully denervated medial rectus muscle, resulting in an unbalanced pulling of the eyeball to the temporal side by the functional lateral rectus muscle. The eyeball is unable to turn vertically if the inferior oblique, superior rectus, and inferior rectus muscles have lost their nerve supply. If the parasympathetic component of the third nerve is lost, the pupil remains dilated (compared to the contralateral pupil).

OCULOMOTOR (III) NERVE.

OCULOMOTOR NUCLEI$_A$
AXONS$_B$/NERVE$_{B^1}$

GENERAL SOMATIC
EFFERENT PATHWAY ★
LAT. NUCLEI$_C$/AXONS$_{C^1}$
INF. RECTUS M.$_{C^2}$
MED. RECTUS M.$_{C^3}$
INF. OBLIQUE M.$_{C^4}$

MED. NUCLEUS$_D$/AXON$_{D^1}$
SUP. RECTUS M.$_{D^2}$
UNPAIRED NUC.$_E$/AXON$_{E^1}$
LEV. PALP. SUP. M.$_{E^2}$

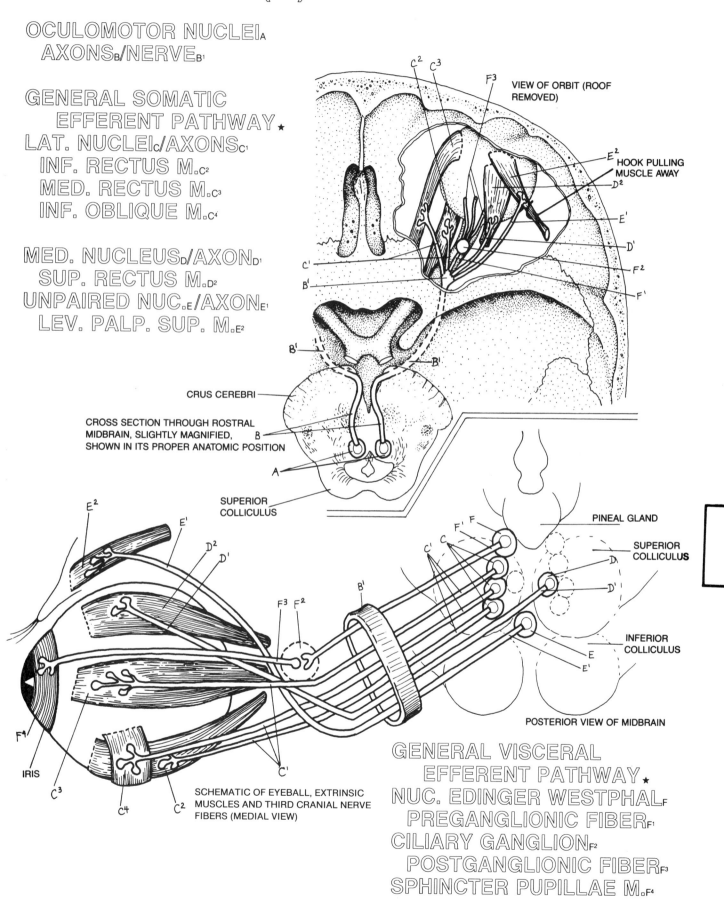

VIEW OF ORBIT (ROOF REMOVED)

HOOK PULLING MUSCLE AWAY

CRUS CEREBRI

CROSS SECTION THROUGH ROSTRAL
MIDBRAIN, SLIGHTLY MAGNIFIED,
SHOWN IN ITS PROPER ANATOMIC POSITION

SUPERIOR
COLLICULUS

PINEAL GLAND

SUPERIOR
COLLICULUS

INFERIOR
COLLICULUS

POSTERIOR VIEW OF MIDBRAIN

IRIS

SCHEMATIC OF EYEBALL, EXTRINSIC
MUSCLES AND THIRD CRANIAL NERVE
FIBERS (MEDIAL VIEW)

GENERAL VISCERAL
EFFERENT PATHWAY ★
NUC. EDINGER WESTPHAL$_F$
PREGANGLIONIC FIBER$_{F^1}$
CILIARY GANGLION$_{F^2}$
POSTGANGLIONIC FIBER$_{F^3}$
SPHINCTER PUPILLAE M.$_{F^4}$

The nuclei of the trochlear (IV) and abducens (VI) nerves are situated in the general somatic efferent column caudal to the oculomotor complex and innervate extraocular muscles.

Color titles A through A³ and related structures, using shades of the same color. For orientation, recall the explanation in the preceding plate.

The *trochlear nucleus* (A; *trochlea,* "pulley") lies ventral to the cerebral aqueduct at the level of the inferior colliculus of the midbrain. The *axons* (A¹) of this nucleus take a unique course by projecting posteriorly around the cerebral aqueduct, then crossing to the opposite side before emerging at the junction of the superior medullary velum with the midbrain. The intracranial path of the fibers of this nerve constitute the longest of any cranial nerve. The trochlear *nerve* (A²) proceeds around each side of the brain stem to enter the superior orbital fissure and the orbital cavity. This nerve supplies the *superior oblique muscle* (A³), which is directed anteriorly from its origin and turns about 120 degrees through a connective-tissue sling (trochlea) to insert on the superior surface of the sclera. Acting alone, the muscle medially rotates the eyeball while simultaneously depressing (turning it downward) and abducting it (turning it laterally). Lesions of the fourth nerve are rarely seen; when experienced, patients report walking downstairs to be a major difficulty.

Color titles B through B³ and related structures.

The *abducens nucleus* (B) is found in the caudal portion of the pontine tegmentum, in the floor of the fourth ventricle adjacent to the midline. The facial nerve fibers (not shown; see Plate 5-7) swing over the abducens nucleus, forming the facial colliculus. The *axons* (B¹) project from the nucleus of cranial nerve VI in an anterolateral direction through the pons to exit on the anterior surface of the brain stem at the medullary-pontine junction. The abducens *nerve* (B²) then passes anteriorly to the orbital cavity through the superior orbital fissure. It innervates the *lateral rectus muscle* (B³), contraction of which turns the eyeball laterally (outwardly). In consensual lateral eye movements, the medial rectus muscle (innervated by the third nerve) of one eye and the lateral rectus muscle (innervated by the sixth nerve) of the contralateral eye normally contract together. A lesion of the sixth nerve creates crosseye or convergent strabismus.

TROCHLEAR (IV) AND ABDUCENS (VI) NERVES.

GENERAL SOMATIC
EFFERENT ★
TROCHLEAR NUCLEUS_A
AXONS_{A^1}/NERVE_{A^2}
SUPERIOR OBLIQUE M._{A^3}
ABDUCENS NUCLEUS_B
AXONS_{B^1}/NERVE_{B^2}
LATERAL RECTUS M._{B^3}

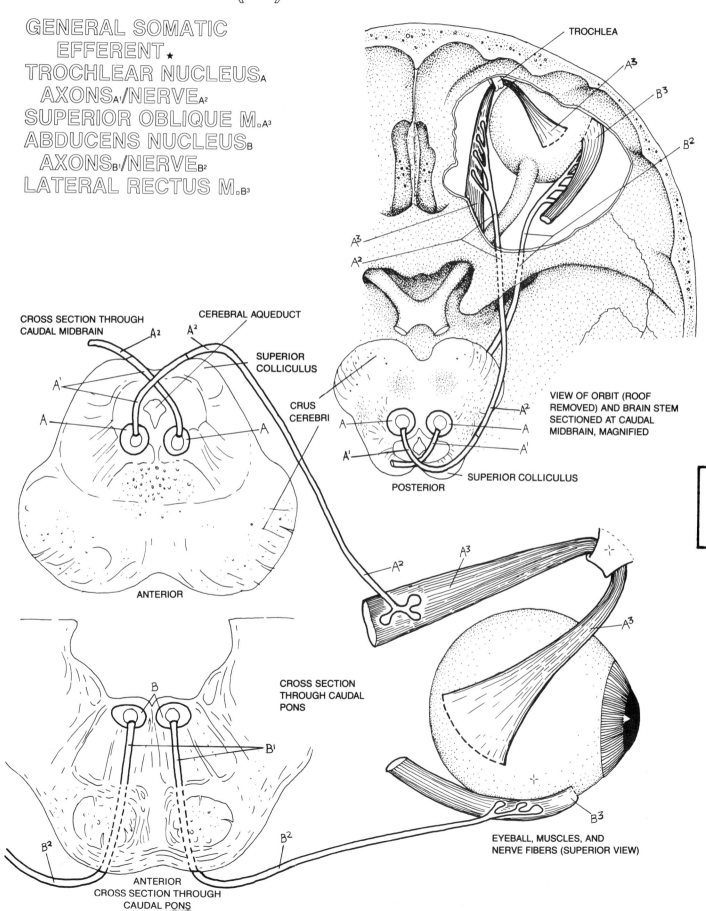

TROCHLEA

CROSS SECTION THROUGH
CAUDAL MIDBRAIN

CEREBRAL AQUEDUCT

SUPERIOR
COLLICULUS

CRUS
CEREBRI

ANTERIOR

VIEW OF ORBIT (ROOF
REMOVED) AND BRAIN STEM
SECTIONED AT CAUDAL
MIDBRAIN, MAGNIFIED

POSTERIOR

SUPERIOR COLLICULUS

CROSS SECTION
THROUGH CAUDAL
PONS

ANTERIOR
CROSS SECTION THROUGH
CAUDAL PONS

EYEBALL, MUSCLES, AND
NERVE FIBERS (SUPERIOR VIEW)

TRIGEMINAL (V) NERVE: SENSORY COMPONENT

The trigeminal (*tri-*, "three"; *gemini,* "twins") or fifth nerve is the largest of the cranial nerves and includes both sensory and motor components. In this plate, only the sensory (general somatic afferent) nuclei and related axons will be considered. Here we also introduce the dermatome as it applies to the trigeminal nerve. A dermatome (*derma,* "skin"; *tome,* "cut up") is an area of skin supplied by the sensory root of a single cranial nerve or the posterior root of a single spinal nerve. Of the cranial nerves, the fifth is the only one whose sensory fibers relate to dermatomes of the head.

Color titles A through D⁴ and related structures. Using light colors, color titles B⁵, C⁴, and D⁵ and related areas in the illustration at the lower right.

The *sensory root* (A³) fibers enter the pons and terminate in one of three sensory nuclei of the trigeminal nerve: fibers that conduct facial touch, pain, and temperature sensation end in the *spinal trigeminal nucleus* (A); fibers that conduct facial two-point discriminative touch, position sense, and pressure sensation end in the *main sensory nucleus* (A¹); and proprioceptive fibers reach the cell bodies of origin in the *mesencephalic nucleus* (A²). These nuclei and related central pathways are shown and discussed in Plate 6-12.

The cell bodies of the primary sensory neurons of the trigeminal nerve, with one exception (A¹), are contained within the *trigeminal ganglion* (A⁴; also called semilunar or Gasserian), located on the medial wall of the middle cranial fossa. The central processes of these sensory neurons form the majority of the sensory root. The peripheral processes enter the ganglion as three distinct nerves coming from three different sites of origin. For practical purposes, these sensory nerves will be followed peripherally, although the conduction of impulses is directed centrally.

The superiormost and smallest branch is the *ophthalmic (first) division* of the fifth (V) nerve (B; ophthalmic nerve; often called V₁, pronounced "vee one"). It enters the orbit through the superior orbital fissure in company with the ophthalmic artery and the third, fourth, and sixth cranial nerves. Before entering the orbit, the V₁ division divides into three branches, the *nasociliary* (B¹), *lacrimal* (B²), and *frontal* (B³). The nasociliary nerve sends a root to the

ciliary ganglion (of the parasympathetic division of the VNS), long ciliary nerves to the eyeball, fibers to the paranasal sinuses, and cutaneous fibers to the skin medial to the eye. The lacrimal nerve contains sensory fibers from the lacrimal gland. The major portion of the frontal nerve passes through and out of the orbit via the supraorbital foramen as the *supraorbital nerve* (B⁴), largely supplying the *V₁ dermatome* (B⁵).

The *maxillary division* (C; maxillary nerve or V₂) leaves the skull through the foramen rotundum, sends a root to the pterygopalatine ganglion in the fossa of the same name, sends *nasal branches* (C¹) to the nasal cavity and *superior alveolar nerves* (C²) to the oral cavity, upper teeth, and adjacent maxillary sinus. Some of the terminal branches of the maxillary division exit the skull through the infraorbital foramen as the *infraorbital nerve* (C³) to supply the skin of the face in the *V₂ dermatome* (C⁴).

The *mandibular division* (D; mandibular nerve or V₃) is the only division of the trigeminal nerve to contain motor fibers (Plate 6-13). This division enters the foramen ovale at the base of the skull and descends into the infratemporal fossa medial to the vertical ramus of the mandible. Some sensory fibers project to the otic ganglion, the external ear, and upper V₃ dermatome as the *auriculotemporal nerve* (D¹). Other fibers supply the oral cavity, including the tongue (general sensation excluding taste), as the *lingual nerve* (D²) and the roots of the lower teeth as the *inferior alveolar nerve* (D³). Some fibers exit the mental foramen in the lower jaw as the *mental nerve* (D⁴) to supply the lower part of the *V₃ dermatome* (D⁵).

Symptoms from lesions of the sensory divisions of the fifth cranial nerve depend on the peripheral branch or the specific sensory nucleus that has been affected. Inflammation of the trigeminal ganglion, as in herpes zoster, may cause vesicles to appear within one or more of the trigeminal dermatomes. Interruption of the ophthalmic fibers from the cornea represents one cause of absence of the corneal (blink) reflex in both eyes. In the condition called tic douloureaux ("painful twitch") or trigeminal neuralgia, excruciating stabs of pain radiate along a single branch of the fifth nerve. The slightest stimulation, even a gentle breeze, can initiate an agonizing experience. The cause is unknown.

TRIGEMINAL (V) NERVE: SENSORY COMPONENT.

SPINAL TRIGEM. NUC.$_A$
MAIN SENS. NUC.$_{A^1}$
MESENCEPH. NUC.$_{A^2}$
SENSORY ROOT$_{A^3}$
TRIGEMINAL GANGLION$_{A^4}$

OPHTHALMIC (V_1) DIVISION:$_B$
NASOCILIARY$_{B^1}$/LACRIMAL$_{B^2}$
FRONTAL$_{B^3}$/SUPRAORBITAL$_{B^4}$

MAXILLARY (V_2) DIVISION:$_C$
NASAL$_{C^1}$/SUP. ALVEOLAR$_{C^2}$
INFRAORBITAL$_{C^3}$

MANDIBULAR (V_3) DIVISION:$_D$
AURICULOTEMP.$_{D^1}$/LINGUAL$_{D^2}$
INF. ALVEOL.$_{D^3}$/MENTAL$_{D^4}$

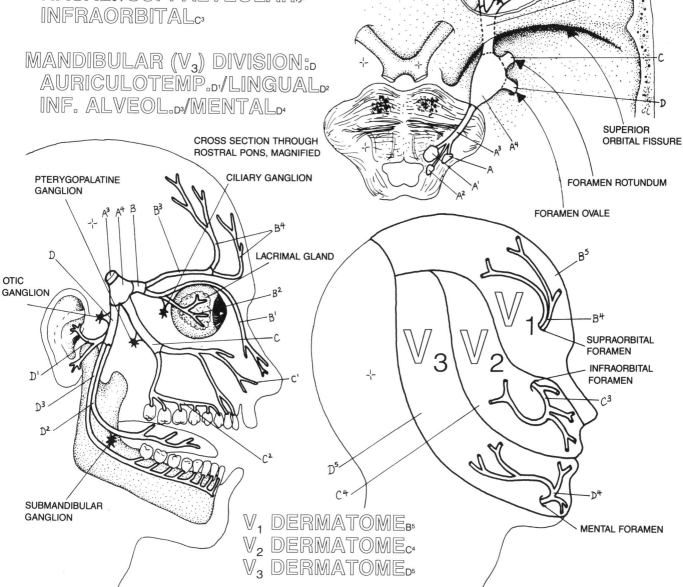

VIEW OF ORBIT FROM ABOVE (ROOF REMOVED)

CILIARY GANGLION

SUPERIOR ORBITAL FISSURE

FORAMEN ROTUNDUM

FORAMEN OVALE

CROSS SECTION THROUGH ROSTRAL PONS, MAGNIFIED

PTERYGOPALATINE GANGLION

CILIARY GANGLION

LACRIMAL GLAND

OTIC GANGLION

SUBMANDIBULAR GANGLION

SUPRAORBITAL FORAMEN

INFRAORBITAL FORAMEN

MENTAL FORAMEN

V_1 DERMATOME$_{B^5}$
V_2 DERMATOME$_{C^4}$
V_3 DERMATOME$_{D^5}$

In Plate 6-11 we have shown how sensations reach the central nervous system via branches of the trigeminal nerve from the skin, mucous membranes of the nasal and oral cavities, tongue, and teeth. Now we examine the fibers of the sensory root, their entrance into the brain stem, and the pathway of impulses after they leave two of the three sensory nuclei of the trigeminal nerve within the brain stem. The central pathway for fibers from the mesencephalic nucleus have not been established.

Color titles A through J at the upper left and the related structures in the brain stem first; then continue with the lowest cross section and work up. Read the text after completing the first pathway (B through J).

The *sensory root* (A) of the fifth nerve conducts fibers to the pons. The central processes of the *primary sensory neurons* (B) concerned with facial touch, temperature, and pain penetrate the mid pons and turn caudally to form the spinal trigeminal tract (descending spinal tract of the fifth cranial nerve). Along the course of these descending fibers, the central processes turn medially to synapse with cells of the adjacent *spinal trigeminal nucleus* (B^1; often called spinal nucleus of V).

In the lowest cross section at the right, note that *axons* (B^2) from these cells give *collaterals* (B^3) to the ipsilateral *reticular formation* (E). They then cross anteriorly and medially to ascend in the contralateral *medial lemniscus* (G) as the *ventral trigeminothalamic tract* (F; also known as the trigeminal lemniscus). These ascending fibers reach and synapse in the *ventral posterior medial nucleus* (H) of the thalamus. *Thalamocortical fibers* (I) ascend to the *postcentral gyrus* (J; areas 3, 1, and 2 or primary sensory cortex) of the parietal lobe.

Color titles C^2 through I^2 and color the structures labeled C^2, C^3, and K in the cross section second from the bottom and upward, including structures I^1 and I^2.

The central processes of *primary sensory neurons* (C) conveying impulses related to touch, position sense, and two-point discrimination converge on the oblong *main (principal) sensory nucleus* (C^1) in the mid pons, located rostral to and continuous with the spinal trigeminal nucleus. *Uncrossed axons* (C^2) of the main sensory nucleus ascend as the *dorsal trigeminothalamic tract* (K) to the ventral posterior medial nucleus of the thalamus, where *thalamocortical fibers* (I^1) conduct related impulses on to the postcentral gyrus. *Crossed axons* (C^3) of the main sensory nucleus project toward the contralateral medial lemniscus at the level of the pons and ascend to the ventral posterior medial nucleus of the thalamus. Again, *thalamocortical fibers* (I^2) send impulses to the primary sensory cortex.

The *primary sensory neurons* (D) conveying proprioceptive impulses from the muscles of mastication are located in the *mesencephalic nucleus of V* (D^1), which extends from the pons, at the level of the origin of the trigeminal nerve, through the mesencephalon (hence its name). This nucleus is a singular example of primary sensory neurons (pseudounipolar neurons) located within the CNS instead of a ganglion.

The trigeminal system is associated with a number of important reflexes, including blinking, tearing of the eyes, sneezing, and vomiting. The afferent limb of these reflexes includes the sensory nuclei just presented. Fibers from these nuclei ascend and descend in the reticular formation, giving off collaterals (not shown) to the motor nuclei of the brain stem, the axons of which provide the efferent limb of these reflexes. For example, a small particle comes in contact with the cornea, stimulating afferents of the ophthalmic division of V. The protective closure of the eye involves contraction of the orbicularis oculi muscle, initiated by the motor division of the facial (VII) nerve, completing the reflex. Dust particles inhaled into the nasal cavity stimulate afferents of the maxillary division of V. These afferents synapse with neurons of the reticular formation, which in turn facilitate action potentials in anterior horn cells of the spinal cord. Here arise nerves innervating the muscles of respiration (diaphragm and intercostal muscles), the sudden, uncontrollable contraction of which causes the sneeze.

TRIGEMINAL (V) NERVE: CENTRAL PATHWAYS.

SENSORY ROOT A
PRI. SENS. NEUR. B/SP.
   TRIGEM. NUC. B1
PRI. SENS. NEUR. C/MAIN
   SENS. NUC. C1
PRI. SENS. NEUR. D/MESEN.
   NUC. D1
SPINAL TRIGEM. NUC. AXON B2
COLLATERAL B3/RETIC. FORM. E
VENT. TRIGEM. THAL. TR. F
MEDIAL LEMNISCUS G
VENT. POST. MED. NUC. THAL. H
THALAMOCORTICAL FIBER I
POSTCENTRAL G. J

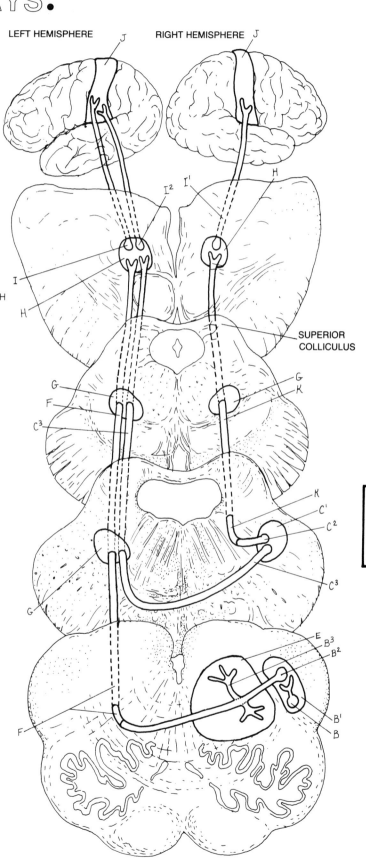

LEFT HEMISPHERE   RIGHT HEMISPHERE

SUPERIOR
COLLICULUS

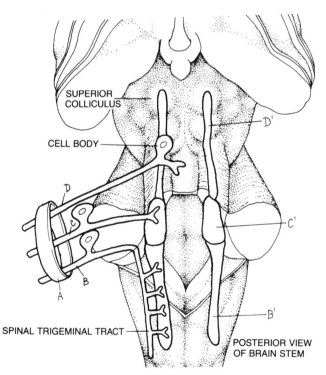

SUPERIOR
COLLICULUS

CELL BODY

SPINAL TRIGEMINAL TRACT

POSTERIOR VIEW
OF BRAIN STEM

MAIN SENS. NUC. AXON
   (UNCROSSED) C2
DORSAL TRIGEM. THAL. TR. K
MAIN SENS. NUC. AXON
   (CROSSED) C3
THALAMOCORTICAL FIBER I1, I2

The motor component (special visceral efferent) of the trigeminal nerve is small compared with the sensory nuclei. The term *special visceral* is based on the embryonic origin of branchiomeric muscles, that is, ones that arise from branchial (gill) arches in the ventral head region. The motor (branchiomotor) nucleus of the fifth cranial nerve supplies the muscular derivatives of the first branchial or mandibular arch, specifically the muscles of mastication, the tensor tympani of the middle ear, the tensor veli palatini of the pharynx (not shown), and the mylohyoid and anterior digastric muscles in the floor of the mouth (not shown).

Color titles and structures A through H¹, starting with the illustration at the upper left.

The *motor nucleus* (A) is composed of multipolar neurons grouped in a rounded mass medial to the main sensory nucleus. The *axons* (B) from this nucleus leave the lateral aspect of the pons with the sensory root, slip under the trigeminal ganglion, and exit the skull through the *foramen ovale* (C) with the mandibular division (V₃) sensory fibers (not shown). These efferents, the motor root of the trigeminal *nerve* (B¹), enter the infratemporal fossa to supply the muscles of mastication, giving *branches* (B²) to the *temporalis* (D), *masseter* (E), and *medial* (F) and *lateral pterygoid* muscles (F¹; *ptery,* "wing"). One branch passes through the otic ganglion and enters the middle ear to innervate the *tensor tympani* (G) and the nearby tensor veli palatini on the medial side of the auditory tube (not shown). The muscles of mastication insert on the mandible; with the exception of the lateral pterygoid, they re-

tract the lower jaw, closing the mouth. The tensor tympani, inserting on the malleus, dampens movement of the tympanic membrane (eardrum) in response to excessive sound. The tensor veli palatini elevates the soft palate, and the mylohyoid and anterior digastric muscles, in part, elevate the hyoid bone as part of the swallowing mechanism.

It is interesting to note that the motor root of the fifth nerve contains some afferent fibers whose cell bodies (not shown) lie within the trigeminal ganglion. The function of these fibers is not known.

The motor nucleus of the fifth nerve receives input from cortical levels, the precentral gyrus being one known source. Descending fibers, the *corticobulbar tract* (H; fibers running from the precentral gyrus to the brain stem), send *collaterals* (H¹) to this nucleus, establishing voluntary control. Many of the corticobulbar fibers terminate on neurons of the reticular formation, which in turn project fibers to the motor nucleus of the fifth nerve. In addition, the mesencephalic nucleus of the fifth nerve contributes the afferent limb for reflex control of the jaw muscles.

Since the axons of neurons in the motor nucleus leave the CNS and terminate directly on effectors, the cells of the motor nucleus can be classified as lower motor neurons (recall Plate 2-3). Lesions of the motor nucleus or its nerve cause a loss of reflex contraction of the chewing muscles (jaw jerk), denervation atrophy (muscle degeneration due to separation from nerve supply), and weakness or paralysis of the affected muscles. In the event of a unilateral lesion, the jaw may deviate, upon protrusion, to the side of the damaged nerve.

TRIGEMINAL (V) NERVE: MOTOR COMPONENT.

MOTOR NUCLEUS$_A$
AXONS$_B$/NERVE$_{B^1}$/BRS.$_{B^2}$
FORAMEN OVALE$_C$
EFFECTORS ★
TEMPORALIS$_D$
MASSETER$_E$
MEDIAL PTERYGOID$_F$
LATERAL PTERYGOID$_{F^1}$
TENSOR TYMPANI$_G$
CORTICOBULBAR TR.$_H$
COLLATERAL$_{H^1}$

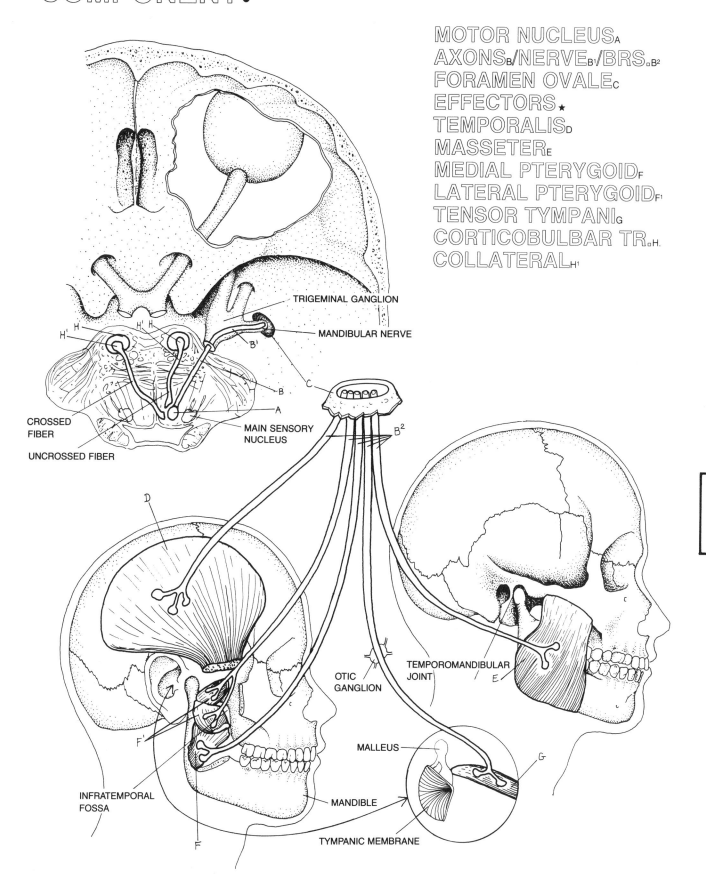

TRIGEMINAL GANGLION

MANDIBULAR NERVE

CROSSED
FIBER

UNCROSSED FIBER

MAIN SENSORY
NUCLEUS

D

OTIC
GANGLION

TEMPOROMANDIBULAR
JOINT

E

MALLEUS

G

INFRATEMPORAL
FOSSA

F

MANDIBLE

TYMPANIC MEMBRANE

FACIAL (VII) NERVE: SPECIAL VISCERAL MOTOR COMPONENT

The facial (VII) nerve contains axons from several cell columns, including general somatic afferent (skin behind the ear), special visceral afferent (taste receptors), and general visceral efferent (salivary glands, lacrimal gland). Also present are special visceral efferent axons to the muscles of facial expression, certain muscles of the floor of the mouth, and a muscle of the middle ear. The special visceral efferent component is the subject of this plate.

Color titles A through N and related structures, beginning with Figure 1. Finish each figure completely before going to the next.

The special visceral efferent nucleus of the seventh nerve consists of a group of cells in the mid pons, between the motor nucleus of cranial nerve V rostrally and the nucleus ambiguus caudally (not shown; see Plate 6-4). Interestingly, motor nuclei V and VII and the nucleus ambiguus all innervate branchial muscles.

The *motor nucleus* (A) of cranial nerve VII is immediately posterior to the superior olivary nucleus and lateral to the *reticular formation* (B; Figure 1). *Collaterals* (C^1) from the *corticobulbar tract* (C) synapse directly or indirectly, via *neurons* (B^1) of the reticular formation, with the motor nucleus. The rostral part of the nucleus, supplying the more superior facial muscles (in the forehead and around the eyes), is supplied by both crossed and uncrossed corticobulbar collaterals; thus a lesion of the corticobulbar fibers or upper motor neurons seldom produces weakness or paralysis of these muscles, whereas the facial muscles in the lower half of the face on the contralateral side may be paralyzed.

After leaving the nucleus of the seventh nerve, the *motor root* (A^1) travels rostrally (not shown), posteriorly, and medially toward the midline, then swings around the abducens nucleus (the arc is called the genu), forming the facial colliculus. The motor root proceeds through the pons laterally and anteriorly to exit the brain stem, with the sensory root (intermediate nerve; includes general visceral motor; Plates 6-15, 6-16), at the cerebellopontine angle.

Passing a short distance through the posterior cranial fossa, the motor and sensory roots, in company with the VIII nerve, enter the *internal auditory meatus* (D) in the petrous portion of the temporal bone (recall Plate 6-2), which contains the internal and middle ear (Figure 2). Emerging laterally from the meatus, the two roots (motor and sensory), now called the *facial nerve* (A^2) and enclosed within the *facial canal* (E), proceed laterally in the roof of the internal ear and then bend posteriorly at a sharp angle (Figure 2). It is here that the cell bodies of the sensory neurons of VII are located, appropriately called the *geniculate ganglion* (F). The axons responsible for different functions are routed in either anterior or posterior directions at the ganglion (Figure 2). The anteriorly directed fibers are presented in Plate 6-15; here we are concerned with the posteriorly directed fibers (facial nerve), which, contained within the facial canal, bend caudally, in an arc, to pass through the posterior wall of the middle ear (tympanic) cavity (Figure 4). In this caudally directed canal, a *nerve* (H^1) is given off to the *stapedius muscle* (H), a dampener of excess movement of the stapes.

Emerging from the *stylomastoid foramen* (G; inferior opening of the facial canal), the facial nerve turns anteriorly to enter the parotid (salivary) gland, within which it divides into a number of branches including (from above to below) the *temporal* (J), *zygomatic* (K), *buccal* (L), *marginal mandibular* (M), and *cervical* (N). Each of these branches forms smaller filaments, which supply the *muscles of facial expression* (I). The muscles of the scalp as well as a muscle of the neck are innervated by this nerve (as are two muscles in the floor of the mouth, the stylohyoid and the posterior belly of the digastric; not shown).

The facial nerve is vulnerable to injury at several points along its path—for example, at the entrance to the internal auditory meatus (due to a tumor of the VIII nerve or its sheath), in the facial canal (infection of the middle ear cavity), and in the substance of the parotid gland (tumor or surgery). The signs of a facial nerve lesion vary according to the site of the lesion; peripheral lesions are characterized by facial muscle paralysis (Bell's palsy) on the affected side (drooping of the corners of the eye and mouth). Central lesions are more complicated, often involve major descending tracts and one or more neighboring cranial nerve nuclei.

FACIAL (VII) NERVE: SPECIAL VISCERAL MOTOR COMPONENT.

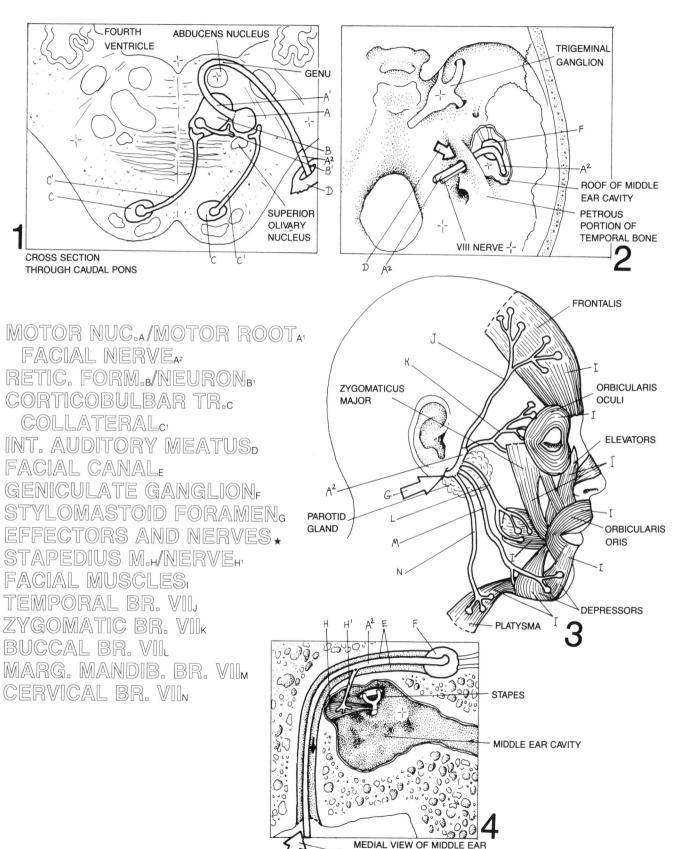

1 CROSS SECTION THROUGH CAUDAL PONS

FOURTH VENTRICLE
ABDUCENS NUCLEUS
GENU
A'
A
B
A²
B'
D
C'
C
SUPERIOR OLIVARY NUCLEUS
C C'

2
TRIGEMINAL GANGLION
F
A²
ROOF OF MIDDLE EAR CAVITY
PETROUS PORTION OF TEMPORAL BONE
VIII NERVE
D A²

MOTOR NUC.A/MOTOR ROOTA¹
FACIAL NERVEA²
RETIC. FORM.B/NEURONB¹
CORTICOBULBAR TR.C
COLLATERALC¹
INT. AUDITORY MEATUSD
FACIAL CANALE
GENICULATE GANGLIONF
STYLOMASTOID FORAMENG
EFFECTORS AND NERVES ★
STAPEDIUS M.H/NERVEH¹
FACIAL MUSCLESI
TEMPORAL BR. VIIJ
ZYGOMATIC BR. VIIK
BUCCAL BR. VIIL
MARG. MANDIB. BR. VIIM
CERVICAL BR. VIIN

3
FRONTALIS
J
K
I
ORBICULARIS OCULI
I
ZYGOMATICUS MAJOR
ELEVATORS
I
A²
G
I
ORBICULARIS ORIS
PAROTID GLAND
L
M
N
I
DEPRESSORS
PLATYSMA
I

4 MEDIAL VIEW OF MIDDLE EAR CAVITY AND ITS MEDIAL WALL
H H' A² E F
STAPES
MIDDLE EAR CAVITY
G

FACIAL (VII) NERVE: GENERAL VISCERAL MOTOR COMPONENT

The general visceral efferent component of the facial (VII) nerve is part of the intermediate nerve and consists of parasympathetic neurons innervating the lacrimal, parotid, sublingual, and submandibular glands, the intrinsic glands of the nasal and oral cavities, and the smooth musculature of related blood vessels. You will recall a similar motor component of the III nerve (Plate 6-9) innervating the intrinsic smooth muscles of the eye. A survey of Plates 8-1 and 8-2 (efferent component of the visceral nervous system) may be helpful in understanding the basic pattern of parasympathetic innervation.

Color titles A through I and the related structures, starting with the upper illustration. The superior salivatory nucleus (A) is highly magnified here.

The *superior salivatory nucleus* (A), caudal to the motor nucleus of the facial nerve and just rostral to the pontomedullary junction, sends preganglionic fibers anterolaterally to join the sensory root of the facial nerve. Within the geniculate ganglion in the roof of the tympanic cavity, the fibers separate into three small bundles.

One bundle of *preganglionic fibers* (B) is directed anteriorly as the *greater petrosal nerve* (C; *petrosal,* "rocky"; referring to the petrous part of the temporal bone in which it lies). Leaving this area, it crosses the floor of the middle cranial fossa under the trigeminal ganglion and is joined by postganglionic fibers of the sympathetic division of the VNS (deep petrosal nerve). These fibers, collectively constituting the *nerve of the pterygoid canal* (D), penetrate the anterior wall of the middle cranial fossa through the pterygoid canal just below and medial to the foramen rotundum. Entering the pterygopalatine fossa (lateral to the posterior nasal cavity and nasopharynx), the preganglionic fibers synapse with the postganglionic neurons of the *pterygopalatine ganglion* (E). Fibers of *postganglionic neurons* (F) travel with sensory and sympathetic fibers to terminate in effectors (glands, vascular musculature) of the *oral cavity mucosa* (G) and *nasal mucosa* (H; mucous membrane or lining). Postganglionic fibers also ascend laterally to the orbital cavity, in company with sympathetic fibers (retro-orbital plexus, not shown), to innervate the *lacrimal gland* (I).

Color titles B¹ through M and related structures in both illustrations.

Certain *preganglionic fibers* (B¹) project anteriorly from the geniculate ganglion in a small bundle lateral to and smaller than the greater petrosal nerve. These fibers are joined by the somewhat larger tympanic branch of the IX cranial nerve, with which they form the *lesser petrosal nerve* (J). This nerve travels in parallel with the greater petrosal nerve to the foramen ovale. Here the lesser nerve descends through the foramen and enters the infratemporal fossa to synapse with postganglionic neurons of the *otic ganglion* (K). Fibers of *postganglionic neurons* (L) leave the ganglion, join with sensory fibers of the auriculotemporal nerve (a branch of cranial nerve V) to reach the *parotid gland* (M), and innervate its vascular and glandular elements.

Color titles B² through S and related structures in the upper and lower illustrations.

Certain *preganglionic fibers* (B²) turn posteriorly at the geniculate ganglion and join the facial nerve in the facial canal (recall Plate 6-14). Proceeding caudally in the posterior wall of the tympanic cavity, these preganglionic fibers spring anteriorly from the facial canal to form the *chorda tympani nerve* (N). This nerve crosses the malleus of the ear ossicles and slips through the small petrotympanic fissure to join the *lingual nerve* (O; a branch of V₃ or mandibular division of the fifth nerve) somewhat below the trunk of the mandibular division. The preganglionic fibers follow the course of the lingual nerve to a point medial to the third molar in the lateral aspect of the floor of the mouth. Here they synapse with neurons in the *submandibular ganglion* (P). *Postganglionic fibers* (Q) project to the *sublingual* (R) and *submandibular glands* (S).

FACIAL (VII) NERVE: GENERAL VISCERAL MOTOR COMPONENT.

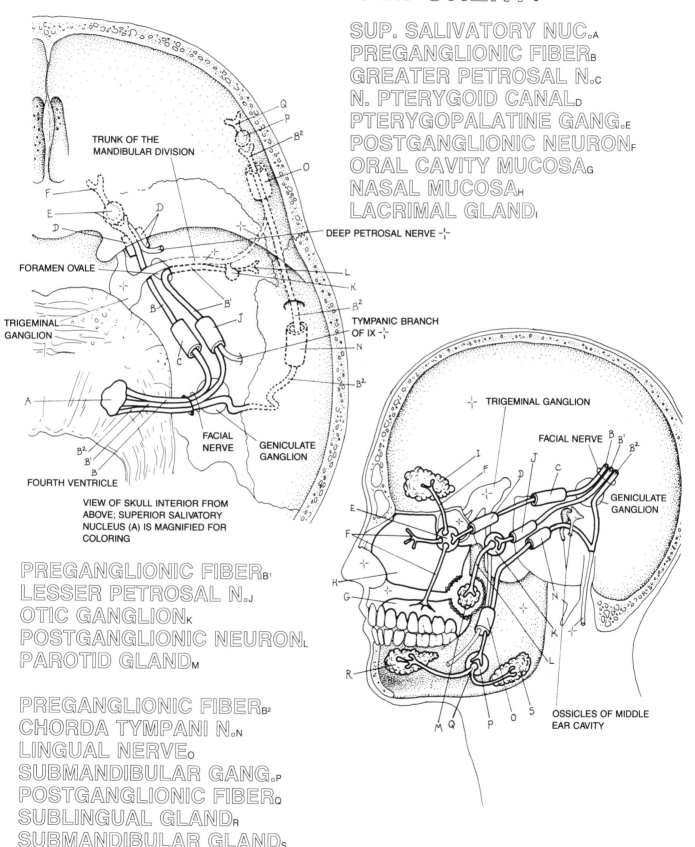

SUP. SALIVATORY NUC. A
PREGANGLIONIC FIBER B
GREATER PETROSAL N. C
N. PTERYGOID CANAL D
PTERYGOPALATINE GANG. E
POSTGANGLIONIC NEURON F
ORAL CAVITY MUCOSA G
NASAL MUCOSA H
LACRIMAL GLAND I

DEEP PETROSAL NERVE -|-

TRUNK OF THE MANDIBULAR DIVISION

FORAMEN OVALE

TRIGEMINAL GANGLION

TYMPANIC BRANCH OF IX -|-

FACIAL NERVE

GENICULATE GANGLION

FOURTH VENTRICLE

VIEW OF SKULL INTERIOR FROM ABOVE; SUPERIOR SALIVATORY NUCLEUS (A) IS MAGNIFIED FOR COLORING

TRIGEMINAL GANGLION

FACIAL NERVE

GENICULATE GANGLION

OSSICLES OF MIDDLE EAR CAVITY

PREGANGLIONIC FIBER B1
LESSER PETROSAL N. J
OTIC GANGLION K
POSTGANGLIONIC NEURON L
PAROTID GLAND M

PREGANGLIONIC FIBER B2
CHORDA TYMPANI N. N
LINGUAL NERVE O
SUBMANDIBULAR GANG. P
POSTGANGLIONIC FIBER Q
SUBLINGUAL GLAND R
SUBMANDIBULAR GLAND S

FACIAL (VII) NERVE: SENSORY COMPONENT

The sensory component of the facial (VII) nerve is part of the intermediate nerve because of its relationship (intermediate) between the seventh and the eighth nerves as they emerge from the brain stem at the cerebellopontine angle. The sensory component contains both general somatic afferents (from the external ear) and special visceral afferents (from certain taste receptors). The peripheral portions of the sensory fibers from the ear are not shown.

Color the heading Central Pathways/Connections, titles A through E², and related structures in the upper illustration.

The cell bodies of the sensory neurons belonging to the facial nerve are situated in the *geniculate ganglion* (A). The *general somatic afferent neuron* (B) component receives touch, pain, and temperature input from a small area of skin on the ear (not shown). The central processes of these neurons project from the geniculate ganglion to the *spinal trigeminal nucleus* (D). *Axons* (D²) from *neurons* (D¹) in this nucleus are directed to the thalamus via the ventral trigeminothalamic tract (recall Plate 6-12).

The *special visceral afferent neurons* (C) receive taste input primarily from the tongue and palate. The central processes of these neurons project to the lower pons, where they form the tractus solitarius (not shown) and enter the *nucleus solitarius* (E) of the upper medulla, along with sensory fibers from the ninth and tenth cranial nerves. By pathways that are not well established, the *neurons* (E¹) of the nucleus solitarius project their *axons* (E²) to the ventral posterior medial nucleus of the thalamus (not shown) and other brain stem stations. Thalamocortical projections (not shown) ascend to the postcentral gyrus, in which taste representation is included within the area subserving the facial (V_1, V_2, V_3) dermatomes.

Color the heading Peripheral Pathways, titles F through I, and related structures, including structures A and C, in the lower illustration.

Taste (gustatory) receptors are found predominantly on the tongue, but they are also present on the palate, pharynx, epiglottis, and even the esophagus. Though the receptors for taste have a wide distribution within these areas, the known varieties of taste are specifically localized on the tongue. For example, sweet is experienced on the tip, bitter on the back, and salty and sour on the sides. A minimal number of receptors are located in the center of the tongue.

The *taste receptor areas of the palate* (F) synapse with the peripheral processes of special visceral afferent neurons that join the *palatine nerves* (G) to the pterygopalatine ganglion, the *nerve of the pterygoid canal* (H) to the middle cranial fossa, and the *greater petrosal nerve* (I) to their cell bodies in the geniculate ganglion.

Color titles J through R and related structures in the lower illustration.

The *presulcal taste receptor area* (J) is located in the anterior two-thirds of the tongue, anterior to the sulcus terminalis. The receptors for taste (*taste buds,* L) are found on surface projections called *circumvallate papillae* (K). Each taste bud, likened to the petals of a flowering bud, consists of about 40 to 50 *neuroepithelial cells* (M) intertwined with *supporting cells* (N). At the base of the bud are mitotically active *basal cells* (O), which replace the older neuroepithelia about every ten days. The apex of each bud is open to the surface through a taste pore. The apical surfaces of the supporting and receptor (neuroepithelial) cells are characterized by microvilli, the collection of which form the "gustatory hairs" visualized by lower-power light microscopy. Substances brought to the tongue are partly dissolved in mucus, which fills the taste pores. Contact of these substances with the microvilli stimulate the formation of action potentials at synaptic sites along the lower halves of the receptor cells. These action potentials are conducted centrally by special visceral afferent neurons, the axons of which join the *lingual nerve* (P) just outside the tongue. These axons ascend to the level of the *chorda tympani nerve* (Q), joining the latter through the middle ear cavity and into the facial canal. Here they join with the *facial nerve* (R) and proceed to the geniculate ganglion.

FACIAL (VII) NERVE: SENSORY COMPONENT.

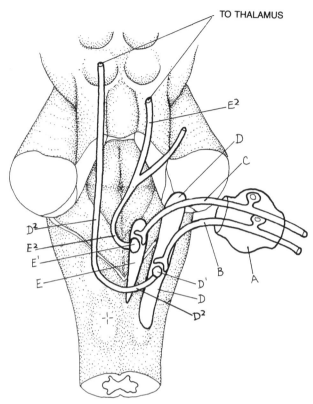

TO THALAMUS

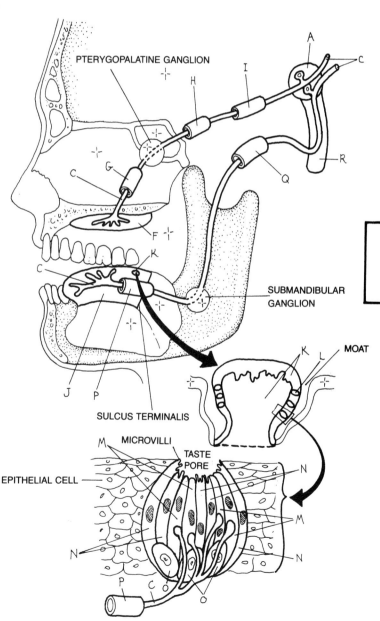

CENTRAL PATHWAYS/
CONNECTIONS ★
GENICULATE GANGLION$_A$
GEN. SOMATIC AFF. NEURON$_B$
SPEC. VISCERAL AFF.
NEURON$_C$
SPINAL TRIGEM. NUC.$_D$
NEURON$_{D1}$/AXON$_{D2}$
NUC. SOLITARIUS$_E$
NEURON$_{E1}$/AXON$_{E2}$

PERIPHERAL PATHWAYS ★
PALATINE TASTE RECEPTOR
AREA$_F$
PALATINE N.$_G$
N. PTERYGOID CANAL$_H$
GREATER PETROSAL N.$_I$
PRESULCAL TASTE
RECEPTOR AREA$_J$
CIRCUMVALLATE PAPILLA$_K$
TASTE BUD$_L$
NEUROEPITHELIAL CELL$_M$
SUPPORTING CELL$_N$
BASAL CELL$_O$
LINGUAL N.$_P$
CHORDA TYMPANI N.$_Q$
FACIAL N.$_R$

PTERYGOPALATINE GANGLION

SUBMANDIBULAR GANGLION

SULCUS TERMINALIS

MOAT

MICROVILLI
TASTE PORE
EPITHELIAL CELL

The auditory portion of the ear collects and converts sound waves to nerve impulses. The vestibular portion responds to changes in head position and movement to maintain balance and equilibrium. The structures concerned with audition or hearing will be covered in this plate.

Color the heading External Ear, titles A and B, and the related structures in the upper illustration. Color title C, the heading Middle Ear, titles D through F, and related arrow and structures in the upper illustration.

The external ear consists of an *auricle* (A), an *external auditory meatus* (B), and a *tympanic membrane* (C; eardrum or drumhead). The auricle collects sound waves and funnels them through the external auditory meatus to the tympanic membrane, which is stretched across the entrance to the *middle ear cavity* (D; tympanic cavity). The *malleus* (E; "hammer") of the middle ear is attached to the tympanic membrane. The malleus articulates with the *incus* (E^1; "anvil"), which in turn articulates with the *stapes* (E^2; "stirrup"). The footplate of the stapes is attached to the membrane covering the *oval window* (H). The tympanic cavity communicates with the nasopharynx via the *auditory tube* (F; Eustachian or pharyngotympanic tube), which provides for equalization of air pressure on both sides of the tympanic membrane.

Color titles G through J at the middle right and related structures in the upper illustration. Color the headings Cochlea of the Inner Ear and Organ of Corti, titles K through V, and related structures in the middle and lower illustrations. Color the titles W, X, and Y and related structures in all three illustrations, as applicable.

The inner ear, located within the petrous portion of the temporal bone, consists of a series of fluid (perilymph)-filled passageways carved in bone: the bony labyrinth. A series of membranous, endolymph-filled passageways, called the membranous labyrinth, fits within the bony labyrinth. In this plate we are concerned with the anteriormost parts of the bony labyrinth (the vestibule and cochlea) and membranous labyrinth (cochlear duct); the more posterior parts can be studied in Plate 6-19.

The *cochlea* (I) consists of two elongated tubes coiled around a central, bony pillar. Like a cornucopia, the cochlea has an expanded part, the base, and a narrow part, the apex. The base is adjacent to the *vestibule* (G), a relatively large cavity of the bony labyrinth separated from the more medial middle ear cavity, in part, by the oval window. The vestibule opens into the upper tube or *scala vestibuli* (K) of the snail shell–like cochlea. The scala vestibuli coils around a pillar of bone (*modiolus*, M) two and one-half turns to the apex (helicotrema) of the cochlea, where it communicates with a second (lower) tube, the *scala tympani* (L). This tube coils around the modiolus below the scala vestibuli and terminates in the base of the cochlea at the membrane-covered *round window* (J) adjacent to the lower part of the middle ear cavity. A small shelf of bone (*osseous spiral lamina*, M^1) projects from the modiolus between the scala vestibuli above and the scala tympani below, giving it and the modiolus the appearance of the spiral flange and the shaft of a screw, respectively.

The membranous, triangular, endolymph-filled *cochlear duct* (N; also called *scala media*), closed at both ends, runs between the two tubes. The thin, cellular roof of the cochlear duct is the vestibular (*Reissner's*) *membrane* (O). The floor is the ligamentous *basilar membrane* (P). The cochlear duct contains the organ of Corti, the complex receptor of hearing. It consists of one row of *inner hair cells* (S) and three to five rows of *outer hair cells* (T), supported by *pillar* (U) and *phalangeal cells* (V) attached to the basilar membrane. It is overlain by a gelatinous *tectorial membrane* (R) attached to the *limbus* (Q), a fibrous projection of the spiral lamina. The hair cells exhibit cilia (stereocilia or "hairs") at their apices. Afferent fibers running in the spiral lamina make synaptic contact at the bases of the hair cells. The vast majority of these fibers synapse with the inner cells. These afferents are *peripheral fibers* (X) of bipolar cell bodies (*spiral ganglion*, W) located within the modiolus. The central processes of these cells form the cochlear division of the vestibulocochlear nerve, commonly called the *cochlear* or auditory *nerve* (Y).

To recapitulate, sound waves induce vibrations of the tympanic membrane. The resulting oscillations of the ossicles vibrate the membranous covering of the oval window, moving the perilymph in the tubes of the cochlea. Fluid movement in the scala tympani causes the basilar membrane to vibrate. With this movement, the "hairs" of the inner and outer hair cells become embedded in the tectorial membrane and bend. Action potentials are thereby generated at the base of the hair cells and conducted through the nerve cells of the spiral ganglia to the brain.

AUDITORY SYSTEM: THE EAR.

EXTERNAL EAR ★
AURICLE$_A$
EXT. AUD. MEATUS$_B$
TYMPANIC MEMBRANE$_C$

MIDDLE EAR ★
MIDDLE EAR CAVITY$_D$
MALLEUS$_E$/INCUS$_{E^1}$/STAPES$_{E^2}$

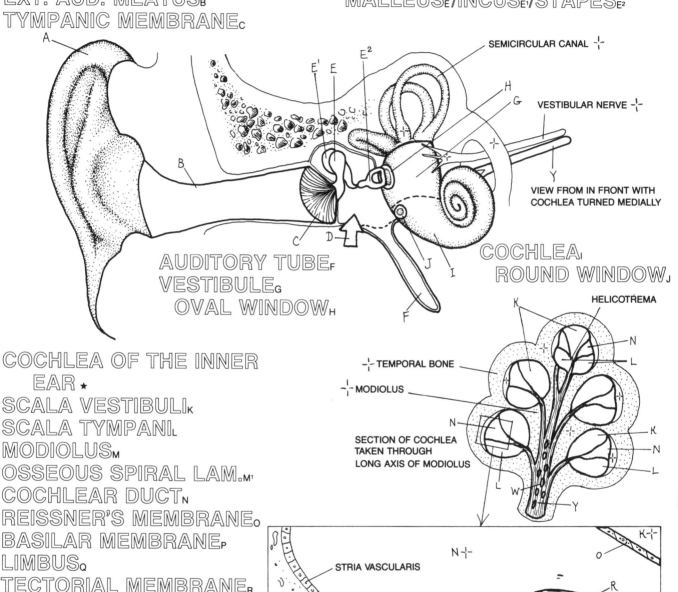

SEMICIRCULAR CANAL
VESTIBULAR NERVE

VIEW FROM IN FRONT WITH
COCHLEA TURNED MEDIALLY

AUDITORY TUBE$_F$
VESTIBULE$_G$
OVAL WINDOW$_H$

COCHLEA$_I$
ROUND WINDOW$_J$

HELICOTREMA
TEMPORAL BONE
MODIOLUS

SECTION OF COCHLEA
TAKEN THROUGH
LONG AXIS OF MODIOLUS

COCHLEA OF THE INNER EAR ★
SCALA VESTIBULI$_K$
SCALA TYMPANI$_L$
MODIOLUS$_M$
OSSEOUS SPIRAL LAM.$_{M^1}$
COCHLEAR DUCT$_N$
REISSNER'S MEMBRANE$_O$
BASILAR MEMBRANE$_P$
LIMBUS$_Q$
TECTORIAL MEMBRANE$_R$
ORGAN OF CORTI ★
INNER HAIR CELL$_S$
OUTER HAIR CELL$_T$
PILLAR CELL$_U$
PHALANGEAL CELL$_V$
SPIRAL GANGLION$_W$
PERIPH. PROCESS$_X$
COCHLEAR NERVE FIBERS$_Y$

STRIA VASCULARIS
SUPPORT CELLS
HAIRS

CROSS SECTION THROUGH COCHLEAR DUCT

The cochlear nerve (part of the VIII cranial nerve) conducts impulses generated in the organ of Corti to the cochlear nuclei. In this plate we examine the central pathways from these nuclei to intermediate cell stations of the brain stem and thalamus and on to the cerebral cortex.

Color titles A through G³ and the related structures, starting with the nerve at the lower left. Color titles B³ through M and related structures, beginning at the ventral cochlear nucleus. Use similar shades of one color for B, B¹, and B² and contrasting shades of the same color for B³, B⁴, and B⁵. Note the lowest cross section is shown at different levels: upper medulla on the left, lower pons on the right.

The *central processes of the spiral ganglion* (A¹) neurons form the *cochlear nerve* (A), which leaves the petrous portion of the temporal bone via the internal auditory meatus and runs a short course to the cerebellopontine angle. On entering the rostral medulla, each axon of the nerve bifurcates, sending a branch to each of the *cochlear nuclei, dorsal* (B) and *ventral* (B³). These nuclei are found in the rostral medulla and the caudal pons (not shown in the pons). The dorsal and ventral nuclei are situated posterolateral and anterolateral to the inferior cerebellar peduncle, respectively.

Efferents (B¹) from the dorsal cochlear nucleus form the *dorsal acoustic stria* (C) to cross the pontine tegmentum to a contralateral relay cell complex, the *superior olivary nucleus* (D). Giving a *collateral* (B²) to the olivary nucleus, the efferent fibers contribute to the ascending *lateral lemniscus* (E). The lateral lemniscus is the major brain stem auditory pathway; it is located in the lateral tegmentum (see Plate 5-43), from the rostral medulla to its termination in the inferior colliculus and (with some fibers, path not shown) the medial geniculate body. Some ascending dorsal cochlear efferents in the lateral lemniscus terminate in the *nuclei of the lateral lemniscus* (F), arranged adjacent to and along the extent of the lateral lemniscus; others continue on to the ipsilateral *inferior colliculus* (G). Some *axons* (F¹) of neurons in the lateral lemniscal nuclei *decussate* to the contralateral side of the mid pons and ascend with the lateral lemniscus to the inferior colliculus on that side.

Efferents (B⁴) from the ventral cochlear nucleus may project to the ipsilateral dorsal cochlear nucleus (not shown) or arc around the inferior cerebellar peduncle. The latter form the *intermediate acoustic stria* (H) to the ip-

silateral (not shown) or contralateral superior olivary nucleus. These fibers continue on as part of the lateral lemniscus to terminate in the lateral lemniscal nuclei or the ipsilateral inferior colliculus.

Efferents (B⁵) from the ventral cochlear nucleus may also form the ventral acoustic stria or *trapezoid body* (I), running transversely through the caudal pons. Collaterals of these efferents terminate in the ipsilateral superior olivary nucleus (not shown) or in the *nuclei of the trapezoid body* (J). The trapezoid nuclei and the neighboring ventral cochlear efferents and their collaterals constitute the trapezoid body complex (I and J). The trapezoid body fibers may synapse in the contralateral superior olivary nucleus or bend rostrally to contribute to the lateral lemniscus and ascend to the lateral lemniscal nuclei or inferior colliculus. No fibers from the cochlear nuclei ascend in the ipsilateral lemniscus.

In the midbrain, most of the lateral lemniscal fibers terminate in the inferior colliculus, an important relay center for impulses particularly concerned with auditory reflexes, such as involuntarily jumping in response to a loud noise. From each inferior colliculus, some *axons* (G¹) pass to the contralateral colliculus via the *commissure of the inferior colliculus* (G²); other efferents form the *brachium of the inferior colliculus* (G³) and project to the *medial geniculate body* (K) of the thalamus.

Neurons of the medial geniculate body send *axons* (K¹) to the superior temporal gyrus of the cerebral cortex. These axons form a large bundle called the *auditory radiation* (L), composing the sublenticular part of the internal capsule (recall Plate 5-33) and the lateral part of the corona radiata. The axons of the auditory radiation terminate in *area 41* (M; Heschl's gyrus or the primary auditory cortex) on the superior temporal gyrus.

In addition to this extensive afferent pathway, there is also an efferent tract, the olivocochlear bundle (not shown). This tract projects to the hair cells of the organ of Corti from contralateral brain stem nuclei, including one of the nuclei of the superior olivary complex. Such a pathway represents an inhibitory feedback mechanism on auditory input; stated in more familiar jargon, we can "turn off" what we don't want to hear.

Destruction of the cochlear nuclei or nerve causes complete deafness on the affected side. Lesions of the lateral lemniscus or area 41 cause minimal bilateral deafness, a condition difficult to detect clinically because of the extensive crossed and uncrossed fibers shown here.

AUDITORY SYSTEM: COCHLEAR (VIII) NERVE AND PATHWAYS.

COCHLEAR N.A
  CENT. PROC. SPIRAL
    GANG.A¹
DORSAL COCHLEAR NUC.B
  EFFERENT AXONB¹
    COLLATERALB²
DORSAL ACOUSTIC STRIAC
SUP. OLIVARY NUC.D
LAT. LEMNISCUSE
NUC. LAT. LEMNISCUSF
  DECUSS. AXONF¹
INF. COLLICULUSG
  EFFERENT AXONG¹
  COMMISSUREG²
  BRACHIUMG³
VENT. COCHLEAR NUC.B³
  EFFERENT AXONB⁴
  EFFERENT AXONB⁵
INTERMED. ACOUSTIC STRIAH
TRAPEZOID BODYI
NUC. TRAPEZOID BODYJ
MED. GENICULATE BODYK
  EFFERENT AXONK¹
AUDIT. RADIATIONL
AREA 41M

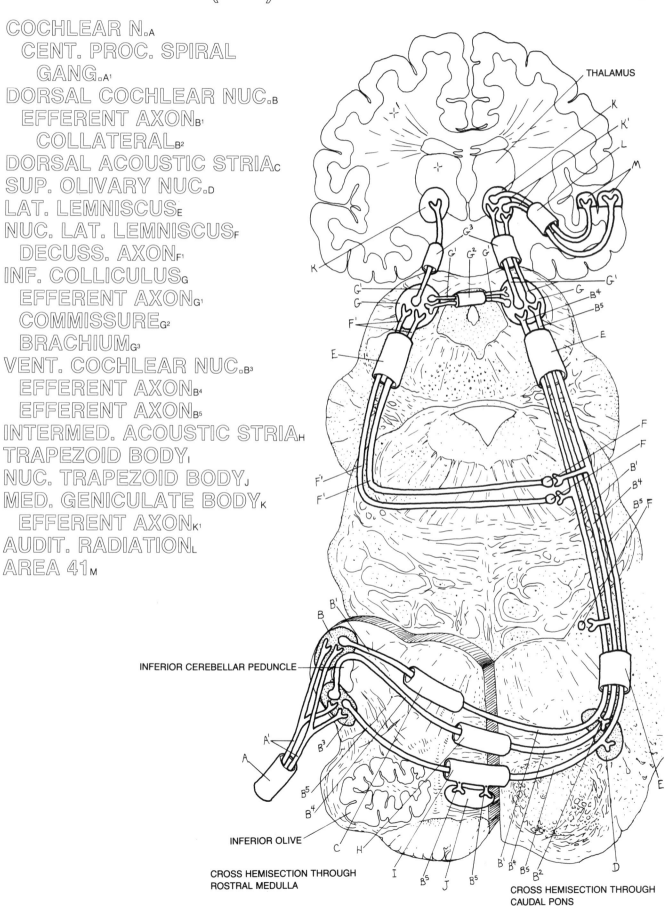

THALAMUS

INFERIOR CEREBELLAR PEDUNCLE

INFERIOR OLIVE

CROSS HEMISECTION THROUGH
ROSTRAL MEDULLA

CROSS HEMISECTION THROUGH
CAUDAL PONS

The vestibular division of the inner ear includes the bony labyrinth made up of the vestibular and semicircular canals, as well as the membranous labyrinth consisting of the semicircular ducts, utricle, and saccule.

Color the titles A through H¹ and related structures in the upper right and center illustrations. Then color the titles B¹ through S and related structures in all applicable illustrations.

The structures of the bony labyrinth are formed from and located within the petrous portion of the temporal bone. Within the *vestibule* (A) are two membranous sacs: the *utricle* (B) and the *saccule* (C). The utricle, filled with endolymph, is in communication with semicircular ducts posteriorly and laterally and with the saccule (via the utriculosaccular duct) anteriorly.

Three arched, semicircular ducts, oriented at about right angles to one another, are secured within the bony *semicircular canals* (D). The *anterior* (F) and *posterior semicircular ducts* (G) arise from the posterior-superior aspect of the utricle via a *common duct* (E). The anterior duct arches anterolaterally, tilted somewhat laterally from the sagittal plane. The posterior duct arches posterolaterally along the axis of the petrous portion of the temporal bone, midway between the sagittal and coronal planes of the skull. The *lateral semicircular duct* (H), unlike the other two ducts, is more horizontal and arches laterally and anteriorly from just below the common duct to the anterolateral surface of the utricle. The semicircular ducts are open at both ends to the utricle; one end of each is dilated and forms the *ampulla* (F¹, G¹, H¹; flask). The bony canals are also enlarged at these sites and are likewise called ampullae.

The inner lining of the ducts and ampullae, utricle, and saccule is composed of a single layer of flat (squamous) or cuboidal cells supported by vascular connective tissue. This connective tissue is thickened on the floor and adjacent lateral wall of the utricle, the anterior wall of the saccule, and the ampullae of the semicircular ducts. This thickening contains the receptor sites, called the *maculae* (B¹, C¹; spot or thickening) in the utricle and saccule, and the *cristae ampullaris* (I; *crista,* "ridge") in the ampullae.

Each of these receptor sites basically consists of sensory *hair cells* (J; cells having apical processes appearing like hair shafts when viewed with the light microscope) sur-rounded by *supporting cells* (M). The bases of these sensory cells offer synaptic sites for the terminals of afferent nerve fibers. The apex of each hair cell is characterized by modified microvilli, called *stereocilia* (K; *stereo,* "solid"; the reference to a true cilium is incorrect, based on electron microscopic studies), and one true cilium, called a *kinocilium* (L; *kino,* "move"). These "cilia" are shown only in the section through the macula; both kinds exist in the cristae as well. The hairs of the sensory cells of the maculae are embedded in a flat *gelatin*like *mass* (N) containing calcite (calcium carbonate) bodies called *otoliths* (O). The hairs of the receptor cells of the cristae are embedded in a calcite-free gelatinous, mucopolysaccharide material which characteristically forms a dome or *cupula* (P).

In both maculae and cristae, the kinocilium transmits mechanical stimuli received from the movement of the overlying gelatinous mass to the adjacent stereocilia. Excitation of the receptor cells occurs when the stereocilia bend in the direction of the kinocilium; inhibition occurs with bending in the opposite direction.

The utricular and saccular maculae are sensitive to gravitational changes, which cause the relatively heavy otoliths to bend the "hairs" of the receptor cells during movement. The utricular macular cells are sensitive to up and down ("jumping") or vertical movements of the head, while saccular macular cells are more sensitive to forward and backward ("stop and go") movements of the head. In fulfilling these functions, the macular receptors report static balance or position of the head as well as linear (not angular) acceleration of it.

The receptor cells of the cristae of the semicircular ducts are responsive to angular acceleration (bending, rotation) of the head. With these kinetic changes, the movement of endolymph bends the "hairs" of the receptor cells, initiating a stimulus.

Bending of the "hairs" induces release of a transmitter substance at synaptic sites with afferent nerve endings. Some of the endings are bulbous (terminal boutons), and others surround the base of the receptor cells. The afferents are the *peripheral processes* (Q) of the bipolar cells of the *vestibular ganglion* (R) located in the internal auditory meatus. The *central processes* (S) of the neurons constitute the vestibular nerve or the vestibular division of the vestibulocochlear nerve.

VESTIBULAR SYSTEM: INNER EAR.

VESTIBULE A
UTRICLE B
SACCULE C
SEMICIRC. CANAL D
COMMON DUCT E
ANT. S. C. DUCT F/AMPULLA F1
POST. S. C. DUCT G/ AMPULLA G1
LAT. S. C. DUCT H/AMPULLA H1

DIRECTION OF VIEW OF VESTIBULAR APPARATUS IN MIDDLE ILLUSTRATION

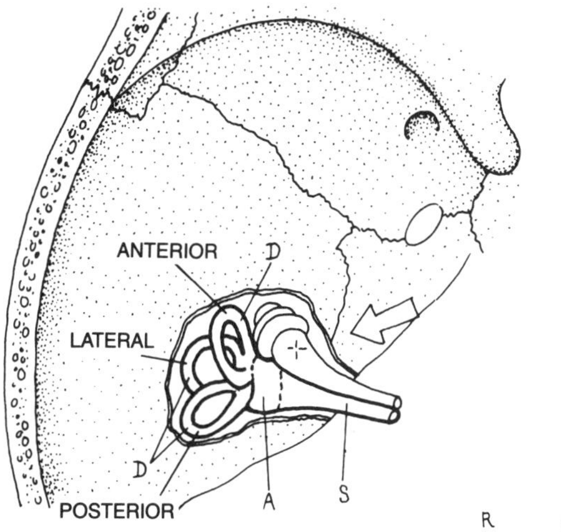

ANTERIOR
LATERAL
POSTERIOR
D
A
S

POSTERIOMEDIAL ASPECT OF VESTIBULAR APPARATUS

H
H'
E
F
F'
I
Q
R
S
PSEUDOUNIPOLAR
NEURON
CELL BODIES
COCHLEAR NERVE
B'
A
C'
G
G'
A + B
A+C
COCHLEAR DUCT
OVAL WINDOW
ROUND WINDOW
L
K
N
O
J
M
P

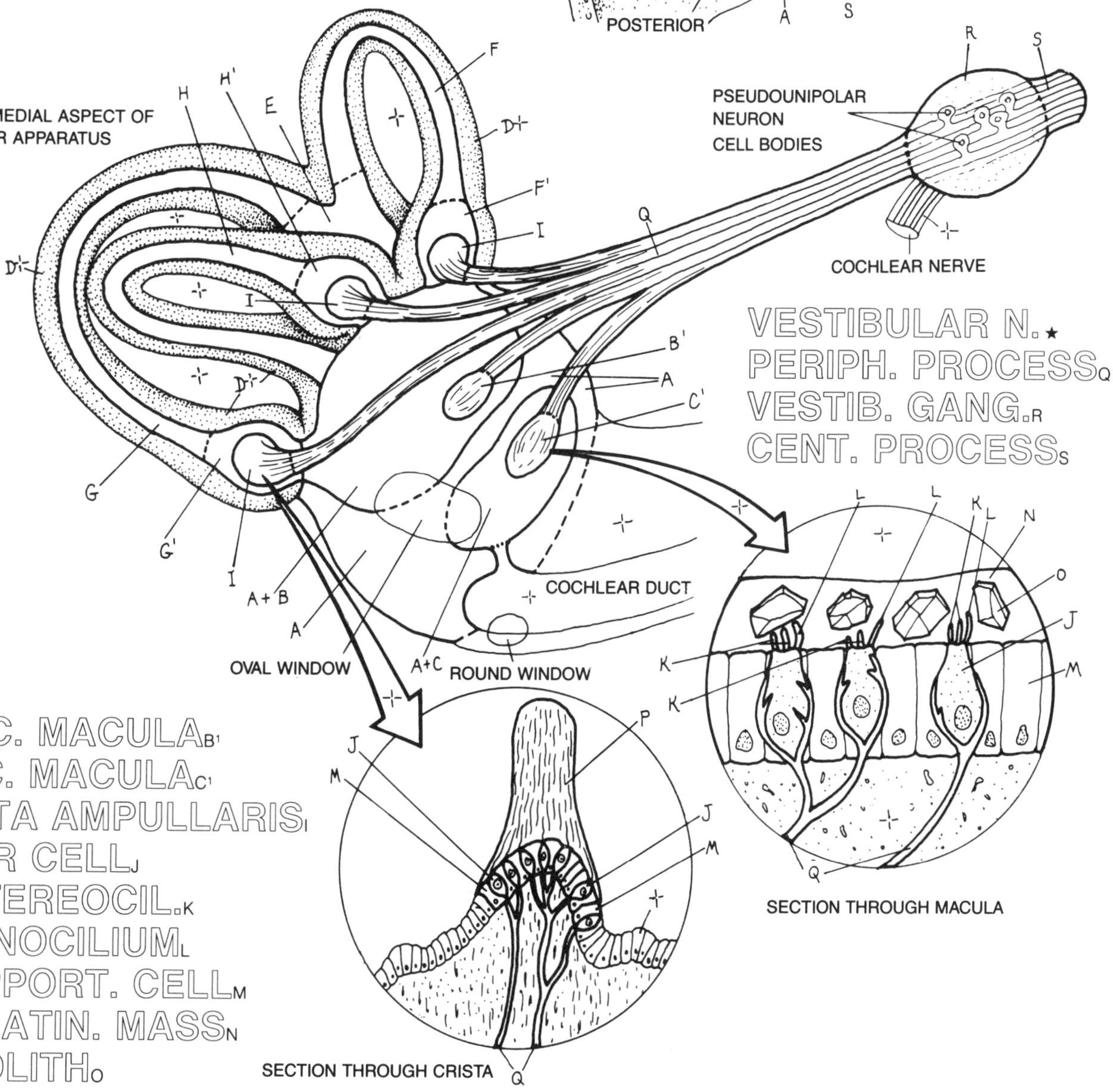

VESTIBULAR N.★
PERIPH. PROCESS Q
VESTIB. GANG. R
CENT. PROCESS S

SECTION THROUGH MACULA

SECTION THROUGH CRISTA

UTRIC. MACULA B1
SACC. MACULA C1
CRISTA AMPULLARIS I
HAIR CELL J
STEREOCIL. K
KINOCILIUM L
SUPPORT. CELL M
GELATIN. MASS N
OTOLITH O
CUPULA P

In this plate we examine the afferent and efferent fibers constituting the vestibular component of the VIII cranial nerve. The vestibular nuclear complex and some of the more important related central pathways are shown as well. The complexity of the pathways for maintenance of equilibrium and balance reflect the influence of this system throughout the brain.

Color heading Vestibular Nuclei and Relations, titles A through I and L, and related structures in the upper illustration. Note that it consists of two hemisections: lower pons on the left, upper medulla on the right. Then color the same structures, as applicable, in the lower illustration. Consider using the same color for a vestibular nucleus and its axons; use contrasting colors among the nuclei.

The *vestibular nerve* (A) enters the brain stem at the cerebellopontine angle and proceeds posteromedially through the upper medulla, where its fibers synapse among the *medial* (B), *lateral* (C), *superior* (D), and *inferior vestibular nuclei* (E). These nuclei are grouped closely together (area acoustica, not labeled) along the floor of the fourth ventricle, from the level of the abducens nucleus in the mid pons to the level of the inferior olive in the mid medulla. Significant relationships of the vestibular nuclei include the *inferior cerebellar peduncle* (F) and the more medial, smaller bundle, the *juxtarestiform body* (G; *juxta,* "near"; *restiform body,* alternative name for inferior cerebellar peduncle). Also note the genu of the facial nerve fibers around the *abducens nucleus* (L), the *medial longitudinal fasciculus* (H; abbreviated MLF), and the *reticular formation* (I).

Color the heading Projections, the remaining titles, and related structures.

The vestibular nerve consists largely of the central processes of bipolar *afferent neurons* (A^1), the cell bodies of which constitute the superior and inferior ganglia known collectively as the *vestibular ganglion* (A^2). These cells (recall Plate 6-19) are located in the internal auditory meatus of the petrous portion of the temporal bone. Upon entering the brain stem, the central processes terminate among the vestibular nuclei, with some fibers projecting to the cerebellum via the juxtarestiform body. These latter fibers constitute the vestibulocerebellar tract (not shown), which projects to the cortex of the floccular nodular lobe and uvula of the vermis. Powerful reciprocal projections, the *cerebellovestibular fibers* (G^1), arising in both cerebellar cortex and the fastigial nucleus (recall Plate 5-15), reach all four of the vestibular nuclei via the juxtarestiform body.

Axons from the vestibular nuclei spread widely throughout the brain stem, forming the secondary pathway of this system. Medial vestibular *axons* (B^1) contribute ascending and descending fibers, both crossed (not shown) and uncrossed, to the MLF, some of which terminate at the *oculomotor* (J), *trochlear* (K), and abducens nuclei and some of which terminate in the cervical cord (not shown). Other medial vestibular axons (not shown) project to the reticular formation, from which fibers descend to visceral motor nuclei in the brain stem. These connections provide a basis for vomiting reflexes initiated by excessive vestibular stimulation, often manifested in the extreme by diseases of the inner ear.

Axons of the lateral vestibular nucleus (C^1) give rise to the *vestibulospinal tract* (M; recall Plate 4-10), which facilitates extensor muscle tone, maintaining an upright posture against the force of gravity. Also, axons from this nucleus project as uncrossed ascending and descending fibers of the MLF; some of these fibers reach the oculomotor and trochlear nuclei of the midbrain. *Superior vestibular axons* (D^1) ascend ipsilaterally in the MLF; some of them terminate in the oculomotor and trochlear nuclei. Axons from the superior nucleus, excitatory in nature, join the afferent fibers of the vestibular nerve and terminate about the hair cells of the maculae and cristae (not shown). *Inferior vestibular axons* (E^1) both ascend and descend in the MLF within the brain stem.

Projections from the vestibular nuclei, close to the medial lemniscus, are known to reach the thalamus (not shown). Some investigators believe that thalamocortical fibers convey vestibular impulses to the superior temporal gyrus, anterior to the auditory projections.

To complete a survey of vestibular structure and function, see Plates 4-10, 5-6, 5-7, and 6-19.

VESTIBULAR SYSTEM: NERVE (VIII) AND PATHWAYS.

VESTIBULAR NUC./
   RELATIONS ★
VESTIB. N.$_A$/AFF. NEUR.$_{A^1}$
   GANG.$_{A^2}$
VESTIB. NUC.:★MED.$_B$
   LAT.$_C$/SUP.$_D$/INF.$_E$
INF. CEREBELL. PED.$_F$
JUXTARESTIFORM BODY$_G$
   CEREBELLOVESTIB.
      FIBERS$_{G^1}$
MED. LONGITUD. FASC.$_H$
RETICULAR FORMATION$_I$

PROJECTIONS ★
MED. VESTIB. AXON$_B$TO MLF$_H$/ OCULOM. NUC.$_J$/
   TROCH. NUC.$_K$/ABDUCENS NUC.$_L$
LAT. VESTIB. AXON$_{C^1}$ TO MLF$_H$/ VESTIB. SP. TR.$_M$
SUP. VESTIB. AXON$_{D^1}$ TO MLF$_H$/
   OCULOM. NUC.$_J$/
      TROCH. NUC.$_K$/VESTIB. N.$_A$
INF. VESTIB. AXON$_{E^1}$ TO MLF$_H$

GENU OF FACIAL
NERVE

CROSS
HEMISECTION
THROUGH PONS

CROSS HEMISECTION
THROUGH ROSTRAL MEDULLA

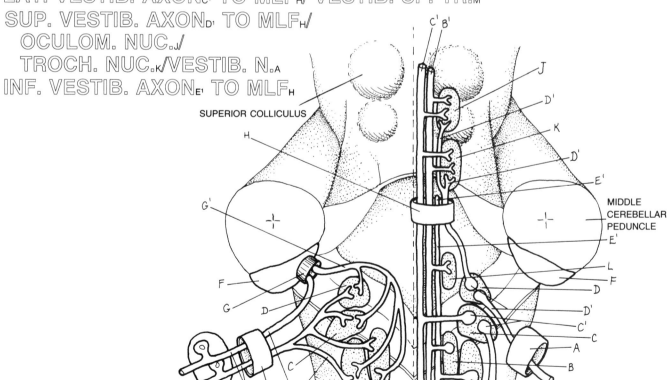

SUPERIOR COLLICULUS

MIDDLE
CEREBELLAR
PEDUNCLE

The glossopharyngeal (IX) cranial nerve (*glosso-*, "tongue"; *pharynx*, "throat") is a mixed nerve. Its sensory component consists of general visceral afferent fibers from the pressoreceptors of the carotid sinus, chemoreceptors of the carotid body, and the mucous membranes of the palate, tonsils, pharynx, auditory tube, and tympanic cavity; special visceral afferents from taste receptors on the post-sulcal region (posterior one-third of the tongue; and general somatic afferents from the external ear and auditory meatus. The motor component of this nerve is considered in Plate 6-22.

Color the titles A through N and related structures, starting with the lower drawing and using shades of the same color for structures sharing the same subscript.

General somatic afferent neurons (A^1) of the glossopharyngeal nerve arise in the *skin* of the *external auditory meatus* and in back of the *ear* (A). Axons of these neurons join the auricular branch of the vagus or the facial nerves. Those fibers ascending with the *auricular branch of the vagus nerve* (B) join the *glossopharyngeal nerve* (E) within the *jugular foramen* (D) and enter the *superior (petrosal) ganglion* (C). The central processes of these neurons penetrate the brain stem and enter the *spinal trigeminal nucleus* (F).

General visceral afferent neurons (G^2), conveying pain and other poorly localized sensations from the *palate* (G) and *pharynx* (G^1), join the *pharyngeal branch* (H) of the glossopharyngeal nerve. Similarly, such neurons from the *tonsils* (G^3; including palatine, lingual, tubal, and pharyngeal tonsils) join the glossopharyngeal nerve via the *tonsillar branch* (I). The pain of tonsillitis is conveyed by these and other branches of the IX nerve, including the tympanic plexus (discussed in Plate 6-22; *plexus*, an interwoven network of fibers), which also conveys pain and temperature sensations from the mucous membranes of the middle ear and auditory tube (not shown). Herein lies the basis for the fact that the pain of tonsillar inflammation is sometimes referred to the middle ear cavity.

Certain general visceral afferent fibers originate among specialized pressure receptors (*carotid sinus*, G^4) located in a thickened part of the wall (seen externally as a swelling) of the common carotid artery close to its bifurcation into internal and external branches. These fibers compose the afferent limb of a reflex controlling systemic blood pressure. Posterior to and often wedged in the bifurcation is a small mass (the *carotid body*, G^5) consisting of specialized epithelioid cells, a complex of small vessels, and nerves supported by connective tissue. The carotid body (a chemoreceptor) is concerned with acid-base balance (pH) and concentrations of oxygen and carbon dioxide in the blood. The afferents of the carotid body and sinus make up the *sinus nerve* (J), which ascends with other afferents to join the root of IX.

Special visceral afferent fibers (K^1) of the glossopharyngeal nerve make synaptic contact with the taste receptor cells (as shown in Plate 6-16) on the area of the tongue posterior to the sulcus terminalis (*post-sulcal region*, K). *Lingual branches* (L) of the IX nerve carry these fibers upward between the internal and external carotid arteries lateral to the muscular pharyngeal wall to join pharyngeal and tonsillar branches of IX and form one nerve bundle. This bundle joins with the sinus nerve and reaches the *inferior (petrosal) ganglion* (M) just below the superior ganglion at the entrance to the jugular foramen.

The special and general visceral afferent fibers enter the brain stem and terminate in the *nucleus solitarius* (N). This cigar-shaped nucleus, located in the posterolateral medulla, receives special visceral afferents in its rostral part (gustatory nucleus, not shown) from those cranial nerves (VII, IX, and X) conducting sensations from the tongue and pharynx. The more caudal part of the nucleus receives general visceral afferent fibers from the IX and X nerves, including axons from the gastrointestinal tract, esophagus, and respiratory tract. The entire nucleus is intimately associated with the pontomedullary reticular formation and cardiorespiratory centers in the medulla. Its efferent fibers project to the ventral posterior medial nucleus of the thalamus and to numerous areas of the brain stem (not shown).

GLOSSOPHARYNGEAL (IX) NERVE: SENSORY COMPONENT.

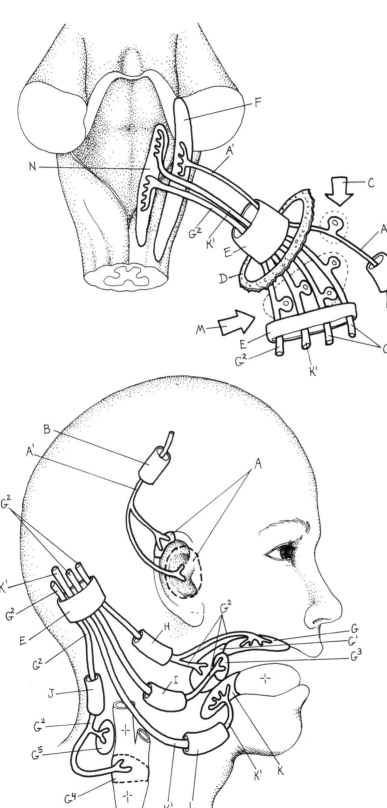

SKIN OF EXT. EAR_A
GEN. SOM. AFF. NEURON_A'
AURIC. BR. VAGUS N._B
SUP. GANGLION_C
JUGULAR FORAMEN_D
GLOSSOPHARYNGEAL N._E
SPINAL TRIGEM. NUC._F

PALATE_G/PHARYNX_G'
GEN. VISC. AFF. NEUR._G²
PHARYNGEAL BR._H

TONSIL_G³
TONSILLAR BR._I

CAROTID SINUS_G⁴
CAROTID BODY_G⁵
SINUS N._J

POSTSULCAL
TASTE REGION_K
SPEC. VISC. AFF.
NEURON_K'
LINGUAL BR._L
INF. GANGLION_M
NUC. SOLITARIUS_N

The motor component of the glossopharyngeal (IX) nerve consists of special visceral efferent fibers to the stylopharyngeus and the superior constrictor muscles of the pharynx (derivatives of one or more of the branchial or embryonic gill arches, discussed in Plate 6-3), and general visceral efferent (parasympathetic division of the VNS) fibers to the parotid (salivary) gland. The sensory component of this nerve has been presented in Plate 6-21.

Color titles A through D² and the related structures associated with the special visceral efferent neuron.

The cell bodies of the *special visceral efferent neurons* (B) are located in the rostral part of the *nucleus ambiguus* (A; recall Plate 6-4), lying in the reticular formation of the upper medulla. The *axons* (B¹) exit the cerebellopontine angle as part of several rootlets of the *glossopharyngeal nerve* (C; recall Plate 6-21), pass through the jugular foramen, and descend with the vagus lateral to the pharyngeal wall, between the internal jugular vein and the internal carotid artery (relations not shown). The glossopharyngeal nerve slips between the superior and middle constrictor muscles, sending motor fibers (*nerve to stylopharyngeus,* D) to the adjacent *stylopharyngeus muscle* (D¹). In association with the vagus (X) nerve, via the pharyngeal plexus (not shown), motor fibers may also be sent to the *superior constrictor muscle* (D²) of the pharyngeal wall. These muscles contribute to the sequential, rhythmic contractions of the palatal and pharyngeal muscles during swallowing. Denervation of these efferent fibers and the closely related vagal efferents cause paralysis of the affected muscles and some difficulty in swallowing (dysphagia).

Color titles E through M and the related structures associated with the general visceral efferent neuron.

The cell bodies of the *general visceral efferent neurons* (F) of the IX nerve are located in the *inferior salivatory nucleus* (E; recall Plate 6-4), a poorly defined neuronal cell group in the upper, posterior medulla. The general visceral efferent or parasympathetic *preganglionic axons* (F¹) exit the jugular foramen and turn upward to pass through a fissure in the temporal bone and enter the middle ear cavity. Here the fibers ascend the promontory (a convex bulge accommodating the first turn of the cochlea) of the medial wall of the cavity as part of the *tympanic plexus* (G). This network of fibers includes sensory fibers from the mucous membranes of the middle ear, the mastoid air cells, and the auditory tube. The preganglionic fibers pierce the roof of the middle ear cavity and join a small branch from the facial nerve (recall Plate 6-15), the two forming the *lesser petrosal nerve* (H). This nerve continues anteriorly to the *foramen ovale* (I) and descends into the infratemporal fossa along with the mandibular division (nerve) of the trigeminal nerve (recall Plate 6-2). Here the preganglionic fibers synapse with the cell bodies of the *postganglionic neurons* (K) in the *otic ganglion* (J). The *postganglionic axons* (K¹) travel with the *auriculotemporal nerve* (L; a branch of the mandibular division of the trigeminal nerve). This nerve reaches the *parotid gland* (M) between the external auditory meatus posteriorly and the ramus of the mandible anteriorly. The parotid is the largest of the salivary glands, lying in front of and slightly below the ear immediately posterior to the masseter muscle (recall Plate 6-13). It contributes a thin, watery secretion rich in amylase, an enzyme important for the initial digestion of starches.

GLOSSOPHARYNGEAL (IX) NERVE: MOTOR COMPONENT.

NUCLEUS AMBIGUUS$_A$
SPEC. VISC. EFF. NEUR.$_B$/AXON$_{B1}$
GLOSSOPHARYNGEAL N.$_C$
N. TO STYLOPHARYNGEUS$_D$
STYLOPHARYNG. M.$_{D1}$/SUP. CONSTR. M.$_{D2}$

INF. SALIVATORY NUC.$_E$
GEN. VISC. EFF. NEURON$_F$
PREGANG. AXON$_{F1}$
TYMPANIC PLEXUS$_G$
LESSER PETROSAL N.$_H$
FORAMEN OVALE$_I$
OTIC GANGLION$_J$
POSTGANG. NEURON$_K$
AXON$_{K1}$
AURICULOTEMPORAL N.$_L$
PAROTID GLAND$_M$

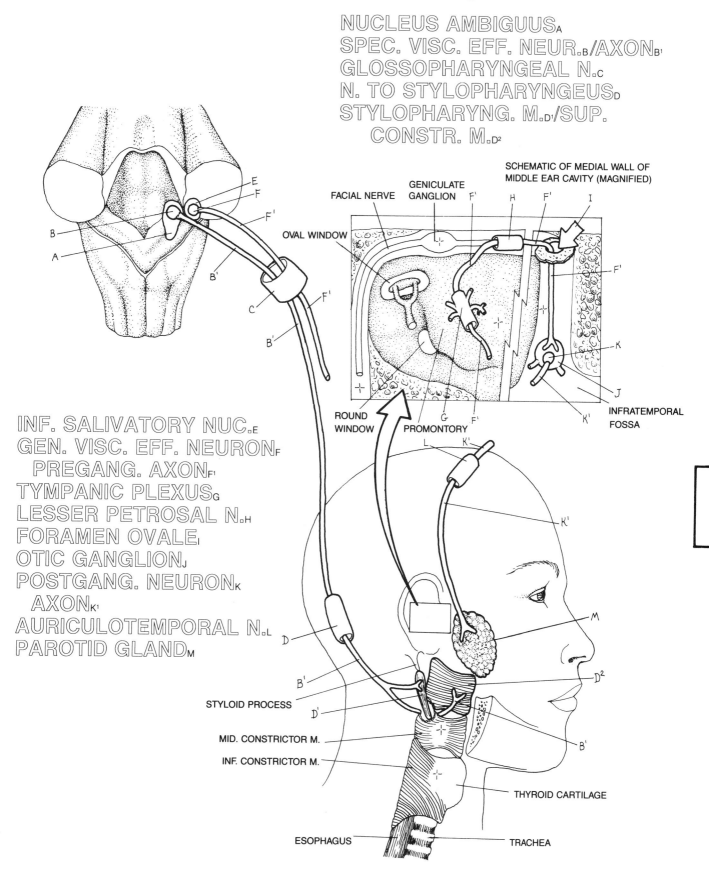

SCHEMATIC OF MEDIAL WALL OF
MIDDLE EAR CAVITY (MAGNIFIED)

FACIAL NERVE
GENICULATE GANGLION
OVAL WINDOW
ROUND WINDOW
PROMONTORY
INFRATEMPORAL FOSSA

STYLOID PROCESS
MID. CONSTRICTOR M.
INF. CONSTRICTOR M.
THYROID CARTILAGE
ESOPHAGUS
TRACHEA

The sensory component of the vagus (X) nerve consists of three parts. The general somatic afferent part receives cutaneous sensations from the external ear. The general visceral afferent part conducts visceral sensations from the thoracic and abdominal viscera as well as the pharynx and larynx. In addition, special visceral afferent fibers come from taste receptors at the base of the tongue and epiglottis (not shown).

Visceral receptors provide the basis for feelings of fullness and emptiness of the stomach, urinary bladder pressure, upper and lower bowel pressure, and so on. They and their vagal afferent fibers are concerned with visceral reflexes, such as hunger, satiety, vomiting, secretion, etc. Not included in the sensory repertoire of the vagus is visceral pain. For example, thoracic and abdominal pain associated with smooth muscle contractions or spasms is conducted by visceral afferents in company with the sympathetic visceral motor fibers. These afferents enter the spinal cord by way of spinal nerves T1 through L3. Pelvic and perineal pain fibers travel with the pelvic splanchnic (parasympathetic) nerves associated with spinal nerves S2, S3, and S4.

Color titles A through E and the related structures associated with the general somatic afferent neuron.

General sensory input from the *external ear* (A) can be conducted centrally by somatic afferents from cranial nerves V, VII, IX, and X as well as upper cervical spinal branches (great auricular nerve and other nerves, not shown). The basis for this curious fact lies in the embryological development of the first and second branchial arches, from which the external ear is derived. The *general somatic afferents* (A^1) of the *vagus nerve* (C) make up the *auricular branch* (B). These fibers pass through a small canal in the petrous portion of the temporal bone to reach their cell bodies in the *superior ganglion* (D), immediately caudal to the jugular foramen.

The central processes of these neurons join one of the many rootlets entering the medulla caudal to, but along the same line as, the glossopharyngeal nerve, posterior to the inferior olive. These fibers terminate in the *spinal trigeminal nucleus* (E).

Color titles F through N^1 and the related structures associated with the general visceral afferent fibers.

General visceral afferent fibers (G) in the abdominal and thoracic cavities arise from sites as far caudally as the proximal descending colon of the large intestine. Along the *gastrointestinal tract* (F) and related glands (liver, pancreas, gallbladder), vagal afferents travel with vagal preganglionic efferents (next plate), sympathetic postganglionic fibers (not shown; see Plate 8-4), and blood vessels. Assembling on the abdominal aorta (not shown), the afferents ascend to be incorporated in the anterior and posterior *vagal trunks* (F^1); only one is shown passing with the esophagus to enter the thoracic cavity.

Afferents from the *esophagus* (H) join the *esophageal plexus* (H^1), and fibers from the *heart* (I) form the *cardiac plexus* (I^1). Axons originating in the *lungs and bronchial tree* (J) ascend in the thorax via the *pulmonary plexus* (J^1). All of these branches contribute to the well-defined vagus nerves, which ascend in sheaths with the common carotid arteries and internal jugular veins in the neck (not shown).

Afferents from the *larynx* (K) form the *superior laryngeal nerves* (K^1), and fibers from the *pharynx and palate* (L) contribute to the *pharyngeal plexus* (L^1), all of which join the vagus nerve at the angle of the mandible. The general visceral afferents find their cell bodies in the *inferior ganglion* (M). The central processes of these cell bodies traverse the jugular foramen, contribute to the rootlets of the vagus, and penetrate the brain stem to enter the *tractus solitarius* (N) and the adjacent *nucleus solitarius* (N^1; recall Plate 6-21).

VAGUS (X) NERVE: SENSORY COMPONENT.

EXTERNAL EAR_A
GEN. SOM. AFF. NEURON_{A¹}
AURICULAR BR._B
VAGUS N._C
SUP. GANGLION_D
SPINAL TRIGEM. NUC._E

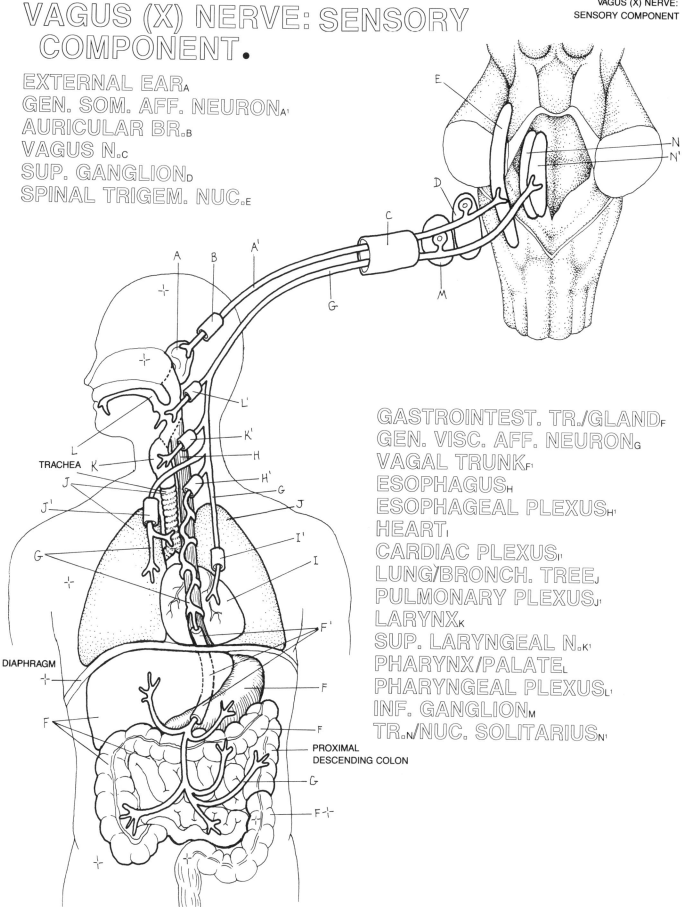

GASTROINTEST. TR./GLAND_F
GEN. VISC. AFF. NEURON_G
VAGAL TRUNK_{F¹}
ESOPHAGUS_H
ESOPHAGEAL PLEXUS_{H¹}
HEART_I
CARDIAC PLEXUS_{I¹}
LUNG/BRONCH. TREE_J
PULMONARY PLEXUS_{J¹}
LARYNX_K
SUP. LARYNGEAL N._{K¹}
PHARYNX/PALATE_L
PHARYNGEAL PLEXUS_{L¹}
INF. GANGLION_M
TR._N/NUC. SOLITARIUS_{N¹}

TRACHEA

DIAPHRAGM

PROXIMAL
DESCENDING COLON

The motor component of the vagus (X) nerve has both general visceral efferent fibers (parasympathetic preganglionics) to numerous motor ganglia in the abdominal and thoracic viscera and special visceral efferents to branchiomeric muscles of the head and neck.

Color titles A through G¹ and the related structures associated with the special visceral efferent pathway.

The *special visceral efferent fibers* (B¹) of the *vagus nerve* (D) originate from *cell bodies* (B) in the *nucleus ambiguus* (A; recall Plate 6-4). The most caudal of these fibers constitute the cranial root of the accessory nerve. The rest of the special efferent fibers join the vagus nerve at the *jugular foramen* (C). At the level of the inferior ganglion (recall Plate 6-23), fibers begin leaving the parent nerve to form the *pharyngeal plexus* (F), in association with the cranial root of the accessory nerve, to innervate the *muscles of the palate and pharynx* (F¹). Other special visceral efferents continue to descend in the vagus nerve within the *carotid sheath* (E). On the left side, the special efferent fibers bend around the arch of the aorta; on the right, they bend around the subclavian artery, both sets reversing their course as major parts of the *recurrent laryngeal nerves* (G). These ascend between the esophagus and the trachea to the thyroid gland, sometimes in the capsule of the latter, and continue upward to innervate the branchiomeric *muscles of the larynx* (G¹; derivatives of the fourth and sixth branchial arches).

The recurrent laryngeal nerves innervate the muscles that move the parts of the larynx, including the vocal folds (cords), necessary to normal respiration and speech. In surgical operations on the neck, and especially thyroidectomies (partial or total removal of the thyroid gland), these nerves are quite vulnerable to injury. Unilateral paralysis of the laryngeal muscles partially obstructs the airway, and speech becomes tiring (dysphonia). Bilateral paralysis of the laryngeal muscles causes the vocal folds to close (adduct), narrowing the airway to a thin slit and causing suffocation.

Color titles H through O and the related structures associated with the general visceral efferent fibers.

Light colors for viscera and dark colors for fibers are recommended.

The general visceral efferent *(preganglionic) fibers* (I¹) of the vagus nerve arise from the *cell bodies* (I) in the *dorsal motor nucleus* (H) in the floor of the fourth ventricle in the rostral medulla (recall Plate 5-6). The axons emerge from the medulla, posterior to the inferior olive, in eight to ten rootlets, with their sensory and special visceral efferent counterparts. The fibers leave the skull through the jugular foramen, dropping down through the neck in the carotid sheath, in company with the common carotid artery and the internal jugular vein.

Following a course virtually identical to its visceral afferent fellows (recall Plate 6-23), the motor fibers are distributed to *postganglionic neurons* (J) in small *intramural ganglia* (K; *murus,* "wall") in the walls of the viscera. Here the postganglionic fibers leave the cell bodies of origin and follow a short course to the *glands* (K¹) and *smooth muscle of the mucosa* (K²) and the deeper double- or triple-layered *muscular coat* (K³).

The viscera innervated by the general visceral efferents (I¹) include the *bronchial tree* (L; causing secretion of glands and contraction of bronchial smooth muscle, resulting in bronchial constriction), the *heart* (M; the specialized conducting tissue in the SA and AV nodes as well as the cardiac muscle of the atria, resulting in slowed heart rate), the *esophagus* (N; glandular secretion and peristaltic contractions, referred to as secretomotor activity), and the abdominal *gastrointestinal tract* (O). These efferents also innervate related extrinsic glands (secretomotor activity of the liver, pancreas, and gallbladder). Overall, these vagal fibers contribute to routine visceral secretomotor activity. They function synergistically with sympathetic fibers to create a balanced pattern of visceral function.

In cases of gastric hypersecretion and ulcerations of the stomach, the vagal trunks near the esophageal orifice of the diaphragm may be transected (vagotomy) to reduce, sometimes temporarily, the secretomotor activity of the stomach. Transections of the vagi in the neck are serious primarily due to interruptions in the fibers to the laryngeal muscles. Disturbances in esophageal and gastrointestinal motility and irregular, often accelerated heart rate follow such transections.

VAGUS (X) NERVE: MOTOR COMPONENT.

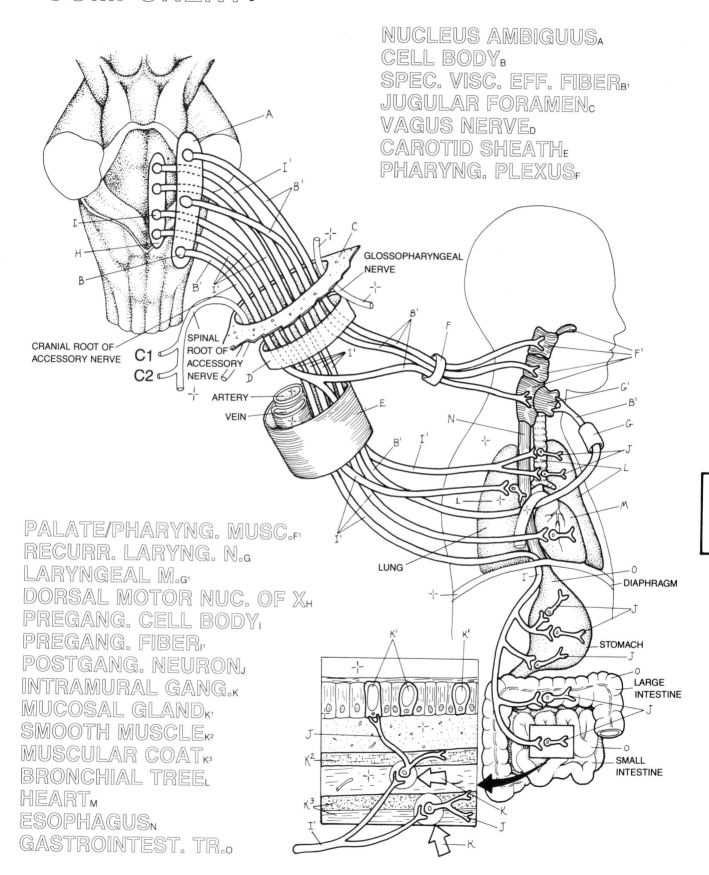

NUCLEUS AMBIGUUS_A
CELL BODY_B
SPEC. VISC. EFF. FIBER_B'
JUGULAR FORAMEN_C
VAGUS NERVE_D
CAROTID SHEATH_E
PHARYNG. PLEXUS_F

GLOSSOPHARYNGEAL
NERVE

CRANIAL ROOT OF
ACCESSORY NERVE

C1
C2

SPINAL
ROOT OF
ACCESSORY
NERVE

ARTERY

VEIN

LUNG

DIAPHRAGM

STOMACH

LARGE
INTESTINE

SMALL
INTESTINE

PALATE/PHARYNG. MUSC._F'
RECURR. LARYNG. N._G
LARYNGEAL M._G'
DORSAL MOTOR NUC. OF X_H
PREGANG. CELL BODY_I
PREGANG. FIBER_I'
POSTGANG. NEURON_J
INTRAMURAL GANG._K
MUCOSAL GLAND_K'
SMOOTH MUSCLE_K2
MUSCULAR COAT_K3
BRONCHIAL TREE_L
HEART_M
ESOPHAGUS_N
GASTROINTEST. TR._O

ACCESSORY (XI) NERVE: CRANIAL AND SPINAL ROOTS

The accessory (XI) nerve consists of a relatively small cranial root or division (also called the internal branch) and a larger spinal root (external branch). The nerve is named because of the functional and structural continuity of the cranial root with (accessory to) the vagus nerve.

Color the headings Middle Medulla and Fourth Cervical Segment, titles A through J, and related structures. Start with the upper left illustration.

The *special visceral efferent neurons* (B) of the *cranial root* (C) of the accessory nerve have their origins in the caudal part of the *nucleus ambiguus* (A) of the medulla. The *axons* (B^1) leave the brain stem close to the lower fibers of the vagus and integrate with that nerve as it passes through the *jugular foramen* (D). These fibers, entirely or in part with those of the vagus nerve, form the recurrent laryngeal nerve, which supplies the intrinsic muscles of the larynx (see Plate 6-24; follow the course of the recurrent laryngeal nerve fiber from its origin in the nucleus ambiguus). These special visceral efferents of the cranial root also contribute to the pharyngeal plexus (not shown).

The *spinal root* (G) of the accessory nerve arises from *motor neurons* (F) in the *anterior horn* (E) of the upper five or six cord segments. The *axons* (F^1) of these neurons enter and turn upward from the ventral roots of spinal nerves C5 through C1 within the dural sheath of the spinal cord in the vertebral canal. They ascend through the *foramen magnum* (H) to the level of the cranial root of the accessory nerve. Here they bend laterally and pass through the jugular foramen with the vagus nerve. The spinal root then turns posteriorly and caudally, crosses the first cervical vertebra, giving off fibers that enter the deep surface of the *sternocleidomastoid muscle* (I; *sterno,* "sternum"; *cleido,* "clavicle") near its origin at the mastoid process (behind the earlobe; not shown) of the temporal bone. The balance of the fibers descend across the posterior part of the angle of the neck (posterior triangle), joined by small motor branches from C3 and C4, to pass along and supply the deep surface of the *trapezius muscle* (J).

The sternocleidomastoid rotates and tilts the head to the same side. Paralysis of the muscle prevents rotation of the head in the direction of the affected side. A sustained contracture of this muscle is called wry neck or torticollis.

The trapezius is a mooring muscle for the scapula and elevates it (military "braced" posture); it draws the two scapulae together. An injury to the spinal accessory nerve (as may be caused by a tight shoulder harness during a sudden stop in an automobile accident) may cause weakness or paralysis of this muscle and subsequent drooping of the shoulders on the affected side.

ACCESSORY (XI) NERVE: CRANIAL AND SPINAL ROOTS.

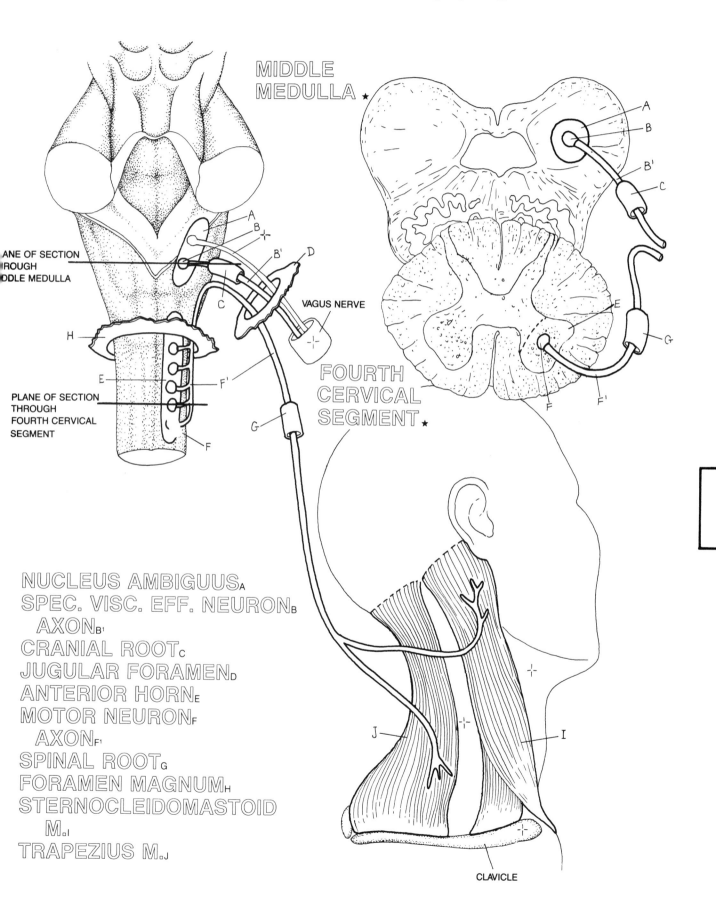

MIDDLE MEDULLA ★

ANE OF SECTION
ROUGH
DDLE MEDULLA

PLANE OF SECTION
THROUGH
FOURTH CERVICAL
SEGMENT

VAGUS NERVE

FOURTH
CERVICAL
SEGMENT ★

NUCLEUS AMBIGUUS_A
SPEC. VISC. EFF. NEURON_B
    AXON_B¹
CRANIAL ROOT_C
JUGULAR FORAMEN_D
ANTERIOR HORN_E
MOTOR NEURON_F
    AXON_F¹
SPINAL ROOT_G
FORAMEN MAGNUM_H
STERNOCLEIDOMASTOID
    M._I
TRAPEZIUS M._J

CLAVICLE

The hypoglossal (XII) nerve is a motor nerve innervating the intrinsic and extrinsic muscles of the tongue. Its neurons belong to the general somatic efferent column of cranial nerve nuclei, similar to nerves III, IV, and VI.

Color the titles A through E and related structures. Start with the illustration at the upper right. Note the relationships of this nerve with the fibers of C1, C2, and C3 that contribute to the ansa cervicalis. As they only have close relationships with and are not part of the hypoglossal nerve, coloring them here is not recommended.

The *nucleus* (A) of the *hypoglossal nerve* (B) is located in the medulla on the floor of the fourth ventricle, near the midline, at the level of the inferior olive. The *general somatic efferent fibers* (A^2) of these *cells* (A^1) emerge from the brain stem between the inferior olive and the pyramids in several *rootlets* (B^1). These rootlets converge into one bundle as they pass through the *hypoglossal canal* (C). At the level of the inferior ganglion of the vagus (not shown), a branch of the first cervical nerve joins the hypoglossal nerve and shares the same sheath. Lying between the internal carotid artery and the internal jugular vein, the hypoglossal and its cervical nerve companion descend. About three centimeters above the bifurcation of the common carotid artery, the two nerves arch forward. At that point, some of the cervical nerve fibers continue their almost vertical descent as the superior root of the ansa cervicalis. The hypoglossal nerve and the remaining first cervical nerve fibers penetrate the suprahyoid region (floor of the mouth) where the cervical fibers innervate the geniohyoid muscle (not shown). The hypoglossal fibers innervate the *intrinsic muscles* (D; arising from and being inserted within the tongue) and *extrinsic muscles* (E; arising outside of the tongue). These muscles not only give bulk to the tongue but also provide it with considerable mobility, enhancing its effectiveness as a mechanical aid to the digestive process. It is the tossing action of the tongue that propels food to the oral pharynx as the first stage of swallowing (deglutition). Afferents to the XII nucleus (not shown) come from muscle spindles in the tongue muscles. The location of the sensory cell bodies is not clear.

Brain stem lesions above the level of the hypoglossal nucleus but involving central pathways to the nucleus produce deviation of the tongue, on protrusion, to the contralateral side of the lesion. Lesions of the nucleus and peripheral lesions of the hypoglossal nerve cause deviation of the tongue, on protrusion, to the ipsilateral side of the lesion. Bilateral peripheral lesions paralyze the muscles of the tongue, resulting in difficult mastication and swallowing.

HYPOGLOSSAL (XII) NERVE.

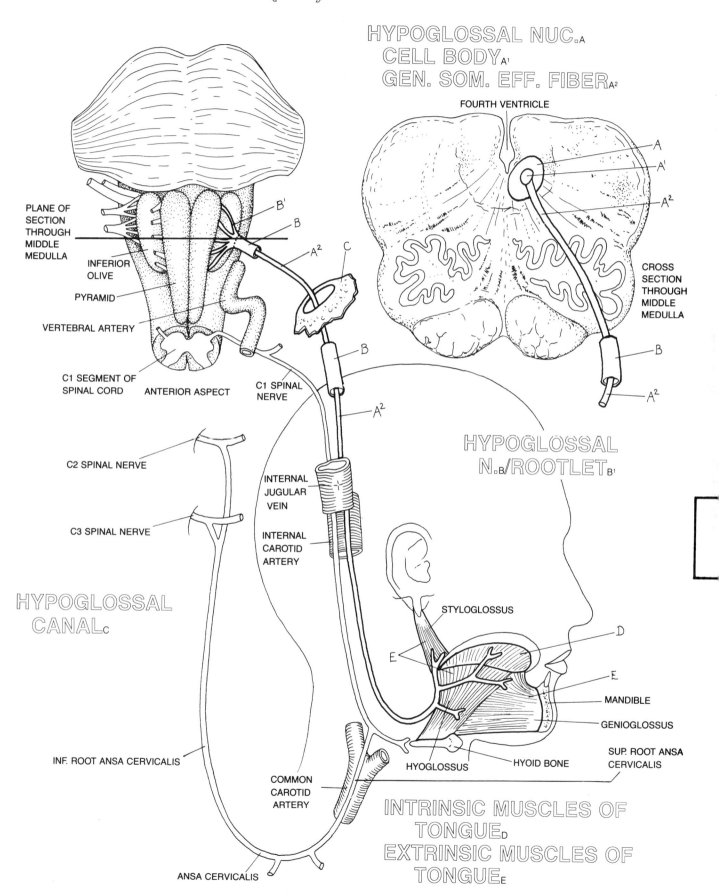

HYPOGLOSSAL NUC.A
CELL BODYA¹
GEN. SOM. EFF. FIBERA²

FOURTH VENTRICLE

A
A¹
A²

CROSS
SECTION
THROUGH
MIDDLE
MEDULLA

B

A²

PLANE OF
SECTION
THROUGH
MIDDLE
MEDULLA

B'
B
A²
C

INFERIOR
OLIVE

PYRAMID

VERTEBRAL ARTERY

C1 SEGMENT OF
SPINAL CORD   ANTERIOR ASPECT

C1 SPINAL
NERVE

B

A²

HYPOGLOSSAL
N.B/ROOTLETB¹

C2 SPINAL NERVE

C3 SPINAL NERVE

HYPOGLOSSAL
CANALC

INTERNAL
JUGULAR
VEIN

INTERNAL
CAROTID
ARTERY

STYLOGLOSSUS

D

E

E

INF. ROOT ANSA CERVICALIS

MANDIBLE

GENIOGLOSSUS

SUP. ROOT ANSA
CERVICALIS

COMMON
CAROTID
ARTERY

HYOGLOSSUS   HYOID BONE

ANSA CERVICALIS

INTRINSIC MUSCLES OF
TONGUED
EXTRINSIC MUSCLES OF
TONGUEE

COMPOSITION OF A SPINAL NERVE

Cranial nerves have been presented in Unit Six. Spinal nerves arise by roots from the spinal cord and branch into peripheral nerves that are distributed throughout the body in characteristic patterns. In this plate we examine the formation of spinal nerves and the composition of spinal and peripheral nerves.

Color titles A, B, C, and F and related structures in the small illustration at the upper right. Then color the rest of the titles through G² and the related structures in the main illustration. Color the headings Effector and Receptor and the related structures at the bottom of the plate. Although structures D¹, D², and G² are axons of identical construction and appearance, they receive separate colors to illustrate their functional differences.

A *spinal nerve* (A) is formed from *posterior* (B) and *anterior roots* (F). The posterior root (sensory or dorsal root) consists largely of the *central processes* (D²) of sensory neurons, the *cell bodies* (D³) of which produce a swelling, called the *spinal ganglion* (C; dorsal root or posterior root ganglion) along the distal part of the posterior root. The *peripheral processes* (D¹) of the sensory neurons are diverted into the posterior root at the bifurcation of the spinal nerve and extend to their cell bodies of origin within the spinal ganglion. The peripheral processes are axonal in structure but dendritic in function; they are often termed axons. These peripheral axonal processes constitute the sensory fibers of spinal and peripheral nerves and conduct impulses from receptors located throughout the body. The spinal ganglia consist of numerous pseudounipolar neuronal cell bodies (recall Plate 2-3) connected to their processes by an *axonal stalk* (D⁴). Each cell body is surrounded by metabolically supportive *satellite cells* (E) that are continuous (not illustrated) with the Schwann cells enveloping the peripheral and central axonal processes.

The central axonal processes composing the posterior root largely continue into the posterior horn of the spinal cord or adjacent white matter (exception noted ahead). These fibers are variable in diameter and coverings. Those of the *lateral division* (B¹) of the posterior root consist of smaller, often unmyelinated fibers, while those of the larger *medial division* (B²) consist of myelinated fibers. This arrangement of fibers is clinically useful, as the lateral division, containing the smaller pain fibers, can often be

selectively transected in the hope of alleviating intractable pain.

The *anterior root* (F; motor or ventral root) joins the posterior root, forming the spinal nerve, within the framework of the vertebral column (intervertebral foramen). It largely consists of *axons* (G²) of multipolar motor neurons (G), the *cell bodies* (G¹) of which are located in the anterior and lateral horns of the spinal cord (cell body shown is highly magnified). These motor axons conduct motor commands from their cell bodies to effectors throughout the body—specifically, the neuromuscular junctions with muscle cells. Fibers of the anterior root vary in size and coverings as well as function. For instance, almost 30 percent of anterior root fibers examined have been shown to be sensory. These central processes of sensory neurons gain access to the spinal cord by way of the anterior root. The role of these fibers is not clear.

Color the heading Coverings, titles H through L, and related structures where applicable. Light colors for K and L are recommended. Gray or black is recommended for I. The fascicles can be left uncolored, or you may cover them with the J color overlaid by dots of the colors used for D¹ and G².

The axons of motor and sensory neurons outside the brain and spinal cord are enveloped by *Schwann cells* (H). The majority of these fibers also exhibit a variable number of layers of *myelin* (I). External to the Schwann cell covering, a layer of collagen fibers form a sheath called the *endoneurium* (J). Groups of endoneurium-ensheathed axons form variably sized bundles segregated by perineurial *septa* (K¹; *septum*, "wall"); groups of axon bundles called fascicles are enveloped in layers of connective tissue called *perineurium* (K). Penetrating the cell layers and fine fibers of the perineurium are small vessels (not shown) that conduct blood to and from the capillaries of the endoneurial sheath, and sensory and visceral motor nerve filaments.

Groups of perineurium-enveloped fascicles are bound by a variably thick *epineurium* (L). Consisting of loose, intertwining collagen fibers, fat cells, and cells of the general connective tissues, epineurial sheaths bind spinal nerves and their larger peripheral branches. All these connective-tissue coverings have important insulating, protective, and nutrient functions.

COMPOSITION OF A SPINAL NERVE.

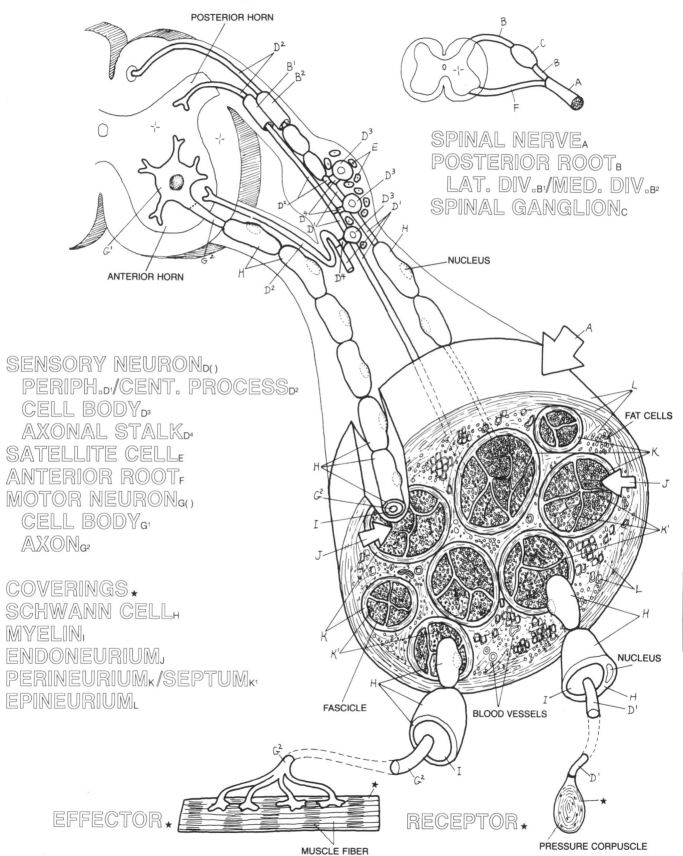

POSTERIOR HORN

SPINAL NERVE A
POSTERIOR ROOT B
LAT. DIV. B1/MED. DIV. B2
SPINAL GANGLION C

NUCLEUS

ANTERIOR HORN

FAT CELLS

SENSORY NEURON D( )
    PERIPH. D1/CENT. PROCESS D2
    CELL BODY D3
    AXONAL STALK D4
SATELLITE CELL E
ANTERIOR ROOT F
MOTOR NEURON G( )
    CELL BODY G1
    AXON G2

COVERINGS ★
SCHWANN CELL H
MYELIN I
ENDONEURIUM J
PERINEURIUM K/SEPTUM K1
EPINEURIUM L

NUCLEUS

FASCICLE

BLOOD VESSELS

EFFECTOR ★

RECEPTOR ★

MUSCLE FIBER

PRESSURE CORPUSCLE

Axons of the peripheral nervous system are ensheathed by specialized supporting cells named after Theodor Schwann, an eminent German anatomist and physiologist. In all axons one micrometer in diameter or larger, Schwann cells produce one or more layers (lamellae) of a phospholipid substance called myelin around their axons. Such axons are called myelinated or medullated. Myelin around the axons of the CNS is produced by oligodendrocytes (recall Plate 2-6). Myelin is not present or is very scarce around dendrites and cell bodies of the CNS and the ganglion cells of the PNS.

Myelin consists of cholesterol, cerebrosides (components of fatty acids), some phospholipids (including sphingomyelin), and glycoproteins and water. Its macromolecular structure is similar to that of all unit membranes (cell membrane, organelle membranes, etc.), consisting of proteins embedded in a double layer of lipid. Myelination of axons begins in the fourth month of fetal development and continues into puberty and beyond. Peripheral nerve injury causes demyelination (see Plate 7-5); if regeneration follows, remyelination occurs. Demyelinating diseases or injuries of the CNS (multiple sclerosis, etc.) are generally more severe in that they involve progressively larger areas of neuronal destruction.

This plate is concerned with the myelination process and the relationship of the Schwann cell to unmyelinated axons.

Color titles A through C and related structures, starting with Figure 1 and ending with Figure 3 and its related inset. Use a light color for B¹. After completing Figure 3, color the heading Myelin Lamella, titles B⁴ through E, and related structures in Figure 4, including the related inset.

The *Schwann cell* (B; Figure 1) consists of a *nucleus* (B³) and a mass of *cytoplasm* (B²) surrounded by a *cell membrane* (B¹). In the earliest stages of myelination, a flattened Schwann cell wraps around an *axon* (A) as shown in Figures 2 and 3. The opposing sides of the Schwann cell meet and overlap; the initial part of the interfacing cell membranes is called the *internal mesaxon* (C). The Schwann cell rolls around the axon for 2 to 100 rotations like a jelly roll (Figure 3). As the layers of cell membrane overlap, the cytoplasm appears to be squeezed out, causing the opposing inner layers of plasma membrane to appear as one *major dense line* (B⁴; Figure 4).

This dense line is the myelin lamella; the condensation of lipid and protein within the lamella creates the dense, black image characteristically seen in electron micrographs. In the innermost and outermost layers of the Schwann cell, the cytoplasm is retained and the major dense line is not seen. Near the node of Ranvier (E; Figure 4), the cell membranes form a series of loops filled with cytoplasm; these loops abut against the axon and may play a supportive role.

On either side of the major dense line are the interfacing outer layers of the cell membranes, making up the minor dense lines (B⁵). The end or edge of the outermost layer of cell membrane forms an *external mesaxon* (D) with the underlying cell membrane. The total number of myelin lamellae may relate to the size of the axon.

The axon, its lamellae of myelin (myelin sheath), and the supporting Schwann cell constitute an *internode*. Between adjacent internodes, there are short lengths of myelin-free axon called nodes of Ranvier (E; Figure 4). The "gap" between Schwann cells at the node is much smaller than that between oligodendrocytes of the CNS. The absence of the myelin sheath at the node, as well as the accumulation of anions in the gap of the node, may alter its excitability (decrease the threshold for depolarization), resulting in node-to-node transfer of impulse conduction (saltatory conduction; recall Plate 2-8).

Color the heading Unmyelinated Nerve and related structures in Figure 5.

Very small axons are also invested by the cytoplasm of Schwann cells, but many do not undergo the myelination process. The manner in which the Schwann cell invests the small axons varies, but in one case (shown here), the axons are invaginated into the membrane of the Schwann cell, creating a mesaxon between the opposing surfaces. The group of small axons and the linear sequence of Schwann cells that surround them constitute an unmyelinated nerve (also called Remak's fibers).

Myelinated fibers range in diameter from 2 to 22 micrometers and exhibit conduction velocities of 3 to 120 meters per second. Unmyelinated fibers have diameters ranging from 0.2 to 2.0 micrometers and exhibit conduction velocities of less than 2 meters per second; they are restricted to conducting sensations of burning pain and postganglionic motor impulses.

MYELINATION OF AXONS.

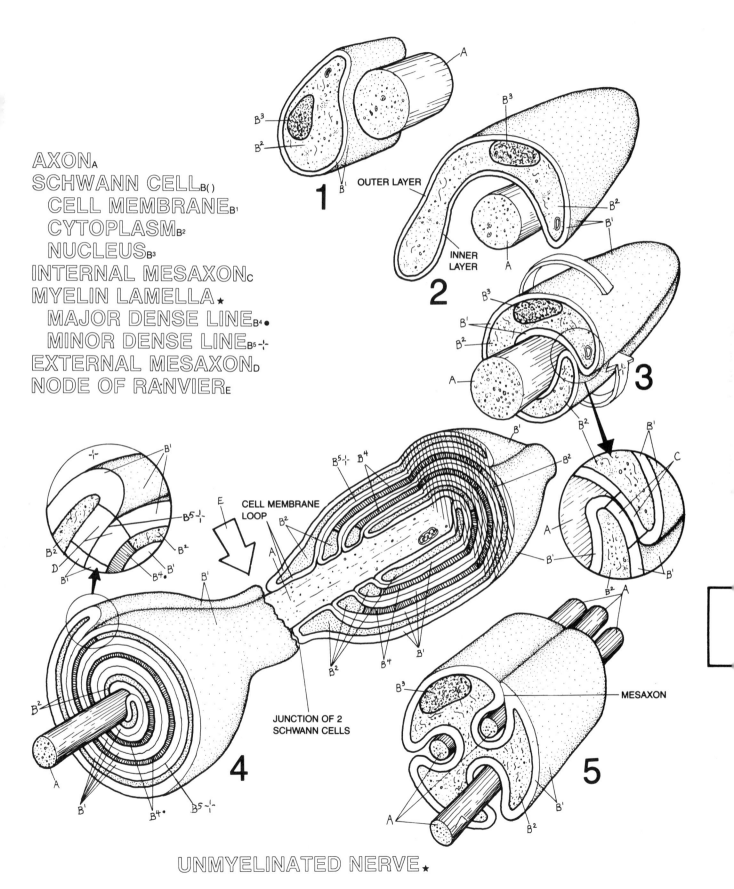

AXON_A
SCHWANN CELL_{B( )}
  CELL MEMBRANE_{B¹}
  CYTOPLASM_{B²}
  NUCLEUS_{B³}
INTERNAL MESAXON_C
MYELIN LAMELLA★
  MAJOR DENSE LINE_{B⁴●}
  MINOR DENSE LINE_{B⁵-¦-}
EXTERNAL MESAXON_D
NODE OF RANVIER_E

OUTER LAYER

INNER LAYER

CELL MEMBRANE LOOP

JUNCTION OF 2 SCHWANN CELLS

MESAXON

UNMYELINATED NERVE★

Spinal nerves, upon exiting the intervertebral foramina, divide into branches along a predictable pattern. These patterns are related to the development of the body part or parts they supply. The simplest arrangement is seen in the body torso, where the peripheral nerves to the thoracic and abdominal walls arise directly from spinal nerves and are arranged segmentally in a series of beltlike patterns. The anterior rami of most spinal nerves form plexuses or networks of spinal nerve axons from which peripheral nerves are projected to the neck, upper and lower limbs, and pelvis.

Color the heading Body Wall, titles A through F[7], and the related structures in the upper illustration.

Each spinal nerve is formed from *anterior* (A) and *posterior roots* (B). As each newly formed *spinal nerve* (C) leaves the intervertebral foramen, it divides into a *posterior ramus* (E) and an *anterior ramus* (F; pl. *rami;* large or first-order branch of a peripheral nerve). In the immediate area of this major division, the spinal nerve (spinal nerves T1–L3 only) gives off a small branch (*white communicating ramus,* D) to the sympathetic chain of ganglia running along each side of the vertebral column. Each spinal nerve receives a small bundle of unmyelinated fibers (*gray communicating ramus,* D[1]) from the sympathetic chain.

The posterior rami of all spinal nerves turn posteriorly at their origin, penetrate the fasciae around the deep muscles of the back, innervate neighboring muscles with *muscular branches* (E[1]), and send *cutaneous branches* (E[2]) to the superficial fascia and overlying skin. These cutaneous branches divide into *medial* (E[3]) and *lateral branches* (E[4]), which overlap with cutaneous branches of the contiguous anterior ramus and the contralateral posterior ramus. These posterior rami, from the base of the skull to the coccyx, give origin to the peripheral nerves of the back (see Plate 7-4).

The anterior rami of spinal nerves T2 through T12 constitute the intercostal (peripheral) nerves. These are arranged circumferentially and segmentally between each pair of ribs, packaged between the internal and innermost intercostal muscles. En route, they give off *muscular branches* (F[1]) to the local intercostal muscles. Laterally, along a plumb line dropped from the middle of the axilla (armpit), the anterior rami send *lateral cutaneous divisions* (F[2]) to the overlying skin. Within the underlying superficial fasciae, these divisions split into *anterior* (F[3]) and

posterior cutaneous branches (F[4]), which overlap with adjacent cutaneous branches. The anterior ramus terminates just short of the sternum by turning superficially to form the *anterior cutaneous division* (F[5]), which divides in the superficial fascia into *medial* (F[6]) and *lateral cutaneous branches* (F[7]). These also overlap with neighboring cutaneous branches.

Color the heading Upper Limb, titles A[1] through J[3], and the related structures in the lower illustration.

The anterior rami of most spinal nerves, intercostal nerves excepted, contribute to interwoven axonal networks, each of which is called a *plexus* (network or tangle). Four plexuses give origin to peripheral nerves of the neck, upper and lower limbs, and pelvis (see Plate 7-4). Here the branches of the brachial plexus to the upper limb are shown to illustrate the merging of fibers to form nerves of multiple spinal nerve origin. The anterior rami represent the *roots of the plexus* (F[8]). These merge into *trunks* (G), which consist of fibers from one or two anterior rami. The trunks split into *divisions* (H), which combine to form *cords* (I). From these cords, as well as from the roots and trunks, *peripheral nerves* (J) project to their destinations. These nerves have a varied composition of two or more spinal nerves (see Plate 7-4).

It is important for the physician to be able to differentiate symptoms and signs arising from lesions of multiple-origin peripheral nerves from those arising from nerve root (radicular) injuries. Compression of a spinal nerve, for example, is likely to be manifested in areas covered by two or more peripheral nerves; a peripheral nerve lesion may involve fibers from several spinal nerves. Sensory loss following a posterior root compression generally follows a dermatomal distribution (area of skin supplied by the posterior root of a single spinal nerve); sensory loss following a peripheral nerve injury may follow quite a different pattern, involving several dermatomes.

Branches of peripheral nerves disbursed to the superficial fasciae are called *cutaneous nerves* (J[1]). These nerves contain sensory fibers from the skin and subcutaneous tissue as well as visceral motor fibers to blood vessels, pilomotor muscles (arrector pili; muscles causing hairs to erect on the skin surface), and sweat glands. Other peripheral nerves may be purely *motor* (J[3]) or *mixed* (J[2]; containing both sensory and somatic/visceral motor fibers).

SPINAL NERVE PATTERNS OF DISTRIBUTION.

BODY WALL ★
ANT.ₐ/POST. ROOT_B
SPINAL NERVE_C
  WHITE COMMUN. RAMUS_D
  GRAY COMMUN. RAMUS_D¹
POST. RAMUS_E
  MUSC. BR._E¹
  CUTAN. BR._E²
  MED. BR._E³
  LAT. BR._E⁴
ANT. RAMUS_F
  MUSC. BR._F¹
  LAT. CUTAN. DIV._F²
  ANT. BR._F³
  POST. BR._F⁴
  ANT. CUTAN. DIV._F⁵
  MED. BR._F⁶
  LAT. BR._F⁷

UPPER LIMB ★
ANT.ₐ/POST. ROOT_B¹
SPINAL NERVE_C¹

BRACHIAL PLEXUS ★
ROOT OF PLEXUS/
  ANT. RAMUS_F⁸
TRUNK_G/DIV._H/CORD_I
PERIPHERAL NERVE_J
  CUTAN. NERVE_J¹
  MIXED NERVE_J²
  MOTOR NERVE_J³

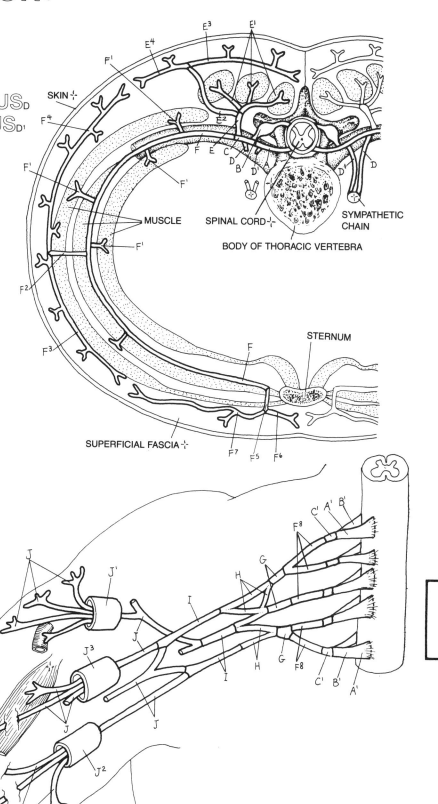

SKIN
MUSCLE
SPINAL CORD
SYMPATHETIC CHAIN
BODY OF THORACIC VERTEBRA
STERNUM
SUPERFICIAL FASCIA

In this plate are presented the formation of the anterior rami of cervical, lumbar, and sacral spinal nerves into plexuses and the pattern of posterior rami in the back.

Color the heading Anterior Rami, titles A through F, and related nerves on the left half of the figure.

The *cervical plexus* (A) is formed from the anterior rami of cervical spinal nerves 1 through 4 (C1–C4). Branches of the plexus supply the sternocleidomastoid (C2) and trapezius (C3 and C4) muscles (recall Plate 6-25) as well as several superficial and deep (prevertebral) muscles of the neck (not shown). The *phrenic nerve* (A^1; from C3, C4, and C5) innervates the thoracic diaphragm, which is responsible for about 75 percent of the respiratory effort. Fibers from C1 through C3 form the ansa cervicalis (recall Plate 6-26), which sends fibers to the infrahyoid muscle group and geniohyoid. Cutaneous nerves supply the skin at the side of the head, the neck, and the shoulder (not shown).

The *brachial plexus* (B) is formed from the anterior rami of cervical spinal nerves 5 through 8 and the first thoracic nerve (C5–T1). This plexus is found in the lower neck and axilla of the upper limb. In addition to its major terminal branches, the plexus gives off several nerves to neighboring muscles and cutaneous areas in the superficial back and the lateral and anterior chest (not shown).

The major nerves are directed to the shoulder, arm, forearm, and hand. The *musculocutaneous nerve* (B^1; C5–C7) supplies the muscles of the anterior arm and the skin of the lateral forearm. The *median nerve* (B^2; C6–T1) supplies muscles of the anterior compartment of the forearm, muscles of the thumb, and the skin of the anterior forearm and two-thirds of the hand. The *ulnar nerve* (B^3; C8–T1) supplies the muscles in the lateral forearm and hand and the skin of the fourth and fifth digits. The *radial nerve* (B^4; C5–C8) supplies a muscle of the posterior arm and muscles (largely extensors) of the posterior compartment of the forearm. It sends cutaneous fibers to the lower lateral arm, the posterior forearm, and the posterior web of skin between the thumb and index finger (not shown). The *axillary nerve* (B^5; C5–C6) runs round the posterior aspect of the humerus at the surgical neck to supply the deltoid muscle of the shoulder, in part, and the skin of the shoulder and upper arm.

The *intercostal nerves* (C; T1–T12) run between the ribs and supply the intercostal muscles and the overlying skin (recall Plate 7-3; the first rib and first intercostal nerve are not shown here). The *lumbar plexus* (D; L1–L4) forms in the posterior abdominal wall and supplies the muscles there. It contributes cutaneous fibers to the anterior and lateral abdominal wall below the level of the navel, including the inguinal region (not shown). It also sends fibers to the skin of the lateral thigh. Its two major branches are the *femoral* (D^1) and the *obturator nerves* (D^2). The femoral nerve supplies the anterior muscles of the thigh and sends cutaneous nerves to the anterior and medial thigh, the knee, and the medial leg. The smaller obturator nerve supplies the adductor muscles of the medial thigh and the overlying skin.

Major contributions from L4 and L5 anterior rami merge as the *lumbosacral trunk* (D^3), which joins in the formation of the *sciatic nerve* (E^1). This is the largest nerve of the body and is formed from the *sacral plexus* (E; L4, L5, S1–S3), on the posterior wall of the pelvis. The sacral plexus sends fibers to the muscles of the pelvis, the buttock, posterior thigh, and entire leg and foot. It also sends cutaneous fibers to the skin of the posterior thigh, leg, and foot. The *pudendal nerve* (E^2) from the sacral plexus supplies the external genitals, anal sphincter, and skin around the anus. The *coccygeal plexus* (F) consists of small loops of fibers from S4, S5, and Co1 spinal nerves; they supply the skin around the coccyx.

Color the heading Posterior Rami, titles G through K, and the related nerves on the right side of the illustration. Dotted lines are muscular branches of the posterior rami; cutaneous branches are solid lines.

The *cervical* (G) posterior rami (C1–C4) pass into the deep neck to supply suboccipital and other local muscles. The *greater occipital nerve* (G^1) supplies the cutaneous area at the back of the head. Other cervical cutaneous nerves, including those of *thoracic* (H) posterior rami T1 through T6, come up to the skin along a vertical line about 3 centimeters lateral to the cervical and thoracic spines (except for C7 and C8, which have no cutaneous branches). The lower thoracic and *lumbar* (I) posterior rami project their cutaneous branches more laterally than those above. The muscular branches of these rami supply the deep muscles of the back, called the erector spinae group. The posterior rami of L4 and L5 send only muscular branches. The *sacral* (J) and *coccygeal* (K) posterior rami supply the skin of the medial aspect of the buttock and over the coccyx. In addition, the upper three sacral fibers supply deep muscles.

SPINAL NERVES AND PLEXUSES.

ANTERIOR RAMI ★
CERVICAL PLEXUS (C1–C4) A
  PHRENIC N. A¹
BRACHIAL PLEXUS (C5–T1) B
  MUSCULOCUTANEOUS N. B¹
  MEDIAN N. B²
  ULNAR N. B³
  RADIAL N. B⁴
  AXILLARY N. B⁵
INTERCOSTAL N.
  (T1–T12) C
LUMBAR PLEXUS
  (L1–L4) D
  FEMORAL N. D¹
  OBTURATOR N. D²
LUMBOSACRAL TRUNK D³
SACRAL PLEXUS
  (S1–S3) E
  SCIATIC N. E¹
  PUDENDAL N. E²
COCCYGEAL PLEXUS
  (S4–Co1) F
POSTERIOR RAMI ★
  CERVICAL BR. G
    GR. OCCIPITAL N. G¹
  THORACIC BR. H
  LUMBAR BR. I
  SACRAL BR. J
  COCCYGEAL BR. K

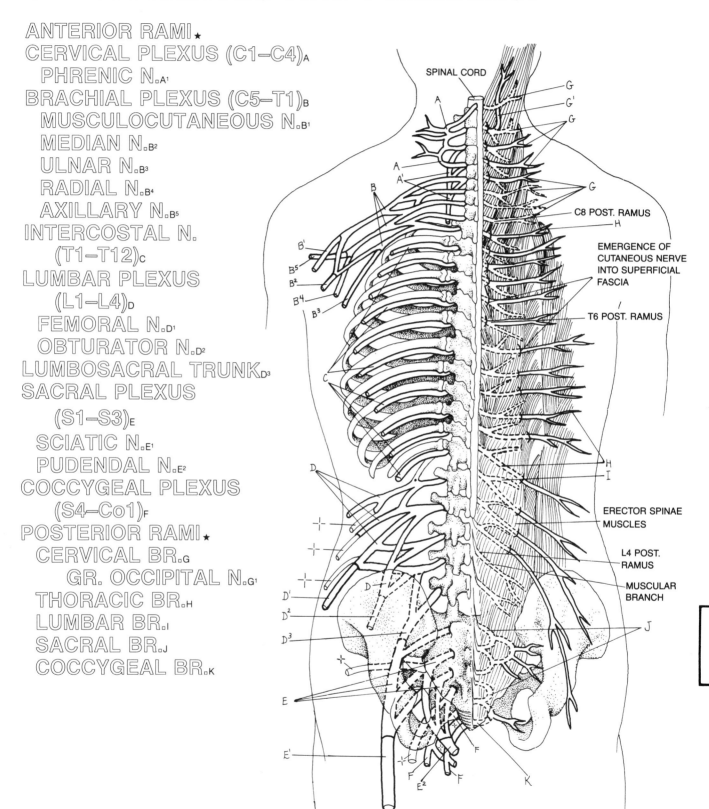

SPINAL CORD

G'
G'
G
G
C8 POST. RAMUS
H
EMERGENCE OF
CUTANEOUS NERVE
INTO SUPERFICIAL
FASCIA
T6 POST. RAMUS
H
I
ERECTOR SPINAE
MUSCLES
L4 POST.
RAMUS
MUSCULAR
BRANCH
J

A
A
A'
B
B'
B⁵
B²
B⁴
B³
C
D
D'
D²
D³
E
E'
F
E²
F
F
K

When neurons are subjected to injury or disease, they may undergo degeneration. Although this entails destruction of parts of neurons, and sometimes death of entire cells with their supporting structures, the capacity for regeneration is very powerful. It is important to understand both degenerative and regenerative processes, not only for their intrinsic biological importance but also because of their central role in the diagnosis and treatment of all neurological diseases. Damage and degeneration in peripheral nerves is more likely to be followed by regeneration and recovery than injury in the brain and spinal cord. The characteristics of neuronal degeneration are presented in this plate; those of regeneration are covered in the following plate.

Color the heading Normal State, titles A through F, and related structures in the motor neuron at left. Then color the heading Injured State, titles G through I, and related structures in the neuron at right. For A^1, B^1, C^1, and D^1, use a paler shade of the colors used for A, B, C, and D. In both neurons, the axon and related structures are magnified to illustrate detail.

Three areas of the neuron reflect a lesion (such as a cut from a blade): the cell body, the segment proximal to the cut, and the segment distal to the cut. Each of these parts and their components—including the *cell body* (A) and its *nucleus* (B), the *endoplasmic reticulum* (C), the *axon* (D) as well as the *Schwann cell* (E) and *myelin* (F)—respond to the insult, often in different ways. The degenerative changes in the cell body are referred to as *chromatolysis* (G; *chroma*, "color"; *lysis*, "dissolution") and begin to appear after the first day of injury. The changes become clearly evident after one week. In lesser degrees of damage, the chromatolytic changes are reversible weeks to months after the moment of injury. With damage to the plasma membrane, extracellular water enters the cell and causes swelling (*swollen cell body*, A^1). The nucleus, normally centered, is moved to the side and is said to be *eccentric* (B^1). The endoplasmic reticulum becomes swollen and *disperses* (C^1) around the periphery of the cell body; in some cases it disappears completely. These and other changes in the appearance of organelles reflect significant metabolic alterations under way in the cell. If these changes are severe, the entire neuron will die.

The degeneration process within the proximal segment of the cut axon is called *retrograde degeneration* (H); it is characterized by *axonal fragmentation* (D^1) extending back toward the cell body for one or more nodes of Ranvier. The myelin breaks down into beads (*myelin bead*, F^1) and is phagocytosed by *proliferating Schwann cells* (E^1). The closer the site of injury to the cell body, the greater the risk of cell death. Within 12 hours or so, the plasma membrane encloses the cut end of the axon.

The degeneration of the distal segment of the axon is called *Wallerian degeneration* (I; also called anterograde degeneration). The events that take place here occur three to five days after injury and continue distally from the site of injury to the effector or receptor. As with the degenerating proximal segment, axonal fragmentation occurs as the axon swells with fluid, its cell membrane ruptures, and its cellular contents disintegrate. The Schwann cells multiply to as much as ten times their original number. The cells become elongated and overlap along the length of the distal segment, seen with the light microscope as longitudinal bands (bands of Büngner, not shown). The newly formed basement membrane of these cells (a thin layer of fine fibers adjacent to the plasma membrane at the basal surface of the cell) becomes separated from the plasma membrane, creating longitudinal spaces between them called Schwann tubes (see next plate). It is through these tubes that regenerating axons may grow. The myelin breaks up into fragments or beads, which are subsequently phagocytosed, along with the axon fragments, by the proliferating Schwann cells.

The terminals of degenerating motor and sensory axons disintegrate as part of the process. End organs, both receptor cells and effector muscle cells, tend to atrophy irreversibly if not innervated within a period of a year or two. However, this is functionally significant only if several motor units (recall Plate 2-12) are denervated. Atrophy of a number of sensory end organs within a confined area may be reflected as a detectable diminution of sensation. Injury to whole peripheral nerves or their roots involve hundreds or thousands of axons, resulting in significant sensory loss, muscle weakness, or paralysis before regeneration occurs.

Degeneration in a neuron may affect the adjacent neuron across a synapse (in the CNS or in VNS ganglia), resulting in transneuronal atrophy (not shown). In this process, denervation hypersensitivity occurs which is due to an increase in receptor sites that follows the loss of the presynaptic terminal and its neural transmitter.

NEURONAL DEGENERATION.

NORMAL STATE★
CELL BODY_A
   NUCLEUS_B
   ENDOPLAS. RETIC._{□C}
AXON_D
SCHWANN CELL_E
MYELIN_F

INJURED STATE★
CHROMATOLYSIS_G
SWOLLEN CELL BODY_{A¹}
ECCENTRIC NUC._{□B¹}
DISPERSED ENDOPLAS.
  RETIC._{□C¹}
AXON FRAGMENT_{D¹}
PROLIF. SCHWANN CELL_{E¹}
MYELIN BEAD_{F¹}

RETROGRADE
   DEGENERATION_H
WALLERIAN DEGENERATION_I

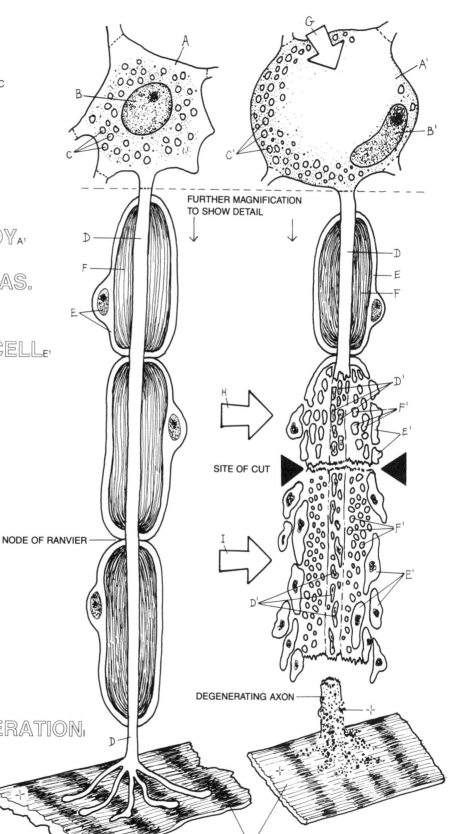

FURTHER MAGNIFICATION
TO SHOW DETAIL

NODE OF RANVIER

SITE OF CUT

DEGENERATING AXON

MUSCLE FIBER

Regeneration of axons of the PNS, both motor and sensory, after injury is more the rule than the exception. Still, there are many obstacles to reinstatement of nerve function, including a relatively long distance from site of injury to effector or receptor, the axon reaching the wrong terminal, heavy scar tissue formation at the injury site, inadequate circulation, poor nutritional state, and atrophy of effector or receptor before reinnervation occurs. In this plate, some aspects of axonal and nerve regeneration are presented.

Color titles A through J^1 and related structures. Consider using the same colors for structures colored on the previous plate that bear the same subscript and exponent. D^1, D^4, and E^2 are not used here.

At the same time degeneration is taking place in the neuronal processes, steps toward regeneration are beginning, providing the cell injury is not too severe. An increase in ribonucleic acid (RNA) synthesis in the *nucleus* (B) brings about an increase in the protein within the *cell body* (A), especially the *endoplasmic reticulum* (C). The newly formed protein in the cell body flows down the *axon* (D) to provide substance for new *axon sprouts* (D^2) and the *regenerating axon* (D^4) from the cut end of the axon. The growing tips of the sprouts are called *growth cones* (D^3). There may be as many as 50 growth cones from a single axon.

You will recall from Plate 7-5 that *proliferation* (E^1) of *Schwann cells* (E) is a hallmark of the axonal degenerative process. Longitudinal cords of these cells (bands of Büngner) form along the path of the degenerating axon

and myelin. Many of the newly developed axon sprouts find these cords and make passage through the linear sequence of these cells in *Schwann cell tubes* (E^3), the spaces formed between the *plasma membrane* (E^4) and the surrounding *basement membrane* (E^5) of the Schwann cell. In this environment, a regenerating axon (a successful axon sprout) can grow at the optimal rate of 3 to 4 millimeters per day. Within ten days after finding a Schwann cell tube, a regenerating axon can be seen with one or more new lamellae of *myelin* (F). If a patent Schwann cell tube is available adjacent to a healthy axon in a regenerating nerve, the axon may form a *collateral* (D^5), which may, with the invitation of a chemical stimulus, enter the tube and grow. Such a phenomenon is especially likely if excessive amounts of *endoneurial* (J) connective tissue (*scar tissue,* J^1) bars the growth of axon sprouts from the parent cell body. If the mass of scar tissue is excessive, the Schwann cell tubes become distorted or closed, and the regenerating axons cease further longitudinal growth and form a nonfunctional convoluted ball of axon sprouts (*neuroma,* D^6). Related to this is the interesting fact that crush injuries of axons are more amenable to functional restoration than complete transections.

In the CNS, where Schwann cells are absent, axonal injury is followed by a proliferation of oligodendrocytes and astrocytes. Instead of forming a pathway for regenerating axons, they tend to create a block for the new growth sprouts. Axons of the CNS have the potential to regenerate only if they can cross the glial scar. Glial scarring, the great density of fibers per unit area in the CNS, and the complexity of regenerating functional synapses may be among the factors inhibiting CNS axonal regeneration.

AXONAL REGENERATION.

CELL BODYA
  NUCLEUSB
  ENDOPLAS. RETIC.C
AXOND
AXON SPROUTD2
  GROWTH CONED3
REGEN. AXOND4/COLLAT.D5
NEUROMAD6
SCHWANN CELLE
  PROLIF. SCHWANN CELLE1
SCHWANN CELL TUBEE3
  PLASMA MEMB.E4
  BASEMENT MEMB.E5
MYELINF
ENDONEURIUMJ
  SCAR TISSUEJ1

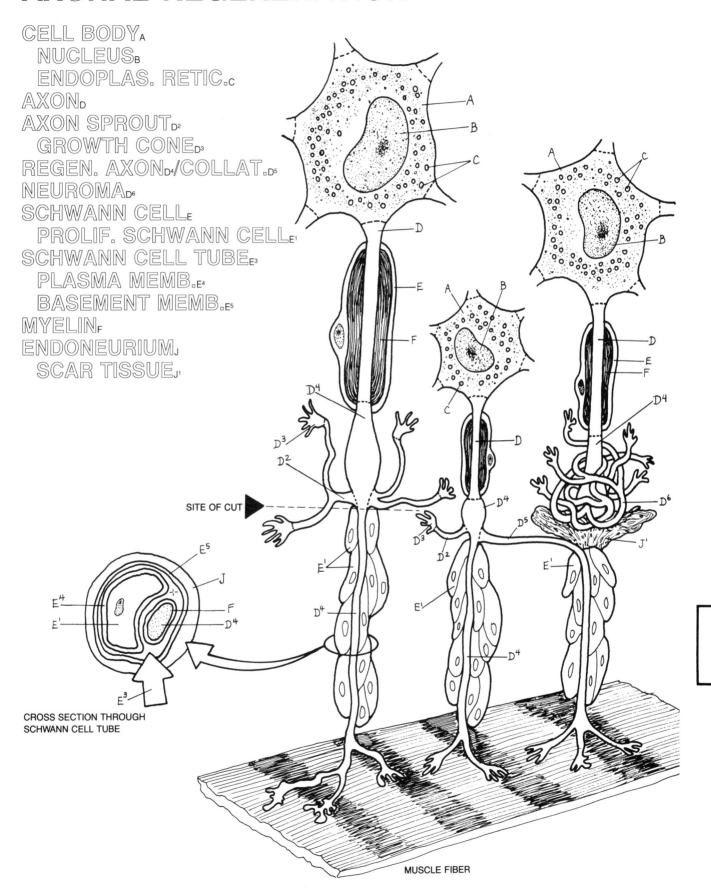

SITE OF CUT

CROSS SECTION THROUGH
SCHWANN CELL TUBE

MUSCLE FIBER

The visceral nervous system (VNS) consists of both visceral afferent and visceral efferent neurons. Visceral afferent fibers conduct sensory input from viscera to the brain and spinal cord (recall Plate 6-23; see sensory references in index under visceral nervous system). Visceral efferent neurons innervate smooth muscle, cardiac muscle, and glands. The VNS regulates the activity of the internal organs, and it achieves this function by constant interaction with the central and peripheral nervous systems. For example, many of the VNS neurons exist in the brain and spinal cord and require cortical, hypothalamic, brain stem, and spinal cord input. The visceral afferent axons composing the afferent limb of visceral reflexes, as well as most visceral efferent axons, run with their somatic counterparts in cranial and spinal nerves.

The outflow (efferent component) of the VNS is divided into two divisions, sympathetic (*sym-*, "with"; *pathos*, "feeling") and parasympathetic. The divisions perform integrated and usually opposed actions to achieve their mutual ends: harmony and synergy of visceral function. They are not antagonistic in their activity; for the most part there is a gentle play between the two divisions except in time of stress. Through its innervation, the sympathetic division provides a widespread response, whereas, the parasympathetic is characterized by more confined areas of innervation. The former expends energy; the latter conserves it.

The efferent pathway is characterized by a two-neuron unit with the neurons synapsing in a motor ganglion. The first neuron and its axon are called preganglionic; the second neuron and its axon are called postganglionic.

Color the titles and related structures associated with the cranial outflow of the parasympathetic division. Choose a group of colors on one side of the color spectrum, planning a contrasting group for the sympathetic division of the VNS. Then color the lowest set of titles and structures associated with the sacral outflow of the parasympathetic division.

Preganglionic neurons (A^1) of the parasympathetic division are found in the brain stem and the sacral region of the spinal cord (craniosacral division or outflow). In the cranial area, the preganglionic neurons are associated with the III, VII, IX, and X cranial nerves (recall Unit 6). The *preganglionic axons* (A^2) are relatively long, projecting to *cranial ganglia* (A^3) (or *intramural ganglia*, A^4, in the case of the vagus and sacral nerves) located in the vicinity or wall of the organ innervated. The *postganglionic neurons* (A^5) are characterized by short *axons* (A^6). The pre- and postganglionic axons of the parasympathetic division liberate the *neurotransmitter acetylcholine* (B) upon stimulation.

The *preganglionic neurons* (A^1) of the sacral outflow have their cell bodies in the lateral horns of sacral segments 2, 3, and 4 of the spinal cord. The *axons* (A^2) of these neurons are relatively short and generally find their *intramural ganglia* (A^4) in the walls of the target organ. The *axons* (A^6) of the *postganglionic neurons* (A^5) are correspondingly short. The *neurotransmitter* of both neurons is *acetylcholine* (B).

Color the titles and related structures associated with the thoracolumbar outflow of the sympathetic division. Use a color for D that contrasts highly with the color used for B.

The *preganglionic neurons* (C^1) of the thoracolumbar outflow have their cell bodies in the lateral horns of the 12 thoracic and upper 2 or 3 lumbar segments of the spinal cord. The preganglionic *axons* (C^2) that terminate in *paravertebral ganglia* (C^3; sympathetic chain) are relatively short. The *postganglionic axons* (C^6) of *cell bodies* (C^5) located in these ganglia are considerably longer. Preganglionic fibers terminating in *prevertebral ganglia* (C^4) are relatively long; the postganglionic axons departing the ganglia vary in length. The *neurotransmitter* of sympathetic preganglionic fibers is *acetylcholine* (B). The postganglionic fibers of this division, with one exception (fibers to sweat glands), liberate *norepinephrine* (D).

Acetylcholine release by the parasympathetic postganglionic fibers generally encourages secretomotor activity of the gastrointestinal tract, reduction of heart and respiratory rates, and increased blood flow to the viscera. Norepinephrine enhances blood flow to skeletal muscle and increases heart and respiratory rates, blood pressure, and the blood sugar level, providing a mechanism for stress reactions.

PLAN OF THE EFFERENT COMPONENT OF THE VISCERAL NERVOUS SYSTEM.

PARASYMPATHETIC DIV._A( )
CRANIAL OUTFLOW.★
PREGANG. NEURON_{A^1}
  AXON_{A^2}
NEUROTRANS.: ACH_B
CRANIAL GANG._{A^3}
INTRAMURAL GANG._{A^4}
POSTGANG. NEURON_{A^5}/
  AXON_{A^6}
NEUROTRANS.: ACH_B

SYMPATHETIC DIV._C( )
THORACOLUMBAR
  OUTFLOW.★
PREGANG. NEURON_{C^1}/
  AXON_{C^2}
NEUROTRANS.: ACH_B
PARAVERT. GANG._{C^3}
PREVERT. GANG._{C^4}
POSTGANG. NEURON_{C^5}/
  AXON_{C^6}
NEUROTRANS.: NOREP._D

PARASYMPATHETIC DIV._A( )
SACRAL OUTFLOW.★
PREGANG. NEURON_{A^1}/AXON_{A^2}
NEUROTRANS.: ACH_B
INTRAMURAL GANG._{A^4}
POSTGANG. NEURON_{A^5}/AXON_{A^6}
NEUROTRANS.: ACH_B

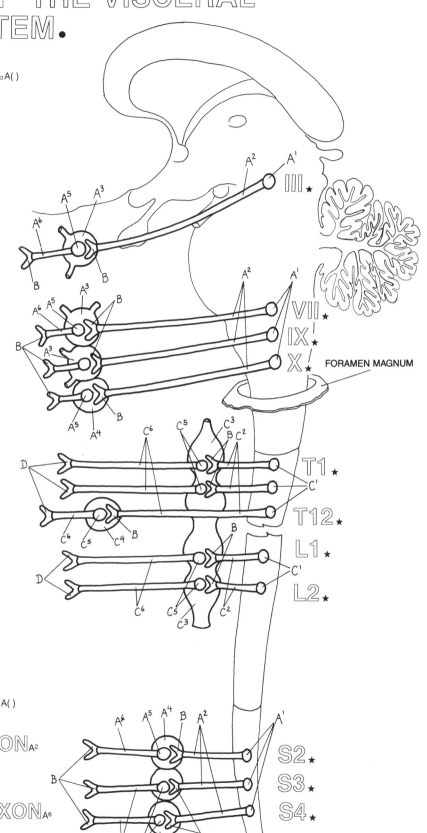

FORAMEN MAGNUM

III ★
VII ★
IX ★
X ★
T1 ★
T12 ★
L1 ★
L2 ★
S2 ★
S3 ★
S4 ★

The parasympathetic division of the VNS conserves energy by slowing the contraction of heart muscle and generally enhancing the contraction of smooth muscle and the secretion of glands. It facilitates digestive activity, maintains the moisture of the surfaces of the mucous and serous membranes lining the internal cavities, and stimulates contraction of the urinary bladder.

Color titles A through G^5, the heading Cranial Outflow, and the related structures. Then color the heading Sacral Outflow, titles H through H^5, and related structures. Shades of the same color are recommended for structures with the same subscript but different exponents. Note that only one of the multiples of ganglion/cell body/axon ($G^3/G^4/G^5$ and $H^3/H^4/H^5$) supplied by one preganglionic input (G^1, H^1) is labeled; all should be colored.

The cerebral cortex influences parasympathetic activity by way of *efferent fibers from the frontal lobe* of the cerebral *cortex* (A) to the brain stem and spinal cord, particularly to the *anterior nucleus* (B^1) and the *periventricular nucleus* (B^2) of the hypothalamus. Axons of the periventricular nucleus project down the brain stem via the *dorsal longitudinal fasciculus* (C) and other pathways (not shown). The hypothalamus integrates ascending and descending VNS-related input and regulates parasympathetic activity by way of its descending fibers.

Preganglionic fibers (D^1) from the *nucleus of Edinger Westphal* (D) are directed to the *ciliary ganglion* (D^2) in the orbit (recall Plate 6-9). Axonal *fibers* (D^4) of *postganglionic neurons* (D^3) in this ganglion penetrate the eyeball to innervate the ciliary muscles and pupillary constrictor muscles of the iris. Contraction of the ciliary muscles results in an increase in the diameter of the lens, an accommodation for near vision. Pupillary constriction protects the retina from bright light.

The *superior salivatory nucleus* (E) sends *preganglionic fibers* (E^1) to the *pterygopalatine* (E^2) and *submandibular ganglia* (E^3) (recall Plate 6-15). *Postganglionic fibers* (E^5) of *neurons* (E) in the pterygopalatine ganglion promote secretions of the lacrimal gland and glands of the nasal and oral mucous membranes. Fibers from the submandibular ganglion stimulate watery secretions from the submandibular and sublingual salivary glands.

Preganglionic fibers from the *inferior salivatory nucleus* (F) run to the *otic ganglion* (F^2) (recall Plate 6-22). *Postganglionic fibers* (F^4) of *neurons* (F^3) there stimulate watery secretions of the parotid salivary gland. The mumps virus causes inflammation and stenosis (narrowing) of the duct of this gland, causing its swelling. Parasympathetic stimulation of this gland at such a time puts added pressure on the small, inflamed ducts, causing considerable pain (conducted via the trigeminal nerve).

Preganglionic fibers (G^1) from the *dorsal motor nucleus* (G) create a remarkably extensive projection pattern as part of the *vagus nerve* (G^2; recall Plates 6-23 and 6-24). These fibers synapse in *intramural ganglia* (G^3) located in a diverse array of organs from the neck to the abdominal cavity, including the bronchial tree and lungs, heart, esophagus and gastrointestinal tract (to the descending colon), liver, gallbladder, pancreas, and kidneys.

Postganglionic fibers (G^5) leave their cell bodies (*neurons,* G^4) in these ganglia and travel a short distance to the cardiac or smooth muscle fibers and glands in the organ wall. In the thorax, vagal stimulation reduces the heart rate, slows the respiratory rate, constricts the bronchial passageways, increases bronchial secretion, and enhances esophageal peristalsis (rhythmic contraction). It induces secretomotor activity in the alimentary canal from esophagus to anal canal. It is remarkable that such a relatively small group of neurons (dorsal motor nucleus of the vagus nerve) in the floor of the fourth ventricle supplies axons to all the thoracic viscera as well as three-fourths of the alimentary canal.

The sacral outflow of the parasympathetic division begins in *neurons of the lateral horn* (H) of the sacral segments 2, 3, and 4 of the spinal cord. *Preganglionic fibers* (H^1) from these areas form the *pelvic splanchnic nerves* (H^2; also called *nervi erigentes*) and project to pelvic and perineal viscera, including the sigmoid colon, rectum, urinary bladder, and reproductive organs. *Postganglionic neurons* (H^4) in the *intramural ganglia* (H^3) of these organs project *fibers* (H^5) to local smooth muscles and glands. These fibers stimulate contraction of the urinary bladder musculature during urination. In sexual activity, parasympathetic-induced dilatation of vessels in the penis and clitoris brings about erection of these organs.

VNS: PARASYMPATHETIC DIVISION.

CORTICAL EFF.$_A$
HYPOTHALAMUS$_{B(\ )}$
  ANT. NUC.$_{B^1}$
   PERIVENT. NUC.$_{B^2}$
DORSAL LONG. FASC.$_C$

CRANIAL OUTFLOW ★
NUC. EDINGER WESTPHAL$_D$
PREGANG. FIBER$_{D^1}$
CILIARY GANG.$_{D^2}$
POSTGANG. NEUR.$_{D^3}$/FIBER$_{D^4}$

SUP. SALIV. NUC.$_E$
PREGANG. FIBER$_{E^1}$
PTERYGOPAL. GANG.$_{E^2}$
SUBMANDIB. GANG.$_{E^3}$
POSTGANG. NEUR.$_{E^4}$/FIBER$_{E^5}$

INF. SALIV. NUC.$_F$
PREGANG. FIBER$_{F^1}$
OTIC GANG.$_{F^2}$
POSTGANG. NEUR.$_{F^3}$/FIBER$_{F^4}$

DORSAL MOTOR NUC.$_G$
PREGANG. FIBER$_{G^1}$
VAGUS N.$_{G^2}$
INTRAMURAL GANG.$_{G^3}$
POSTGANG. NEUR.$_{G^4}$/FIBER$_{G^5}$

SACRAL OUTFLOW ★
LAT. HORN MOTOR NEUR.$_H$
PREGANG. FIBER$_{H^1}$
PELVIC SPLANCH. N.$_{H^2}$
INTRAMURAL GANG.$_{H^3}$
POSTGANG. NEUR.$_{H^4}$/FIBER$_{H^5}$

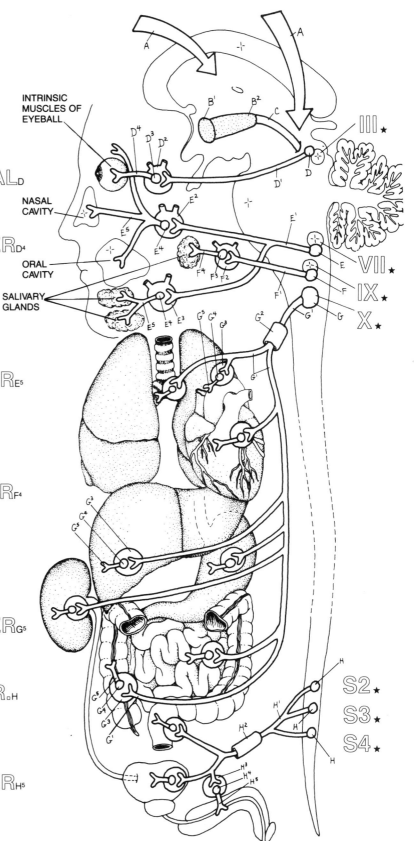

INTRINSIC MUSCLES OF EYEBALL

NASAL CAVITY

ORAL CAVITY

SALIVARY GLANDS

III ★
VII ★
IX ★
X ★

S2 ★
S3 ★
S4 ★

The sympathetic division of the VNS expends energy by accelerating the heart and respiratory rates, diverting blood from the gastrointestinal tract to the brain and the skeletal muscles, and so on. Such activation is characteristic of crisis behavior; however, "routine" sympathetic activity balances and synergizes with parasympathetic activity to maintain a metabolic steady state (homeostasis).

The sympathetic division is presented in this and the following plates; although they are not subscripted for color coordination, you may wish to color them together.

Color titles A through B and related structures in the upper illustration. Use a light color for A⁴.

Postganglionic cell bodies are located in one of two sympathetic ganglia, the paravertebral and the prevertebral. The paravertebral ganglia (also called the sympathetic chain) are paired ganglionated cords lying on the lateral surfaces of the vertebral column, extending from the base of the skull (first cervical vertebra) to the coccyx. In general, these ganglia are segmentally related to the adjacent vertebrae, except for the cervical region; thus there are 11 to 12 thoracic, 3 to 4 lumbar, and 4 to 5 sacral ganglia in each chain.

In the cervical region, several ganglia become fused into three bodies. The largest, the *superior cervical ganglion* (A¹), lies lateral to vertebrae C2 and C3. The *middle cervical ganglion* (A²) is smaller, often located lateral to the vertebral body of C6. The *inferior cervical ganglion* (A³) is usually found at the C7 vertebral level, often fused with the first thoracic ganglion as the stellate ganglion. The ganglia caudal to the stellate constitute the thoracolumbosacral component of the *chain* (A⁴) on each side of the vertebral column. At the level of the coccyx, the left and right chains are fused into a single *ganglion impar* (A⁵; *impar,* "unpaired").

The *prevertebral ganglia* (B) consist of irregular masses of postganglionic cell bodies and fibers arranged on the anterior surfaces of the abdominal aorta and its principal visceral branches lying in front of the vertebral column (hence, "prevertebral"). The major groups of these ganglia are named after the neighboring arteries: celiac, superior mesenteric, and inferior mesenteric.

Color title B¹, the heading Pathway, titles C through I, and related structures, including A⁴ and B in the lower illustration.

Sympathetic *preganglionic neurons* (C) send their *axons* (C¹) through the *anterior roots* (D) to the *spinal nerves* (D¹). These myelinated fibers form the *white communicating ramus* (E) to the sympathetic chain of ganglia. Upon entering the chain, these fibers may follow one of four courses: (1) They may ascend to synapse with the cell bodies of postganglionic neurons at higher levels in the chain. This is particularly true in the cervical levels, where there are no white communicating rami. (2) They may descend to synapse at lower levels in the chain, especially fibers entering the chain at vertebral levels L1 to L3. (3) They may synapse at the level entered. (4) They may pass through the chain to synapse in a more distant ganglion.

Most *axons* (F¹) of *paravertebral postganglionic neurons* (F) leave the chain via the *gray communicating rami* (G) to enter the spinal nerve. Although white communicating rami may be limited to thoracic and lumbar levels, gray rami are found at all levels of the sympathetic chain (C1 to the ganglion impar). The axons that join spinal nerves innervate the smooth musculature of peripheral blood vessels, sweat glands of the subcutaneous tissues, and arrector pili (hair) muscles. Many postganglionic fibers leaving the superior cervical ganglion form a plexus around neighboring arteries to reach head and neck vessels, pupillary dilator muscles, and glands. Other postganglionic fibers (not shown) are directed as tiny filaments to thoracic viscera or visceral nerve plexuses serving the thoracic viscera, such as the cardiac plexus.

Preganglionic fibers that pass through the sympathetic chain without synapsing arise from neurons at levels T5 to L2 of the spinal cord. Upon exiting the chain, they form *thoracic* or lumbar *splanchnic nerves* (B¹). These are directed caudally and anteriorly along the sides of the thoracic vertebrae (not shown), slip through the fibers of the diaphragm, and terminate among the prevertebral ganglia on the anterior surface of the abdominal aorta. The *axons* (H¹) of these *prevertebral postganglionic neurons* (H) join with vagal motor and sensory fibers and reach their target organs by accompanying neighboring arteries.

Relatively recent studies have shown that the pathways just cited may be overly simplistic. Dopaminergic *interneurons* (I) may intervene between pre- and postganglionic neurons in the sympathetic chain.

VNS: SYMPATHETIC GANGLIA.

PARAVERTEBRAL GANG.□A( )
SUP. CERV. GANG.□A¹
MID.□A²/INF. CERV. GANG.□A³
GANG. CHAIN_A⁴
GANG. IMPAR_A⁵
PREVERTEBRAL GANG.□B
THOR. SPLANCHNIC N.□B¹

PATHWAY ★
PREGANG. NEURON_C/AXON_C¹
ANT. ROOT_D
SPINAL NERVE_D¹
WHITE COMMUN. RAMUS_E
PARAVERT. POSTGANG.
    NEURON_F/AXON_F¹
GRAY COMMUN. RAMUS_G

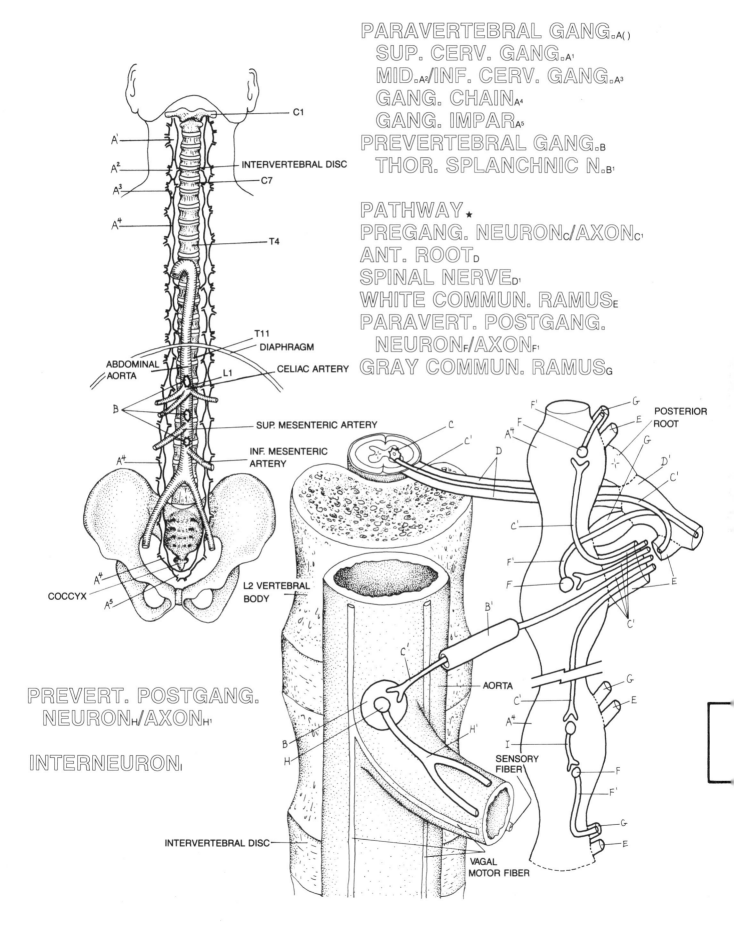

C1
A'
INTERVERTEBRAL DISC
A²
C7
A³
A⁴
T4
T11
DIAPHRAGM
ABDOMINAL AORTA
CELIAC ARTERY
L1
B
SUP. MESENTERIC ARTERY
INF. MESENTERIC ARTERY
A⁴
COCCYX
A⁴
A⁵
L2 VERTEBRAL BODY

PREVERT. POSTGANG.
    NEURON_H/AXON_H¹

INTERNEURON_I

C
C'
D
F'
F
A⁴
G
E
POSTERIOR ROOT
G
D'
C'
F'
F
E
C'
B'
AORTA
G
C'
E
A⁴
I
SENSORY FIBER
F
H'
B
H
INTERVERTEBRAL DISC
F¹
G
E
VAGAL MOTOR FIBER

In this plate the arrangement of sympathetic postganglionic neurons, the projection of their axons, and the target effectors and responses are considered.

Color titles A through A² and related structures in the upper half of the illustration, beginning with A in the T1–T5 part of the spinal cord.

Many *preganglionic fibers* (A), entering the upper five thoracic levels (T1–T5) of the paravertebral ganglia, ascend to the inferior, middle, and superior cervical ganglia, within which they synapse with *postganglionic neurons* (A¹). Many of the postganglionic axons leaving the *superior cervical ganglion* (B) form a network of fine filaments about the internal and external carotid arteries and their branches en route to their destinations: dilator muscles of the iris, lacrimal glands, salivary glands, and small blood vessels in the oral and nasal cavities. Blood vessels, arrector pili muscles, and sweat glands of the face and scalp receive sympathetic innervation from filaments around the facial and scalp arteries. Postganglionics from the superior cervical ganglion form the *superior cervical cardiac nerve* (B¹), which joins the cardiac plexus (a network of vagal, sensory, and sympathetic postganglionic fibers to the heart and great vessels). Superior cervical postganglionic fibers also join cranial nerves IX, X, XI, and XII (not shown) and form the gray communicating rami of spinal nerves C1 through C4 (not shown).

The *middle cervical ganglion* (C) sends postganglionic axons to the thyroid gland, the cardiac plexus (via the *middle cervical cardiac nerve,* C¹), the trachea and esophagus, and the gray communicating rami of spinal nerves C5 through C7 (not shown). The *inferior* (stellate) *cervical ganglion* (D) directs axons to the cardiac plexus via the *inferior cervical cardiac nerve* (D¹) and to the gray communicating rami for spinal nerves C7, C8, and T1 to the upper limb (not shown). Postganglionic axons from the upper five thoracic levels of the *thoracolumbosacral chain* (E) contribute to the *pulmonary plexus* (A²) (a network of vagal, sensory, and sympathetic fibers to the lungs and bronchi). They induce relaxation of smooth muscle in the bronchial tree and inhibit bronchial mucosecretion, thus making the respiratory effort easier.

Color titles F through K⁴ and related structures, beginning with F arising from the T5–T9 levels of the spinal cord.

A bundle of axons of *T5–T9 preganglionic neurons* (F) transit the chain to form the *greater splanchnic nerve* (F¹), projecting to the *celiac* (I) and *superior mesenteric ganglia* (J). A smaller number of axons of *T10 and T11 preganglionic neurons* (G) form the *lesser splanchnic nerve* (G¹), directed to the superior mesenteric ganglia; a very small number of axons from *T12 neurons* (H) form the *least splanchnic nerve* (H¹) to the inferior mesenteric ganglia.

Postganglionic fibers (F³, G², H²) to the gastrointestinal tract generally inhibit motility and secretion but stimulate contraction of the pyloric and ileocecal sphincter muscles. They are vasoconstrictive to gastrointestinal vessels. Preganglionic fibers terminate among secretory cells in the *adrenal medulla* (F²) instead of neurons. These cells secrete epinephrine and norepinephrine, the latter being the neurotransmitter of sympathetic postganglionic axons (recall Plate 8-1).

Axons of some *L1 and L2 preganglionic neurons* (K) pass to the *inferior mesenteric ganglia* (L) as *lumbar splanchnic nerves* (K¹). Fibers of *postganglionic neurons* (H²) emerge from these ganglia to innervate the large intestine and kidneys; other *postganglionic fibers* (K²) descend into the pelvis as the *superior hypogastric plexus* (K³). These fibers join the *pelvic plexus* (K⁴; composed of pelvic splanchnic nerves of parasympathetic origin and afferent fibers), terminating in pelvic and perineal viscera. They stimulate muscular contraction and glandular secretion in the male reproductive tracts (ejaculation). They also enhance contraction of uterine and uterine duct musculature.

Postganglionic fibers composing the gray communicating rami of spinal nerves L2 to S3 (not shown) largely project to the blood vessels, sweat glands, and arrector pili muscles of the lower limb.

Sympathetic activity promotes sweating, erection of the hair shafts (perhaps enhancing sensitivity and conservation of body heat), and peripheral vasoconstriction (a notable exception being the coronary arteries of the heart). Certain circulatory disorders, such as Raynaud's phenomenon, are characterized by periods of sustained vasoconstriction, resulting in pain and skin changes. Sympathectomy of the first two or three thoracic paravertebral ganglia often helps the condition in the hand.

VNS: SYMPATHETIC DIVISION.

PREGANG. NEUR. T1–T5 A
POSTGANG. NEUR. A1
SUP. CERV. GANG. B
SUP. CERV. CARD. N. B1
MID. CERV. GANG. C
MID. CERV. CARD. N. C1
INF. CERV. GANG. D
INF. CERV. CARD. N. D1
THORACOLUMBOSAC.
CHAIN E
POSTGANG. NEUR./
PULM. PLEXUS A2

PREGANG. NEUR. T5–T9 F
GRTR. SPLANCH. N. F1
PREGANG. NEUR. T10, T11 G
LESS. SPLANCH. N. G1
PREGANG. NEUR. T12 H
LEAST SPLANCH. N. H1
ADRENAL MEDULLA F2
CELIAC GANG. I
POSTGANG. NEUR. F3
SUP. MES. GANG. J
POSTGANG. NEUR. G2
PREGANG. NEUR. L1, L2 K
LUMBAR SPLANCH. N. K1
INF. MES. GANG. L
POSTGANG. NEUR. H2, K2
SUP. HYPOGAST. PLEX. K3
PELVIC PLEX. K4

PUPILLARY DILATOR
BLOOD VESSEL
SWEAT GLAND
SALIVARY GLAND
UTERINE TUBE

C1 C2 C3 C4 C5 C6 C7 C8
T1 T2 T3 T4 T5 T6 T7 T8 T9 T10 T11 T12
L1 L2 L3 L4 L5
S1 S2 S3 S4 S5
Co1

The adult brain requires 750 milliliters (almost a quart) of oxygenated blood every minute to maintain normal activity. Of the total amount of oxygen delivered to the body tissues by the arteries, 20 percent is consumed by the brain alone. Under normal conditions, cessation of blood flow to the brain for 5 to 10 seconds is sufficient to cause temporary changes in neuronal activity. Interruption of flow for 5 to 10 minutes can produce irreversible neuronal damage. Delivery of blood to the brain is accomplished by two pairs of arteries. In this plate, the origin, course, and distribution of one pair—the internal carotid arteries—and their branches are illustrated in a schematic anterior view. A lateral view of the course of the internal carotid artery and its branches are also shown, in a drawing from a carotid arteriogram.

Color titles A through K and the related vessels, receptors, and plaques in the central illustration and the circled magnified portions of the bifurcation of the carotid arteries. Then color the vessels in the drawing of the carotid arteriogram at the lower left. Color title L and its representation as well.

The largest systemic artery, the *aorta* (A), leaves the base of the heart in a sweeping arch to supply the entire body with oxygenated blood. The aortic arch lies anterior to the formation of the paired primary bronchi from the bifurcation of the trachea at the level of the fourth thoracic vertebra. To the right of the midline, the aortic arch gives off a large vessel, the *brachiocephalic artery* (B), which runs a short distance rostrally and laterally before dividing to form the more central *right common carotid artery* (C) and the more lateral subclavian artery (shown but not to be colored). The latter vessel will be considered in the next plate.

The origin of the *left common carotid artery* (C¹) is different from that on the right, as there is no left brachiocephalic artery. The left common carotid artery arises directly from the aorta, slightly to the left of the midline. The left subclavian artery also arises directly from the aorta immediately lateral to the left common carotid artery.

The right and left common carotid arteries ascend in the neck, each lateral to the trachea, sharing a common sheath with the internal jugular vein and vagus nerve (not shown). At the level of the laryngeal prominence ("Adam's apple") of the thyroid cartilage (C5 vertebral level), each common carotid artery divides into *external* (D) and *internal carotid arteries* (E). The external carotid arteries supply the facial region and anterior neck and are not considered here. At the root of the internal carotid artery, a swelling or thickening in the arterial wall, called the *carotid sinus* (F), incorporates pressure receptors connected to the sinus nerve (a part of the glossopharyngeal nerve; recall Plate 6-21). These receptors are part of the afferent limb of the blood pressure–regulating cardiovascular reflex.

The point of carotid bifurcation is of interest for another reason, for here atherosclerosis (*athero,* "gruel"; *sclerosis,* "hardening") frequently occurs. This disease process involves the formation of granular, lipid-containing, plate-like *atheromatous plaques* (G) in the inner layer of certain arteries. These plaques can build up in the internal carotid arteries to such an extent that they obstruct the blood supply to the brain (cerebrovascular disease). Cardiovascular surgeons can often remove these plaques from the carotid bifurcation by a technique known as endarterectomy, restoring the blood supply to the brain.

The internal carotid artery enters the skull through the *carotid foramen* (L), passes upward and anteriorly through the petrous portion of the temporal bone (petrous part), ascends into and curves anteriorly through the large cavernous (venous) sinus (cavernous part), and turns upward into the middle cranial fossa (cranial part). Here, just caudal to the optic nerve, the cavernous part of the internal carotid artery sends off the *ophthalmic artery* (H), which enters the orbit along the optic nerve to supply the orbital structures, including the eyeball. The internal carotid gives off the posterior communicating (see Plate 9-3) and anterior choroidal arteries (not shown) and then divides into its major terminal branches, the *anterior cerebral* (I) and *middle cerebral arteries* (J). The *anterior communicating artery* (K) can be seen connecting the paired anterior cerebral arteries.

In the next plate, the second major arterial (vertebral-basilar) system to the brain is considered.

BLOOD SUPPLY TO THE BRAIN: INTERNAL CAROTID ARTERIES.

AORTA_A
BRACHIOCEPHALIC A._B
R. COM. CAROTID A._C
L. COM. CAROTID A._{C¹}
R./L. EXT. CAROTID A._D
R./L. INT. CAROTID A._E
CAROTID SINUS_F
ATHEROM. PLAQUE_G
OPHTHALMIC A._H
ANT. CEREBRAL A._I
MID. CEREBRAL A._J
ANT. COMMUN. A._K
CAROTID FORAMEN_L

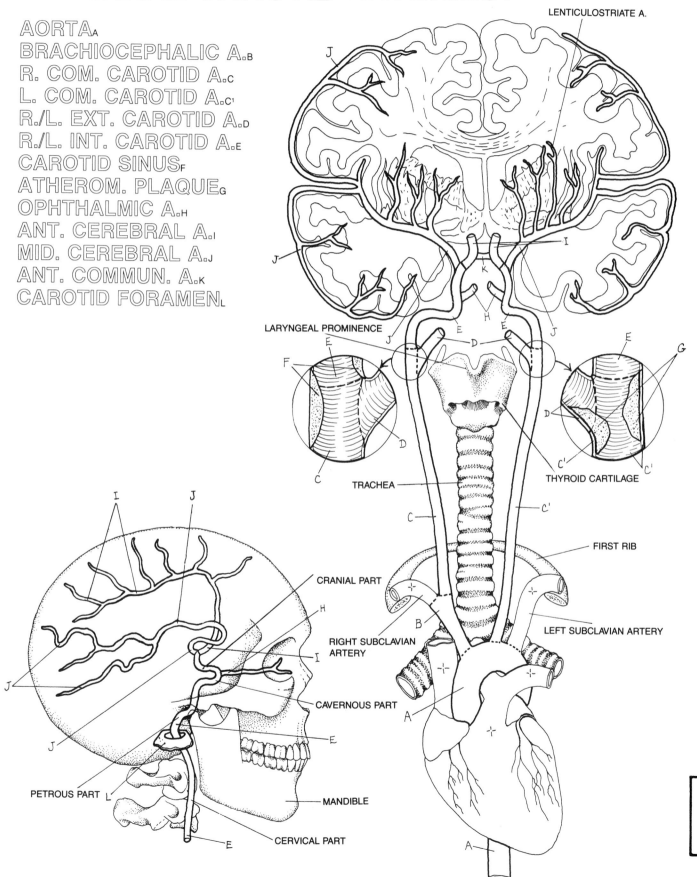

LENTICULOSTRIATE A.

LARYNGEAL PROMINENCE

THYROID CARTILAGE

TRACHEA

FIRST RIB

LEFT SUBCLAVIAN ARTERY

CRANIAL PART

RIGHT SUBCLAVIAN ARTERY

CAVERNOUS PART

PETROUS PART

MANDIBLE

CERVICAL PART

BLOOD SUPPLY TO THE BRAIN: VERTEBRAL ARTERIES

The vertebral arteries represent another significant source of blood to the brain. This plate shows a lateral view of the vertebral-basilar arterial system as it ascends through the neck and enters the skull. Its relationship to the common and internal carotid arteries is also seen. Illustrations drawn from vertebral-basilar arteriograms, in both lateral and anterior-posterior projections, are included.

Color titles A through H and related structures in the upper illustration. Then color the vessels in the drawings of the lateral and anteroposterior views of the vertebral and basilar arteries and their largest branches.

The *vertebral artery* (D) arises from the superior surface of the first part of the subclavian artery. You will recall from the previous plate that the *right subclavian artery* (C) is one of the branches of the *brachiocephalic artery* (B). The brachiocephalic artery arises directly from the arch of the *aorta* (A). The left subclavian artery (not shown) arises from the aortic arch just lateral to the origin of the left common carotid artery (not shown; see Plate 9-1). Each vertebral artery dives deep toward the lower cervical vertebrae, medial and posterior to the scalenus anterior muscle and lateral and posterior to the common carotid artery. It enters and ascends through the transverse foramina (in the transverse processes) of the upper six cervical vertebrae. After passing through the atlas, it bends sharply medial to approach the *foramen magnum*

(H) and turns upward to pass through it. In its passage through the transverse foramina, the vertebral artery gives one or two branches to the spinal cord (not shown).

As the vertebral artery enters the posterior fossa of the cranial cavity, it lies on the ventral lateral aspect of the medulla. In its rostral course along the brain stem, it gives off some important branches, which can be seen in Plates 9-3 and 9-6: anterior and posterior spinal arteries, medullary arteries, and the posterior inferior cerebellar arteries. The left and right vertebral arteries merge on the anterior aspect of the caudal pons to form the *basilar artery* (E). Branches of this artery can be seen in Plates 9-3, 9-6, and 9-7: anterior inferior cerebellar arteries, pontine arteries, and superior cerebellar arteries. The basilar artery terminates at the caudal midbrain by bifurcating into the *posterior cerebral arteries* (F). By way of the *posterior communicating arteries* (G) from the first part of the posterior cerebral vessels, the vertebral-basilar system has access to the carotid system.

Arteriograms of the cerebellar and spinal branches of the vertebral arteries are used to search for space-occupying lesions associated with the posterior cranial fossae and cervical spinal cord, respectively. As these avascular masses form, they may distort the normal pattern of these vessels. Introduction of contrast medium into the vertebral system is usually accomplished by injection into the subclavian artery or percutaneous (through the skin) catheterization through the femoral artery of the thigh.

BLOOD SUPPLY TO THE BRAIN: VERTEBRAL ARTERIES.

AORTA_A

AORTAA
BRACHIOCEPHALIC A.B
R. SUBCLAVIAN A.C
R. VERTEBRAL A.D
BASILAR A.E
POST. CEREBRAL A.F
POST. COMMUN. A.G
FORAMEN MAGNUMH

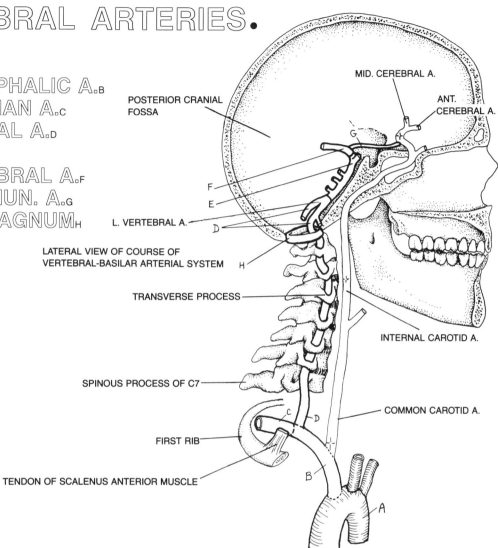

MID. CEREBRAL A.

ANT. CEREBRAL A.

POSTERIOR CRANIAL FOSSA

L. VERTEBRAL A.

LATERAL VIEW OF COURSE OF VERTEBRAL-BASILAR ARTERIAL SYSTEM

TRANSVERSE PROCESS

INTERNAL CAROTID A.

SPINOUS PROCESS OF C7

COMMON CAROTID A.

FIRST RIB

TENDON OF SCALENUS ANTERIOR MUSCLE

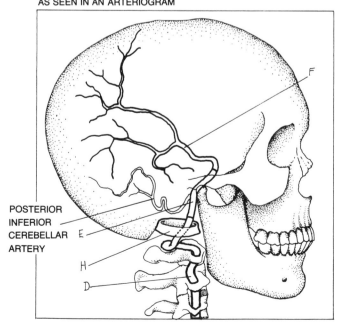

LATERAL VIEW OF VERTEBRAL-BASILAR ARTERIAL SYSTEM AS SEEN IN AN ARTERIOGRAM

POSTERIOR INFERIOR CEREBELLAR ARTERY

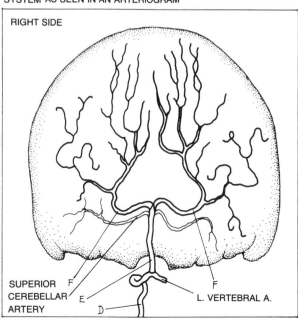

ANTERIOR-POSTERIOR VIEW OF VERTEBRAL-BASILAR ARTERIAL SYSTEM AS SEEN IN AN ARTERIOGRAM

RIGHT SIDE

SUPERIOR CEREBELLAR ARTERY

L. VERTEBRAL A.

BLOOD SUPPLY TO THE BRAIN: CIRCULUS ARTERIOSUS

The circulus arteriosus or circle of Willis is located on the anterior-inferior surface of the upper brain stem. It is a vascular loop formed from the vertebral-basilar and internal carotid arterial systems. Under normal conditions, there is no or very little mixing between left and right vessels of the loop. Following massive constriction of one of the vessels of the loop, some collateral flow occurs across the midline, as evidenced by widening of the communicating vessels.

The circulus arteriosus, its branches, and its associated vessels are shown in situ on the anterior-inferior surface of the brain stem at the left side of the plate. The brain is intact on the left; the anterior third of the temporal lobe and the cerebellum have been removed on the right.

Color the heading Circulus Arteriosus, titles A through E, and the related vessels in the illustration at the lower right. Then color these vessels (A through E) on the brain stem at the upper left. Note that the vessels are labeled on one side only.

The rostral portion of the circulus arteriosus consists of the two *anterior cerebral arteries* (A), which arise from the terminal part of the *internal carotid arteries* (B). The paired anterior cerebral vessels are joined just anterior to the optic chiasm by the *anterior communicating artery* (C), completing the rostral part of the loop. The anterior cerebral arteries proceed anteriorly between the hemispheres; their distribution can be seen on Plate 9-4.

The *posterior communicating arteries* (D) arise at the junction of the internal carotid and *middle cerebral arteries* (G). These posterior communicating vessels are directed inferiorly and posteriorly on either side of the hypothalamic surface and the stalk of the pituitary gland, and they anastamose (connect) with the initial segment of the *posterior cerebral arteries* (E). The posterior cerebral vessels originate from the bifurcation of the *basilar artery* (K). The irregular loop (or circle) thus formed surrounds the inferior surface of the diencephalon, including the optic chiasm, pituitary stalk, and mammillary bodies.

Color the heading Related Arteries, titles F through P, and the related structures in the illustration at the right and then in the illustration at left. Use a light, pastel color for the dotted circles (P) representing areas where aneurysms are often found. The percentages indicate the frequency of occurrence of aneu- rysms (among all intracerebral aneurysms) at these sites.

The circulus arteriosus gives rise to several arteries that supply both central and cortical brain areas. *Central arteries* (F), coming off the circle at several sites, as well as the *lenticulostriate branches* (H) of the middle cerebral arteries, penetrate and supply the diencephalon, the corpus striatum, and the internal capsule (not shown; see Plate 9-5). Obstruction of these small vessels brings on serious neurological deficits due to inadequate collateral circulation within their areas of distribution. Cortical branches, such as the anterior, middle, and posterior cerebral arteries, are larger and branch more freely. Occlusion of one of these vessels can accordingly be partially compensated for by anastamotic vessels.

The basilar artery is formed by the union of the left and right *vertebral arteries* (I). Located inferior to the circulus arteriosus on the anterior-inferior surface of the pons, the basilar artery is the connecting vessel between the vertebral and carotid systems. It terminates at the pontine-midbrain junction by dividing into the posterior cerebral arteries. Branches of the basilar artery include (from caudal to rostral) the *anterior inferior cerebellar arteries* (L), which supply the inferior aspect of the cerebellum anterolaterally and communicate with branches of the *posterior inferior cerebellar artery* (J; from the vertebral artery); the *labyrinthine arteries* (M) to the internal ear; the *pontine arteries* (N) to the pons; and the *superior cerebellar arteries* (O) to the pons, pineal gland, and superior part of the cerebellum.

Saclike outpocketings or localized dilatations of arteries are known as *aneurysms* (P; "widenings"). Such abnormalities, usually congenital (a developmental defect existing at birth) in origin, range from microscopic dimensions to the size of baseballs. They are frequently found to be associated with vessels of the circulus arteriosus (dotted areas). About 90 percent of such aneurysms occur in the anterior part of the circle. In the last few years, visualization of cerebral aneurysms has been enhanced by the technique of digital subtraction angiography (in which the vessels in front and in back of the vessel to be studied are eliminated from the angiogram by a digital computer). Aneurysms can often be treated surgically. Rupture of aneurysms may occur spontaneously or may be related to short periods of increased blood pressure; subsequent hemorrhage can result in serious neurological deficits or in death.

BLOOD SUPPLY TO THE BRAIN: CIRCULUS ARTERIOSUS.

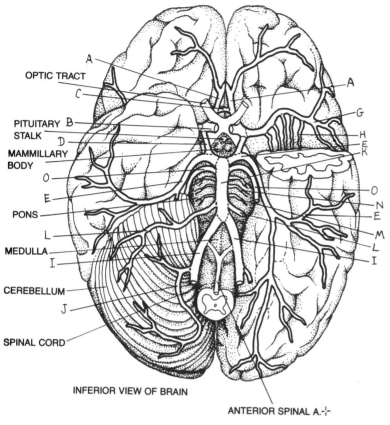

OPTIC TRACT

PITUITARY STALK

MAMMILLARY BODY

PONS

MEDULLA

CEREBELLUM

SPINAL CORD

INFERIOR VIEW OF BRAIN

ANTERIOR SPINAL A.-¦-

CIRCULUS ARTERIOSUS.★
ANT. CEREBRAL A.ₐ
INT. CAROTID A.ʙ
ANT. COMMUN. A.c
POST. COMMUN. A.ᴅ
POST. CEREBRAL A.ᴇ

RELATED ARTERIES.★
CENTRAL A.ꜰ
MID. CEREBRAL A.ɢ
    LENTICULOSTRIATE A.ʜ

VERTEBRAL A.ɪ
    POST. INF. CEREBELL. A.ᴊ
BASILAR A.ᴋ
    ANT. INF. CEREBELL. A.ʟ
    LABYRINTHINE A.ᴍ
    PONTINE A.ɴ
    SUP. CEREBELL. A.ₒ

SITE OF ANEURYSM/
    PERCENTAGEₚ

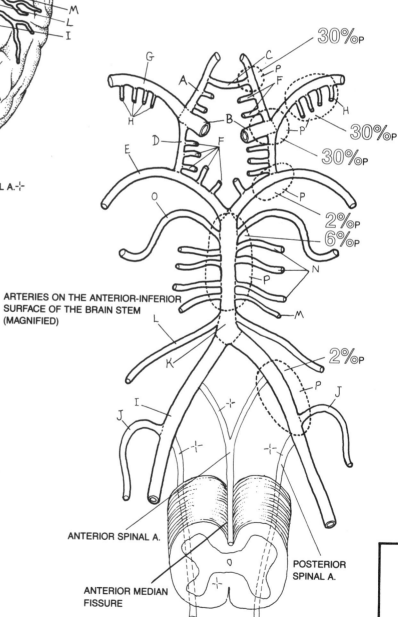

ARTERIES ON THE ANTERIOR-INFERIOR
SURFACE OF THE BRAIN STEM
(MAGNIFIED)

30%ₚ
30%ₚ
30%ₚ
2%ₚ
6%ₚ
2%ₚ

ANTERIOR SPINAL A.

POSTERIOR SPINAL A.

ANTERIOR MEDIAN FISSURE

BLOOD SUPPLY TO THE CEREBRAL HEMISPHERES

The cerebral hemispheres receive their blood supply from both the internal carotid and the vertebral-basilar systems via the anterior, middle, and posterior cerebral arteries. In this plate, three views of the brain illustrate the interrelated distribution of branches of these three arteries.

Color titles A through B² and the related vessels in each of the three illustrations, beginning with Figure 1 at the upper left and ending with Figure 3. The area vascularized by the anterior cerebral artery is stippled in each of the three views and labeled B¹. For B¹, use a very light shade of the color used for B.

The *anterior cerebral artery* (B) is one of two terminal branches of the *internal carotid artery* (A). It runs anteriorly in the longitudinal cerebral fissure between the two hemispheres (Figures 1 and 3). Its *branches* (B) supply the medial surface and a small part of the lateral convexity of the frontal lobe (Figure 2). The artery sweeps upward around the genu of the corpus callosum (Figure 1) to nourish the remainder of the medial and part of the lateral hemispheric surface as far caudally as the parieto-occipital sulcus (Figure 2). A number of small and medium-sized vessels, the anterior medial striate arteries, are given off by the anterior cerebral and *anterior communicating arteries* (B²; Figure 3). These striate arteries supply parts of the basal ganglia, the septal nuclei, and internal capsule.

Color titles D and D¹ and the related vessel and area of distribution in all three figures, as you did above.

The *middle cerebral artery* (D) is one of the two terminal branches of the internal carotid artery. It runs later-

ally along the base of the hemisphere (Figure 3) and through the lateral sulcus (Figure 2) before dividing into branches that supply the insula and most of the lateral surface of the frontal, parietal, temporal, and occipital lobes. It also covers the anterolateral-inferior surface of the frontal lobe (Figure 3). Note that the middle cerebral artery provides almost all of the oxygen and nourishment for the lateral surface of the cerebral hemisphere. Occlusion of the branches of this vessel may deprive such functionally important cortical areas as those connected with somatosensory, auditory, motor, and speech activities.

Color the remaining titles and the related vessels and areas of distribution in each of the three illustrations, as applicable. For F¹, use a very light shade of the color used for F.

The *posterior cerebral artery* (F) arises as the terminal branch of the *basilar artery* (E; Figure 3). The *posterior communicating artery* (C) connects the posterior cerebral and internal carotid arteries. The proximal part of the posterior cerebral artery curves over the lateral surface of the crus cerebri to reach the undersurface of the hemisphere. Its branches supply the entire occipital lobe and the inferior and medial surfaces of the temporal lobe. The *calcarine branch* (F²) of the posterior cerebral artery nourishes the primary visual cortex. Since deep branches of the posterior cerebral artery also supply the tectum, medial and lateral geniculate bodies, and pulvinar, note that virtually all these brain centers involved in the central processing of visual information receive their blood by a single major artery, the posterior cerebral.

BLOOD SUPPLY TO THE CEREBRAL HEMISPHERES.

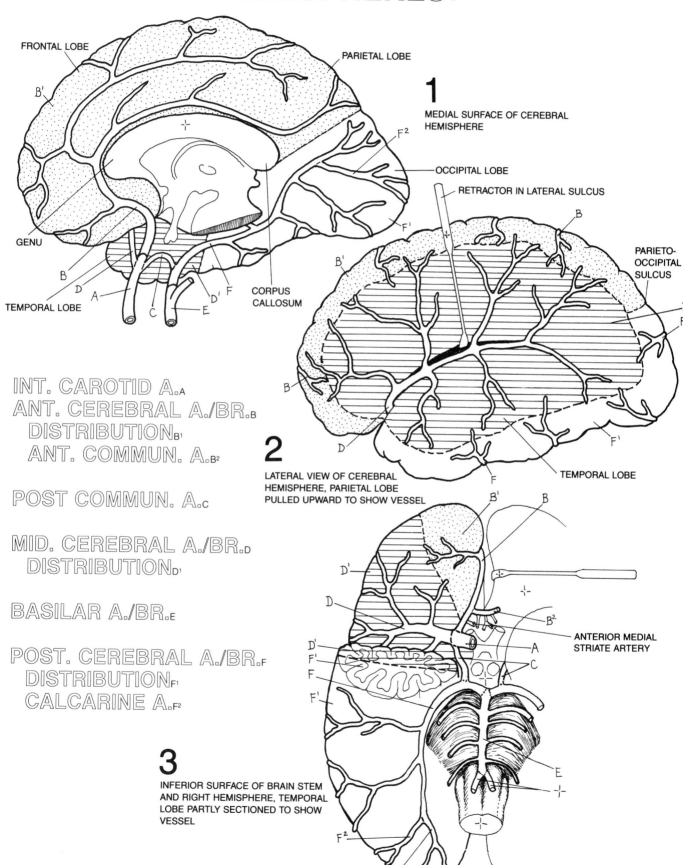

FRONTAL LOBE

PARIETAL LOBE

B'

1
MEDIAL SURFACE OF CEREBRAL HEMISPHERE

F^2

OCCIPITAL LOBE

GENU

RETRACTOR IN LATERAL SULCUS

B

PARIETO-OCCIPITAL SULCUS

B

D

A

C

E

D'

F

F^1

TEMPORAL LOBE

CORPUS CALLOSUM

B'

D'

F

INT. CAROTID A. A
ANT. CEREBRAL A./BR. B
    DISTRIBUTION B'
ANT. COMMUN. A. B²

POST COMMUN. A. C

MID. CEREBRAL A./BR. D
    DISTRIBUTION D'

BASILAR A./BR. E

POST. CEREBRAL A./BR. F
    DISTRIBUTION F'
CALCARINE A. F²

B

D

F

2
LATERAL VIEW OF CEREBRAL HEMISPHERE, PARIETAL LOBE PULLED UPWARD TO SHOW VESSEL

TEMPORAL LOBE

F^1

B'

B

D'

D

A

B^2

D'

F'

F

A

C

ANTERIOR MEDIAL STRIATE ARTERY

F^1

E

3
INFERIOR SURFACE OF BRAIN STEM AND RIGHT HEMISPHERE, TEMPORAL LOBE PARTLY SECTIONED TO SHOW VESSEL

F^2

F

The vascular supply to structures of the deep forebrain is of great clinical significance. Even modest vascular accidents (hemorrhage or thrombosis) can produce severe, often lasting injury or even death. This plate offers a semi-schematic view of the deep forebrain vessels branching from the three major cortical arteries. The origin of these cortical arteries can be seen in Plate 9-4.

Color titles A through H and the related structures in the upper illustration at left; structure H can be colored in the lower illustration. It is not recommended that structures A–H be colored in the lower illustration; here only blood vessels are colored. Color titles I through M² and the related vessels in the lower illustration; K and K¹ can also be colored in the illustration at the upper right. Shades of the same color are recommended for structures with the same subscript but different exponents.

The basal ganglia, including the *caudate nucleus* (A), the *globus pallidus* and *putamen* (B), and the *amygdala* (C), the *basal forebrain area* (D), the *internal capsule* (E), and the diencephalon—represented here by the *thalamus* (F) and *hypothalamus* (G)—are among the critical structures supplied by the deep branches of the cortical arteries.

The *anterior cerebral artery* (J), a terminal branch of the *internal carotid artery* (I), sends *medial striate arteries* (J^1; one shown) to the area of the anterior limb of the internal capsule and head of the caudate nucleus. These vessels reach their target area via the *anterior perforated substance* (H; recall Plate 6-5). *Anterior communicating arteries* (J^2) from the anterior cerebral artery give off *anterior medial arteries* (J^3). These arteries enter the anterior perforated substance to supply the preoptic and supraoptic nuclei (not shown) of the hypothalamus, the head of the caudate nucleus, and the anterior limb of the internal capsule.

The *middle cerebral artery* (K), also a terminal branch of the internal carotid artery, runs laterally in the lateral fissure, giving off delicate, hairlike arteries to the basal ganglia and internal capsule. These are the lateral striate arteries, which include the *lenticulostriate arteries* (K^1). The lenticulostriate arteries, known clinically as the "stroke arteries," are frequently the site of occlusion (thrombosis) or rupture (hemorrhage). They are prone to catastrophic vascular accidents for two reasons: They are much smaller than their artery of origin (the middle cerebral artery), thus experiencing relatively high flow forces directly from their parent vessel, and their relatively thin walls make them susceptible to rupture. In the event of the rupture of these vessels, the motor pathways compressed within the internal capsule are largely deprived of blood, resulting in paralysis on the opposite side of the body (hemiplegia).

The *posterior cerebral artery* (M) originates as a terminal branch of the *basilar artery* (L) and communicates with the internal carotid artery via the *posterior communicating artery* (M^1). The posterior cerebral artery sends *thalamic branches* (M^2) to the posterior thalamus, including the geniculate bodies and pulvinar, and the posterior limb of the internal capsule. If these vessels are occluded or ruptured, contralateral anesthesia and hemiplegia occur. An unusual complication of such an occlusion or hemorrhage is the thalamic pain syndrome, characterized by severe and intractable pain following the slightest touch of the affected part of the body. The cause is not clear but may be due to the loss of inhibitory neurons in the nucleus reticularis thalami (recall Plate 5-19). These neurons normally inhibit sensory relays from the thalamus to the cerebral cortex.

BLOOD SUPPLY TO THE DEEP FOREBRAIN.

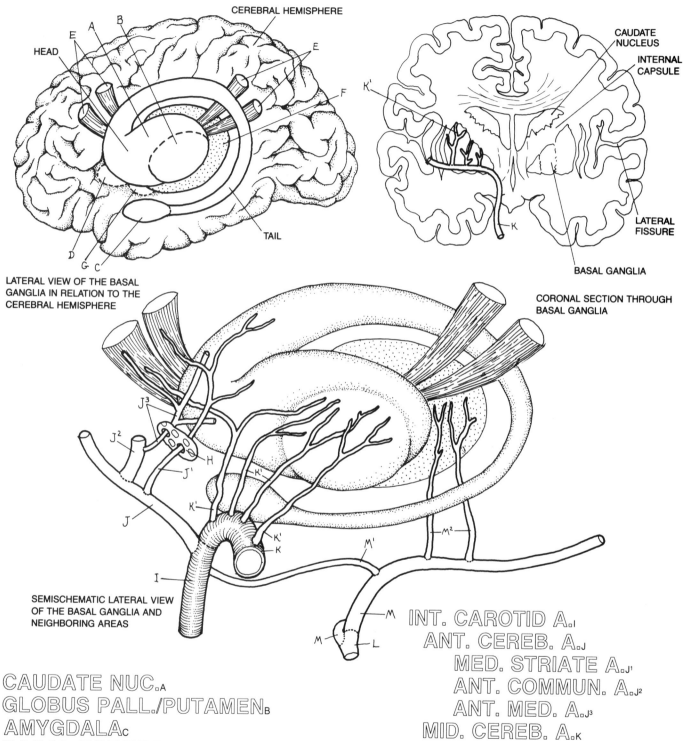

CEREBRAL HEMISPHERE

HEAD

TAIL

LATERAL VIEW OF THE BASAL
GANGLIA IN RELATION TO THE
CEREBRAL HEMISPHERE

CAUDATE
NUCLEUS

INTERNAL
CAPSULE

LATERAL
FISSURE

BASAL GANGLIA

CORONAL SECTION THROUGH
BASAL GANGLIA

SEMISCHEMATIC LATERAL VIEW
OF THE BASAL GANGLIA AND
NEIGHBORING AREAS

CAUDATE NUC.A
GLOBUS PALL./PUTAMENB
AMYGDALAC
BASAL FOREBRAIND
INT. CAPSULEE
THALAMUSF
HYPOTHALAMUSG
ANT. PERF. SUBST.H

INT. CAROTID A.I
ANT. CEREB. A.J
MED. STRIATE A.J¹
ANT. COMMUN. A.J²
ANT. MED. A.J³
MID. CEREB. A.K
LENTICULOSTR. A.K'
BASILAR A.L
POST. CEREB. A.M
POST. COMMUN. A.M¹
THALAMIC A.M²

The blood supply to the brain stem and cerebellum is derived from the vertebral-basilar arterial system. In this plate we examine the specific vessels vascularizing the medulla and cerebellum. Deficits resulting from hemorrhage or thrombosis of two of these vessels are illustrated. This and the following plate should be colored in sequence.

Color titles A through E² and the related vessels in the illustration at the upper left.

The cerebellum is supplied by the *posterior inferior cerebellar arteries* (D) from the rostral parts of the paired *vertebral arteries* (A), the *anterior inferior cerebellar arteries* (E¹) from the *basilar artery* (E), and the *superior cerebellar arteries* (E²), also branches of the basilar artery near its rostral bifurcation.

The posterior inferior cerebellar artery runs on the inferior surface of the cerebellum and sends branches to the lower portions of the vermis, tonsil, and neighboring area (recall Plate 5-13). The anterior inferior cerebellar artery is directed to the inferior surface of the cerebellum by way of the cerebellopontine angle. Here it lies close to the seventh and eighth cranial nerves (not shown), supplying them. Thrombosis of this artery often produces facial paralysis and loss of hearing in association with cerebellar defects. The superior cerebellar artery approaches the cerebellum at the level of the midbrain. Its branches include both cortical and central (perforating) arteries, supplying most of the cerebellar hemispheres, the superior and middle cerebellar peduncles, and the cerebellar nuclei.

The medulla is supplied by *bulbar arteries* (A¹) directly from the vertebral artery; *medullary branches* (B¹) of the *anterior spinal arteries* (B); branches (not shown) of the *posterior spinal arteries* (C); and branches of the posterior inferior cerebellar artery. Frequently the posterior spinal arteries arise from the posterior inferior cerebellar arteries.

Color the heading Inferior Alternating Hemiplegia, titles F through G¹, and the related areas in the illustration at the upper right and those of the magnified tongue and the human figure. Color vessels B and B¹ in the upper cross section. Do not color the vessels beyond the site of the thrombus on the affected side. Color area H a very light color.

In the cross section through the mid medulla, a medullary branch of the anterior spinal artery can be seen supplying the central portion of the caudal medulla. A thrombosis (obstruction of a vessel due to a clot) or hemorrhage of this artery produces a significant unilateral area of vascular insufficiency (*area of lesion,* H). Such a lesion (injury, wound) can affect the *hypoglossal nucleus or nerve* (F) as well as the great mass of descending fibers constituting the *pyramid of the medulla* (G). Ischemia (insufficient blood) to the twelfth cranial nerve produces a paralysis of the muscles of the tongue on the same side as the lesion. Upon protrusion, the *tongue deviates ipsilaterally* (F¹). Loss of blood to the medullary pyramid produces a weakness (paresis) or paralysis on the opposite side of the body, called *contralateral hemiplegia* (G¹; *hemi-,* "half"; *plegia,* "paralysis"), more prominent in the distal than in the proximal part of the limbs. Such muscles are more stiff and rigid than normal (spasticity), and the deep tendon reflexes (for example the knee or ankle jerk) are increased in intensity (hyperreflexia). A person with this condition walks (or relearns to walk) by swinging the leg out and around in an arc from the hip joint since there is more control here than at the knee or ankle joint. An affected arm is usually carried in a close-in flexed position. The clinical syndrome, combining both of these lesions, is known as "inferior alternating hemiplegia."

Color the vessels in the cross section at the lower left, the heading PICA Syndrome, and the title and area labeled I. Use a light color for I. Note the nuclei and tracts often affected in the area of the vascular lesion.

A PICA syndrome, brought on by obstruction of the posterior inferior cerebellar artery (PICA), is characterized by sudden onset of dizziness and vomiting (the vestibular nuclei and dorsal motor nucleus of the vagus nerve, respectively). Ipsilateral facial numbness (spinal trigeminal system) and sensory deficits on the contralateral side of the body (spinothalamic tract) are seen, as well as contralateral arm and leg involvement (inferior cerebellar peduncle). Difficulty in swallowing (dysphagia) and speech (dysarthria) reflect a *lesion* (I) to the nucleus ambiguus as well as the dorsal motor nucleus of the tenth cranial nerve. A wide spectrum of signs and symptoms follow such a vascular disturbance, and each case carries its own signature, depending on the number of structures involved and the degree to which they have been affected.

BLOOD SUPPLY TO THE MEDULLA AND CEREBELLUM.

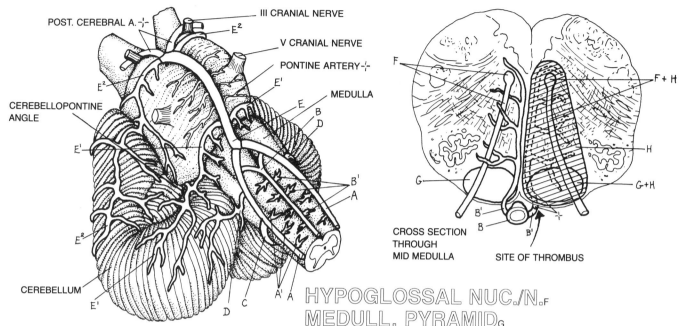

III CRANIAL NERVE
POST. CEREBRAL A. -¦-
E^2
V CRANIAL NERVE
PONTINE ARTERY -¦-
E^1
MEDULLA
E^2
CEREBELLOPONTINE ANGLE
E
B
D
E^1
B^1
A
E^2
CEREBELLUM
E^1
A^1 A
D C

CROSS SECTION THROUGH MID MEDULLA

F
F + H
G
H
B^1
G + H
B
B^1

SITE OF THROMBUS

VERTEBRAL A.$_A$
BULBAR A.$_{A^1}$
ANT. SPINAL A.$_B$
MEDULLARY A.$_{B^1}$
POST. SPINAL A.$_C$
POST. INF. CEREBELL. A.$_D$

BASILAR A.$_E$
ANT. INF. CEREBELL. A.$_{E^1}$
SUP. CEREBELL. A.$_{E^2}$

HYPOGLOSSAL NUC./N.$_F$
MEDULL. PYRAMID$_G$

INF. ALT. HEMIPLEGIA ★
AREA OF LESION$_H$
IPSILAT. DEVIATION OF TONGUE$_{F^1}$
CONTRALAT. HEMIPLEGIA$_{G^1}$

F^1
G^1
G^1

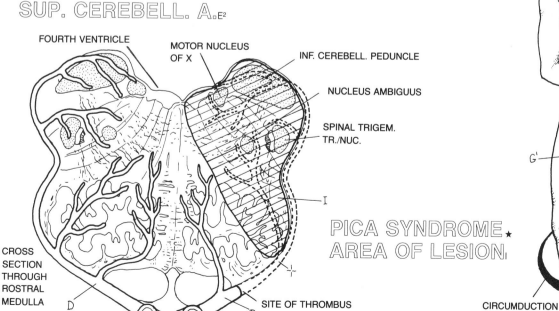

FOURTH VENTRICLE
MOTOR NUCLEUS OF X
INF. CEREBELL. PEDUNCLE
NUCLEUS AMBIGUUS
SPINAL TRIGEM. TR./NUC.
I

PICA SYNDROME ★
AREA OF LESION$_I$

CROSS SECTION THROUGH ROSTRAL MEDULLA
D
D
A
SITE OF THROMBUS

CIRCUMDUCTION

BLOOD SUPPLY TO THE PONS
AND MIDBRAIN

As a continuation of the previous plate, the vessels supplying the pons and midbrain are illustrated, as well as selected deficits resulting from thrombosis or hemorrhage of two of these arteries.

Color titles A through F¹ and the related vessels in the illustration at the upper left. Consider using the same colors as on the previous plate for vessels A, B, C, and E. As before, vessels not related to the areas being examined are not colored.

Along the course of the *vertebral* (A) and *basilar arteries* (B), branches that supply the brain stem and the cerebellum are given off. The branches supplying the medulla and cerebellum are the topic of Plate 9-6. As two of the three pairs of cerebellar vessels also contribute arteries to the pons and midbrain, they are illustrated again. Interruption of any one of these vessels cause significant cerebellar signs, such as loss of balance, muscular weakness, loss of coordination, and proprioceptive abnormalities, in addition to any pontine or midbrain signs of dysfunction.

The pons is supplied by small branches of the *anterior inferior cerebellar artery* (C), a series of *pontine arteries* (D) from the basilar artery, and branches of the *superior cerebellar artery* (E). Branches of the anterior inferior cerebellar artery reach the caudal parts of the pons, while the superior cerebellar artery sends branches to the rostral pons. The central pons receives paramedian, short circumferential, and long circumferential branches of the pontine arteries (see cross section at upper right).

The midbrain is vascularized by paramedian and circumferential branches of the superior cerebellar and *posterior cerebral arteries* (F), as well as branches of the *posterior communicating arteries* (F¹).

Color the heading Middle Alternating Hemiplegia, titles G, H, and G¹, related structures in the cross section at upper right, and the arrow representing an abnormal adduction of the eye. As in the previous plate, the crosshatched area (H) represents the tissue rendered ischemic by thrombosis and should be given a light color. The dotted vessel following the site of thrombosis is not to be colored.

Thrombosis of one or more of the paramedian branches of the pontine arteries results in a *lesion* (H) that may affect the sixth cranial or *abducens nerve and nucleus* (G) as well

as the masses of corticobulbospinal fibers descending through the pons into the pyramid of the medulla. The clinical picture of this "middle alternating hemiplegia" includes involuntary *adduction of the ipsilateral eye* (G¹) due to loss of the sixth nerve and paralysis of the lateral rectus muscle of the eyeball. In addition, a contralateral hemiplegia (not shown; see Plate 9-6) is caused by ischemia to the pontine segment of the large corticobulbospinal tract.

Color the heading Superior Alternating Hemiplegia, titles I through I³, and the related structures and arrow on the lower half of the page.

Branches of the posterior cerebral artery are a principal source of blood to the midbrain. Ischemia in the paramedian *area* (J) characteristically involves the *oculomotor nerve and nucleus* (I) and the great descending (corticopontobulbospinal) tract in the crus cerebri. The resulting neurological condition is called "superior alternating hemiplegia." With ischemia to the third cranial nerve, the superior, inferior, and medial rectus, inferior oblique, and levator palpebrae superioris muscles of the eye and eyelid are weakened or paralyzed, as are the muscles of accommodation and pupillary constriction. The intensity of the ipsilateral eye signs may vary, but in general, the clinical signs are *ptosis* (I¹; drooping eyelid due to the loss of the levator palpebrae muscle) and a *pupillary dilatation* (I²; mydriasis; due to loss of pupillary constrictor muscles). The affected eye is capable of little or no vertical movement (reflecting paralysis of the superior and inferior rectus muscles) and characteristically assumes an *abducted* (I³; pulled away from the midline) position. Associated with these signs is contralateral hemiplegia (secondary to ischemia of the crus cerebri).

In a variation of the midbrain lesion, the third nerve and red nucleus are primarily involved, resulting in ipsilateral oculomotor paralysis and tremors of the opposite arm (Benedikt's syndrome).

The scope of clinical signs resulting from partial or complete obstruction of parts of the vertebral-basilar system is, of course, much greater than these illustrated here. Such signs and symptoms range from dizziness or giddiness without other symptoms to profound coma and death. Muscular weakness or flaccid paralysis are additional consequences of basilar occlusion.

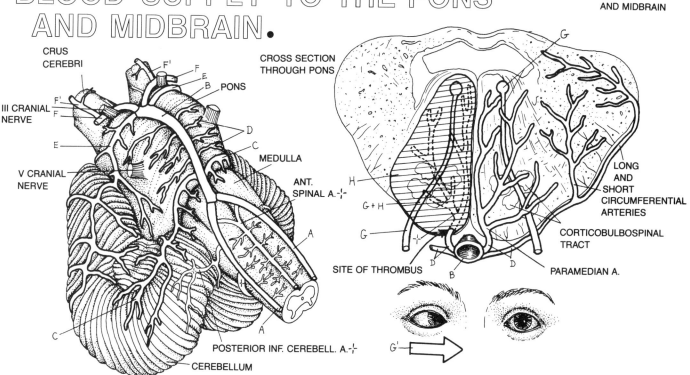
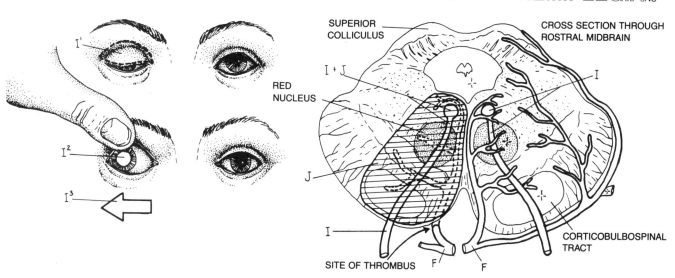

In this plate the major veins draining the external surface and deep portions of the cerebral hemisphere and some of their connections are presented. These veins drain into larger channels, called dural sinuses (see Plate 9-9), formed within the dura mater, the thickest and outermost of the meninges enveloping the brain and spinal cord (see Plate 9-10). Consider coloring this and the next plate together.

Color the headings Cerebral Veins and Superficial Group, titles A through A⁴, and the related vessels in the upper illustration. Color the heading Sinuses, titles B through B³, and the related sinuses.

The capillaries of the hemispheres drain into the cerebral veins. These veins can be divided into two groups, superficial and deep. The superficial veins drain the cortical surface; the deep veins drain the interior parts of the hemispheres, including the basal ganglia and the diencephalon.

The superficial group of veins consists of the *inferior* (A) and *superior cerebral veins* (A¹) and their tributaries. The inferior cerebral veins lie on and drain the inferior lateral surface of the hemisphere, emptying into the *transverse sinus* (B) within the dura mater. The superior cerebral veins lie on and receive blood from the superior hemispheric surfaces. These veins flow into the *superior sagittal sinus* (B¹) in the dura mater along the midline. Blood from the lateral surface of the hemisphere flows through the *middle cerebral vein* (A²), which lies along the lateral sulcus between the temporal lobe inferiorly and the frontal and parietal lobes superiorly. The middle cerebal vein connects with the transverse sinus posteriorly via the *inferior anastomotic vein* (*of Labbe;* A⁴) and the *cavernous sinus* (B²) anteriorly. The middle cerebral vein has direct access to the superior sagittal sinus via the *superior anastomotic vein* (*of Trolard;* A³). Both of these anastomotic veins are useful landmarks for anatomists and surgeons.

Color the heading Venous Outflow, titles C through C⁵, and related vessels.

The *internal jugular vein* (C) is the largest extracranial vessel draining the brain and is the inferior continuation of the *sigmoid sinus* (B³). It descends in the carotid sheath of the anterior lateral neck. Deep to the insertion of sternocleidomastoid muscle (not shown), the vein joins with the subclavian vein to form the brachiocephalic vein (not shown) on each side. These veins, left and right, merge just above the right side of the heart, forming the superior vena cava (not shown), which enters the superior part of the right atrium.

The cavernous sinus has special significance among the dural sinuses. Located on either side of the sella turcica (housing the pituitary gland) in the middle cranial fossa, immediately posterior to the superior orbital fissure, the cavernous sinus is traversed by the internal carotid artery, cranial nerves III, IV, and VI, and the ophthalmic division of V (see next plate). The cavernous sinus is particularly important for its connections with extracerebral vessels, offering collateral routes for venous drainage of the brain. In the event of a thrombosis of the internal jugular vein, for example, blood can flow back to the cavernous sinus and leave the brain via (1) the *superior ophthalmic vein* (C¹) to the deep facial veins; (2) the *pterygoid plexus* (C³) of veins in the infratemporal fossa through small *emissary veins* (C²) perforating the skull; (3) the intercavernous sinus (not shown) to the contralateral cavernous sinus, and out the internal jugular vein via the inferior and superior petrosal and transverse sinuses; (4) the superficial middle cerebral vein to the superior sagittal sinus and the veins of the other side; (5) the *basilar venous plexus* (C⁴) at the base of the skull, where it communicates with the vertebral venous plexus (not shown); and (6) the *occipital vein* (C⁵) by way of emissary veins, and on to the deep cervical vein.

Color the heading Deep Group of Cerebral Veins, titles D through D⁵, and related vessels in the illustration at the lower left.

The deep group of cerebral veins can be seen on the superior surfaces of the caudate nuclei and thalami just under the corpus callosum. The *thalamostriate* (D), *septal* (D¹), and *choroidal veins* (D²) drain the superior thalamus, septal region, and choroid plexus, respectively. These vessels form the *internal cerebral veins* (D³) at the anterior poles of the thalami. These veins merge just posterior to the pineal gland to form the *great vein of Galen* (D⁵), with the *basal veins* (D⁴) coming from around the crura cerebri. The great vein of Galen joins with the inferior sagittal sinus to form the straight sinus (not shown; see Plate 9-9).

VENOUS DRAINAGE OF THE CEREBRAL HEMISPHERES.

CEREBRAL VEINS. ★
  SUPERFIC. GROUP. ●
  INF. CEREBRAL V. ₐA
  SUP. CEREBRAL V. $_{A^1}$
  MID. CEREBRAL V. $_{A^2}$
  SUP. ANASTOMOTIC V. $_{A^3}$
  INF. ANASTOMOTIC V. $_{A^4}$

SINUSES. ★
  TRANSVERSE SINUS $_B$
  SUP. SAG. SINUS $_{B^1}$
  CAVERNOUS SINUS $_{B^2}$
  SIGMOID SINUS $_{B^3}$

VENOUS OUTFLOW. ★
  INT. JUGULAR V. $_C$
  SUP. OPHTHALMIC V. $_{C^1}$
  EMISSARY V. $_{C^2}$
  PTERYGOID PLEXUS $_{C^3}$
  BASILAR VENOUS PLEXUS $_{C^4}$
  OCCIPITAL V. $_{C^5}$

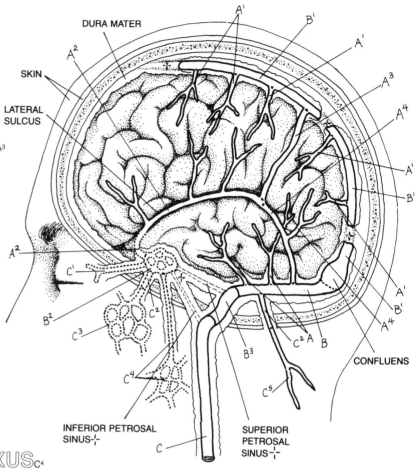

DEEP GROUP OF
  CEREBRAL VEINS.
THALAMOSTRIATE V. $_D$
SEPTAL V. $_{D^1}$
CHOROIDAL V. $_{D^2}$
INT. CEREB. V. $_{D^3}$
BASAL V. $_{D^4}$
GR. V. OF GALEN $_{D^5}$

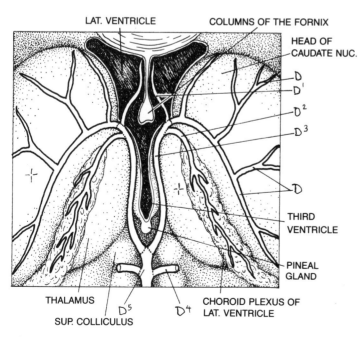

HORIZONTAL SECTION THROUGH
ROOF OF THIRD VENTRICLE (MAGNIFIED)

The large channels draining the superficial and deep cerebral veins are formed within the dura mater and are called dural sinuses. They are lined with the same thin, flat cellular layer (endothelium) seen in all blood vessels. The dural sinuses drain into the internal jugular vein, into veins passing through foramina of the skull, or into emissary veins exiting the skull. The emissary veins communicate with the diploic veins of the cranial bones and, directly or indirectly, with veins of the scalp. They represent an important mode of collateral venous drainage in the event of internal jugular obstruction. The most important of the outflow channels have been discussed in Plate 9-8. It may prove helpful to look at Plate 9-10 for orientation of the meninges before coloring this plate.

Color titles A through L and related vessels in the main illustration. Use a light color for J. Structures J and K can also be colored in the lower illustration. Note the other dural structures as well as the tributaries of the dural sinuses; these should not be colored.

Blood draining from the deeper brain tissues ultimately flows into the internal cerebral veins, which merge just posterior to the pineal gland to form the *great vein of Galen* (A; recall Plate 9-8). This vein enters the *straight sinus* (B), located along a line where the falx cerebri splits to form the tentorium cerebelli. The straight sinus also receives drainage from the *inferior sagittal sinus* (C), located on the free edge of the falx. The inferior sagittal sinus drains the falx cerebri and very few, if any, veins from the brain.

The straight sinus is directed posteriorly and downward; as it approaches the internal occipital protuberance, it bends to form the *left transverse sinus* (F). In some instances it communicates directly with the dilated termination of the *superior sagittal sinus* (D), called the *confluens* (D^1). There is considerable variation in the sinus arrangement here. The *occipital sinus* (E) exits the inferior surface of the confluens and runs in the falx cerebelli to the foramen magnum, where it communicates with the basilar plexus of veins.

The superior sagittal sinus arises in the anterior origin of the falx cerebri and arches posteriorly in that membrane along the latter's attachment to the median plane of the skull. It terminates by bending laterally as the *right transverse sinus* (F^1) or by joining the confluens. It receives several superior cerebral veins, and small venous pools, called lacunae, on either side. Small fingerlike projections of arachnoid (arachnoid villi; see Plate 9-10) project into these lacunae or the sinus itself, providing a means for cerebrospinal fluid to enter the venous system. Fractures of the skull may cause rupture of the superior sagittal or other dural sinuses. Such hemorrhages lead to pooling of venous blood under the dura (subdural hematoma), compressing the brain.

The transverse sinuses are found in the outer margins of the tentorium cerebelli. At the junction between the occipital bone and the petrous portion of the temporal bone, the transverse sinus becomes the *sigmoid sinus* (G). The transverse sinus receives the inferior anastomotic and the superficial inferior cerebral veins (not shown) and communicates with the occipital vein by way of emissary veins. At its termination, the transverse sinus receives the *superior petrosal sinus* (H).

The sigmoid sinus is directed anteriorly and downward to the jugular foramen, where it becomes the bulb of the *internal jugular vein* (L). Here it is joined by the *inferior petrosal sinus* (I).

On each side of the pituitary gland (see lower illustration) is a relatively large sinus characterized by trabeculae of connective-tissue fibers within its lumen. This is the *cavernous sinus* (J); left and right cavernous sinuses are connected by the *intercavernous sinus* (K).

Color the heading Contents of the Cavernous Sinus, titles M through Q, and related structures in the lower illustration. For orientation, see Plate 5-37.

The cavernous sinus is traversed by the *oculomotor* (N) and *trochlear nerves* (O), the *ophthalmic* (P) and *maxillary divisions* (P^1) of the *trigeminal nerve,* and the *abducens nerve* (Q), as well as the serpentine, cavernous part of the *internal carotid artery* (M; recall Plate 9-1). The artery carries a plexus of interconnecting sympathetic (postganglionic) filaments from the superior cervical ganglion.

The cavernous sinus has access to numerous tributaries and venous plexuses (recall Plate 9-8), of which the superior ophthalmic vein, sphenoparietal sinus (along the posterior edge of the anterior cranial fossa), pterygoid plexus, and basilar plexus are shown in the upper illustration.

DURAL SINUSES.

GR. V. OF GALEN_A

STRAIGHT SINUS_B
INF. SAG. SINUS_C
SUP. SAG. SINUS_D
    CONFLUENS_{D^1}
OCCIPITAL SINUS_E

L._F/R. TRANSV. SINUS_{F^1}
SIGMOID SINUS_G
SUP. PETROSAL SINUS_H
INF. PETROSAL SINUS_I
CAVERNOUS SINUS_J
INTERCAVERNOUS SINUS_K
INT. JUGULAR V._L

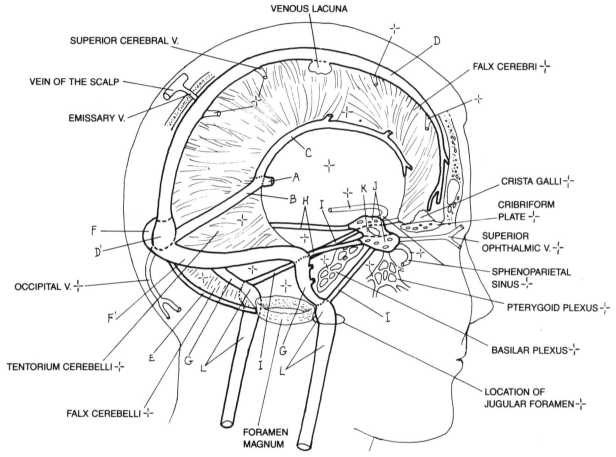

VENOUS LACUNA
SUPERIOR CEREBRAL V.
VEIN OF THE SCALP
EMISSARY V.
D
FALX CEREBRI
C
CRISTA GALLI
A
B H I K J
CRIBRIFORM PLATE
F
D'
SUPERIOR OPHTHALMIC V.
SPHENOPARIETAL SINUS
OCCIPITAL V.
PTERYGOID PLEXUS
F'
I
BASILAR PLEXUS
TENTORIUM CEREBELLI
E G L I G L
LOCATION OF JUGULAR FORAMEN
FALX CEREBELLI
FORAMEN MAGNUM

CONTENTS OF THE
    CAVERNOUS SINUS ★
INT. CAROTID A._M
OCULOMOTOR N._N
TROCHLEAR N._O
OPHTHALMIC DIV.
    TRIGEM. N._P
MAXILLARY DIV.
    TRIGEM. N._{P^1}
ABDUCENS N._Q

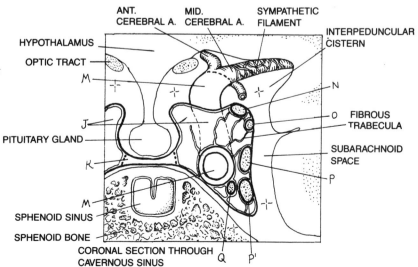

ANT. CEREBRAL A.   MID. CEREBRAL A.   SYMPATHETIC FILAMENT
HYPOTHALAMUS
OPTIC TRACT
INTERPEDUNCULAR CISTERN
M
N
J
O FIBROUS TRABECULA
PITUITARY GLAND
SUBARACHNOID SPACE
K
P
M
SPHENOID SINUS
SPHENOID BONE
Q P'
CORONAL SECTION THROUGH CAVERNOUS SINUS

The connective tissue layers of the brain and spinal cord are called the *meninges* (sing. *meninx*, "membrane"). They offer support and protection to the central nervous system and provide a space for the circulation of cerebrospinal fluid (CSF) around the brain and spinal cord. The dural sinuses have been considered on Plate 9-9. The meninges of the spinal cord are presented in Plate 9-13.

Color the heading Meninges, titles A through C, and related structures. Use a light color for A, and consider not coloring B². Then color the titles D and E and the related vessels. Start at upper left.

The *dura mater* (A; also called *pachymeninx; pachy,* "thick") is the outermost and thickest of the meningeal layers. The superficial or outer fibers (endosteal layer) of this fibrous tissue line the inner surface of the cranial bones. The deeper or inner fibers (meningeal layer) encapsulate the brain, split away from the endosteal fibers to enclose transiting cranial nerves and vessels as well as the venous sinuses, and form septa (fibrous sheets) that compartmentalize the brain within the cranial vault.

The midline, vertical septum within the longitudinal cerebral fissure is the *falx cerebri* (A¹; *falx,* "scythe"). It arises from left and right meningeal layers that bend away from the endosteal dura and merge as a fused sheet—anteriorly, at the crista galli (between the cribriform plates of the ethmoid bone; recall Plate 6-2) projecting off the floor of the anterior cranial fossa; anteriorly, superiorly, and posteriorly, from the midline of the cranial roof; and posteriorly, from the internal occipital protuberance. The falx arches over the corpus callosum, filling the longitudinal fissure between the left and right hemispheres. Along its origin from the cranial roof, the falx encloses the *superior sagittal sinus* (D). Along the posterior two-thirds of its concave, inferior surface (adjacent to the corpus callosum), it encloses the inferior sagittal sinus (not shown).

Between the occipital lobes and the cerebellum, the falx cerebri separates into left and right sheets that break away laterally to cover the cerebellum like a tent, *tentorium cerebelli* (A²). Running along the junction of the falx and the tentorium in the sagittal plane is the straight sinus. The left and right halves of the tentorium cerebelli support the occipital lobes and blend posterolaterally with the endosteal dura along the junction of the occipital and parietal bones. Here each tentorial layer encloses the transverse sinus. Laterally, the tentorium blends with the dura of the petrous portion of the temporal bone, at which point the sigmoid sinus leaves the tentorium. Anteriorly, the tentorium has a free rounded edge. The space between the free border of the tentorium posteriorly and the dorsum sellae (posterior wall of the sella turcica, which holds the pituitary gland) anteriorly is the incisura (also called tentorial notch). The midbrain passes through the incisura. This opening has clinical significance because the free edge of the tentorium may cut into the brain stem secondary to a space-occupying lesion.

A small vertical sheet of dura, the falx cerebelli (not shown; see Plate 9-9), descends from the tentorium midline between the two cerebellar hemispheres. A horizontal sheet of dura also covers the sella turcica; this tiny membrane is called the *diaphragma sellae* (A³).

The dura mater receives its main blood supply from the *middle meningeal artery* (E), a branch of the internal maxillary artery from the external carotid. This vessel runs along the outer surface of the dura on the temporal bone. It or its branches are subject to rupture with temporal bone fractures. In this event, the blood tends to pool in a progressively increasing mass between the dura and the cranial bone (epidural hematoma), compressing the cerebral hemispheres and often causing serious neurological damage.

The *arachnoid* (B) is a delicate, transparent membrane overlying the brain and spinal cord. Closely applied to the dura, it is separated from the underlying *pia mater* (C) by the *subarachnoid space* (B²), which is characterized by crossing fibrous bands called trabeculae. In certain areas around the brain, the subarachnoid space is enlarged, forming cisterns (cisternae). Fingerlike extensions of the arachnoid (*arachnoid villi,* B²; also called granulations) project into superior sagittal and other sinuses, permitting CSF flow into the venous system.

The pia mater is a highly vascular, loose connective tissue closely applied to the brain and spinal cord. It invests the small vessels penetrating the brain and spinal cord. It contributes to the roof of the third ventricle and to the formation of the choroid plexuses of the lateral, third, and fourth ventricles. The pia mater and arachnoid are known collectively as the leptomeninges (*lepto-,* "slender").

CRANIAL MENINGES.

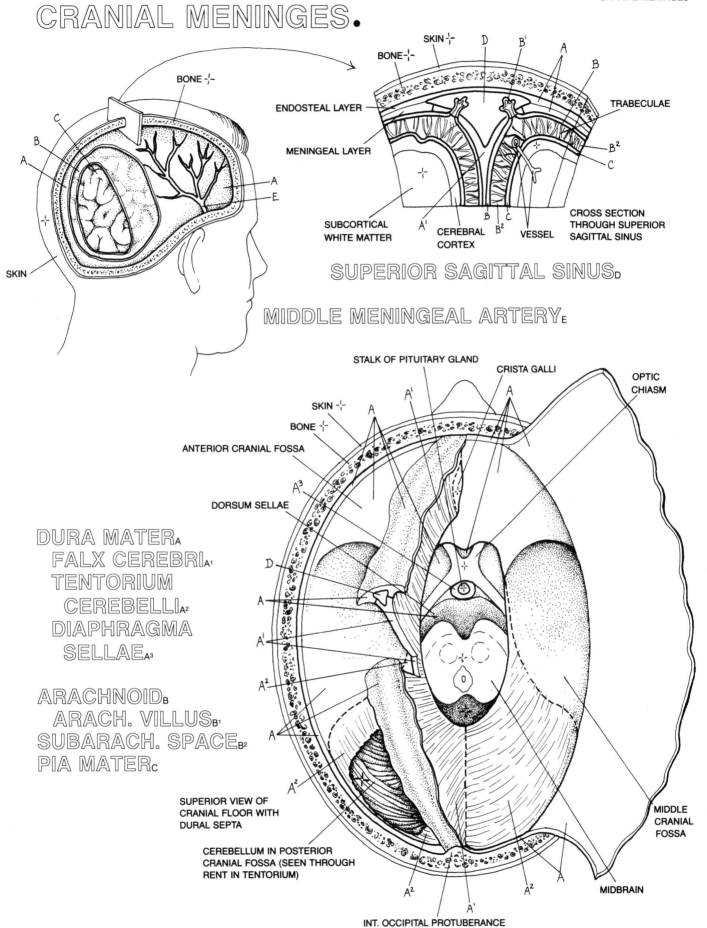

BONE -¦-

C

B

A

SKIN

SKIN -¦-

BONE -¦-

ENDOSTEAL LAYER

MENINGEAL LAYER

D

B¹

A

B

TRABECULAE

B²

C

A

A¹

B

C

B²

VESSEL

SUBCORTICAL
WHITE MATTER

CEREBRAL
CORTEX

CROSS SECTION
THROUGH SUPERIOR
SAGITTAL SINUS

A

E

SUPERIOR SAGITTAL SINUS_D

MIDDLE MENINGEAL ARTERY_E

STALK OF PITUITARY GLAND

CRISTA GALLI

OPTIC
CHIASM

SKIN -¦-

BONE -¦-

ANTERIOR CRANIAL FOSSA

A³

DORSUM SELLAE

A

A¹

A²

A

A²

A¹

A

A²

A²

D

A

A¹

A²

A

DURA MATER_A
FALX CEREBRI_A1
TENTORIUM
CEREBELLI_A2
DIAPHRAGMA
SELLAE_A3

ARACHNOID_B
ARACH. VILLUS_B1
SUBARACH. SPACE_B2
PIA MATER_C

SUPERIOR VIEW OF
CRANIAL FLOOR WITH
DURAL SEPTA

CEREBELLUM IN POSTERIOR
CRANIAL FOSSA (SEEN THROUGH
RENT IN TENTORIUM)

INT. OCCIPITAL PROTUBERANCE

MIDDLE
CRANIAL
FOSSA

MIDBRAIN

The ventricular system consists of a series of interconnected cavities originating from the central canal of the embryonic neural tube. These cavities are lined with ependymal cells and contain cerebrospinal fluid (CSF), which is produced from specialized tissues (choroid plexus; see Plate 9-12) within the ventricles.

Color the central canal heading, titles A through D, and the related cavities in the illustration at the upper right. Then color titles A^1 through D^1 and the related structures in the upper left and lower right illustrations. The specific brain structures labeled in the illustration at the lower right (amygdala, calcar avis, thalamus and so on), included to show their relationship to the ventricular system, are not in true scale.

The central canal of the embryonic *forebrain* (A) forms the *lateral ventricles* (A^1 through A^6), the *interventricular foramina* (A^7), and the *third ventricle* (A^8 and A^9). The lateral ventricle is pulled into each lobe of a hemisphere as the latter enlarges during embryonic and fetal development. In this way, the *anterior horn* (A^2) forms in the frontal lobe, the *body* (A^3) in the parietal lobe, the *inferior horn* (A^4) in the temporal lobe, and the *posterior horn* (A^6) in the occipital lobe. The posterior and inferior horns meet the body in a region called the *atrium* (A^5; also called the trigone).

Some of the important relations of the lateral ventricles include the following structures, which can be seen in the Atlas of Brain Sections in Unit Five. The walls of the anterior horn are formed by the septum pellucidum medially, the head of the caudate nucleus laterally and inferiorly, and the corpus callosum rostrally. The lateral floor and wall of the body are also formed by the caudate nucleus, its medial floor by the thalamus, and its roof by the corpus callosum (see Plates 5-38 and 5-44). The inferior horn projects into the temporal lobe, the amygdaloid nucleus lying at its tip (Plate 5-41). The inferior horn is semilunar in shape, with the concave floor and medial wall formed by the bulge of the hippocampus (Plate 5-38). The tail of the caudate extends along the roof of the inferior horn (Plate 5-24).

The atrium, located in the base of the junction between the temporal and occipital lobes (Plate 5-46), has a slight swelling (collateral eminence, not shown) in its floor due to the indentation of the collateral sulcus on the outer inferior surface of the temporal lobe (Plate 5-30). The posterior horn (Plate 5-47) extends into the occipital lobe. The calcarine fissure on the medial surface of the occipital lobe creates a bulge called the calcar avis (bird's spur) on the medial wall of the posterior horn (Plate 5-47). The roof of the posterior horn is the corpus callosum; the optic radiation projects along the lateral wall.

CSF is formed by choroid plexuses in the body, atrium, and inferior horn of the lateral ventricle. This fluid flows out of the lateral ventricles into the third ventricle by way of the interventricular foramina (of Monro). These foramina are located just anterior to the thalamus and posterior to the columns of the fornix (Plates 5-39 and 5-44).

The third ventricle is a thin cavity between the left and right thalamus and hypothalamus (Plate 5-38). The floor of the third ventricle, formed by the hypothalamus, is characterized by an *infundibular recess* (A^9) surrounded by the infundibular stalk of the pituitary gland (Plates 5-20 and 5-37). CSF is formed by the choroid plexus, which constitutes part of the roof of the third ventricle. The third ventricle extends posterosuperiorly into the stalk of the pineal gland (pineal recess); posteroinferiorly, it continues into the midbrain as the cerebral aqueduct.

The *cerebral aqueduct* (B^1), formed from the central canal of the embryonic *midbrain* (B), is short (2 cm) and narrow (2 mm in diameter) and separates the tectum (superior and inferior colliculi) from the more anterior-inferior tegmentum. It has no choroid plexus and opens posteroinferiorly into the fourth ventricle. Because of its constricted lumen, it is subject to obstruction from infection, trauma, or space-occupying lesions.

The *fourth ventricle* (C^1) is formed in the embryonic *hindbrain* (C). Its floor is the pontine and medullary tegmentum; its roof is the thin superior and inferior medullary vela (Plates 5-8 and 5-44). The choroid plexus is located in the inferior velum. Laterally, the fourth ventricle is drawn into the cerebellar hemispheres, forming recesses. At the tips of these lateral recesses are the *foramina of Luschka* (C^3), through which CSF flows into the adjacent subarachnoid spaces (Plate 9-12). CSF can also enter the subarachnoid space via the *foramen of Magendie* (C^2), lying in the midline toward the posterior (caudal) end of the fourth ventricle. The fourth ventricle narrows caudally to become the *central canal of the spinal cord* (D^1), a vestige of the embryonic *spinal cord* (D) canal.

VENTRICULAR SYSTEM.

SCHEME OF CENTRAL CANAL
   OF THE EMBRYONIC: ★
   FOREBRAIN$_A$
   MIDBRAIN$_B$
   HINDBRAIN$_C$
   SPINAL CORD$_D$

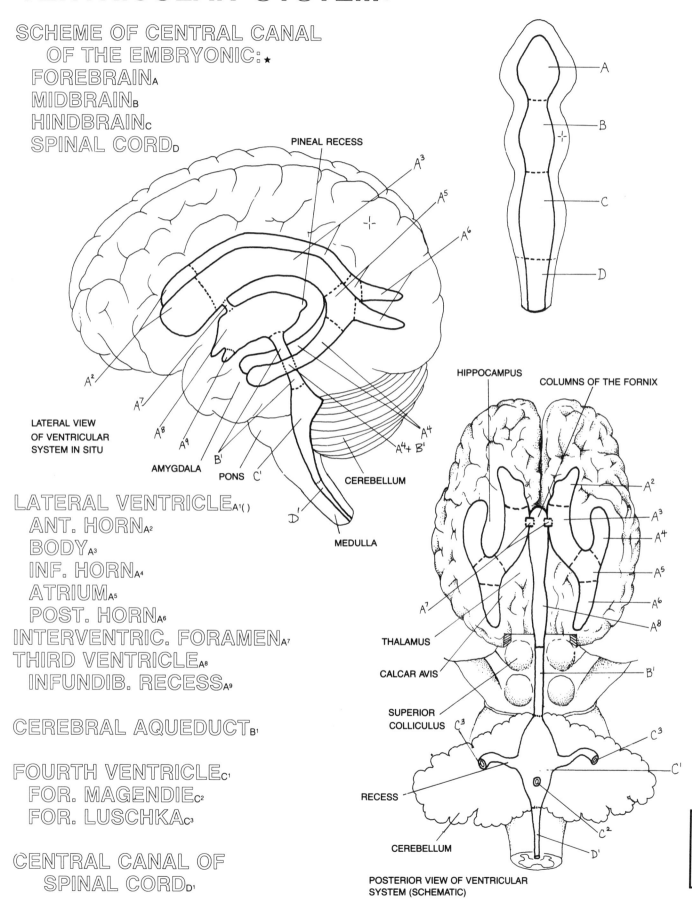

PINEAL RECESS

LATERAL VIEW
OF VENTRICULAR
SYSTEM IN SITU

AMYGDALA
PONS
CEREBELLUM
MEDULLA

HIPPOCAMPUS
COLUMNS OF THE FORNIX

THALAMUS
CALCAR AVIS
SUPERIOR
COLLICULUS
RECESS
CEREBELLUM

POSTERIOR VIEW OF VENTRICULAR
SYSTEM (SCHEMATIC)

LATERAL VENTRICLE$_{A^1()}$
   ANT. HORN$_{A^2}$
   BODY$_{A^3}$
   INF. HORN$_{A^4}$
   ATRIUM$_{A^5}$
   POST. HORN$_{A^6}$
INTERVENTRIC. FORAMEN$_{A^7}$
THIRD VENTRICLE$_{A^8}$
   INFUNDIB. RECESS$_{A^9}$

CEREBRAL AQUEDUCT$_{B^1}$

FOURTH VENTRICLE$_{C^1}$
   FOR. MAGENDIE$_{C^2}$
   FOR. LUSCHKA$_{C^3}$

CENTRAL CANAL OF
   SPINAL CORD$_{D^1}$

Cerebrospinal fluid (CSF) surrounds the brain and spinal cord, offering a means of protection, support, nutrition, and removal of neuronal metabolic by-products. Cerebrospinal fluid is a clear, acellular fluid, similar to blood plasma in its basic chemical constitution, differing only in concentration: CSF has less protein and fewer potassium and calcium ions; it has more sodium, chloride, and magnesium ions.

Color titles A through N and related structures in the two small inset illustrations and the main illustration.

Cerebrospinal fluid is formed within the *choroid plexuses* (A) of the lateral, third, and fourth ventricles. These plexuses consist of a spongy mass of tissue (see inset below the forebrain) composed of *capillaries* (B), *pia mater* (C), and *ependymal cells* (D). They produce as much as 700 milliliters of CSF every 24 hours. An equal amount is absorbed by the *superior sagittal sinus* (G) or the neighboring venous lacunae from the subarachnoidal space through projections of *arachnoid* (E) called *arachnoid villi* (E[1]; also called granulations). These villi reach the sinus or lacuna by penetrating the *dura mater* (F; upper inset). In this way, CSF is directed into the venous system. With aging, these villi increase in size and number; some may become calcified. Obstructions to flow throughout the ventricular system or subarachnoid space or cisterns results in a condition of progressively enlarging ventricles (hydrocephalus).

Cerebrospinal fluid in the *lateral ventricles* (H) flows into the *third ventricle* (I) via the *interventricular foramina* (H[1]). The CSF flow circulates through the *cerebral aqueduct* (J) into the large *fourth ventricle* (K). Here the CSF can enter the very narrow *central canal* (M) of the spinal cord. It can also enter the *subarachnoid space* (N) via three apertures in the roof of the fourth ventricle, the median *foramen of Magendie* (L) and the lateral foramina of Luschka (not shown; see Plate 9-11).

Color the heading Cisterns, titles O through P, and the related cisterns and dural sac in the main illustration.

The subarachnoid space is characterized by trabeculae of connective-tissue fibers. In certain areas around the brain, the subarachnoid spaces are much enlarged and the trabeculae are absent. These are the subarachnoid cisterns.

The major cisterns include the *superior* (O; or cistern of the great cerebral vein), located between the cerebellum and the splenium of the corpus callosum, containing the pineal gland and the great cerebral vein of Galen (recall Plate 9-8); the *cerebellomedullary* (O[1]; or cisterna magna), between the caudal cerebellum and the medulla; the *pontine* (O[2]), located primarily in the anterior median groove along the entire rostral-caudal extent of the pons; the *interpeduncular* (O[3]), between the crura cerebri; and the *chiasmatic* (O[4]), surrounding the optic chiasm.

The spinal cord terminates at the first or second lumbar vertebral level as the conus medullaris. The fibrous component of the pia mater continues caudally from the conus as the filum terminale. The dura mater and arachnoid continue caudally to the second sacral vertebral level, forming an enlarged subarachnoid space called the *dural sac* (P). The filum terminale continues through the sac, picks up dural and arachnoid investments at the second sacral level, and attaches to the posterior surface of the first coccygeal vertebra.

It is within the dural sac, generally at the fourth lumbar level, that lumbar punctures are performed for CSF testing and anesthetic agents as well as contrast media (fluids rendered especially opaque) are introduced for fluoroscopic study of the spinal cord and spinal nerve roots.

Color titles B[1] and Q and the related structures in the illustration at the lower left.

Neurons of the brain and spinal cord are protected from many harmful chemical and biological agents by the "blood-brain barrier." This protective device has many elements, ranging from tight junctions between endothelial cells in the capillaries of the brain, restricting permeability of the larger molecules, to neuroglia. The lumina of the larger blood *vessels* (B[1]) penetrating the brain tissue are lined with an inner layer of endothelium reinforced by fibromuscular tissue. These vessels are enclosed by an investment of pia mater. As the artery narrows to capillary dimensions within the brain, it loses its fibromuscular coat and pial investment. Neuroglia, especially *astrocytes* (Q), extend processes to these capillaries, to which they attach by end feet (recall Plate 2-6).

FLOW OF CEREBROSPINAL FLUID.

CHOROID PLEXUS_A
CAPILLARY_B
PIA MATER_C
EPENDYMAL CELL_D

ARACHNOID_E
ARACH. VILLUS_E1
DURA MATER_F
SUP. SAGITTAL SINUS_G

LATERAL VENTRICLE_H
INTERVENTRIC.
FORAMEN_H1
THIRD VENTRICLE_I
CEREBRAL AQUEDUCT_J
FOURTH VENTRICLE_K
FOR. MAGENDIE_L
CENTRAL CANAL_M
SUBARACH. SPACE_N

CISTERNS ★
SUPERIOR_O
CEREBELLOMEDULLARY_O1
PONTINE_O2
INTERPEDUNCULAR_O3
CHIASMATIC_O4

DURAL SAC_P

VESSEL_B1
ASTROCYTE_Q

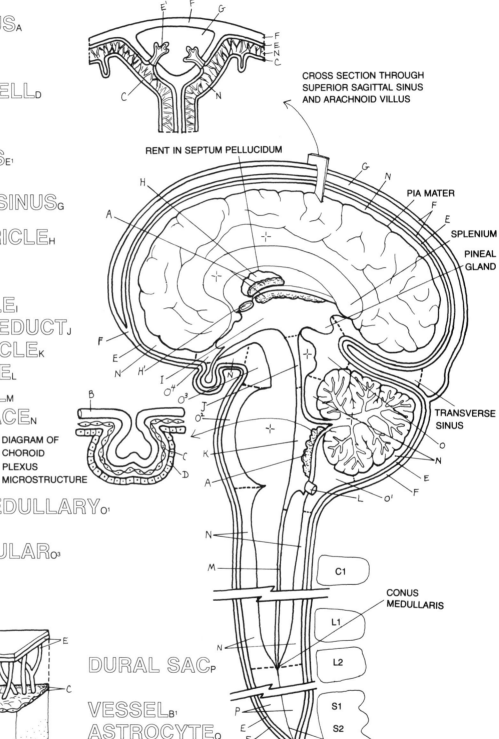

CROSS SECTION THROUGH
SUPERIOR SAGITTAL SINUS
AND ARACHNOID VILLUS

RENT IN SEPTUM PELLUCIDUM

PIA MATER

SPLENIUM

PINEAL
GLAND

TRANSVERSE
SINUS

DIAGRAM OF
CHOROID
PLEXUS
MICROSTRUCTURE

CONUS
MEDULLARIS

C1
L1
L2
S1
S2

FILUM TERMINALE

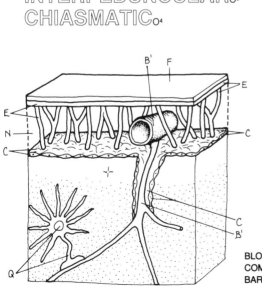

BLOCK OF TISSUE ILLUSTRATING
COMPONENTS OF BLOOD-BRAIN
BARRIER

The spinal cord is richly supplied with blood by a veritable network of arteries and drained, in part, by an extensive venous plexus associated with the vertebral column. The sources of arterial blood to the cord can be traced to the segmental vessels of the thorax and abdomen (intercostal and lumbar branches of the thoracic and abdominal aorta; not shown), cervical and vertebral arteries of the neck, and sacral arteries of the pelvis (not shown). The veins of the spinal cord tend to follow the arteries, except that they are more numerous and tend to merge into complex networks.

Color the heading Arteries, titles A through D, and the vessels in the upper illustration. Vessel A can also be colored in the illustration at the lower right.

The anterior surface of the spinal cord is supplied by the *anterior spinal artery* (A) and its *branches* (A^1). It is considered to be the longest identifiable artery in the body; its continuity is maintained by a series of segmental vessels joining it at several levels bilaterally. It is formed rostrally by two arteries that arise from the intracranial portion of the vertebral arteries (recall Plate 9-3). These paired spinal arteries (not shown) descend to merge at the vertebral level of C3 to form the unpaired anterior spinal artery. As this vessel descends within the anterior median fissure, it is variably supplied by a series of *radicular arteries* (C^1; *radi,* "root") from segmental vessels, such as spinal branches of thyrocervical, costocervical, intercostal, and lumbar arteries (*segmental artery,* C). The radicular arteries approach the cord from the sides, riding over the spinal roots. Branches of the anterior spinal artery penetrate into the gray matter via the various sulci.

The paired *posterior spinal arteries* (B) also arise from the vertebral arteries (recall Plate 9-3); they descend near the dorsal root entry zones. They receive posterior branches of the radicular arteries mentioned above. The spinal cord is literally cradled in a loosely woven network of vessels, some of which encircle the cord like a halo or crown (*arterial vasocorona,* D). In this way vessels reach the gray and white matter of the cord.

Color the heading Meninges, titles E through H^1, and the related structures in the illustrations at the lower right and left. Yellow (the color of epidural fat) is recommended for F.

The dura mater surrounding the brain (not shown) continues downward and completely envelopes the spinal cord.

The outer or *periosteal layer of dura* (E) is closely adherent to the walls of the vertebral (spinal) canal, serving as its periosteum. The inner or *meningeal layer of dura* (E^1) forms a closed tube around the cord and continues caudally as far as the second sacral vertebra, at which level it encloses the filum terminale (recall Plate 9-12). Extensions of the dura pass laterally like *sleeves* (E^2) along the spinal roots to become continuous with the epineurial sheaths of the spinal nerves. The limited space between the inner and outer dural layers is called the *epidural space* (F). It contains aggregates of adipose tissue and the *internal vertebral venous plexus* (N). This space is often used as a site for the administration of anesthetic agents in the lumbar or sacral regions (caudal block), especially in obstetrics.

The spinal cord is closely covered by a thin layer of *arachnoid* (G) and an inner layer of *pia mater* (H). The *subarachnoid space* (I-$\vdots$-) contains most of the vessels to the cord. It is this same space that becomes the dural sac caudal to the termination of the spinal cord (recall Plate 9-12). Between dural sleeves, along the length of the spinal cord, the pia mater thickens and extends laterally across the subarachnoid space to the meningeal layer of dura mater. These *denticulate ligaments* (H^1) suspend the cord within the canal—somewhat like the vertical support cables supporting the roadway of a suspension bridge—and separate the anterior and posterior roots.

Color the heading Veins, titles J through P, and related vessels in the illustration at the lower left. Vessels N can be colored in the illustration at the lower right.

The spinal veins, like their arterial counterparts, consist of a single *anterior spinal vein* (J) and paired *posterior spinal veins* (L) interconnected by a venous *vasocorona* (K). These veins are drained by anterior and posterior *radicular veins* (M), which are the tributaries of the *internal vertebral venous plexus* (N). This plexus of veins, located in the epidural space, runs the length of the spinal cord. It receives the basilar plexus at the base of the skull (recall Plates 9-8 and 9-9). Between each pair of vertebrae, *intervertebral veins* (O) drain into *segmental veins* (P; such as the lumbar and intercostal veins) as well as the external vertebral venous plexus (not shown). In the neck, the radicular veins join the vertebral veins.

BLOOD SUPPLY AND MENINGES OF THE SPINAL CORD.

ARTERIES ★
ANT. SPINAL A.ₐ/BR.ₐ₁
POST. SPINAL A.ᵦ/BR.ᵦ₁
SEGMENTAL A.ᴄ
   RADICULAR A./BR.ᴄ₁
ARTER. VASOCORONA/BR.ᴅ

MENINGES ★
PERIOST.ₑ/MENING. DURAₑ₁
DURAL SLEEVEₑ₂
EPIDURAL SPACEꜰ
ARACHNOIDɢ
PIA MATERₕ
   DENTICULATE LIG.ₕ₁

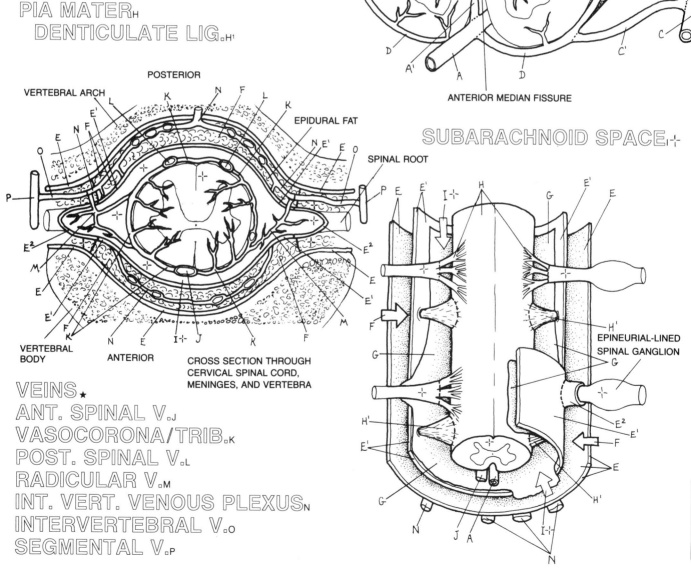

ANTERIOR MEDIAN FISSURE

POSTERIOR
VERTEBRAL ARCH
EPIDURAL FAT
SPINAL ROOT

SUBARACHNOID SPACE ╫

VERTEBRAL BODY
ANTERIOR
CROSS SECTION THROUGH CERVICAL SPINAL CORD, MENINGES, AND VERTEBRA

EPINEURIAL-LINED SPINAL GANGLION

VEINS ★
ANT. SPINAL V.ⱼ
VASOCORONA/TRIB.ₖ
POST. SPINAL V.ₗ
RADICULAR V.ₘ
INT. VERT. VENOUS PLEXUSₙ
INTERVERTEBRAL V.ₒ
SEGMENTAL V.ₚ

INDEX

Entries are generally arranged as follows: by individual name (e.g., abducens nerve), by group (e.g., nerve, nucleus, tract, gyrus), and by region of the brain (e.g., diencephalon, thalamus, cerebral cortex). When seeking a term belonging to a general group, such as a nerve, nucleus, or lemniscus, look for the group entry first. If it is not listed there, look up the individual name. Structures that begin with "anterior," "posterior," and so on are listed under the group to which they belong and not individually. Thus, *superior colliculus* is listed under *colliculus*.

For organizational purposes, structures/areas belonging to a common system (e.g., visual system) or anatomical region (e.g., thalamus) will also be listed under that system or region. Thus, if you wish to scan the index listings of all structures/areas in the midbrain, look up midbrain. Only the major, and not a complete set of, references are listed under the entries of common regions. Thus, the *inferior colliculus* is listed under *midbrain*, but a more complete set of references can be found under *colliculus*.

Italicized numbers indicate the principal reference and/or the reference in which definition of a term can be found.

296